MARKETING MANAGEMENT:
AN INTERNATIONAL PERSPECTIVE

INTERNATIONAL MARKETING SERIES
Series Editor: Professor Christian Pinson, INSEAD

MARKETING MANAGEMENT: AN INTERNATIONAL PERSPECTIVE

Edited by
Kamran Kashani and Dominique Turpin

MACMILLAN
Business

First published 1999 by
MACMILLAN PRESS LTD
Houndmills, Basingstoke, Hampshire RG21 6XS
and London
Companies and representatives throughout the world

ISBN 0–333–75007–1 hardcover
ISBN 0–333–75008–X paperback

A catalogue record for this book is available from the British Library.

This book is printed on paper suitable for recycling and made from fully managed and sustained forest sources.

10 9 8 7 6 5 4 3 2 1
08 07 06 05 04 03 02 01 00 99

Editing and origination by
Aardvark Editorial, Mendham, Suffolk

Printed in Great Britain by
TJ International Ltd

Contents

List of Exhibits   vii
Case Writers and Associates   xiv
Preface   xv
Acknowledgements   xvii

SECTION I   INTRODUCTION TO MARKETING   1

Introduction to Marketing   3
    The Job of the Marketing Manager   3
    The Marketing Mission   3
    Putting It All Together   14
    Cases in Section I   15
    Learning Points   15

    Case 1.1   *The Skisailer: Marketing a Young Investor's Dream*   17
    Case 1.2^R   *Delissa in Japan*   35

SECTION II   MARKETING DECISIONS: THE FIVE 'PS'   53

Introduction: The Five 'Ps'   55
    Segmentation and Positioning Decisions   55
    Product Management Decisions   56
    Pricing Decisions   60
    Distribution Decisions   64
    Communication Decisions   68
    Conclusions   73
    Learning Points   73

    Case 2.1   *Konica Corp.*   75
    Case 2.2   *Kirin Brewery Co. Ltd (A)*   104
    Case 2.3   *Daewoo Motor Company UK (A)*   134
    Case 2.3   *Daewoo Motor Company UK (B)*   147
    Case 2.4^R   *Interdrinks*   160
    Case 2.5   *Salomon: The Monocoque Ski*   191
    Case 2.6   *Hong Kong & Shenzhen Bank (A)*   216
    Case 2.6   *Hong Kong & Shenzhen Bank (B)*   222
    Case 2.6   *Hong Kong and Shenzhen Bank (C)*   225

Case 2.6   *Hong Kong & Shenzhen Bank (D)*   241
Case 2.6   *Hong Kong and Shenzhen Bank (E)*   245
Case 2.6   *Hong Kong and Shenzhen Bank (F)*   247
Case 2.7   *Computron Inc., 1994*   248
Case 2.8R   *Pharma Swede: Gastirup*   256
Case 2.9R   *Jordan A/S*   280
Case 2.10   *GPS One-hour Service (C): Moving Abroad*   298
Case 2.11   *Make Yourself Heard: Ericsson's Global Brand Campaign*   326
Case 2.12R *Mediquip S.A.*   345

SECTION III   INTERNATIONAL MARKETING: GLOBAL INTEGRATION STRATEGY   355

International Marketing: Global Integration and Strategy   357
  Forces   359
  P&G Goes Global   361
  Global Marketing: The Issues   363
  Global Strategy: A Framework for Analysis   366
  The Case of Integrated Solutions Inc.   369
  Cases in Section III   370
  Learning Points   371

Case 3.1   *Libby's Beverages: Um Bongo Fruit Drink*   373
Case 3.2   *Hilti Corporation (A)*   411
Case 3.3R   *Haaks Europe*   418

SECTION IV   INTERNATIONAL MARKETING: STRATEGY IMPLEMENTATION   423

International Marketing: Strategy Implementation   425
  Chapter Coverage   426
  Structure   426
  Tasks   431
  Process   433
  Behavior   435
  Skills   437
  Cases in Strategy Implementation   439
  Learning Points   440

Case 4.1R   *Alto Chemicals Europe (A)*   441
Case 4.1R   *Alto Chemicals Europe (B)*   453
Case 4.2   *Sony Europa (A)*   456

List of Exhibits

CASE 1.2

Exhibit 1	Illustration of Skisailer from Product Brochure	30
Exhibit 2	Skisailer Market Potential	32
Exhibit 3	Skisailer Achievable Sales Estimate	33
Exhibit 4	World Market of Alpine and Cross-country Skis	34

CASE 2.1

Exhibit 1	Konishiroku Photo Industry (Konica) Selected Data	84
Exhibit 2	World Amateur Photographic Exposures (units in bns)	86
Exhibit 3	Japanese Photography Exposures (bn shots)	87
Exhibit 4	Japanese Amateur Total Photographic Expenditures (¥100 mn)	88
Exhibit 5	The World Photofinishing Industry (US$100 mn)	89
Exhibit 6	Photofinishing Sales in Japan (¥ bn)	90
Exhibit 7	Sales of Data Processing by Type of Outlet (% of total value)	91
Exhibit 8	Photofinishing Prices in Japan (¥)	92
Exhibit 9	Sales of Still Cameras in Japan (¥ mn)	93
Exhibit 10	Sales of Cameras in Japan by Sex and Age Group (%)	94
Exhibit 11	Sales of Photographic Film in Japan by Sex and Age Group	95
Exhibit 12	Market Shares in the 35mm SLR Camera Industry in Japan (1975–86)	96
Exhibit 13	Sales of Color Negative Film in Japan by Size, Sensitivity and Prints (Film for Amateurs Only)	97
Exhibit 14	Konishiroku Photo Industry Product Line for Color Print Film (Film for Amateurs Only)	98
Exhibit 15	Konishiroku Photo Industry Product Line for Color Print Film (Film for Amateurs Only)	99
Exhibit 16	Comparative Retail Prices for Color Print Film in Japan 1987*	100
Exhibit 17	Photographic Subjects for Color Prints by Sex and Age Group	101
Exhibit 18	Photographic Subjects for Color Prints by Season* (ISO100, Color Prints 1980–86)**	102
Exhibit 19	Fuji Photo Film Selected Data	103

CASE 2.2

Exhibit 1	The World Beer Industry (1987)	118
Exhibit 2	Selected Financial Data	119
Exhibit 3	Comparative Market Shares in the Japanese Beer Industry (1949–87*)	120
Exhibit 4	Segmentation of the Beer Market in Japan by Product Categories and Brewers in 1987 (× 10,000 kiloliters)	121
Exhibit 5	Comparative Marketing Expenditures of the Major Japanese Brewers 1983–87 (¥ bn)	122
	Comparative Advertising Expenditures per Media, 1987 (in %)	123
Exhibit 6	Sapporo Breweries' Selected Financial Data	124
Exhibit 7	Asahi Breweries' Selected Financial Data	125
Exhibit 8	Positioning Map for Beer Products	126
Exhibit 9	Asahi's Super Dry Label	127
Exhibit 10	Kirin's Lager Beer Label	128
	Consumer Opinions on Dry Beer in Japan	129

CASE 2.3A

Exhibit 1	New Car Market Shares and Distribution Structure by Manufacturer: 1992–94	140
Exhibit 2A	Overview of Segmentation of the UK Car Market	141
Exhibit 2B	Market Share by Model: Lower- and Upper-medium Segments (1993)	142
Exhibit 2C	Private Buyers – Main Reasons for Purchase	143
Exhibit 2D	Price Ranges of Competing Models: August 1994	144
Exhibit 3	Largest UK Franchised Dealer Groups	145
Exhibit 4	Brand and Retail Advertising for Top Car Manufacturers	146

CASE 2.3B

Exhibit 1	Daewoo Launch Advertising	152
Exhibit 2	New Car Registrations in UK by Marque: 1994–97	157
Exhibit 3	Daewoo New Model Pricing	159

CASE 2.4

Exhibit 1	Switzerland and IDC's Geographic Coverage*	173
Exhibit 2	Partial Organization Chart	174
Exhibit 3	Income Statement (in thousand Sfrs)	175
Exhibit 4	Balance Sheet (in thousand Sfrs)	176

Exhibit 5	IDC's Product Line	177
Exhibit 6	1997 Sales by Outlet (in thousand Sfrs)	178
Exhibit 7	1997 Sales by Outlet (in thousands of bottles)	179
Exhibit 8	Average Ex-factory Prices by Outlet* in 1997 (Sfrs)	180
Exhibit 9	Variable Manufacturing Costs* (in Sfrs)	181
Exhibit 10	Advertising and Promotion Expenditures (in thousand Sfrs)	182
Exhibit 11	Swiss Soft Drink and Mineral Water Consumption (millions of liters)	183
Exhibit 12	National Market Shares of Top Bottling Companies (1997, liters)	184
Exhibit 13	Representative Consumer Prices (in Sfrs)	185
Exhibit 14	Share of Food Chains in Total Consumer Purchases (%)	186
Exhibit 15	Estimated Sales of Competitors Within IDC's Region	187
Exhibit 16	Breakdown of Selling Expenses (Sfrs 000s)	188
Exhibit 17	Age and Service Profile of Salesmen	189
Exhibit 18	Performance Evaluation Form	190

CASE 2.5

Exhibit 1	Salomon S.A., Sales and Profits (FF mn)	205
Exhibit 2	Growth of Sales and R&D Expenditures Index (1983–84 = 100)	206
Exhibit 3	Salomon S.A., Five-Year Financial Summary	207
Exhibit 4	Ski Sales in the 1980s (millions of pairs)	209
Exhibit 5	1986–87 Sales by Country (thousands of pairs)	210
Exhibit 6	The Market Price Structure in the Ski Market	211
Exhibit 7	Sales by Manufacturers (thousands of pairs)	212
Exhibit 8	Types of Ski Structure	213
Exhibit 9	The Ski Purchasing Process	214
Exhibit 10	The Ski Concept: Progressive Profile	215

CASE 2.6A

| Exhibit 1 | Organization Chart of the Hong Kong & Shenzhen Bank | 221 |

CASE 2.6C

Exhibit 1	Step 1a: Summary of Clients' Expectations	226
Exhibit 2A	Step 1a: Division's Performance	228
Exhibit 2B	Step 1a: Division's Performance	229
Exhibit 2C	Step 1a: Division's Performance	230
Exhibit 2D	Step 1a: Division's Performance	231

CASE 2.6C

Exhibit 3A	Step 1b: Sensitiveness of the Employees Towards Quality	232
Exhibit 3B	Step 1b: Sensitiveness of the Employees Towards Quality	233
Exhibit 3C	Step 1b: Sensitiveness of the Employees Towards Quality	234
Exhibit 3D	Step 1b: Sensitiveness of the Employees Towards Quality	235
Exhibit 3E	Step 1b: Sensitiveness of the Employees Towards Quality	236
Exhibit 3F	Step 1b: Sensitiveness of the Employees Towards Quality	237
Exhibit 3G	Step 1b: Sensitiveness of the Employees Towards Quality	238
Exhibit 3H	Step 1b: Sensitiveness of the Employees Towards Quality	239
Exhibit 3I	Step 1b: Sensitiveness of the Employees Towards Quality	240

CASE 2.6D

Exhibit 1	Examples of Company Charters	243
Exhibit 2	The Hong Kong & Shenzhen Bank's Quality Chart	244

CASE 2.7

Exhibit 1	Estimated Price for the 1000X Computer for the Slavisky Experimental Pilot Plant based on 'Usual' Calculations	254
Exhibit 2	1993 Market Share for Companies Selling Medium-priced Computers to the Polish Market (US$)	255

CASE 2.8

Exhibit 1	Pharma Swede (Sales in $ mn)	270
Exhibit 2	Partial Organization Chart	271
Exhibit 3	The Development of a New Drug	272
Exhibit 4	Product Pricing and Government Relations	273
Exhibit 5	The Oral Osmotic Delivery System (OROS)	274
Exhibit 6	Sales and Market Shares in Major European Markets* (Sales in $ mn)	275
Exhibit 7	Retail Prices in Europe (Daily Treatment Cost)	276
Exhibit 8	Price Setting and Reimbursement in the EU	277
Exhibit 9	Relative Retail Prices of Gastirup	279

CASE 2.9

Exhibit 1	Selected Financial Results (millions of Norwegian kroner)	290
Exhibit 2	Sales Budget Total: 330 mn kroner	292

Exhibit 3   The World Market for Toothbrushes (data unavailable for
              some countries)   293
Exhibit 4   Jordan Market Share by Country   294
Exhibit 5   Major Competitors in Toothbrushes: Selected Financial and
              Operating Statistics ($ mn)   295
Exhibit 6   Major Competing Brands of Toothbrushes   296
Exhibit 7   British Toothbrush Market   297

CASE 2.10

Exhibit 1A   Representation of the GPS Group   310
Exhibit 1B   GPS Consolidated Profit & Loss 1992–96   311
Exhibit 2   The Spirit of GPS   312
Exhibit 3   Photos of GPS Stores   313
Exhibit 4   Quick Look at the Optical Industry   315
Exhibit 5   Costs and Income of a Typical Grand Optical or La Générale
              d'Optique Store in France   318
Exhibit 6   Grand Optical Facts and Figures as per December 1996   319
Exhibit 7   Overview of International Competitors   320
Exhibit 8   Positioning of the International Optical Chains   322
Exhibit 9   Quantitative Market Data   323
Exhibit 10   Competitors' Profiles per Market (as evaluated by the IMD
              MBA project team)   324

CASE 2.11

Exhibit 1   Partial Organization Chart: Ericsson Group and Mobile Phones
              and Terminals   336
Exhibit 2   Mobile Phones: Global Market Shares   337
Exhibit 3   Pan-European Press Advertising 1995   338
Exhibit 4   James Bond Tie-in Advertising: Austria 1997   339
Exhibit 5   Global Brand Campaign Billboard Advertising 1998   340
Exhibit 6   Global Brand Campaign TV Commercial Storyboards 1998   341
Exhibit 7   European Region's Product Campaign Press Advertising 1998   342
Exhibit 8   Local Product Campaign Press Advertising 1997   343
Exhibit 9   Radio Systems Press Advertising 1998   344

CASE 2.12

Exhibit 1   Account Management Analysis Forms (condensed version)   352

CASE 3.1

Exhibit 1	Nestlé's 1988 Sales Breakdown	386
Exhibit 2	Partial Corporate Nestlé Organization Chart	387
Exhibit 3	Segmentation of the US Beverage Market, 1988	388
Exhibit 4	US Competitive Overview: Who is Who in Shelf-stable Juice	389
Exhibit 5	1988 Dollar Volume and Share Trends: Total US Juice/Drinks Category (US$ thousands)	391
Exhibit 6	Libby's US Division Reporting Structure	392
Exhibit 7	Juicy Juice: Sample Labels	393
Exhibit 8	Juicy Juice Positioning (Based on 1987 Creative)	394
Exhibit 9	Juicy Juice Storyboard	395
Exhibit 10	Hawaiian Punch Storyboard	396
Exhibit 11	Juicy Juice Consumer Profile	397
Exhibit 12	Highlights of 1989 Marketing Plan Juicy Juice	398
Exhibit 13	Segmentation of the UK Beverage Market, 1988 (US$ mn)	399
Exhibit 14	Um Bongo Brik Paks	400
Exhibit 15	Um Bongo Commercial Storyboard	401
Exhibit 16	UK Consumer Data on Um Bongo*	402
Exhibit 17	Spanish Fruit Juice and Drinks Market* 1988	403
Exhibit 18	Portuguese Fruit Juice and Drinks Market* 1988	404
Exhibit 19	US Um Bongo Research: Interpretative Summary and Selected Findings	405

CASE 3.2

| Exhibit 1 | The Hilti Product Line | 416 |
| Exhibit 2 | Global Strategy | 417 |

CASE 3.3

| Exhibit 1 | Haaks International Partial Organization Chart | 422 |

CASE 4.1A

Exhibit 1	Stabilizer Market Segments (1989)	450
Exhibit 2	Stabilizer Marketing Organization	451
Exhibit 3	Partial Job Definitions	452

CASE 4.1C

Exhibit 1	Sony Product Innovations	475
Exhibit 2	History of Sony's Operations in Europe	476
Exhibit 3	Relations Between European Country Management and Sony Tokyo	477
Exhibit 4	European Consumer Electronics Market Size and Shares of Major Producers	478
Exhibit 5	European Consumer Electronics Sales Trends by Product Category	479
Exhibit 6	European Consumer Electronics Sales Trends by Country and Region	480
Exhibit 7	Per Capita Expenditure on Consumer Electronics (1992)	481
Exhibit 8	Shares of Consumer Electronics by Channel	482
Exhibit 9	Partial Organization Chart: European Sales and Marketing Operations	483
Exhibit 10	The Butterfly Concept	484
Exhibit 11	SymphONY Europa	485
Exhibit 12	Shin Takagi's Career History at Sony	486
Appendix	Partial Text of Organization Announcement	487

Case Writers and Associates

Case 1.1   Dominique Turpin and Kamran Kashani

Case 1.2[R]   Juliet Burdet-Taylor and Dominique Turpin

Case 2.1   Dominique Turpin

Case 2.2   Dominique Turpin with Joyce Millar

Case 2.3   Debra Riley, under the supervision of Sean Meehan

Case 2.4   Srinivasa Rangan and Janet Shaner under the supervision of Kamran Kashani

Case 2.5   Francis Bidault

Case 2.6   Dominique Turpin and Giana Klaas

Case 2.7   Ralph Z. Sorenson, revised by Dominique Turpin

Case 2.8[R]   Kamran Kashani with Robert C. Howard and Janet Shaner

Case 2.9[R]   David H. Hover and Janet Shaner under the supervision of Per V. Jenster and Kamran Kashani

Case 2.10   Els van Weering under the supervision of Jacques Horovitz

Case 2.11   Kamran Kashani

Case 2.12[R]   Kamran Kashani

Case 3.1   Kamran Kashani with Robert C. Howard

Case 3.2   Peter Killing

Case 3.3[R]   Kamran Kashani with Janet Shaner

Case 4.1[R]   Kamran Kashani

Case 4.2   Kamran Kashani and J.B.M. Kassarjian

Preface

This book intends to respond to a growing interest in the internationalization of business and the challenges of conducting marketing in markets other than one's own. In a shrinking world of business, thanks to ease of transportation, instant communications, rapid deregulation of financial markets and trade, this book introduces the students of international marketing and management to the excitement, challenges and opportunities of global markets and offers a practical means of learning about international marketing issues.

This book is primarily designed for international marketing teaching purposes but it can also serve to cover more general management issues in international business such as cross-cultural management, strategic alliances and partnerships. The cases are based on our personal observations of companies and their operations in countries where the IMD faculty has done consulting or research. We have used every case presented in this book successfully with both IMD MBA participants and executives. Taken together, they cover subjects in different international marketing contexts: evaluating the potential of different markets around the globe, launching or re-launching a product or service in a global context, managing the marketing mix in an international or new

environment, implementing a global marketing strategy, dealing with cross-cultural marketing issues, managing alliances and partnership strategies in international marketing.

The cases in this book are not intended to be examples of 'best practices' or, for that matter, of ineffective management. We selected them for their general interest and pedagogical value, the overall picture of doing business overseas they paint, and the specific issues on international marketing they present. All the cases in this book are comprehensive and are based on real business situations. They include selected information about the companies, the events and circumstances they operate in. All cases are especially designed for teaching – they highlight the issues important in developing a management framework by engaging participants in probing discussions. Most importantly, this book features real management issues. The views of the managers and the experiences of the companies, different as they are from each other and from those of academic scholars, are invaluable because they are based on the field experiences of real world marketers.

The structure of the book has the following flow of topics: it begins with an overview and an examination of marketing fundamentals before progressing to the more advanced issues in global marketing. The four parts of the book are organized as follows:

Section I: Introduction to Marketing provides a general picture of international marketing issues, market analysis and decisions. It introduces the students to the complexity of the international environment and provides a general overview of key managerial issues in international marketing such as evaluating the size of a new market for an innovative product or seizing the opportunities for growth in different markets.

Section II: Marketing Decisions introduces the students to the key decision areas in marketing, the so-called '5 Ps': segmentation and positioning; product and service policy; pricing; distribution; and communication.

Section III: International Marketing – Integration & Planning focuses on issues coming out of companies trying to adapt their international marketing towards a coherent integrated strategy. The introductory chapter highlights some of the pertinent issues here, such as local versus global bias in marketing decision-making, and sets the stage for the cases that follow.

Section IV: International Marketing – Organization & Strategy Implementation examines important issues left out of most international marketing case books: not only the organizational structure (which is usually covered) but also elements of strategy implementation. This latter set of issues deals with how a management team undertakes actions necessary to implement a given strategy. Implementation issues are especially critical when a given strategy cuts across many organizational, cultural and market divisions – as is often the case in international marketing.

An Instructor's Manual is available for adopters of this book.

KAMRAN KASHANI
AND DOMINIQUE TURPIN

Acknowledgements

We would like to thank our colleagues at IMD for their generous support of our effort to produce this book. Many people have contributed to the realization of our project, but special mention should be made of Persita Egeli-Farmanfarma, IMD Case Administrator, Gordon Adler, IMD Senior Writer, and his assistant Cheryl Petroski, and our proofreader, Michelle Perrinjaquet, for providing us with the assistance necessary to put this book together. We are equally grateful to Janet Shaner, Research Associate, who worked on updating many of the cases that appear in this book. Her work has resulted in exciting new and timely teaching material. Our thanks also go to several of our current and former colleagues for contributing their fine cases to this collection. They are Professors Francis Bidault, Jacques Horovitz, Per Jenster, J.B.M Kassarjian, Peter Killing, Christopher Lovelock, Sean Meehan and Ralph Z. Sorenson. We are also grateful to the research staff who assisted them in developing these cases.

As always, we owe special thanks to our families for their understanding and unwavering support during the completion of this project.

Introduction to Marketing

Introduction to Marketing

The Job of the Marketing Manager

Over the last few decades, the marketing function has been dramatically transformed from a narrow to a much broader and strategic function. In its earliest form, marketing was defined as a limited function restricted to sales or advertising for the local market. The responsibilities of the marketing manager were often limited to selling the factory output and managing the physical distribution of the goods to the distributor. Competition was mainly local and relatively friendly. Today, in many industries, these days are over! The job of the marketing manager is now strategic and diffused within the same organization. A broader look and knowledge of the business is required. In particular, the marketing manager must have a large view of the business activities needed to serve its customers and a strategic sense of the business as a whole. Consequently, the function of the marketing manager has come to encompass many different skills: managing market intelligence, spotting new business opportunities, as well as monitoring existing and new competitors, managing the marketing mix, interact-ing with global customers and the different functions within the firm, and spearheading the customer orientation spirit within the whole organization. In other words, the scope of the marketing function has evolved from a pure functional job to a much broader and strategic managerial function.[1]

The Marketing Mission

If the job of the marketer has greatly evolved during the last few decades, the mission remains unchanged: the marketing manager must first identify customer needs (sometimes these needs are unarticulated by the customers themselves), and mobilize the company resources to serve these needs for a profit for his or her firm. Products, technologies, systems and people are just the means used by the marketing manager and his or her team to satisfy market needs and add value to customers. This fundamental concern for the customer is at the heart of the success of leading companies such as Sony, Procter & Gamble, Tetra Pak, Singapore Airlines or Amazon.com. For these firms, to satisfy customer needs is the key success factor for the growth and survival of their respective

---

1. Kamran Kashani, 'Marketing Futures: Priorities for a Turbulent Environment', *Long Range Planning Journal*, **28**(4): 87–98.

3

organizations. In the eyes of these firms, the 'customer is king!'.

Many companies today still have difficulties in building and maintaining a market orientation. The 'production' spirit often characterizes companies built on 'technical excellence at all costs'. These organizations will typically claim that they manufacture superior products that the world will one day buy. These companies may be right in the short term. In the long term, with limited market input and no customer feedback, they are likely to be left in the dark by the competition since technical superiority only works as long as customers recognize its value. Matsushita Electric Co. Ltd, the world's largest producer of consumer electronics, recently experienced this challenge. Adding technical features to its camcorders was perceived by its engineers as the major means to gain market share and beat the competition. But after a brisk launch of the first generation of camcorders, sales quickly stagnated. What Matsushita engineers failed to recognize was that customers were confused by the complexity of its products. Plenty of 'buttons' and technical 'gadgets' were designed for 'enhanced technical value' but feedback from the marketplace indicated that customers were massively looking to buy 'user friendly' products. Customers were also adamant about the instruction manuals of these camcorders. Manuals were perceived by customers as being written by technical specialists for other technicians rather than being written in everybody's language. Following a review of customer feedback, Mat-sushita decided to redesign its cameras for more user friendliness and to start writing instruction manuals together with customers' input. No need to say that following this move, Matsushita sales for camcorders started to boom.

Another challenge often faced by companies is the confusion between sales and marketing orientation. Sales orientated companies very much focus on maximizing sales – often at the expenses of customer satisfaction. Their major preoccupation is to convince customers that their products are needed. These companies are usually not very inclined to adapt their products to their customer target. These organizations are likely to spend a great amount of time and effort on mounting huge advertising campaigns and building a sales force that will sell the factory production. In order to achieve its quota, the sales force may be tempted to drop the price in order to maximize orders. They may also be inclined to rely on too much 'hard sales' and dubious ethical selling techniques. The final result is likely to be dissatisfied customers, negative word of mouth and no repeat sales.

While sales is often the sole responsibility of the sales force, in contrast, market orientation is everybody's job. Customers are likely to form an opinion on the market orientation of your organization every time a contact is established between the customer and the firm. Every one of these contacts is what Jan Carlzon, the former CEO of Scandinavian Airlines, called a *'moment of truth'*.[2] For example, every second lost by a customer waiting for

---

2. Jan Carlzon, *Moments of Truth*, HarperCollins (1989).

a call to be answered or lost to repeated dialing when the line is busy, is likely to tarnish the goodwill and credibility of the company and may eventually result in lost business.

Corporate culture, complacency, lack of attention to detail, are several of the numerous forces that cause many companies to lose sight of the customer. While most companies compete in mature industries with commodity products, identifying and satisfying customer needs remain the only way to grow and prosper.

Analysis for Marketing Decisions

Market analysis encompasses what is often referred to as the '5Cs Analysis': Context, Customer, Competition, Company, Channels and Cost analysis.

Context Analysis

Identifying customer needs focuses on understanding who needs a particular product or service, for what purpose, where, when and how this particular product or service will be used. However, identifying and satisfying customer needs may not be enough for an organization to gain a sustainable competitive advantage. To survive as an organization, it is imperative to outperform the present or future competition. Consequently, before making any decision on what product/service to offer, to whom, at what price, through which channels, with which communication tools, marketers need to have a full understanding of the environment in which they are operat-

ing: the context (political, legal, socioeconomic, sociocultural, ethnical, and so on) in which they want to operate, the customers they aim to serve, the competition they will fight as well as a fair understanding of the company's own capabilities.

Introducing a new product

Context analysis is particularly useful when a company decides to launch a brand new product concept or move into a new market. Take the example of Mibrovale, a medium-sized Australian winery that recently decided to export wine to the rest of the world. Which markets should it go after: France? where wine consumption is highest but local competition is well entrenched and cultural acceptance of Australian wine can be questionable. Japan? where consumption of imported wines is booming but where French and Italian wines have a very dominant share. The UK? where awareness for Australian wines is high but where Australian competitors have already built solid positions. To maximize its chances of success, this Australian company looked at key entry factors such as: wine consumption per capita; level of awareness for Australian wines; share of imports as a percentage of total wines consumed; level of competition; import taxes, etc. After compiling and analyzing all these data, Mibrovale felt that entering Ireland and the UK would maximize its chances of success.

Entering into a new market

Many fast moving consumer goods companies have been moving recently into China with the expectation that if every 1.2 billion Chinese buys one of their products, their future will be ensured for many years. Quite a large number of companies, such as San Miguel of the Philippines, Philips of the Netherlands or Peugeot of France, have found that the market is often much smaller and more sophisticated than they had anticipated. The reality of the Chinese market is often much more complex than originally planned. In 1998, Peugeot, the French car manufacturer, decided to pull out of this market because it had badly underestimated the sophistication of the Chinese automotive markets. Long negotiations with the Chinese government took longer than expected. Changes in taxation, import legislation and unexpected competitive pressure made Peugeot's Chinese dream a nightmare: the passenger car model that Peugeot had decided to introduce into the People's Republic of China was ill chosen. Rather than to develop or adapt a car model to the Chinese market the way Volkswagen did, Peugeot chose to launch an established car model developed more than a decade ago for the French market. The car did not sell well as Chinese customers were very quick to compare Peugeot's sedan model with more sophisticated models offered by Japanese and other Western competitors.

Customer Analysis

Understanding who buys our products, when, how and why are some of the fundamental questions linked to customer analysis. In marketing, consumer behavior can be analyzed along the following dimensions: identification of needs; search for information; evaluation of the potential options; purchasing decisions; evaluation of the purchasing act.[3]

In the first step (identification of needs), customers express certain needs activated by different stimuli (that is, need for a new product or to replace an obsolete one). Then, customers look for information on how best to fulfil these needs. Information on where, when and what to buy usually comes in different forms: advertising, promotions, word of mouth, past experiences, and so on and can be influenced by marketers through different communication tools (see below). Once customers are aware of the different alternatives available, they are likely to weigh the different elements of the product available to them and make a purchasing decision according to the attributes they value most. These product attributes can be tangible: perceived performance, convenience, after-sales service, price, or intangible: image, perceptions, emotions, and so on. Finally, as customers use the product, they will form an opinion based on the product real performance versus their original expectations. Their level of satisfaction (from disappointment to delight) may greatly influence the repurchase decision of a similar product in the future.

Another important element of customer analysis is to recognize that the buyer is not necessarily the payer or

---

3. See J.F. Engel, R.D. Blackwell and D.T. Kollat: *Consumer Behavior*, Holt, Rinehart & Winston, 1978, p. 22.

the user of the product. This is particularly true of industrial products. Typically, the more expensive the product, the higher the number of players likely to be involved in the decision-making process. Depending on the nature of the product, the decision-making unit may include:

- The *decider* (who is likely to initiate the purchasing)
- The *specifier* (who writes down the technical specification of the product to be bought)
- The *administrator* (who will write the check to the supplier)
- The *user* (who finally makes use of the product)

Marketers need to realize that each one of the decision-makers involved is likely to have different needs to be addressed and fulfilled by the marketer and his team. (For example, when buying a new aircraft, the CEO of the airline corporation may initiate the purchase. Technicians will specify the specifications of the aircraft needed. The financial officer will weigh the total cost of the aircraft against additional revenues. Finally, the pilot who will fly the plane is likely to be concerned with a mix of technical and safety issues, but probably less by the financial issues linked to this purchase.

Market segmentation

Market segmentation is one of the most important decisions a marketing manager can make. What marketers do need to recognize is that markets are made of buyers and buyers differ in many ways. Segmentation is therefore at the heart of understanding cus-

tomers and building a strategy to serve them. Let's look at the example of Coca-Cola. Even this company, renowned for its global products, had to recognize that all coke drinkers are not alike. One segment of the market – the so-called 'traditionalists' – only values the real thing: 'Classic Coke'; while another segment – the 'health conscious' – values 'Coca-Cola Light' for its lower content of sugar and caffeine. Similarly, Coca-Cola offers its products in different packaging: cans versus glass or plastic bottles, 1.5 liters versus 6.5-ounce containers. All these different offers are designed to meet specific customers' needs or preferences (glass versus plastic bottles), different customer profiles (that is, 1.5 liter for families) or convenience (cans versus glass).

Since any product category – be it ice creams, banking or packaging machines – cannot satisfy all customers, segmentation is at the heart of customer analysis. Companies usually go through the market segmentation process in three parts:

- First, they evaluate the market and divide it into meaningful clusters (or segments) of customers in terms of personal characteristics, needs and preferences, differences in purchasing and buying behavior
- Second, they select particular segment(s) as target(s) for the company's marketing efforts, and
- Third, they design a specific marketing program (product offer, price, communications, distribution) for the specific needs of the targeted segment(s).

Customer analysis and market segmentation offer numerous advantages to the firm:

- It forces an understanding of customer problems by focusing on analyzing customers' differences and preferences
- It forces the firm to make the best use of its limited resources (people, money, technologies)
- It enables management to develop a competitive advantage by forcing it to serve one or more segments with marketing plans uniquely tuned to their specific needs.

Evaluating market segments

Since every individual or business is unique, each potential customer is theoretically and potentially a segment of one! However, it may not be economically viable for the firm to serve every customer as a single segment. Finding out the most relevant segmentation for a firm is best done with reference to the following criteria:

- *Measurability*: Is the segment large enough, or growing fast enough, to justify marketing and other corporate investment and provide a worthwhile return?
- *Accessibility*: Can the firm solve the problem or satisfy the needs of this specific segment with a viable and sustainable marketing plan?
- *Defensibility*: Can the firm make use of its core competencies and defend itself against any competitors' move into this segment?
- *Durability*: Is the segment likely to grow, to shrink or to merge with other segments?

- *Competitive edge:* Can the firm outperform the competition by focusing on the chosen segment(s)?

Re-segmenting the market for competitive advantage

Too many market managers take existing market segmentation for granted. However, *re*-segmenting the market is often a key to marketing innovation and the source of a major competitive advantage. Take the photographic film industry for example. Until recently, the photographic film industry was segmented along technical dimensions such as: back and white versus color pictures, paper versus slides, film sensitivity: ISO100 versus ISO200, ISO400, and so on. Konica was the first film manufacturer to recognize that the industry could be resegmented along innovative customer behavior dimensions. By observing how consumers were using photographic films and targeting new customer segments, Konica was able to increase its revenues significantly and build a new image for itself (see Case 2.1: Konica). Similarly, Asahi Breweries, a Japanese beer producer was able to take the number one spot from Kirin by focusing on customer behavior rather than relying on the traditional segmentation based on technical features (see Case 2.2: Kirin Brewery Co. Ltd).

How Nike re-segmented the athletic shoe market

One classic example of re-segmenting its industry has been Nike. While the athletic shoe industry has been dominated for several decades by Adidas of Germany, the German manufacturer

underestimated competition and customers' preferences in the US market.[4]
Even worse, it underestimated the
entry of new competitors such as Nike,
who were keen to change the rules of
the game in this industry. Prior to
Nike's entry into the athletic shoe
industry, Adidas and Puma had practi-
cally the entire market to themselves.
Adidas' strength had traditionally been
in international and Olympic events in
which participants were amateurs.
Endorsements contracts were often
made with national sports associations
rather than with individual athletes.
During the late 1970s and early 1980s,
the environment affecting the running
shoe industry changed dramatically as
American consumers were increasingly
concerned with physical fitness. Phil
Knight, founder of Nike, challenged
the giants by launching the 'waffle sole',
whose tiny rubber studs made it more
springy than competitive shoes on the
market. While Adidas had already segmented the athletic shoe market by type
of sports, Phil Knight went one step
further by re-segmenting the market
along new dimensions: foot types,
body weights, running speed, training
schedules, sex and different levels of
skills. By the early 1980s, demand for
Nike products was such that 60% of
Nike retailers gave advanced orders,
often waiting six months for delivery.
Within four years, Nike's market share
for running shoes went from zero to
33% while Adidas' share went down
from 50% to 20%. By offering a great
variety of styles, prices and uses, Nike
was able to appeal to many different
customer segments. While all running

shoe manufacturers followed Adidas'
segmentation strategy, Nike just did it
better. Not only did it outpace its competitors in creativity, R&D, and market
research but it carefully built a brand by
investing massively in communications
and individual athlete's sponsorship.

Competition Analysis

To survive as an organization, it is
imperative for the firm to know and
outperform the competition. As illustrated by the Nike–Adidas example,
knowing who is the present and
potential competition is not just as
trivial a question as it sounds. Finding
out existing competition is often not
too difficult. Sources of competitive
information can come from two major
sources: published (industry publications, annual reports, press articles,
patent records, and so on) or from the
field (sales force reports, trade and
suppliers' feedback, and so on).
Exploiting this information is key in
understanding and anticipating competitors' moves. For all major existing
and potential competitors, it is important to identify what customer segment they focus on and what value
proposition they are offering. Marketers need to recognize that competitors would not exist if they were not
providing value to customers.
Consequently the following key critical questions need to be addressed on
a regular basis:

- What are my competitors' current
  goals with regard to profitability,

---

4. For a more detailed description of these events, see: 'Adidas: Letting Market Advantage
Slip Away', in Robert F. Hartley, *Marketing Mistakes*, John Wiley & Sons, 1996.

market share, new product introduction, geographical expansion,
and so on?

- What assumptions do my competitors hold about the industry, about
themselves and ourselves?
- Are my competitors' goals likely to
change over time, why or why not?
- What are their major strengths and
weaknesses?
- What changes in the industry are
my competitors likely to trigger?
- How will they react to our own initiatives?

Finding out what future competitors will be like is more difficult to
evaluate. Yet marketers need to regularly identify and assess who are the
newcomers on the competitive radar
screen to avoid being caught off-
guard. As we have often found out in
our research, newcomers into an
industry are likely to be the true 'revolutionaries': They are usually not
bound by historical considerations on
how the game is being played in the
industry. These new competitors typically look at the customer with fresh
eyes, designing and exploiting new
customer segments, and bringing
innovative customer value propositions to the market. Dell in computers, Walmart in retail, Nintendo in
electronic games, Microsoft in software or Virgin airlines in the transportation industry are all examples of
successful revolutionaries that have
taken the established industry giants
by surprise and made their mark in
their respective industry with innovative products and services.

How a Johnson & Johnson major breakthrough broke down

Johnson & Johnson (J&J), which had
sparked a revolution in the treatment
of coronary-artery disease with a medical device called a stent, recently faced
the challenge we have just described.
In just three years, J&J had captured
90% of a US$1 billion market for a
tiny metal scaffold that opens
obstructed heart vessels only to lose
everything in 1998 to Guidant Corp.
In the autumn of 1998, Guidant
launched a competitive program and
captured 79% of the market in just 45
days![5] What went wrong? According
to Eric Topol, Chairman of cardiology
at Cleveland Clinic, J&J did not sustain the technology and underestimated a fast competitive reaction. This left
the door open for competitors to
come up with better designs. J&J was
also slow in developing next generation versions of its technology and left
the impression among top doctors
that it was banking on a strong patent
to protect its product from competition. Moreover, J&J angered many key
customers with a rigid pricing strategy, offering no discounts even for
accounts that purchased more than
US$1 million of stents a year. When
an alternative became available with
Guidant products, unhappy customers
quickly rushed to shift suppliers. What
J&J failed to anticipate was a strong
and fast reaction from competitors for
a product with fat margins. Now, J&J
is experimenting new products in clinical trials and expects to convince
skeptical doctors that it is truly com-

---

5. For more details, see *The Wall Street Journal Europe*, 'Missing a Beat: How a Breakthrough in Cradia Treatment Broke Down for J&J', September 23, 1998.

mitted to the cardiology market. But Guidant and other competitors are also working on a new generation of products, leaving limited prospects to J&J to go back to an overly dominant position in the market. The J&J example is not an isolated one. In fact, it illustrates the challenges that many marketers in technically orientated industries often experience. In industries with short product life cycles such as fashion, toys or consumer electronics, every new product innovation is a new competitive game.

Company Analysis

According to Richard Teerlink (Chairman of Harley Davidson): 'Complacency, greed and arrogance are the key ingredients for corporate failure.'[6] Regularly reassessing the corporate capabilities is therefore critical for the growth and survival of the organization. 'What differentiates us from our competitors in meeting the needs of our target customers?', 'Where can we improve?', 'How can we serve our customers better', 'Where are our products/services in their life cycles?' 'What is our unique value proposition?' are some of the questions that are being addressed again and again by the best companies.

A marketing corporate audit is often difficult to conduct with objectivity when run internally. Personal interests, internal politics and lack of distance from the day-to-day problems often lead companies to rely on outside consultants or other external marketing experts for an objective

diagnosis of where the company marketing performance stands. A typical approach for company analysis usually follows these three critical steps:

1. Marketing performance evaluation.
2. Marketing diagnosis.
3. Identification of key strengths and weaknesses and actions for improvements.

Marketing performance evaluation

This step looks at how target segments' needs are satisfied (performance of our products/services *vis-à-vis* the competition, before, during, and after the sale; quality, availability, as well as other key dimensions of the value proposition perceived as important by the customer). This analysis is usually performed through customer satisfaction and other market research surveys. Marketing performance evaluation also includes an audit of the corporate performance in terms of: market share, financial profitability by product line, customer segments and geographical coverage. Benchmarking surveys provide very useful feedback on these different dimensions when the corporate performance is compared with the best in the same industry. The PIMS (Profit Impact of Marketing Strategy) is another useful strategic marketing tool. It permits a business to learn from strategy peers who are conducting a large number of strategy experiments from a similar competitive position rather than from industry peers who participate in the same industry but face different strategic situations.

---

6. Quote from a speech to the IMD MBA Class of 1997, October 20 1997.

Marketing diagnosis

The marketing diagnosis enables the marketer to find out the causes of its marketing problems. For example, a small German kitchen accessory manufacturer found that its profits and margins relied heavily on the success of a small number of products for which the demand was stagnating. The company was also losing money on every sales order below DM60 (as the costs to sell these items far exceeded the profits made out of these orders). Another firm in the UK floor accessories industry found that its 50% customer repurchase rate and a 66% coverage of the total available market offered significant potential for improvement. Both companies also found through this marketing diagnosis that, although they were winning more customers than they were losing, concentrating on retaining existing customers represented another important opportunity

Marketing actions

By regularly concluding a complete marketing diagnosis, marketers can then formulate an appropriate marketing plan that builds on existing strengths, copes with areas for improvement and sets priorities for action. For example, our German kitchen accessory manufacturer decided to refocus the efforts of its sales force on the products that generated more margins. Similarly, the UK floor accessory manufacturer decided to work on a new incentive plan to retain existing customers rather than to develop an expensive communications campaign to attract new ones.

Channel Analysis

More and more marketers recognize the importance of **relationship marketing** as channel members (distributors and retailers) are significantly increasing their bargaining power. Consequently, large retailers are considered to be a very special kind of customer. Focusing only on end-users has led some manufacturers to ignore the great influence that channel members play on final sales.

Lego, the Danish-based toy manufacturer of plastic bricks, has been a case in best practices when it comes to managing big and small retailers. Lego has quickly recognized that the needs of these two types of retailer must be managed differently to gain a sustainable competitive advantage in the industry. Thanks to electronic data systems, large retailers are usually better aware of new fashion trends in the industry. They require 'Just in Time' delivery, fast turnover of products and may even work on consignment. By responding to the specific needs of these retailers, Lego has managed to get better shelf space with large retailers.

Small toy shops, on the contrary, do not have the sophisticated electronic data systems used by large retailers. Consequently, they are usually 'late' at capturing end-user trends. Inventory management and sales forecasting are usually major headaches for them. By working on these challenges jointly with small retailers, Lego has also won the respect of small toys retailers. The lesson learnt by the Danish company is that any issue or problem faced by retailers (small or big) is an opportunity to increase sales at the end-user level. The more responsive Lego is to their concerns, the more shelf space may be available to the plastic brick manufacturer.

In other industries – very often technical businesses – the trend has been the reverse, the customer has traditionally been considered to be the distributor only and few businesses have been paying enough attention to the final end-user. Until recently, SKF, the Swedish-based ball-bearing manufacturer used to sell its products *to* distributors rather than *through* distributors. As a result, few people at SKF were worrying a great deal about the final customers: garagists and car owners. Ball-bearings were sold by the ton to distributors and service to the garagists (assortment, availability, ease of installation) was not considered to be a critical issue.[7] By reversing this trend and paying more attention to the needs of the end customer, SKF was able to take the lead in the industry and reap considerable benefits from selling its products *together* with its channel members.

Cost Analysis

Too many marketers often stop the marketing homework at analyzing issues without looking in detail at the numbers. However, a financial or economic analysis is often necessary for managers to evaluate different marketing options. Launching a new product, revising a price, a distribution or a communication strategy have significant financial implications.

Costs and contribution

The logic behind a financial analysis of a marketing plan is to estimate the impact that marketing decisions will have on the bottom line. Profit is the result of the differences between sales revenues and costs. Marketing costs can be divided into **variable** and **fixed** costs. Variable costs are directly linked to volume of products made or sold. For example, costs of materials, salespeople's commissions are classified as **variable costs** since they vary according to sales or production volumes. In contrast, advertising is considered a **fixed cost**, as it remains unchanged regardless of the production or sales volume.

Contribution or margin per unit is the difference between price per unit and variable cost per unit. Similarly, net contribution is equal to unit contribution times volume less fixed cost.

To illustrate these concepts, consider the example of a small brewery producing lager beer. Rental costs of the factory and facilities, including such elements as utilities, insurance and taxes are US$300,000 per annum. Sales force, advertising and other marketing and management costs amount to US$400,000 annually. The costs of leasing machinery with an expected life of five years are US$200,000. The cost of raw materials and labor is US$30 per case (12 bottles) of beer. If the selling price of lager beer is US$36 per case, then we have the following:

---

7. See IMD Case Study: 'SKF Bearings Series: Market Orientation Through Services' by Sandra Vandermerwe and Marika Taishoff.

Fixed
costs   = \$300,000 + \$400,000 +\$200,000
         = \$900,000

Variable
costs per
case   = \$30

Selling
price   = \$36

Unit
contrib-
ution   = \$36 – \$30 = \$6

If the brewery expects to sell 35,000 cases within a year, then estimated costs and revenues will be as follows:

Total variable
costs   = 35,000 × \$30
              = \$1,050,000

Total revenue = 35,000 × \$36
              = \$1,260,000

Total
contribution = \$1,260,000 – \$1,050,000
              = \$210,000

Breakeven analysis

Breakeven is an important tool to calculate the level of sales needed to cover all fixed costs and just that, no profits, no losses, just breaking even. The breakeven volume is found by dividing the fixed costs by the contribution per unit. Using the previous example of our brewery:

Breakeven (in units):
    \$900,000 / \$6 = 150,000 cases

The concept of breakeven can be used to help managers decide on a price of the adequate level of marketing and other fixed costs a business can support. It is then a matter of performing various calculations of the breakeven point using different alternatives as regards to price, advertising support, number of salespeople, and so on.

In reality, companies seldom operate at breakeven level. Profit target is the norm. The breakeven formula can be used to calculate the level of sales required to meet profit goals. If the owner of the brewery wants to reach a \$100,000 profit target, the calculation will be as follows:

Profit target = unit contribution x units sold – fixed costs

or

Units
required = fixed costs + profit target / unit
           contribution
         = \$900,000 + \$100,000 / \$6
         = 166,667 units

Obviously, it would be wrong to take marketing decisions relying solely on these numbers, unless the owner of this brewery considers the total size of the market, its growth rate, customers' preferences, competitive products and possible reactions, channels interests, and so on. In other words, cost analysis cannot substitute for customer and competition, company and channel analysis. Cost analysis can only help the marketing manager to have a better perspective of what is feasible, to narrow down the number of alternatives and to help him or her make a sound decision on what is best for the company.

Putting It All Together

Once the four elements of the marketing analysis – context, customer, competitor and company – have been completed, marketers should be able to get a clearer picture of their competitiveness. Systematic marketing analysis is the first step to developing a sustainable competitive advantage by:

- Creating a unique product or service that will be perceived by customers and distributors as clearly superior
- Developing an appropriate marketing plan (product, price, promotion, place) for our targeted segments
- Getting the necessary resources (money, technology, human talents) to implement the marketing plan.

Cases in Section I

Cases presented in Section I provide many opportunities to apply the concepts presented in this first section: context, customer, competitor and company analysis. In the first case study of this first section, 'The Skisailer', a new product combining windsurfing and skiing runs into trouble in its first year of worldwide sales. A group of MBA students studies the problem and collects market data. The product's inventor is left with the task of taking actions to save his invention from imminent disaster. What should he do?

'Delissa in Japan': Agria, a Swedish milk products cooperative launches its Delissa yogurt in Japan through a joint venture/franchise agreement. At launch, Agria expected to reach between 10% and 15% of the total Japanese yogurt market. Despite repeated surveys and visits from Agria marketing specialists, Delissa fails to reach 3% of the Japanese market after 9 years of operation. Disappointed by Delissa's poor results, the Swedish management begins to wonder whether they should continue doing business in Japan, change franchise or pull out.

Learning Points

The students can expect the following learning points from analyzing and discussing the cases in this section:

- Context, customer, competitor and company analysis
- Market segmentation
- Market entry strategies
- Product re-launch strategies
- Market research methods used in stimulating market potential for a new product
- Diagnosis of specific problems hampering sales of a new product
- Cultural differences and internationalization processes
- Marketing consumer products on an international basis
- Managing a global business
- Strategic alliances across cultural and national boundaries

The Skisailer: Marketing a Young Investor's Dream

This case was written by Professors Dominique Turpin and Kamran Kashani.

David Varilek was given the bad news about the worldwide sales of his invention, the Skisailer. The management at Mistral, the company which had invested in David's innovation, informed him that the first year sales of Skisailer had failed to match the target and that the future of the product was in doubt. Only 708 Skisailers had been sold in the first season the product was on sale. Mistral, which manufactured and marketed the product worldwide, had already invested more than half a million dollars in the project. The management was seriously considering dropping the product from its line next year.

Realizing that such an initial setback could jeopardize the future of his four-year-old invention, David asked a group of MBA students at a leading international school of management in Switzerland to study the market potential for Skisailer and recommend what needed to be done to revive sales. The students had recently completed the first phase of the project. They had presented David with their findings and the 23-year-old inventor was reviewing the information.

The Invention

Skisailer was based on a concept that combined downhill skiing and windsurfing in a new sport: skisailing. As a Swiss native, David Varilek considered himself 'born on skis'. However, he had always been frustrated by not being able to ski on the flat snow fields that surrounded his home in the winter season.

Four years ago, in his own garage, David invented a connection bar which could be fixed onto regular skis while still allowing them to be directed with great flexibility. A windsurfing rig, consisting of a connecting bar and a sail, could then be installed on the connection bar and, with enough wind, flat snow surfaces could become great fun for skiing. The idea was subsequently patented under the Swiss law. A major feature of the invention was that the Skisailer's unique design also allowed 'windskiers' to use regular downhill skis and almost any type of windsurfing rig, an innovation that limited the buyer's expense. The connection bar and the sail were easy to install. Lateral clamps used for attaching the connection bar to the skis did not damage them in any way except for small grooves on the side of each ski. Only 5cm (2 inches) of the ski's length were held rigid and the rest retained normal flexibility. Safety had also been an important consideration when developing the Skisailer; three self-releasing safety mechanisms were installed on the product. (Refer to **Exhibit 1** for an illustration of the Skisailer.)

The Skisailer could be used on either smooth slopes or flat surfaces. The ideal surface for skisailing was on the kind of hard-packed snow usually found on groomed ski slopes, but the Skisailer could also be used on ice where it could achieve speeds of up to 100km/h.[1] Skisailing in deep snow or slightly uphill required stronger wind. For use at high speeds, a safety helmet was recommended.

According to David Varilek, skisailing was as much fun as windsurfing even though it had to be done in cold weather. 'For identical sensations, skisailing is easier to learn and handle than windsurfing,' David claimed. 'You can get on and get off the Skisailer easily, and you are always on your feet. Another great thing with the Skisailer is that you can take advantage of the terrain to perform the same kind of loopings as on sea waves. The Skisailer is a great vehicle for discovering variety in the surroundings.'

Mistral Windsurfing AG

Mistral Windsurfing AG was a company affiliated with the ADIA Group. ADIA, a $1 billion conglomerate with headquarters in Lausanne, Switzerland, had its activities centered around ADIA Interim, a company providing temporary personnel to companies around the world.

A number of years ago, ADIA had acquired Mistral as part of its diversification strategy. The acquisition was seen as an opportunity to enter a rapidly growing industry. Consistency in marketing and product policy over the past ten years had made Mistral a leader in the worldwide windsurfing industry. This success was grounded in technological competence, permanent innovation, high quality standards, a selective international distribution policy and strong financial backing. Thus, in a fiercely competitive market for windsurfing equipment, characterized by the rise and fall of brands and manufacturers, Mistral was occupying a leading position. To Martin Pestalozzi, the President of ADIA, the Skisailer represented a good opportunity to extend Mistral's product line, at a time when Mistral management was increasingly concerned about the future of the windsurf market.

Mistral and the Windsurf Market

The fathers of the modern windsurf were two Californians, Hoyle Schweitzer and James Drake, who had developed the concept and registered the Windsurfer

---

1. 1 kilometre = 0.62 mile.

brand. They had applied for and received a patent for their device which was a cross between a surfboard and a sailboat.

A few years later, Schweitzer bought out Drake and developed his firm, Windsurfing International, from a living-room operation into a multimillion dollar corporation with branches in six countries. Because of its North American patents, Windsurfing International was able to hold a virtual monopoly in the US and Canada for some time when a number of other firms entered the market.

Meanwhile, competition in the European windsurfing equipment market was years ahead of North America. First introduced to the European market by Ten Cate, a Dutch firm, windsurfing enjoyed an unprecedented growth, particularly in France and Germany. Even as the industry matured, it maintained growth in terms of dollar volume though not in units. Interest in windsurfing had grown from a small pool of enthusiasts to a large and growing population, an estimated 2–3 million people internationally.

Established in Bassersdorf near Zurich (Switzerland), Mistral rapidly won an international reputation among windsurfers. Its success was enhanced by two promotional strategies. First, from the start, Mistral had signed up Robby Naish, a young Californian who had won all the major distinctions and titles in this sport. Using Mistral equipment, Robby Naish had become the World Champion at age 12 and had dominated this sport ever since. Last year, he won the world title for the tenth time in a row. Second, Mistral had promoted its brand by supplying several hundred windsurfs free of charge to such leisure organizations as Club Méditerranée which gave the brand visibility around the world.

Mistral also enjoyed an advantage over other windsurf manufacturers by concentrating on the upper price and quality range of the market. Worldwide, Mistral's equipment was considered the best. Robby Naish's name and the high quality and reliability of Mistral's products had helped build an extensive network of distributors in 30 countries. The company had its own subsidiary in the US where it generated about one-third of its global sales and market share. Mistral was also directly represented in a number of European countries such as France, Germany and the Benelux. For the rest of the world, Mistral used exclusive agents who were responsible for selling Mistral products in specific regions.

Recent Market Developments in Windsurfing

Recently, a number of factors had combined to dampen the sales of windsurfs in the US market. Patent infringement fights had led to the forced withdrawal of Bic and Tiga, both French manufacturers, from the market. With a total sales of 16,000 units, the two companies were among the major brands in the US. Meanwhile, a number of European manufacturers had gone bankrupt, thus reducing even further the supply of and marketing expenditures on windsurfing equipment. Market saturation had also contributed to the decline of sales from 73,000 units two years ago to 62,000 last year.

In Europe, where windsurfing had grown at spectacular rates over the years, the market was showing the signs of a slowdown. According to the French market research group ENERGY, windsurfing equipment sales in France had risen from less than 600 units to more than 115,000 units over the span of a decade. However, cool weather conditions as well as general market saturation had reduced French sales to 65,000 units last year. In Germany, the second largest market after France, sales had also declined to below 60,000 units from the high levels of a few years ago. Sales had leveled off in Italy at around 35,000 units, in Holland at 45,000 units, and in Switzerland at 15,000 units.

European sales were dominated by European brands. In France, for example, Bic and Tiga together accounted for 45,000 sales. Mistral was the top imported brand. In Germany, Klepper was the leading local brand; Mistral was a distant fourth in market share. Last year, the distribution of Mistral's global sales of 45,620 units was: the US, 25%; Europe, 30%; and the rest of the world, 45%. Windsurfing equipment accounted for 60% of the company's $52 million sales, while the rest was divided between sportswear (20%), and spare parts and accessories (20%).

The Skisailer and Mistral's Diversification Policy

Mistral Windsurfing AG had contacted David Varilek three years ago after ADIA management learned about the Skisailer from a four-page article in a major Swiss magazine. David Varilek was interested in establishing a relationship with Mistral as the company was the world leader in windsurfing equipment.

The Skisailer seemed an appropriate product diversification for Mistral. The Skisailer could also fit in with the new line of winter sportswear and other ski-related products that Mistral's management was planning to develop. Mistral had full support from ADIA to launch the project.

A contract for development, manufacturing and distribution of the Skisailer was formally signed between David Varilek and Mistral. For the duration of the agreement, all Skisailer patent and trademark rights would be transferred to Mistral, but David would serve as technical adviser to the company and would receive in return a 2% royalty on sales. It was also agreed that David would demonstrate the Skisailer in competitions and exhibitions where Mistral was participating. Should total sales fall short of 5,000 units by the end of the second year, either party could terminate the agreement, with trademarks and patents reverting back to David Varilek. Mistral could also counter any competitive offer made to David, a so-called 'first right of refusal'.

Introducing the Skisailer

Soon after the contract was signed, two prototypes of the Skisailer were developed at Mistral for presentation at ISPO, the largest European sports exhibition held annually in Munich, Germany. Early the following year, Mistral engineers developed several innovations that were added to the Skisailer. For example, the connecting bar and mounting blocks were strengthened to resist shocks and low temperatures. The equipment was also modified to accommodate the Mistral windsurf sailing rig.

In Munich at ISPO, the Skisailer was widely acclaimed as a truly innovative product that would certainly win public enthusiasm. However, at this early stage of development, the product still lacked promotional support. No pamphlet, video or pictures had been developed to present the product and educate potential users. David thought that the pictures used to introduce the product to Mistral's distributors were not attractive enough to trigger interest and buying. Nevertheless, some distributors liked the product and placed immediate orders.

The formal launch of Skisailer got underway last year. Mistral produced 2,000 Skisailers – consisting of a mast foot, sail (available from its standard windsurf line) and the connecting bar. They were to be distributed worldwide through the company's network of wholesalers and independent sports shops in large and medium-sized cities. For example, in Lausanne, Switzerland, a city of 250,000 inhabitants with 30 skishops and 3 windsurf equipment stores, Skisailer was sold in three locations. Of the three stores, two specialized in ski equipment and the third sold windsurfing products.

Skisailer was priced $410 at retail; the price included the bar connection and its mounting blocks, but excluded the sail and mast – which cost an additional $590. Retail margins on the Skisailer and its rig were set at 35%. The wholesale margins were also 35%. Skisailer cost Mistral $85 per unit to produce and ship to distributors; the cost for the sailing rig was around $200.

It seemed to David that the first year promotional budget of $15,000 set for Skisailer was too low. Mistral management had already turned down a $35,000 proposal from David to produce a promotional video showing Skisailer in action. Nevertheless, David decided to arrange for the shooting of such a video on his own at Mammoth Lake, California. Mistral later refunded David the $10,000 which the video had cost him.

Since the beginning, Mistral had invested more than half a million dollars in Skisailer:

Engineering & Tooling	$214,000
Other Costs	74,000
Development Costs	**288,000**
Inventory – Assembled & Spares	
At Central Warehouse	180,000
At Distributors	68,000
Sub-total	**248,000**
Total	**$536,000**

Market Research Findings

Because of his concern about the future of the Skisailer, David had commissioned the group of MBA students to study the global market for Skisailer and report on their findings. The students had completed the first phase of their study which dealt with estimating the market potential for Skisailer, competing products, ski market developments, and a survey of buyers, retailers and wholesalers. A summary of the findings follows.

Potential Market

Based on interviews with buyers of the Skisailer, the team had learned that the potential customers were likely to be those who did both skiing and windsurfing. Building on industry reports suggesting a total worldwide population of two million windsurfers and 30 million skiers, the team estimated that a maximum of 60% of windsurfers, or a total of 1.2 million individuals, were also skiers. The 'realizable market' for the Skisailer, according to the MBA students, was far below this maximum, however. They identified at least four 'filters' which together reduced the realizable market potential to a fraction of the maximum:

- *Filter 1:* Customer Type. As a relatively new sport, Skisailer appealed to a group of enthusiasts whom the MBA students referred to as 'innovators'. Their study suggested that these buyers were in the 15–25 age bracket, liked sports but, for the most part, could not afford the price tag of the Skisailer. The next most likely group of buyers, called 'early adopters', were older, less sporty, and more image conscious. For this segment, price was not a major factor. The team believed that sufficient penetration of the first segment was necessary before the second group showed any interest in the new product.
- *Filter 2:* Location. Users of the Skisailer reported that ideal skisailing conditions, such as flat ice- or snow-covered fields, were not always accessible. This location factor, the team believed, tended to reduce the potential for the product.
- *Filter 3:* Climate. According to the MBA students, climate was another inhibiting factor. The Skisailer required not only suitable snow or ice, but also a good wind. The minimum required wind speed was around 20 kilometers/hour. The study identified a number of regions as meeting both the needed snow and wind conditions: Scandinavia and central Europe, certain parts of North America, and parts of Southern Australia.
- *Filter 4:* Competing Products. Four similar products were identified but, according to the student report, all lacked brand image, wide distribution and product sophistication. Although information on competing products was scanty, the students had assembled the following information from different sources:

Brand (Origin)	Retail Price	Total Units Sold	Main Sales Area
Winterboard (Finland)	$395	4,000	Finland, US
Ski Sailer (Australia)	$90	3,500	Australia, US
ArticSail (Canada)	$285	3,000	Canada, US
Ski Sailer (US)	$220	300	US

Based on their initial estimate of the maximum size of the potential market, as well as the limiting effects of the four 'filters', the students arrived at an estimate of 20,000 units as the total realizable market for Skisailer. This volume, they believed, could grow by as much as 10% per year. (Refer to **Exhibit 2** for an estimate of the market potential and **Exhibit 3** for the levels of sales the students believed Skisailer could achieve over the next five years.)

Competing Products

Winterboard

Winterboard, a light windsurfing board with skis, had been invented in Finland. It could be used on both ice and snow, and its performance was said to be impressive. Some rated the Winterboard as the best performing windski after the Skisailer. In terms of sales, Winterboard had been the most successful windski product. Over the last five years, 4,000 units had been sold, mainly in Scandinavia and the US, in regular sports shops. Winterboard was being sold at a retail price of $395, excluding the sailing rig. Retail margins were at 40%. The skis were already integrated into the board and did not need to be purchased as an extra.

According to the research team, Winterboard's management believed that prices, retail margins and advertising expenditures were relatively unimportant in their marketing strategy. The key to success was organizing events, as people wanted sportive social gathering on weekends in the winter. When they had to go out snowsailing in the cold by themselves, they quickly lost interest.

Australian-made 'Ski Sailer'

This product was essentially a simple bar with a mastfoot on it which could be attached to normal ski boots and used with either conventional skis or roller skates. The Ski Sailer had an equalizing slide and joint mechanism, so maneuvers such as parallel turns, jump turns and snowplowing were possible. Any sailing rig could be fitted to the Ski Sailer's mast post.

The US distributor for this product reported cumulative sales of about 3,000 units (30% through ski shops, 70% through surf shops) at a retail price of $90 each. But, he admitted that he had lost interest in the product when he realized that only customers who were tough and resistant to the cold enjoyed windsurfing in the wintertime. This meant a much smaller customer base than for his other leisure/sportswear products.

'ArticSail Board'

This product was essentially a W-shaped surfboard for use on snow, ice or water. It was distributed by Plastiques LPA Ltd in Mansonville, Quebec, Canada, approximately 50 miles from the US–Canadian border.

The ArticSail was especially designed for snow and ice, but it could also be used on water, in which case the rear filler plates would be replaced by two ailerons, also supplied with the board. Adjustable footstraps, included with the board, also had to be repositioned for use on water. The product was made of a special plastic, usable at both normal and very low temperatures. The producer warned users to watch for objects which could damage the underside of the sled.

The company reported a cumulative sales of approximately 3,000 units (600 estimated for last winter), mostly in Canada, at a retail price of $285 (including a 38% retail margin). Promotion expenses were about 15% on Canadian and US sales, mainly spent on a two-man team demonstrating at skisailing resorts.

American-made 'Ski Sailer'

Yet another 'Ski Sailer' had been invented by a young Californian, Carl Meinberg. The American Ski Sailer also used a small board mounted on skis and was similar to the product developed by David Varilek. On his own, the inventor had sold about 50 Ski Sailers retailing at $220 each. During the winter season, Carl Meinberg toured a number of ski resorts, demonstrating the Ski Sailer; he spent the rest of the year selling his invention.

Recent Developments in the World Ski Market

As background to their study, the research team also obtained information on the ski market. (Last year's sales of downhill – also called alpine – and cross-country skis are given in **Exhibit 4**.)

The total world alpine skiing population was estimated at 30 million people. Competition in the ski market was intensive and production capacity exceeded demand by an estimated 25–30%. Prices for skis were under pressure and retailers used discounts to build traffic. Retail profits were mostly made on sales of accessories and skiwear.

In distribution, specialty shops were losing market share to the large chains. Production was concentrated, with seven manufacturers controlling 80% of the market. The falling exchange rate for the US dollar had put the large European producers such as Fischer and Kneissel at a disadvantage in the US market.

Marketing skis depended heavily on successes in world championships and the image associated with the winning skis. Customers in the US appeared to be losing interest in skiing, but these signs had not been observed in Europe and Japan, where the sport remained popular at a stable level.

A recent innovation in skiing was the snowboard, a product with high popularity among younger customers. A snowboard was essentially a single large ski with two ski bindings positioned in a similar way as the footstraps on a windsurf.

The board had been available in the US for many years, but had only recently been introduced in Europe. Snowboard's worldwide sales had doubled every year, reaching an estimated 40,000 last season. One US manufacturer, Burton, accounted for 50% of the market. Many manufacturers of winter products had taken advantage of the opportunity and had started producing their own versions of the snowboard. The product was very popular in the European distribution channels and expectations for further growth were high.

Buyers' Survey

The research team had interviewed a small number of Skisailer customers in Germany, Austria, the Benelux countries, the US and Canada. Highlights of their comments on the advantages and disadvantages of the Skisailer were:

Advantages of the Product

- Sure, skisurfing in winter is great; it's a lot of fun.
- You can do quick maneuvers, nice turns, beautiful power turns and fast changes of the grips. It (the Skisailer) gives a good opportunity to train for windsurfing, as you have to drive the way you surf – with the pressure on the inner ski.
- I did not have any problem with turns.
- It is not difficult to learn if you have some feeling for sailing.
- It simulates surfing in your backyard.
- It is the right device if you want to do something on Sunday afternoon (with no time to drive somewhere in your car).
- Fun, different, new, good.
- It is the only thing with a mountain touch that you can use on the plain.
- It turns. That makes it much more fun than the other products on the market. You can do jives, curve jives, jumps... it is close to sailing a shore boat... it's a lot of fun.
- If the conditions are ideal, it's a lot of fun.

Disadvantages of the Product

- The feet get twisted; sailing on the wind requires exceptional twisting of the legs and knees.
- Both of the white caps at the end of the bar came off and it was virtually impossible to get spare parts.
- Difficult in heavy snow.
- Difficult to find the perfect conditions.
- You use it 3–4 times a season. For this, the price is too high.
- It is uncomfortable to use. You have to loosen up your boots, otherwise the rim of the shoe cuts into your twisted leg.
- If the snow is too deep, you cannot use it. What you want is strong wind.
- The price is too high.
- My problem is that there is hardly any wind in winter.
- In the beginning, I was getting stiff in the unnatural position and my knees hurt, but later I got more relaxed and with time you have a lot of fun.
- In mid-winter, it is too cold to use it; spring is ideal.

Retailers' Opinions of the Mistral Skisailer

A dozen retailers of the Skisailer – in Germany, Canada, Austria and France – were also surveyed. Highlights of their comments were:

Advantages of the Product

- You could sell a lot of them in the first year, but I do not see it as the absolute 'barnstormer'.
- It is a first year novelty.
- It is a lot of fun in the snow… and for people with a lot of money. It is a new gimmick.
- It combines two favorite sports – skiing and windsurfing.
- It is better than all self-built products… you have full movability.
- Easy to use. It is an original idea.
- You can use your ski, it is flexible and easy to store.
- Very thoroughly constructed, very stable.

Disadvantages of the Product

- Unhappy product. Usable only under specific weather conditions.
- It is only a fad.
- You just don't drive with your ski to a lake and try it on the ice.

- Maybe it sells better in a winter shop.
- Your position on the skis is abnormal – the snowboard is a better alternative.
- We do not think that it will be a fast-turning product.
- Impossible to sell – nobody tried it.
- In my environment, there is no space to do it, no lakes, no fields.
- For a backyard product, the price is too high. Even Mistral's good image doesn't help. Maybe this will change if the product is better known.
- Customers watched the video with enthusiasm, but when they learned the price, enthusiasm was nil. We are offering our last piece now at a discount of 40%.
- If you ski and windsurf, your hobbies cost you a lot of money. Often the early user is the sportive freak with a low income. How will you convince him about the product?

Distributors' Comments

The research team interviewed Mistral distributors in ten different countries in Europe and North America. Highlights of comments from five distributors were:

Europe

- We first learned about the Skisailer at ISPO in Munich and ordered some.
- From Mistral we got some folders and the video. If you see it on the video, you want to use the Skisailer right away.
- We did not support the retailers very much because we felt that the Skisailer's marketing was not done professionally from the beginning. For instance, Skisailer deliveries were late.
- The product would have potential if the price were lower and the promotion were done professionally all the way through.
- We bought the Skisailer, which is good for use in our winter climate, after Mistral contacted us two years ago.
- The product is expensive and not really functional.
- Promotion was not good at all, only a few folders and a video which was not free of charge. When there were product breakdowns, spare parts were not available.
- A Finnish competitor now has captured the market with a product that looks like a surfboard with two skis fitted into it. We have the right places for skisailing here!
- We used all our contacts and spent approximately $7,500 last year to promote this product on television.
- The retail price is too high for a product to be used only a few weekends in the winter.

- The snowboard, especially made for surfing on ski slopes, is much more fashionable.
- Surf and ski shops make higher margins on clothing and accessories that are sold in larger quantities.
- You don't create a product first and then look for the market, this is the wrong way around. The Skisailer is more a product for Scandinavia and similar regions in America or Canada.
- We didn't know the product but found the demonstration film to be convincing. Therefore, we organized ski resort demonstrations in the French Alps at racing events where there are many spectators. We also pushed about 40 Skisailers in several retail shops.
- For this product, finding suitable locations where you can have a training session with wind and snow is necessary.
- We estimate that the retailers have sold about half their inventory, but we do not want to get more involved and have the rest sent back to us. Retailers are looking for customer demand which is lacking.

North America

- I cannot see further sales of the Skisailer without more product support. At low temperatures the rubber joints failed, but when we asked for replacements, there was no reply from Mistral. In the end, we had to strip other Skisailers to get the spare parts.
- We have good skisailing conditions (in South Ontario/Quebec) and a group of interested enthusiasts here. The product has been promoted to thousands of people! The folder and video are very good.
- On a trade show in Toronto, the product was well received except for the price, which is a problem.

Conclusion

In reviewing the research team's report, David was searching for clues that could explain the Skisailer's poor performance in its first selling season. Was it the product design that needed further refinement? Or the Skisailer's price, which was perceived by some as being high? Was the absence of high promotional support, which he always suspected to be a problem, a key factor? Or maybe Mistral's selective distribution was the core issue? What else could explain why his invention had failed to match everybody's expectations?

An additional piece of information had heightened the need for immediate action. David had just received the final sales and inventory figures for the Skisailer from Mistral – while 708 units had been sold to the trade, only 80 units had been bought at retail:

UNIT SALES

Country	To Distributors	To Retailers	To End-users
US/Canada	233	98	45
Germany	250	50	10
Switzerland	42	30	1
France	56	40	20
Benelux	60	0	0
Others	67	12	4
Total Shipped	**708**	**230**	**80**

David knew that Mistral management was about to review the future of the Skisailer. He feared that without a convincing analysis and action plan from him, the Skisailer would be dropped from Mistral's line. He was therefore impatiently waiting for the MBA research team's recommendations based on the data already collected.

EXHIBIT 1

Illustration of Skisailer from Product Brochure

PRESENTS

A NEW WAY OF SKIING

The **SKISAILER**™

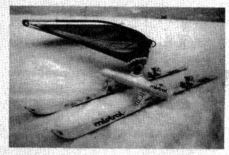

Invented by David Varilek and developed in conjunction
with Mistral Windsurfing AG, Bassersdorf, Switzerland

Contact
Mistral Windsurfing AG
CH – 8303 Bassersdorf/Zürich
Switzerland
Telephone 01/836-8922
Telex 59 266 MWAG CH

EXHIBIT 1 (CONTINUED)

FREEDOM: With the Skisailer, Mistral has developed the ultimate marriage of wind and snow, ski and sail. All the thrills of skiing without the need of mountains or ski-lift passes. More sport and pleasure per hour invested. The boring, grey, winter afternoons when all you can do is gaze at surf photos in the magazines and remember the sunny days on your funboard, are over. Mistral Skisailer – That's funboard surfing in the snow and ski-holidays hanging on the boom.

EASE: Once you have fixed the small rails to your skis in front of the toe-bindings, you are free at any time to 'fly' across the snow-covered countryside. Simple and easy to assemble, the equipment stores neatly in a back-pack, leaving you free to ski, should you wish to switch from wind-power to gravity-power.

FUNCTION: The principal advantages of the Skisailer derive from the basic concept and the light, strong construction of the equipment. The multidirectional freedom of movement of the mast-foot plate allows for all normal ski maneuvers (edging, turning etc.) while the optimum positioning of the mast in relation to the skier allows the maneuvers of sailboarding (jibing, jumping, snow-starts!).

SAFETY: There is no limit to your striving for always more speed, longer jumps and more radical maneuvers. The security of the sport is assured by the triple release security system: the conventional ski bindings, the mast-foot plate connectors and the mast-foot.

FREEDOM: Mit dem Skisailer lässt Mistral den Traum vom Windsurfen im Pulverschnee Wahrheit werden. Vergessen Sie endlose Warteschlangen am Lift und überfüllte Pisten. Die langweiligen, grauen Winternachmittage, an denen die Erinnerungen an die Surferlebnisse des letzten Sommers nur noch beim Betrachten der Fotos in den Magazinen wach werden, sind vorbei. Mistral Skisailer – Funboardfahren im Pulverschnee, Skivergnügen am Gabelbaum.

IT'S SO EASY: Montieren Sie einfach die Funktionsteile vor Ihrer Skibindung. Und los geht's: Snowstart, Raumshots über verschneite Wiesen. Take-Off an einer Bodenwelle, weiche Landung, Slalom zwischen den Schneeflocken, Duck-Jibe, ... Hawaii ist vergessen. Wenn der Wind nachlässt, schalten Sie um von Windkraft auf Schwerkraft, und gehen normal skifahren. Die nicht mehr benötigten Teile passen in Ihren Rucksack.

THE CONCEPT: Der Vorteil des Mistral Skisailers liegt in der superleichten, robusten Konstruktion der Funktionselemente und in der Wirkungsweise des Prinzips. Die allseitige Bewegungsfreiheit der Mastfussplatte ermöglicht Kanteneinsatz und Schwungauslösung wie beim normalen Skilauf. Durch die optimale Positionierung des Riggs auf den Skiern, funktionieren die Funboardmanöver im Schnee bald genauso gut wie auf dem Wasser.

SAFETY FIRST: Ihrem Drang nach immer mehr Speed, noch weiteren Sprüngen und noch heisseren Manbövern können Sie freien Lauf lassen. Selbst bei spektakulären Stürzen schützt Sie ein dreifaches Sicherheitssystem: Ihre Skibindung, der Mastfuss und die Mastfussplatten-Verbinder sind auslösencle Konstruktions-elemente.

LIBERTE: Avec le Skisailer, Mistral réalise enfin le mariage du vent et de la neige, du ski et de la voile. Tous les avantages du ski, sans les inconvénients de la foule et des remontées mécaniques, donnent un rapport plaisir/temps investi incomparable. Fini l'ennui des gris après-midi d'hiver où la seule distraction était de lire des magazines de surf et de se souvenir. Le Skisailer de Mistral c'est du funboard sur neige, des vacances d'hiver accroché au wishbone.

FACILITE: Une fois les petits rails de fixation installés à l'avant des butdes, plus rien ne peut vous empêcher de 'voler' à travers les plaines enneigées, de jiber sur une bosse de neige ou si le vent vous lâche, de ranger votre matériel dans un sac à dos et de skier comme tout le monde.

TECHNICITE: La conception même du Skisailer en est son atout majeur. Les articulations multidirectionnelles de la plaque de soutien du mât permettent une totale liberté de mouvement des skis (prise de carre, virage etc.). D'autre part, la position optimale du mât sur les skis permet de faire toutes les manoeuvres de funboard (snow starts, jibes, sauts).

SECURITE: Celle-ci est assurée en cas de choc par un déclanchement à trois niveaux: aux fixations de ski conventionnelles, aux articulations de la plaque de soutien et au pied de mât. Ainsi toutes craintes dissipées, vos progrès en saut, vitesse et manoeuvres seront encore plus rapides.

EXHIBIT 2

Skisailer Market Potential

Market	Size	%	'Filters'
Potential market	1.2 million	100%	Customer type
Available market	800K	66%	Location Climate
Qualified market	80K	7%	Indirect competition (monoski, skates, etc.)
Served market	40K	3.5%	Direct competition (Winterboard, ArticSail, etc.)
Realizable market	20K	1.7%	Customer type

Source: MBA Student Report.

EXHIBIT 3

Skisailer Achievable Sales Estimate

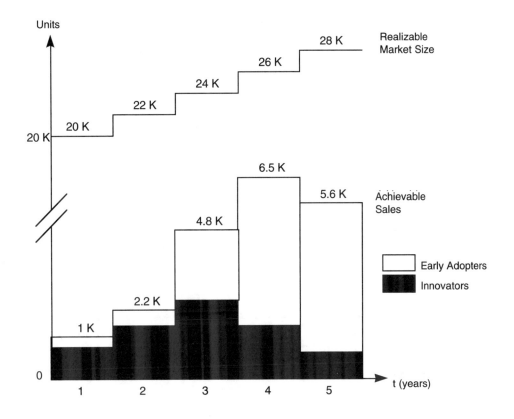

Source: MBA Student Report.

EXHIBIT 4

World Market of Alpine and Cross-country Skis

Alpine Ski Sales	Pairs Sold
Austria, Switzerland, Germany	1,450,000
Rest of Europe	1,550,000
US and Canada	1,600,000
Japan	1,100,000
Other Countries	300,000
Total	**6,000,000**

Cross-country Ski Sales	Pairs Sold
Austria, Switzerland, Germany	700,000
Scandinavia	800,000
Rest of Europe	400,000
US and Canada	750,000
Other Countries	150,000
Total	**2,800,000**

Source: Mistral Windsurfing AG.

CASE 1.2^R

Delissa in Japan

This case was prepared by Research Assistant Juliet Burdet-Taylor and Professor Dominique Turpin. All names and figures have been disguised.

'We can maintain our presence in Japan or we can pull out...'

In the autumn of 1997, Bjorn Robertson, who had recently been named Managing Director of Agria, Sweden's leading dairy products cooperative, met with his team to review the international side of the business. The four men sat around a table piled high with thick reports, Nielsen audits, film storyboards, yogurt cups and a mass of promotional material in Japanese. Agria's 'Delissa' line of fresh dairy products was sold all over the world through franchise agreements. Several of these agreements were up for review, but the most urgent one was the agreement with Nikko of Japan.

'In the light of these results, there are several things we can do in Japan. We can maintain our presence and stay with our present franchisee, we can change our franchisee, or we can pull out. But, let's look first at how badly we are really doing in Japan.' Bjorn Robertson, looked across the conference table at Peter Borg, Stefan Gustafsson and Lars Karlsson, each of whom had been involved with Agria's Japanese business over the past few years.

Robertson read aloud to the others a list of Agria's major foreign ventures featuring the Delissa yogurt brand: 'USA launch date 1977, market share – 12.5%; Germany launch 1980, market share – 14%; UK launch 1982, market share – 13.8%; France launch 1983, market share – 9.5%; Japan launch 1987, market share today – 2–3%.' Robertson circled the figure with his marker and turned to look around at his team. 'Under 3% after 10 years in the market! What happened?' he asked.

History

Agria was founded in 1973 when a group of Swedish dairy cooperatives decided to create a united organization that would develop and sell a line of fresh dairy products. The principal engineers of the organization were Rolf Anderen and Bo Ekman, who had established the group's headquarters in Uppsala, near Stockholm. In 1980, after the individual cooperatives had been persuaded to drop their own trademarks, the Delissa line was launched. This was one of the few 'national' lines of dairy products in Sweden. It comprised yogurts, desserts, fresh cheese and fresh cream. In the two decades that followed, Agria's share rose from 3% to 25% of the Swedish fresh milk products market. Anderen's vision and the concerted efforts of 20,000 dairy farmer members of the cooperative had helped build Agria into a powerful national and international organization.

By 1997, more than 1.1 billion Delissa yogurts and desserts were being consumed per year worldwide. In fiscal year 1996, Delissa had sales of $2.1 billion and employed 4,400 people in and outside Sweden.

Industrial franchising was not very widespread in the 1980s, and few Swedish dairy products firms had invested money abroad. However, Ekman's idea of know-how transfer ventures, whereby a local licensee would manufacture yogurt using Swedish technology and then market and distribute the product using its own distribution network, had enabled Delissa to penetrate over 13 foreign markets with considerable success and with a minimal capital outlay. In contrast, Delissa's biggest competitor worldwide, Danone – a French food conglomerate marketing a yogurt line under the 'Danone' brand name – had gone into foreign markets, mainly by buying into or creating local companies, or by forming regular joint ventures.

By the time Bjorn Robertson took over as European marketing director in 1991, the Delissa trademark – with the white cow symbol so familiar in Sweden – was known in many different countries worldwide. Delissa was very active in sponsoring sports events, and Robertson – himself a keen cross-country skier and sailor – offered his personal support to Delissa's teams around the world.

When he reviewed the international business, Robertson had been surprised by the results of Agria's Japanese joint venture which did not compare to those achieved in most foreign markets. Before calling together the international marketing team for a discussion, Robertson requested the files on Japan and spent some time studying the history of the alliance. He read:

Proposal for Entry into the Japanese Market

In early 1985, the decision was made to enter the Japanese market. Market feasibility research and a search for a suitable franchisee is underway, with an Agria team currently in Japan.

Objectives

The total yogurt market in Japan for 1986 is estimated at approximately 600 million cups (100mn ml). The market for yogurt is expected to grow at an average of at least 8% p.a. in volume for the next 5 years. Our launch strategy would be based on an expected growth rate of 10% or 15% for the total market. We have set ourselves the goal of developing a high quality range of yogurts in Japan, of becoming well known with the Japanese consumer. We aim to reach a 5% market share in the first year and 10% share of market within three years of launch. We plan to cover the three main metropolitan areas, Tokyo, Osaka and Nagoya, within a two-year period, and the rest of the country within the next three years.

Robertson circled the 10% with a red pen. He understood that management would have hesitated to set too high a goal for market share compared to other countries since some executives felt that Japan was a difficult market to enter. But, in 1993, the Japanese operation had not reached its target. In 1997, Delissa's share of the total yogurt market had fallen to 2%, without ever reaching 3%. Robertson wrote a note to the Uppsala-based manager responsible for Far Eastern business stating that he felt Agria's record in Japan in no way reflected the type of success it had had elsewhere with Delissa. He began to wonder why Japan was so different.

The report continued with a brief overview of the Japanese yogurt market:

Consumption
Per capita consumption of yogurt in Japan is low compared to Scandinavian countries. It is estimated at around 5.3 cups per person per year in Japan, versus 110 in Sweden and 120 in Finland. Sales of yogurt in Japan are seasonal, with a peak period from March to July. The highest sales have been recorded in June, so the most ideal launch date would be at the end of February.

Types of Yogurt Available in Japan – 1986
In Japan, yogurt sales may be loosely broken down into three major categories:

- *Plain* (39% of the market in volume):
  Called 'plain' in Japan because the color is white, but it is really flavored with vanilla. Generally sold in 500ml pure pack cups. Sugared or sometimes with a sugar bag attached.
- *Flavored* (45% of the market in volume):
  Differentiated from the above category by the presence of coloring and gelifiers. Not a wide range of varieties, mainly: vanilla, strawberry, almond and citrus.
- *Fruit* (16% of the market in volume):
  Similar to the typical Swedish fruit yogurt but with more pulp than real fruit. Contains some coloring and flavoring.

Western-type yogurts also compete directly in the same price bracket with local desserts – like puddings and jellies – produced by Japanese competitors.

Competition
Three major Japanese manufacturers account for about half of the total real yogurt market:

Snow Brand Milk Products is the largest manufacturer of dairy products in Japan and produces drinking milk, cheeses, frozen foods, biochemicals and pharmaceuticals. Turnover in 1985 was 443.322 million yen ($1 = ¥234 in 1985).

Meiji Milk Products, Japan's second largest producer of dairy foods, particularly dried milk for babies, ice cream, cheese. Its alliance with the Bulgarian government helped start the yogurt boom in Japan. Turnover in 1985 was 410,674 million yen.

Morinaga Milk Industry, Japan's third largest milk products producer processes drinking milk, ice cream, instant coffee. It has a joint venture with Kraft US for cheeses. Turnover in 1985 was 301,783 million yens.

The share of these three producers has remained stable for years and is approximately: Yukijirushi (Snowbrand) 25%; Meiji 19%; Morinaga 10%.

The Japanese also consume a yogurt drink called 'Yakult Honsha' which is often included in statistics on total yogurt consumption as it competes with normal yogurt. On a total market base for yogurts and yogurt drink, Yakult has 31%. Yakult drink is based on milk reconstituted from powder or fresh milk acidified with lactic acid and glucose. Yakult is not sold in shops, but through door-to-door sales and by groups of women who visit offices during the afternoon and sell the product directly to employees.

Along with some notes written in 1985 by Mr Ole Bobek, Agria's Director of International Operations, Robertson found a report on meetings held in Uppsala at which two members of Agria's negotiating team presented their findings to management.

Selecting a Franchisee

We have just returned from our third visit to Japan where we once again held discussions with the agricultural cooperative, Nikko. Nikko is the country's second largest association of agricultural cooperatives; it is the Japanese equivalent of Agria. Nikko is a significant political force in Japan but not as strong as Zennoh, the National Federation of Agricultural Cooperatives which is negotiating with Sodima, one of our French competitors. Nikko is price leader for various food products in Japan (milk, fruit juice, rice) and is active in lobbying on behalf of agricultural producers. Nikko is divided into two parts: manufacturing and distribution. It processes and distributes milk and dairy products, and it also distributes raw rice and vegetables.

We have seen several other candidates, but Nikko is the first one that seems prepared to join us. We believe that Nikko is the most appropriate distributor for Agria in Japan. Nikko is big and its credentials seem perfect for Agria, particularly since its strong supermarket distribution system for milk in the three main metropolitan areas is also ideally suited for yogurt. In Japan, 80% of yogurt is sold through supermarkets. We are, however, frustrated that, after prolonged discussions and several trips to Japan, Nikko has not yet signed an agreement with Agria. We sense that the management does want to go ahead but that they want to be absolutely sure before signing. We are anxious to get this project underway before Danone, Sodima or Chambourcy[1] enter Japan.

The same report also contained some general information on the Japanese consumer, which Robertson found of interest:

---

1. Chambourcy was a brand name for yogurt produced and distributed by Nestlé in various countries. Nestlé, with sales of $52 billion in 1996, was the world's largest food company; its headquarters are in Vevey (Switzerland).

Some Background Information on the Japanese Consumer

Traditionally, Japan is not a dairy products consumer, although locally produced brands of yogurt are sold along with other milk-based items such as puddings and coffee cream.

Many aspects of life in Japan are miniaturized due to lack of space: 60% of the total population of about 120 million is concentrated on 3% of the surface of the islands. The rest of the land mass is mountainous. In Japan, 85% of the population live in towns of which over one third have more than half a million people. This urban density naturally affects lifestyle, tastes and habits. Restricted living space and lack of storage areas mean that most Japanese housewives must shop daily and consequently expect fresh milk products in the stores every day as they rarely purchase long-life foods or drinks. The country is fairly homogeneous as far as culture and the distribution of wealth is concerned. Disposable income is high. The Japanese spend over 30% of their total household budget on food, making it by far the greatest single item, with clothing in second place (10%).

The market is not comparable to Scandinavia or to the US as far as the consumption of dairy products is concerned. There are young housewives purchasing yogurt today whose mothers barely knew of its existence and whose grandmothers would not even have kept milk in the house. At one time it was believed that the Japanese do not have the enzymes to digest milk and that, only a generation ago, when children were given milk, it was more likely to be goat's milk than cow's milk. However, with the market evolving rapidly towards 'Westernization', there is a general interest in American and European products, including yogurt.

Although consumption of yogurt per capita is still low in Japan at the moment, research shows that there is a high potential for growth. When we launch, correct positioning will be the key to Delissa's success as a new foreign brand. We will need to differentiate it from existing Japanese brands and go beyond the rather standardized 'freshness' advertising theme.

Distribution

Traditionally, Japanese distribution methods have been complex; the chain tends to be many layered, making distribution costs high. Distribution of refrigerated products is slightly simpler than the distribution of dry goods because it is more direct.

The Japanese daily-purchase habit means that the delivery system adopted for Delissa must be fast and efficient. Our basic distribution goal would be to secure mass sales retailer distribution. Initially, items would be sold through existing sales outlets that sell Nikko's drinking milk, 'Nikkodo'. The milk-related products and dessert foods would be sold based on distribution to mass sales retailers. The objective would be to make efficient use of existing channels of distribution with daily delivery schedules and enjoy lower distribution costs for new products.

The Japanese Retail Market

The retail market is extremely fragmented with independent outlets accounting for 57% of sales (versus 3% in the US). With 1,350 shops for every 100,000 people, Japan has twice as many outlets per capita as most European countries. Tradition, economics, government regulations and service demands affect the retail system in Japan.

Housewives shop once a day on average and most select the smaller local stores, which keep longer hours, deliver orders, offer credit and provide a meeting place for shoppers. Opening a Western-style supermarket is expensive and complicated, so most retailing remains in the hands of the small, independent, or family business.

Japan has three major metropolitan areas: Tokyo, Osaka and Nogaya, with a respective population of 11, 3, and 2 million inhabitants. Nikko's Nikkodo, with a 15% share of total, is market leader ahead of the many other suppliers. Nikko feels the distribution chain used for Nokkodo milk would be ideal for yogurt. Each metropolitan area has a separate distribution system, each one with several depots and branches. For instance, Kanto (Great Tokyo) – the largest area with over 40 million people – has five Nikko depots and five Nikko branches.

Most of the physical distribution (drivers and delivery vans) is carried out by a subsidiary of Nikko with support from the wholesalers. The refrigerated milk vans have to be fairly small (less than 2 tons) so that they can drive down the narrow streets. The same routes are used for milk delivery, puddings and juices. Our initial strategy would be to accept Nikko's current milk distribution system as the basic system and, at the same time, adopt shifting distribution routes. Japan's complicated street identification system, whereby only numbers and no names are shown, makes great demands on the distribution system and the drivers.

The Franchise Contract

Robertson opened another report written by Ole Bobek, who had headed up the Japan project right from the start and had been responsible for the early years of the joint venture. He left the company in 1990. This report contained all the details concerning the contract between Agria and Nikko. In 1985, Nikko and Agria had signed an industrial franchise agreement permitting Nikko to manufacture and distribute Delissa products under license from Agria. The contract was Agria's standard Delissa franchisee agreement covering technology transfer associated with trademark exploitation. Agria was to provide manufacturing and product know-how, as well as marketing, technical, commercial and sales support. Agria would receive a royalty for every pot of yogurt sold. The Nikko cooperative would form a separate company for the distribution, marketing and promotion of Delissa products. During the pre-launch phase, Per Bergman, Senior Area Brand Manager, would train the sales and marketing team, and Agria's technicians would supply know-how to the Japanese.

By the end of 1986, a factory to produce Delissa yogurt, milk and dairy products had been constructed in Mijima, 60 miles northwest of Tokyo. Agria provided Nikko with advice on technology, machinery, tanks, fermentation processes, and so on. Equipment from the US, Sweden, Germany and Japan was selected. A European-style Erka filling machine was installed which would fill two, four or six cups at a time, and was considered economical and fast.

Robertson opened another report by Bobek entitled 'Delissa Japan – Pre-Launch Data'. The report covered the market, positioning, advertising and media plan, minutes of the meetings with Nikko executives and the SRT International Advertising Agency that would handle the launch, analysis of market research findings, and competitive analysis. Robertson closed the file and thought about the Japanese market. During the planning phase before the launch, everything had looked so promising. In its usual methodical fashion, Agria had prepared its traditional launch campaign to ensure that the new Agria/Nikko venture guaranteed a successful entry into Japan for Delissa. 'Why then,' wondered Robertson, 'were sales so low after nine years of business?' Robertson picked up the telephone and called Rolf Anderen, one of Agria's founders and former chairman of the company. Although retired, Anderen still took an active interest in the business he had created. The next day, Robertson and Anderen had lunch together.

The older man listened to the new managing director talking about his responsibilities, the Swedish headquarters, foreign licensees, new products in the pipeline, and so on. Over coffee, Robertson broached the subject of the Japanese joint venture, expressing some surprise that Delissa was so slow in taking off. Anderen nodded his understanding and lit his pipe:

Yes, it has been disappointing. I remember those early meetings before we signed up with Nikko. Our team was very frustrated with the negotiations. Bobek made several trips, and had endless meetings with the Japanese, but things still dragged on. We had so much good foreign business by the time we decided to enter Japan, I guess we thought we could just walk in wherever we wanted. Our Taiwanese franchise business had really taken off, and I think we assumed that Japan would do likewise. Then, despite the fact that we knew the Japanese were different, Wisenborn – our international marketing manager – and Bobek still believed that they were doing something wrong. They had done a very conscientious job, yet they blamed themselves for the delays. I told them to be patient and to remember that Asians have different customs and are likely to need some time before making up their minds. Our guys went to enormous pains to collect data. I remember when they returned from a second or third trip to Japan with a mass of information, media costs, distribution data, socio-economic breakdowns, a detailed assessment of the competitive situation, positioning statements, and so on. But no signed contract. [Anderen chuckled as he spoke.] Of course, Nikko finally signed, but we never were sure what they really thought about us, or what they really expected from the deal.

Robertson was listening intently, so Anderen continued:

The whole story was interesting. When you enter a market like Japan, you are on your own. If you don't speak the language, you can't find your way around. So you become totally dependent on the locals and your partner. I must say that, in this respect, the Japanese are extremely helpful. But, let's face it, the cultural gap is wide. Another fascinating aspect was the rite of passage. In Japan, as in most Asian countries, you feel you are observing a kind of ritual, their ritual. This can destabilize the solid Viking manager. Of course, they were probably thinking that we have our rituals, too. On top of that, the Nikko people were particularly reserved and, of course, few of them spoke anything but Japanese.

There was a lot of tension during those first months, partly because France's two major brands of yogurt, 'Yoplait' and 'Danone', were actually in the process of entering the Japanese market, confirming a fear that had been on Bobek's mind during most of the negotiation period.

Anderen tapped his pipe on the ashtray and smiled at Robertson,

If its any consolation to you, Bjorn, the other two international brands are not doing any better than we are in Japan today.

What About These Other European Competitors?

The discussion with Anderen had been stimulating and Robertson, anxious to get to the bottom of the story, decided to speak to Peter Borg, a young Danish manager who had replaced Bergman and had been supervising Agria's business in Japan for several years. Robertson asked Borg for his opinion on why 'Danone' and 'Yoplait' were apparently not doing any better than Delissa in Japan. Borg replied:

I can explain how these two brands were handled in Japan, but I don't know whether this will throw any light on the matter as far as their performance is concerned. First, Sodima, the French dairy firm, whose Yoplait line is sold through franchise agreements all over the world, took a similar approach to ours. Yoplait is tied up with Zennoh, the National Federation of Agricultural Cooperative Association, the equivalent of Sodima in Japan. Zennoh is huge and politically very powerful. Its total sales are double those of Nikko. Yoplait probably has about 3% of the total Japanese yogurt market, which is of course a lot less than their usual 15–20% share in foreign markets. However, Zennoh had no previous experience in marketing yogurt.

Danone took a different approach. The company signed an agreement with a Japanese partner, Ajinomoto. Their joint venture, Ajinomoto-Danone Co. Ltd, is run by a French expatriate together with several Japanese directors. A prominent French banker based in Tokyo is also on the board. As you know, Ajinomoto is the largest integrated food processor in Japan, with sales of about $3 billion. About 45% of the company's business is in amino acids, 20% in fats and 15% in oil. Ajinomoto has a very successful joint venture with General Foods for 'Maxwell House', the instant coffee. However, Ajinomoto had had no experience at all in dealing with fresh dairy products before entering this joint venture with Danone. So, for both of the Japanese partners – Ajinomoto and Zennoh, this business was completely new and was probably part of a diversification move. I heard that the Danone joint venture had a tough time at the beginning. They had to build their dairy products distribution network from scratch. By the way, I also heard from several sources that it was distribution problems that discouraged Nestlé from pursuing a plan to reintroduce its Chambourcy yogurt line in Japan. Japanese distribution costs are very high compared to those in Western countries. I suspect that the Danone-Ajinomoto joint venture probably only just managed to break even last year.

'Thanks Peter,' Robertson said. 'It's a fascinating story. By the way, I hear that you just got married to a Japanese girl. Congratulations, lucky chap!'

After his discussion with Borg, Robertson returned to his Delissa-Nikko files. Delissa's early Japanese history intrigued him.

Entry Strategy

The SRT International Advertising Agency helped develop Delissa's entry into what was called the 'new milk-related products' market. Agria and Nikko had approved a substantial advertising and sales promotion budget. The agency confirmed that, as Nikko was already big in the 'drinking milk' market, it was a good idea to move into the processed milk or 'eating milk' field, a rapidly growing segment where added value was high.

Bjorn Robertson studied the advertising agency's pre-launch rationale which emphasized the strategy suggested for Delissa. The campaign, which had been translated from Japanese into English, proposed:

Agria will saturate the market with the Delissa brand and establish it as distinct from competitive products. The concept 'natural dairy food is good to taste' is proposed as the basic message for product planning, distribution and advertising. Nikko needs to distinguish its products from those of early-entry dairy producers and other competitors by stressing that its yogurt is 'new and natural and quite different from any other yogurts'.

The core target group has been defined as families with babies. Housewives have been identified as the principal purchasers. However, the product will be consumed by a wider age bracket from young children to high school students.

The advertising and point-of-sale message will address housewives, particularly younger ones. In Japan, the tendency is for younger housewives to shop in convenience stores (small supermarkets), while the older women prefer traditional supermarkets. Housewives are becoming more and more insistent that all types of food be absolutely fresh, which means that Delissa should be perceived as coming directly from the manufacturer that very day. We feel that the 'freshness' concept, which has been the main selling point of the whole Nikko line, will capture the consumers' interest as well as clearly differentiate Delissa from other brands. It is essential that the ads be attractive and stand out strikingly from the others, because Nikko is a newcomer in this competitive market. Delissa should be positioned as a luxurious mass communication product.

The SRT also proposed that, as Japanese housewives were becoming more diet conscious, it might be advisable to mention the dietary value of Delissa in the launch rationale. Agria preferred to stress the idea that Delissa was a Swedish product being made in Japan under license from Agria Co., Uppsala. They felt that this idea would appeal to Japanese housewives, who associated Sweden with healthy food and 'sophisticated' taste. The primary messages to be conveyed would, therefore, be: 'healthy products direct from the farm' and 'sophisticated taste from Sweden'. Although, it was agreed that being good for health and beauty could be another argument in Delissa's favor, this approach would not help differentiate Delissa from other brands, all of which project a similar image.

In order to reinforce the product's image and increase brand awareness, the SRT proposed that specific visual and verbal messages be used throughout the promotional campaign. A Swedish girl in typical folk costume would be shown with a dairy farm in the background. In the words of the agency: 'We feel that using this scene as an eyecatcher will successfully create a warm-hearted image of naturalness, simplicity, friendliness and fanciful taste for the product coming from Sweden.' This image would be accompanied by the text: 'Refreshing nature of Delissa Swedish yogurt; it's so fresh when it's made at the farm.'

Also included in the SRT proposal:

Advertising

To maximize the advertising effort with the budget available, the campaign should be run intensively over a short period of time rather than successively throughout the year. TV ads will be used as they have an immediate impact and make a strong impression through frequent repetition. The TV message will then be reinforced in the press. The budget will be comparable to the one used for launching Delissa in the US.

Pricing

Pricing should follow the top brands (Yukijirushi, Meiji and Morinaga) so as to reflect a high-class image, yet the price should be affordable to the housewife. The price sensitivity analysis conducted last month showed that the Delissa could be priced at 15% above competitive products.

Launch

In January 1987, Delissa's product line was presented to distributors prior to launch in Tokyo, Osaka and Nagoya. Three different types of yogurt were selected for simultaneous launch:

- plain (packs of 2 and 4)
- plain with sugar (packs of 2 and 4)
- flavored with vanilla, strawberry, and pineapple (packs of 2). (Fruit yogurt, Delissa's most successful offering at home and in other foreign markets, would be launched a year or two afterwards.)

All three types were to be sold in 120ml cups. A major pre-launch promotional campaign was scheduled for the month before launch with strong TV, newspaper and magazine support, as well as street shows, in-store promotions, and test trials in and outside retail stores. On March 1 1987, Delissa was launched in Tokyo, and on May 1, in Osaka and Nagoya.

1990: Delissa After Three Years in Japan

Three years after its launch, Delissa – with 2% of the Japanese yogurt market – was at a fraction of target. Concerned by the product's slow progress in Japan, Agria formed a special task force to investigate Delissa's situation and to continue monitoring the Japanese market on a regular basis. The results of the team's research now lay on Robertson's desk. The task force from Uppsala included Stefan Gustafsson (responsible for marketing questions), Per Bergman (sales and distribution) and Peter Borg (who was studying the whole operation as well as training the Nikko sales force). The team spent long periods in Tokyo carrying out regular audits of the Delissa-Nikko operations, analyzing and monitoring the Japanese market and generating lengthy reports as they did so, most of which Robertson was in the process of studying.

Borg, eager to excel on his new assignment, sent back his first report to headquarters:

Distribution/Ordering System

I feel that the distribution of Delissa is not satisfactory and should be improved. The ordering system seems overcomplicated and slow, and may very well be the cause of serious delivery bottlenecks. Whereas stores order milk and juice by telephone, Delissa products are ordered on forms using following procedure:

Day 1 a.m.:	Each salesman sent an order to his depot.
Day 1 p.m.:	Each depot's orders went to the Yokohama depot.
Day 2 a.m.:	The Yokohama depot transmitted the order to the factory.
Day 2 p.m.:	Yogurt was produced at Nikko Milk Processing.
Day 3:	Delivery to each depot.
Day 4:	Delivery to stores.

Gustafsson agrees with me that the delivery procedure is too long for fresh food products, particularly as the date on the yogurt cup is so important to the Japanese customer. The way we operate now, the yogurt arrives in the sales outlet two or three days after production. Ideally, the time should be shortened to only one day. We realize that, traditionally, Japanese distribution is much more complex and multi-layered than in the West. In addition, Tokyo and Osaka, which are among the largest cities in the world, have no street names. So, a whole system of primary, secondary and sometimes tertiary wholesalers is used to serve supermarkets and retailers. And, since the smaller outlets have very little storage space, wholesalers often have to visit them more than once a day.

I wonder if Nikko is seriously behind Delissa. At present, there are 80 Nikko salesmen selling Delissa, but they only seem to devote about 5% of their time to the brand, preferring to push other products. Although this is apparently not an uncommon situation in many countries, in Japan it is typical – as the high costs there prohibit having a separate sales force for each line.

Borg's report continued:

Advertising

Since we launched Delissa in 1987, the advertising has not been successful. I'm wondering how well we pre-tested our launch campaign and follow-up. The agency seems very keen on Delissa as a product, but I wonder if our advertising messages are not too cluttered. Results of recent consumer research surveys showed only 4% unaided awareness and only 16% of interviewees had any recall at all; 55% of respondents did not know what our TV commercials were trying to say.

A survey by the Oka Market Research Bureau on advertising effectiveness indicated that we should stress the fact that Delissa tastes good... delicious. Agria's position maintains that according to the Oka survey, the consumer believes that all brands taste good, which means the message will not differentiate Delissa. Research findings pointed out that Delissa has a strong 'fashionable' image. Perhaps this advantage could be stressed to differentiate Delissa from other yogurts in the next TV commercial.

Delissa in Japan: Situation in and Leading Up to 1997

In spite of all the careful pre-launch preparation, ten years after its launch in Japan, Delissa had only 3% of the total yogurt market in 1997. Although Agria executives knew the importance of taking a long-term view of their business in Japan, Agria's management in Sweden agreed that these results had been far below expectations.

A serious setback for Agria had been the discovery of Nikko's limited distribution network outside the major metropolitan areas. When Agria proposed to start selling Delissa in small cities, towns and rural areas, as had been agreed in the launch plan, it turned out that Nikko's coverage was very thin in many of these regions. In the heat of the planning for the regional launch, had there been a misunderstanding on Nikko's range?

Robertson continued to leaf through Agria's survey of Japanese business, reading extracts as he turned the pages. A despondent Borg had written:

1994: The Japanese market is very tough and competition very strong. Consumers' brand loyalty seems low. But the market is large with high potential – particularly amongst the younger population – if only we could reach it. Nikko has the size and manpower to meet the challenge and to increase its penetration substantially by 1996. However, Nikko's Delissa organization needs strengthening quickly. Lack of a real marketing function in Nikko is a great handicap in a market as competitive as Japan.

Distribution is one of our most serious problems. Distribution costs are extremely high in Japan, and Delissa's are excessive (27% of sales in 1994 versus 19% for the competition). Comparing distribution costs to production costs and to the average unit selling price to distributors of 54.86 yens, it is obvious that we cannot make money on the whole Delissa range in Japan. Clearly, these costs in Japan must be reduced while improving coverage of existing stores.

Distribution levels of about 40% are still too low, which is certainly one of the major contributing factors for Delissa's poor performance. Nikko's weak distribution network outside the metropolitan areas is causing us serious problems.

1995: Delissa's strategy in Japan is being redefined (once more). The Swedish image will be dropped from the advertising since a consumer survey has shown that some consumers believed that 'fresh from the farm' meant that the yogurt was directly imported from Sweden – which certainly put its freshness into question! Ads will now show happy blond children eating yogurt...

Over time, the product line has grown significantly and a line of puddings has recently been added. Nikko asks us for new products every three months and blames their unsatisfactory results on our limited line.

By 1997, plain yogurt should represent almost half of Delissa's Japanese sales and account for about 43% of the total Japanese market. The plain segment has grown by almost 50% in the past three years. However, we feel that our real strength should be in the fruit yogurt segment, which has increased by about 25% since 1994 and should have about 23% of the market by next year. So far, Delissa's results in fruit yogurt have been disappointing. On the other hand, a new segment – yogurt with jelly – has been selling well: 1.2 million cups three months after introduction. Custard and chocolate pudding sales have been disappointing, while plain yogurt drink sales have been very good.

Robertson came across a more recent memo written by Stefan Gustafsson:

Mid-Year Results

Sales as of mid-year 1996 are below forecast, and we are unlikely to meet our objective of 55 million 120ml cups for 1998. At the present rate of sales, we should reach just over 42 million cups by year-end.

Stores Covered

In 1997, Delissa yogurt was sold mainly in what Nielsen defined as large and super large stores. Delissa products were sold in about 71% of the total stores selling Nikko dairy products. We think that about 7,000 stores are covered in the Greater Tokyo area, but we have found that Nikko has been somewhat unreliable on retailer information.

Product Returns

The number of Delissa products returned to us is very high compared to other countries. The average return rate from April 1996 to March 1997 was 5.06% versus almost 0% in Scandinavia and the international standard of 2–3%. The average shelf life of yogurt in Japan is 14 days. Does the high level of returns stem from the Japanese consumer's perception of when a product is too old to buy (that is, 5–6 days)? The level of return varies greatly with the type of product: 'healthy mix' and fruit yogurt have the highest rate, while plain and yogurt with jelly have the lowest return rate.

Media Planning

Oka's latest results suggest that Delissa's primary target should be young people between 13 and 24 and its secondary target: children. Budget limitations demand that money be spent on advertising addressed to actual consumers (children), rather than in trying to reach the purchasers (mothers) as well.

However, during our recent visit to Japan, we found that Nikko and the agency were running TV spots – that were intended for young people and children – *from 11:15 to 12:15 at night*. We pointed out that far more consumers would be reached by showing the spots earlier in the evening. With our limited budget, careful media planning is essential. Nikko probably was trying to reach both the consumer and distributor with these late night spots. Why else would they run spots at midnight when the real target group is children? Another question is whether TV spots are really what we need.

Looking at some figures on TV advertising rates in Japan, Robertson found that the price of a 15-second spot in the Tokyo area was between 1,250,000 and 2,300,000 yens in 1997 depending on the time it was run, which seemed expensive compared to European rates ($1 = ¥121 in 1997).

Robertson continued to peruse the report prepared by Stefan Gustafsson:

Positioning

I'm seriously wondering whom we are trying to reach in Japan and with what product. The Nielsen and Oka research findings show that plain yogurt makes up the largest segment in Japan, with flavored and fruit in second and third positions. It is therefore recommended that regular advertising should concentrate on plain yogurt, with periodic spots for the second two categories. However, according to Nikko, the company makes only a marginal profit on plain yogurt, thus they feel it would be preferable to advertise fruit yogurt.

In light of this particular situation and the results of the Oka studies, we suggest that plain yogurt be advertised using the existing 'brand image' commercial (building up the cow on the screen) and to develop a new commercial for fruit yogurt based on the 'fashion concept'. We also believe that, if plain yogurt is clearly differentiated through its advertising, sales will improve, production costs will drop and Nikko will start making money on the product.

Last year, to help us understand where we may have gone wrong with our positioning and promotional activities, which have certainly changed rather often, we requested the Oka agency to conduct a survey using in-home personal interviews with a structured questionnaire; 394 respondents in the Keihin (Tokyo-Yokohama) metropolitan area were interviewed between April 11 and April 27, 1997. Some of the key findings are as follows:

Brand Awareness

In terms of unaided brand awareness, Meiji Bulgaria yogurt had the highest level with 27% of all respondents recalling Bulgaria first and 47% mentioning the brand without any aid. Morinaga Bifidus was in second place. These two leading brands were followed by Yoplait and Danone with 4% unaided awareness and 14% and 16% recall at any time.

For Delissa, the unaided awareness was 3% and 16% for recall. In a photo aided test, Delissa plain yogurt was recognized by 71% of all respondents with a score closer to Bulgaria. In the case of fruit yogurt, 78% recognized Delissa, which had the same level as Bulgaria. Awareness of Delissa was higher than Bifidus and Danone but lower than Yoplait. In the case of yogurt drink, 99% of all respondents were aware of Yakult Joy and 44% recognized Delissa (close to Bulgaria).

Interestingly, the brand image of Meiji Bulgaria was the highest of the plain yogurt brands in terms of all attributes except for 'fashionability'. At the lower end of the scale (after Bulgaria, Bifidus and Natulait), Delissa was close to Danone and Yoplait in brand image. Delissa was considered less desirable than the top three, especially as far as the following characteristics were concerned: taste, availability in stores for daily shoppers, frequency of price discounting, reliability of manufacturer, good for health. Delissa's image was 'fashionable'. ['Is this good or bad?' Gustafsson had scribbled on the report. 'Should this be our new platform??? We've tried everything else!']

Advertising Awareness

In the advertising awareness test, half of all respondents reported that they had not noticed advertising for any brand of yogurt during the past six months. Of those who had, top ranking went to Bifidus with 43%, Bulgaria 41% and Delissa in third place with 36%. Danone was fifth with 28% and Yoplait sixth with 26%. Respondents noticed ads for Delissa mainly on TV (94%), followed by in-store promotion (6%), newspapers (4%) and magazines (4%); 65% of the people who noticed Delissa ads could recall something about the contents of the current ads, and 9% recalled previous ads. However, when asked to describe the message of the Delissa ads, 55% of the respondents replied that they did not know what the company was trying to say.

Consumption

77% of all respondents had consumed plain yogurt within the past month: 28% Bulgaria, 15% Bifidus, 5% Yoplait, 4% Danone and 3% Delissa. The number of respondents who had at least tried Delissa was low (22%) vs. 66% for Bulgaria, the best scoring brand. In the plain category, Delissa was third of the brands mainly consumed by respondents. Bulgaria was number 1 and Bifidus number 2. In the fruit segment (under yogurt consumed within the past month), Delissa was in third place (5%) after Yoplait (10%) and Bulgaria (8%). Danone was in fourth place with 3%. ['So where do we go from here?' Gustafsson had scrawled across the bottom of the page.]

Robertson closed the file on Gustafsson's question.

Where Do We Go From Here?

Robertson looked around the table at the other members of his team and asked, 'What happened? We still haven't reached 3% after ten years in Japan!' Bjorn knew that Borg, Gustafsson and Karlsson all had different opinions as to why Delissa had performed badly, and each manager had his own ideas on what kind of action should be taken.

Gustafsson had spent months at Nikko, visiting retailers with members of the sales force, instigating new market research surveys and supervising the whole Nikko-Delissa team. Language problems had made this experience a frustrating one for Gustafsson, who had felt cut off from the rest of the Nikko staff in the office. He had been given a small desk in a huge room along with over 100 people with whom he could barely communicate. The Japanese politeness grated on him after a while and, as no one spoke more than a few words of anything but Japanese, Gustafsson had felt lonely and isolated. He had come to believe that Nikko was not committed to the development of the Delissa brand in Japan. He also felt that the joint venture's market share expectations had been absurd and was convinced the franchisee misrepresented the situation to Agria. He felt that Nikko was using the Delissa brand name as a public relations gimmick to build itself an international image. When he spoke, Gustafsson's tone was almost aggressive:

> I don't know what to think, Bjorn. I know I don't understand our Japanese friends and I was never quite sure that I trusted them, either. They had a disconcerting way of taking control right from the start. It's that extreme politeness. You can't argue with them, and then suddenly they're in command. I remember when the Nikko managers visited us here in Sweden... a busload of them smiling and bowing their way around the plant, and we were bowing and smiling back. This is how they get their way and this is why we had such mediocre results in Japan. Agria never controlled the business. Our distribution set-up is a perfect example. We could never really know what was going on out there because language problems forced us to count on them. The same with our positioning and our advertising, 'We're selling taste; no, we're selling health; no, we're selling fashion – to babies, to grandmas, to mothers.' We thought we were in we control but we weren't, and half the time we were doing the opposite of what we really wanted.
>
> Bjorn, the Japanese will kill Delissa once they've mastered the Swedish technology. Then, they'll develop their own brand. Get out of the joint venture agreement with Nikko, Bjorn. I'd say, get out of Japan altogether.

Robertson next turned his attention toward Borg, who had a different view of the problem. He felt that the Nikko people, trained to sell the drinking milk line, lacked specific knowledge about the eating milk or yogurt business. Borg, who had also taken over sales training in Japan after replacing Bergman, had made several trips a year to train the Nikko people both in marketing the Delissa brand, and in improving distribution and sales. He had also trained a marketing manager. Borg had worked closely with the Japanese at the Tokyo headquarters.

Borg said, 'I understand how Stefan feels... frustrated and let down, but have we given these people enough time?'

'Enough time!' said Gustafsson, laughing. 'We've been there for over ten years and, if you look at our target, we have failed miserably. My question is "have they given us enough support?"' Turning to Gustafsson, Borg continued:

I know how you feel, Stefan, but is 10 years *that* long? When the Japanese go into business abroad, they stay there until they get a hold on the market, however long it takes. They persevere. They seem to do things at their own speed and so much more calmly than we do. I agree on the question of autonomy. It's their very lack of Western aggressiveness that enables them to get the upper hand. Their apparent humility is disarming. But, Bjorn, should we really leave the joint venture now? When I first went to Japan and found fault with everything we were doing, I blamed the whole thing on Nikko. After nearly six years of visits, I think I have learned something. We cannot approach these people on our terms or judge them as we would judge ourselves. We cannot understand them any more than they can understand us. To me, the whole point is not to even *try* and understand them. We have to accept them and then to trust. If we can't, then perhaps we should leave. But, Bjorn, I don't think we should give up the Japanese market so easily. As Stefan says, they can be excruciatingly polite. In fact, I wonder – beneath that politeness – what they think of us.

Lars Karlsson, the product manager, had been looking after the Japanese market only a short time, having been recruited by Agria from Procter & Gamble 18 months earlier.

Bjorn, for me, perhaps the most serious defect in our Japanese operation has been the poor communication between the partners and a mass of conflicting data. I came into the project late and was amazed at the quantity of research and reporting that had taken place over the last ten years by everyone concerned. Many of the reports I saw were contradictory and confusing. As well, the frequent turnover of managers responsible for Japan has interrupted the continuity of the project. And, after all the research we did, has anyone really used the findings constructively? How much is our fault? And another thing, have we been putting enough resources into Japan?

There are so many paradoxes. The Japanese seem to be so keen on the idea of having things Western, yet the successful yogurts in Japan have been the ones with that distinctive Japanese flavor. Have we disregarded what this means? Agria people believe that we have a superior product and that the type of yogurt made by our Japanese competitors does not really taste so good. How can this be true when we look at the market shares of the top Japanese producers? It obviously tastes good to the Japanese. Can we really change their preferences? Or should we perhaps look at our flavor?

It's interesting. Yoplait/Zennoh and Ajinomoto/Danone's joint ventures could be encountering similar problems to ours. Neither has more than 3% of the Japanese yogurt market and they have the same flavor that we do.

Robertson listened to the views and arguments of his team with interest. Soon, he would have to make a decision. Almost ten years after launching Delissa with Nikko, should Agria cancel its contract and find another distributor? Or should the company renew the arrangement with Nikko and continue trying to gain market share? Or should Agria admit defeat and withdraw from Japan completely? Or was it, in fact, defeat at all? Robertson was glad that he had gathered his team together to discuss Delissa's future, their thoughts had given him new insights on the Japanese venture.

Marketing Decisions: The Five 'Ps'

Introduction: The Five 'Ps'

Marketing decisions encompass the key elements of a marketing plan. These decisions concern what is often referred to as the **5 'Ps'**: **Positioning**, **Product**, **Price**, **Place** (distribution) and **Promotion** (communication). These decisions typically deal with the following issues: How should we position our offer? What product line should we consider for our customers? What price should we charge? What is the most effective way to reach our target? Should we go indirect (through distributors) or reach our customers directly? How should we communicate the benefits of our products, through what media?

Segmentation and Positioning Decisions

In Section I, we highlighted the importance for a firm to segment and differentiate products and services to develop a sustainable competitive advantage. The concepts of differentiation and segmentation are very much linked to the concept of **positioning**. Positioning aims at creating a meaningful and distinctive space in the mind of target consumers relative to existing or potential competitive products. For Al Ries and Jack Trout, who popularized this concept, 'positioning is not what you do to the product. Positioning is what you do to the mind of the prospect'.[1]

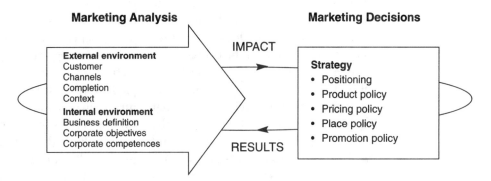

Figure 2.1   Marketing decisions: the five 'Ps'

---

1. See Al Rees and Jack Trout, *Positioning the Battle for Your Mind*, 5th edition, McGraw-Hill, New York, 1986, p. 2.

One of the most classic examples of a positioning strategy is the 7UP 'Uncola' statement. Prior to this campaign, 7UP was confused by consumers as a mixer and not as a soft drink. As a result of this repositioning, 7UP offered itself as an alternative to cola drinks. Another classic example can be found with Avis and its famous: 'We try harder!' With this statement, Avis suggests that it may not be the biggest rent-a-car company but its level of commitment to service is superior to the competition. In the automotive industry, Volvo positions itself in the market as the 'safest most durable car your family can ride'. By making use of this statement, Volvo has established a clear positioning in the mind of potential customers that clearly differentiates its products from the competition. Similarly, Porsche, Jeep and Bentley each have a clear positioning thanks to a unique identity that differentiates their respective brand from the rest of the automotive crowd.

Al Ries and Jack Trout point out that the mind positions brands in the form of a ladder. For hamburgers, the ladder includes McDonald, Burger King and Wendy's. In the express mail business, FedEx, DHL and UPS are likely to come up top-of-mind. Moreover, marketing research suggests that for a specific line of business, the brand with the highest share of mind is also likely to get a leading market share. Being first on this ladder is indeed the source of a competitive advantage. In a bar or a restaurant when we ask for 'a beer', and the waiter in turn asks if we care for a specific brand, our minds only have a few seconds to react and select one brand. Typically, we will pick up the brand positioning as 'top-of-mind'. Companies with a number three or four position on a product ladder are obviously at a disadvantage. What Ries and Trout recommend then is for these firms to identify a key attribute or benefit that the brand can convincingly own. Consequently, very much on the 7UP model, they may be able to create a new ladder in the consumer mind for which, they will be 'Number One'.

Although a positioning strategy has a lot to do with communications strategy – creating a unique space in the mind of potential or existing customers – it should be stressed that such a strategy also requires a consistent product, price and distribution strategy to support and defend the selected positioning statement.

Product Management Decisions

The product is the key element of the marketing mix as decisions on the other elements of the mix are very much dependent on the product and its positioning. For example, a manufacturer of luxury watches (for example Rolex) is likely to have a marketing mix policy consistent with the positioning of its product: the product range is limited to a few models. Price is relatively high. Distribution is selective (restricted to a few points of sales), and the communication strategy focuses on prestigious media, most likely to reach the targeted upper-class customer segment. For service companies such as an airline, the product could be defined as the flying experience (from booking to luggage delivery at the final destination).[2]

It is critical to stress that the product offer is generally not restricted only to the physical product (**generic product**) offered by the company (for example, considering a product like a car, the 'generic product' could be defined as 'basic transportation'). A product is generally much more than the basic function it provides. For an automotive, the product also includes certain quality standards, a warranty, delivery terms, after-sales service, the reputation of the brand, and so on. All these elements make up what is called in marketing jargon: **the augmented product.**

When the product has reached a stage of maturity, the 'augmented product' generally does not offer much opportunity for differentiation. For example, most customers buying an expensive sedan today would expect their car to be provided with the following standard elements: ABS, airbags, a sophisticated hi-fi entertainment system, and so on. To differentiate themselves from the competition and provide better added value to their customer segments, car manufacturers are constantly working on new features to provide the customer with a **potential product** that will fulfill new customer needs. This 'potential product' should include new convenient features and a superior after-sales service.

Service as Key Element of the Product Offer

As the president of Bobst, a major Swiss manufacturer of packaging machines, often likes to point out: 'Although we manufacture big machines, we are first and above all a service company.' As this CEO correctly suggests, most companies today are involved in selling 'solutions' to solve customers' problems rather than pure tangible products. What this statement suggests is that most products encompass two critical elements: first, the functional characteristics of the product (mainly elements linked to the technical performance of the product) and second, the service element (user friendliness, warranty, after-sales service, and so on). One may argue that today, in many industrial sectors, the technical features of mature products do not differ significantly from one company to another. What may then make *the* difference for the customers in preferring one supplier over another is the service component of the offer. For example: How fast and efficient are my suppliers? Do they care when I call them for a problem? How proactive are they in meeting customers' expectations?

The service element is increasingly a critical part of the total offering, as commodity products are often difficult to differentiate purely on functional characteristics. Take the example of BASF, a large German-based chemical company. For years, customers used to buy chemicals from this company purely on a price basis. Recently,

---

2. Some companies even include the chain of their affiliated hotels as part of their product offer.

this company decided to research how it could add more value to its customers by asking how it could better help them solve some of their problems associated with the handling of chemical products. What BASF found was that it was a constant hassle for many customers to clean empty chemicals tanks. Safety and health issues were a major issue for customers. Most of them did not have all the knowledge and the right equipment needed for this kind of operation. Having bought a company that specialized in the cleaning of chemical plants, this German company is now able to provide its customers with a total solution package that includes the cleaning of tanks and the delivery of chemicals 24 hours after any customer order has been placed. What customers appreciated most from BASF is that this firm has gone beyond the sole sales of commodity products to provide a total-solution approach, in a very proactive fashion.

What many companies have realized is that the service element is also an important element of their image. Indeed, at the end of the day, every product/service delivery shapes the corporate identity. Products are associated to specific motivations, emotions and other intangible elements that give an image to the product and the firm attached to it. This symbolic dimension is particularly important for products such as perfumes, fashionable clothes and other luxury products. But it is also linked to consumer products such as cars, or services (for example banks, airlines, consulting practices) and more and more to business to business activities – as highlighted in the previous BASF example.

Brand Equity: The Ultimate Source of Differentiation

Branding is the distinctive signature of a corporation and an integral part of a corporate product. As Franklin Chow, marketing manager of Singapore Airlines puts it: 'Products can be copied, but your image is yours and only yours.' In the airline business, most product features can be copied by the competition. All airlines fly the same planes (Boeings or Airbuses). This element of the product does not offer great opportunities for differentiation. When product innovations are introduced (new reclining seats, new in-flight entertainment, new menus), they are immediately copied by the competition. Yet, Singapore Airlines has built a brand by being always one step ahead of the competition. Many product firsts and a greater attention to detail in its service approach have contributed to its strong brand. Rigorous recruiting, training and retraining, above average wages, high status of staff within the company, consistency in product delivery and communications (the 'Singapore Girl', the distinctive 'Sarong-sebaya' uniform and charm of its staff) are all adding up to differentiate the brand and the company.

As for Sony, Disney or Nike, a strong brand evokes feelings of familiarity, quality, confidence, trust, and security. As a result, a strong brand encourages repeat sales. Strong brand equity also facilitates product line extensions (for example Diet Coke) as well as brand extensions (Toyota Lexus). Companies such as Nestlé may also choose to manage multiple brand names under their corporate brand umbrella to address different product categories (Nescafé for instant coffee, Carnation for infant formulas, Maggi for culinary products, Perrier for mineral water, Kit-Kat for confectionery, Friskies for petfood, and so on).

Finally, brand equity is very much linked to the notion of market power. Not only is branding a key financial asset for the company that can be traded, brand equity also enables the firm to gain stronger bargaining power over the competition and the trade.

Taking Advantage of the Product Life Cycle Concept

Products like living elements go through a life cycle that starts with birth (the product is introduced into the market), and finishes with death (the product is withdrawn). The product life cycle concept is useful for marketers in planning how to make the best use of scarce resources. For the best of efficiencies, every element of the marketing mix needs to be managed carefully and differently during every one of these phases.

The **introductory stage** refers to the full-scale launch of a new product into the marketplace. At that stage, the product line is limited to a few models. Marketing costs at that stage are usually significant. Communication expenditures are high because consumers must be informed about the existence and the benefits of the new product. High distribution margins are also needed to get the interest of dealers to carry an extra product with an unproven track record. Incentives are usually needed to get consumers to try the product.

If it survives the 'introductory stage', the product moves into the **growth stage** of the product life cycle. In this new phase, sales grow up at a faster pace. Product lines are expanded to accommodate more demand. New competitors enter into the market, attracted by its growth opportunities but prices start to fall. Distribution moves from specialized dealership to mass market. Communication focuses on differentiating the product from the competition and brand building. At this stage, most firms have recouped their investment costs and fight for market share and stronger profits.

As growth rates start to stabilize, the product enters the **maturity stage**. In terms of sales, the marketplace reaches a level of saturation. Many product models are available. New customers are more difficult to find. This is generally the longest phase of the cycle. Prices continue to fall. Communication focuses on aggressive promotion or brand building, or both, to retain both dealers and consumers. During the 'maturity stage', marginal players may decide to exit the market because of excessive competition and low margins. The remaining competitors display intensive efforts to retain distribution and market share. Some competitors may attempt to re-segment the industry to rejuvenate the market and re-launch the product sales.

Falling demand for the product signals the beginning of the **decline stage**. More competitors decide to drop out of the market because of poor demand and declining profits. Prices are cut further. The product is not advertised anymore and unprof-

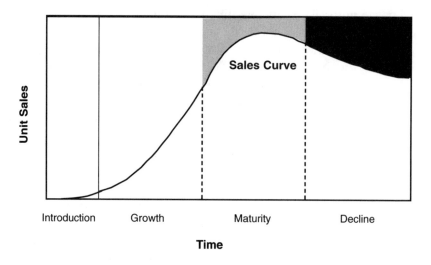

Figure 2.2   Product life cycle

itable distributors are phased out. Surviving competitors may raise prices slightly, since the level of competition is negligible at that stage.

Product Audit

The concept of product life cycle strongly suggests that all products eventually decline in sales and profits. The marketing audit is therefore a useful marketing management exercise whereby the company reviews how each product in its portfolio should be continued, improved, modified or deleted. Some of the key factors to be considered for product audits are:

- *Sales trends:* Is there a persistent decline in sales signaling that the product has reached the critical stage of maturity or decline?
- *Profit contribution:* Is the product generating the expected revenues and profits?

- *Product effectiveness:* Does the product still perform its intended function? Do customers have better alternatives?
- *Substitute products:* Is the market offering new alternatives to our products that the consumer is paying more attention to?
- *Corporate priorities:* Does the product receive enough attention from management in terms of time, financial, techniques and human resources?

Pricing Decisions

Pricing decisions represent one of the most important and complex marketing decisions. Pricing directly affects the profitability of a product category and ultimately the bottom line of the firm. Pricing can also be considered to be a major communications tool. If customers perceive a price to be too high, they are very likely to have a distorted image of the product potential and to consider a competitive alternative. This may lead to a loss of sales and profits for the firm. On the contrary, if prices are too low, sales may grow but profitability and brand equity may suffer, since products with a lower price may be perceived by customers as being inferior.

When deciding on a pricing strategy, a complete evaluation of the market environment[3] is required starting with:

- The context in which the firm is operating
- The cost structure of the firm
- The profit objectives the company has set for itself
- The customers' perception of the value proposition
- The channel incentives
- The competitors' alternative pricing offers.

The context

Pricing plays such a major role in modern economies that it is not rare to see governments impose legislation to control it. This is often the case for products like rice, gasoline, tobacco, alcohol, pharmaceuticals or insurance. By controlling pricing decisions, governments aim at disciplining competition (for example telecommunications in China), generating tax revenues (for example gasoline in Australia), reducing potential price abuse (for example insurance premiums in Korea) or limiting its own deficits (for example healthcare in Italy).

Other context issues also need to be carefully considered. For example, different pricing strategies can be pursued depending on where the product is in its life cycle. When a new product is launched, the firm may choose to price either high (**skimming strategy**) or low (**penetration strategy**). By pricing high, the firm usually aims at quickly recovering its research, development and launching costs. It also usually aims at building a profit reserve that can be later re-invested into production, R&D, or marketing to match competitive threats. As the product enters a new phase of growth and faces more competition, pricing high offers an opportunity to lower prices if competition on price starts to intensify.

A skimming strategy is generally more appropriate when there is a sufficient number of buyers with high demand and a high price supports the image of a superior product. When pricing a new product low (penetration strategy), the firm usually chooses to quickly trigger demand for its product and to make it less attractive for the competition to move in. This strategy is usually favored when production and distribution fall with accumulated production experience and the market is price sensitive.

Cost and pricing

To quote Daniel A. Nimer, President of the DNA Group: 'The purpose of price is not to recover cost but to capture the value of the "product" in the

---

3. See Section I for an analysis of the Cs: 'Context, Customers, Company, Competition, Channels, Cost'.

mind of the customer'.[4] Yet, one of the most common approaches to pricing is to add the different cost elements associated to the development, production and distribution of a product and to add a margin to cover the manufacturer's profit. This **'cost-plus' strategy** is typical of fast moving consumer goods where margins and mark-ups are added to make up the final retail prices. One major danger of the 'cost-plus' approach is that it often does not take into account the customers' price perception. An approach popularized by many Japanese firms is to understand how much is the consumer willing to pay for a particular product and its benefits and then to develop the product with the targeted consumer price in mind (**'customer value pricing' strategy**).

Other concepts linking costs and pricing are also widely used. These include concepts such as profit maximization, breakeven and target-return pricing. **Profit maximization** is a method that sets price when marginal revenue equals marginal cost. The **breakeven** concept helps determine what sales volume must be achieved for a product before total costs equal total revenues and no profits are made. **Target-return pricing** sets price where revenues from sales of a targeted quantity will yield the target return on investment. Also, concepts such as: economies of scale, economies of scope, learning curve, relevant costs are useful in understanding how economic factors impact on price decisions.[5]

Corporate strategy and pricing

Pricing first reflects the financial objectives of the firm and the level of profitability it wants to achieve. Most companies have rules or policies as to what they expect. These financial objectives can be aimed for the long term (for example image, volume, market share) or the short term (for example competitive results, survival, rapid sales maximization). Besides its financial objectives, the firm may also have some corporate image objectives in mind. Indeed, pricing often reflects a factor of communications on the quality of products. By pricing high or low the firm may aim at a distinct positioning in the upper or lower segment of its market. The firm may also have an objective of social responsibility by pricing its products in such a way that they will be perceived as fair by the consumers (for example Wal-Mart's 'Everyday Low Prices').

Customers and pricing

In most economies, pricing is very much the result of demand and offer, according to the principle that the higher the demand, the higher the price. When customers evaluate the possibility of buying a product, they also compare the *cost* associated with the acquisition of the product and the *value* of the benefits that they will derive from the product. Customers also form price perceptions according to former experiences of the same product or service. In practice, they

---

4. HIDA Management Seminar, Boston, September 1983.
5. For more details, see Robert J. Dolan & Hermann Simon, *Power Pricing: How Managing Pricing Transforms the Bottom Line*, Free Press, New York, 1997.

will often estimate a minimum price under which they think the product may be of a questionable quality as well as a maximum price for which the product is perceived as too expensive.

Customers are also likely to compare price alternatives. For example, in making a decision for a trip, consumers may opt for the train, the plane or even their car depending on the costs and value of each alternative. Customers are also often sensitive to price variations and they may form different value perceptions over time: products (for example mobile phones) are generally perceived as more expensive by consumers at the beginning of their product life cycle than when these products reach the phase of maturity. The novelty of a new product is often translated in the short term by a premium price set by the manufacturer.

Elasticity of demand also plays an important role in pricing policy. This concept refers to customers' sensitivity and responsiveness to changes in price. **Elastic demand** means that customers are sensitive to a certain level in price changes. In contrast, **inelastic demand** occurs when an increase or a decrease in price will not significantly affect demand for the product. The reality is still that few marketers can estimate with a great deal of accuracy how consumers respond to changes in price.

To add to the complexity of pricing decisions, we should add that pricing alternatives and value perceptions are to some extent controllable by marketers. Advertising, promotions and other communication tools can indeed influence the image of the product presented to the customers, by emphasizing benefits highly valued by the customer target (ease of use, convenience, design, and so on). This element can be found in the bicycle industry, for example, where special types of mountain bike with front and rear suspension command a premium over regular models. Customer segmentation can also help marketers set different price levels for different customer segments. Clearly, products aimed at the high end of the market are likely to be perceived as 'expensive' (for example Rolex in the case of the watch industry) over products positioned in the low end (for example Casio).

Channels and pricing

Adequate channels of compensation – in the form of attractive margins and trade promotions – and discounts are crucial in ensuring that customers will have access to the right product at the right time. In order to provide the right incentives to distributors and retailers, it is important for marketers to understand how these intermediaries make money and what tasks they perform on behalf of the manufacturer. Indeed, channel members often perform more than just the physical distribution of the product. They may provide advice to the end-user, carry inventories, offer after-sales services, finance part of the sales, and so on. Each of these functions costs money to the channel members and needs therefore to be compensated in one form or another by the manufacturer.

Competition and pricing

Competitive pricing strategies are few but complex to manage. On paper, a firm can decide to price at parity, above or under competition. It may decide to follow or lead, segment or target all customers with one single price policy. In reality, when competition is intense, it is difficult for a firm to raise prices and to sell its products over 'market price'. Charging high prices may also induce competition to enter the market. Similarly, when a firm decides to lower its prices, this move is likely to trigger a competitive response in the form of even lower prices or a price war. Different degrees of competition (monopolies, oligopolies, cartels or intense competition) also directly affect pricing policies and add to the complexity of pricing management.

Most companies choose to avoid fighting the competition on price as much as possible. Firms like GE Plastics, for example, prefer to redefine the value proposition in terms of new customer benefits or to re-segment the market. Nevertheless, there are many real-life circumstances where there is no other choice than to lower prices to the competition level. In order to anticipate possible competitive reactions, marketers need to assess the following factors:

- *Economic* (for example competitors' production capability and productivity reserves)
- *Market* (for example saturation level)
- *Financial factors* (for example capability of the competition to sustain losses)
- *Competitors' corporate objectives* (for example maximization of market share, shareholders value creation, long-term versus short-term orientation, and so on).

Distribution Decisions

Distribution involves all activities that make products available to consumers when and where they want to purchase a product. Distribution decisions are critical as they commit marketers for the long term. Indeed, while it is relatively easy to drop prices by 20% for one week, to drop 20% of a firm's retailers has much longer term repercussions.

Channels of Distribution

Channels of distribution can be short or long depending on how many intermediaries interface between the manufacturer and the end-user. For example:

- Amazon.Com Inc. sells directly to end-users through the Internet
- Nestlé sells food products through a chain of wholesalers and retailers but also goes direct with some selected hypermarket chains
- BMW sells cars to end-users through a network of franchised dealers.

A short distribution circuit may incorporate no intermediary at all, if the manufacturer decides to go direct (for example trading through the Internet). In contrast, long distribution channels use several intermediaries. For example, a manufacturer exporting overseas may use the following distribution agents: an importer, a wholesaler and a retailer. The import agent may take care of all administrative duties linked to import regulations and customs. The distributor will then relay the goods to a network of retailers but does not usually get in touch with the final end-users. This task is left to the retailers who display the goods and ensure the final contact with the customer.

The Role of Channel Members

Channel members can perform many different functions:

- *Physical distribution:* Goods need to be carried from the manufacturer to a warehouse, and then from the warehouse to the retailers' premises. This task typically includes managing logistics and inventories
- *Selling activities:* These include prospecting new customers, arranging displays on the point-of-sales, selling, providing end-users with information and ensuring after-sales services
- *Market feedback:* To remain competitive, manufacturers need regular customer feedback and information from the marketplace. Consumer satisfaction with the product and competitors' reactions are required to develop the next marketing action plan
- *Service:* Installation and after-sales services are generally needed with technical as well as with a large number of consumer products.

Understanding the Trade-offs

Before deciding on their distribution strategy, marketers also need to understand the different trade-offs available to them: direct vs. indirect, exclusive vs. selective vs. intensive distribution.

Direct versus indirect

Marketers may decide to go direct when they want immediate feedback from customers, to receive better margins or be in total control of their marketing mix. However, they may decide to go indirect if someone else can perform the distribution functions better, smarter or cheaper.

Exclusive versus selective or intensive

These decisions very much depend on the strategy of the firm and the nature of the products concerned. For example, exclusive distribution agreements are common in business to business activities where up-front investments in market development are usually quite substantial. Caterpillar, the US-based earth-moving equipment manufacturer is an example of this policy. Thanks to exclusive selling agreements, the manufacturer expects that it will induce strong support by the distributor.

In selective distribution agreements, there is more than one, yet a limited number of retailers for the same product. The objective of the manufacturer is generally to increase selling convenience for the end-user. Selective distribution is a common practice for companies like Rolex, Sony or General Motors.

Finally, manufacturers who want to make their products available as widely as possible practice intensive distribution. Kodak, Nestlé or Procter & Gamble are examples of intensive distribution at the retail level. A key objective of these fast moving consumer goods manufacturers is generally to maximize retail shelf space in order to achieve higher market share.

Choosing Distribution Channels

In choosing the right distribution channel, marketers need to examine and assess the different factors that influence distribution channel decisions. These factors include environmental forces, corporate objectives, market characteristics, customer buyer behavior, product life cycle and economic factors.

Environmental forces

Legislation is one of the major forces that influence the pattern of distribution in a given country. For example, insurance products may only be sold through insurance companies approved by governmental bodies. Similarly, in France, the distribution of pharmaceutical products is exclusively restricted to pharmacists.

Corporate objectives

Marketers have to decide what specific tasks need to be accomplished by the channel members according to their corporate strategy. For example, is the firm a low cost producer or a high-perceived value manufacturer? Take the example of a watchmaker. If the

product – such as Cartier – is positioned in the high end of the market, first-class personal selling at the point of sales is required and outstanding after-sales service must be ensured. The choice of high-class jewelry stores as opposed to mass retailers is consistent with the strategy of Cartier and the positioning of the brand. Finally, the location of the retail store in some prime location should be consistent with the corporate image that Cartier wants to project to its customer target.

Market characteristics

Take the example of Indonesia. This country – made up of 200 million people and numerous islands – can hardly be served by a manufacturer based 10,000 kilometers away from its customers. As a result, Mr Eugene Lim (fictitious name), a distributor of hardware equipment, maintains inventory on behalf of the manufacturer. He provides technical assistance to dealers and end-users. He handles receivables and absorbs occasional bad debts. His sales force calls on end-users. He maintains important relationships with the local authorities. He advertises on behalf of the manufacturer and runs promotional campaigns. In short, Mr Lim does quite a lot for his supplier. No doubt that given the unique characteristics of the local market, few of these functions could be fulfilled more efficiently by the manufacturer himself.

Customer buying behavior

To serve customers best, marketers must have some specific information on who, what, when and where customers are buying. In Europe, for example, a majority of senior citizens still buy from small retailers who are close to their home and provide a personalized service. On the other hand, teenagers generally prefer to enjoy the fun experience of buying in a shopping mall. The result is that a distribution strategy must first be based on an identification of what the customer segments targeted really need and value (for example cheap prices, speed of delivery, personalized service, and so on).

Product life cycle

Generally, the use of new products needs to be explained to consumers. When the first personal computers were introduced to the marketplace, these products were exclusively sold through specialized shops. As the product entered a new phase of rapid growth, distribution was enlarged to large retailers. Finally as the product reached maturity, Dell was one of the first companies to recognize that computers could be sold directly to the end-users.

Economic factors

Every task performed by channel members costs money. Therefore, it is critical for marketers to analyze the economics and needs of every channel member. Marketers must also understand how channel members make money and how their performance can be enhanced. Any opportunity to make channel members more efficient than their competitors is an opportunity for marketers to develop a sustainable competitive advantage. Consequently, marketers must be attentive to all key channel members' constraints (for example technical support, payable time, inventories turnover, slow moving products, and so on).

Managing Channel Conflict and Control

Manufacturers and channel members often have a 'love and hate' relationship. In many industries such as food, toys or consumer electronics, the bargaining power has shifted from large manufacturers to large retailers. Economic considerations can sometimes lead to conflicts between the manufacturer and the channel members, each blaming the other for not stimulating sales enough. They may disagree on how the profits should be split. Manufacturers may also be tempted to opt for intensive distribution to expand market coverage and maximize sales, creating more competition for the existing distribution network. Similarly, a distributor may drop prices to stimulate sales at its own retail level, with the risk of damaging the manufacturer's brand equity.

Consequently, an atmosphere of cooperation and trust must be created and managed over time to avoid potential conflicts.[6] In particular, personal relationships must be developed besides the traditional economic and legal transactions to ensure smooth continuity in the development of the

---

6. See Nirmalya Kumar, 'The Power of Trust in Manufacturer–Retailer Relationship', *Harvard Business Review*, November–December 1996.

trade. While other marketing mix decisions may be changed relatively quickly (for example dropping prices, cutting advertising expenditures), distribution agreements are more long-term bidding and cannot be altered overnight without major consequences. For example, dropping a distributor is likely to result in fewer sales, at least in the short term. Since distribution needs to be adjusted to the product life cycle, one of the key challenges for marketers is to design strong distribution networks for today with enough flexibility to redesign them for tomorrow.

Communication Decisions

Communication is more than just advertising. It encompasses many different traditional tools (such as promotion, publicity, sponsorship, merchandising, public relations, exhibitions, and so on) as well as more recent tools (such as direct marketing and the Internet). Yet, too many marketers forget that their firm also communicates indirectly with their internal and external environment. For example, a user-friendly brochure, the service attitude of employees, a free parking space for visitors, a convenient packaging, a fair price, positive word-of-mouth and a strong brand are also important elements of corporate communications.

Communication is not only restricted to the end-user. Broader target groups can also be reached and influenced such as existing and potential employees, competitors, suppliers, distributors and shareholders. For exam-

ple, the recent privatization of telecommunication companies across markets has led many governments to advertise on TV in order to attract new investors with great success.

Key Elements of the Communication Strategy

Successful communication programs typically follow a '5Ms Approach':

- **Mission:** What are the communication objectives?
- **Message:** What to communicate?
- **Media:** What vehicle should we use?
- **Money:** How much should we spend?
- **Measurement:** How should the results be evaluated?

Mission

The objective of a communication plan is not only to help sales (short term or long term), it is also to pass valuable information and messages to the target audience. Traditionally, communication strategy has one of the major objectives:

To inform:
- Tell the market about a new product or service
- Explain how the product works
- Suggest new uses
- Build corporate image

To persuade:
- Build brand preference
- Encourage product switching
- Change customers' perceptions

To remind:
- When to buy
- Where to buy
- Maintain top-of-mind awareness

For example, a bank may use direct mailing to **explain** some of its new financial products to existing customers. A battery manufacturer may want to **persuade** new customers that its products last longer. A travel agency may want to **remind** existing and potential customers that it is time to book a holiday.

A good communication strategy also focuses on one of several aspects of the components of the 'hierarchy of effects'. This concept suggests that customers go through a 6-step process before buying a product/service:

1. **Awareness:** (Potential) customers must be aware that the product exists
2. **Knowledge:** They must understand the characteristics of the product
3. **Liking:** They must develop a favorable attitude towards it
4. **Preference:** They need to prefer the product to any other alternative
5. **Conviction:** They need to be convinced that the product will fulfil their needs and expectations
6. **Purchase:** They make the purchase and hopefully will buy the product again, if satisfied.

A simplified version of this concept is also known under the acronym of the **AIDA** model that stands for: Awareness, Interest, Desire, Action.

Message

Before deciding on the message and how it should be delivered, marketers need to decide on what customer segment(s) they want to target. Obviously, a different language needs to be used to deliver the message if the target comprises both teenagers and senior citizens. The marketer also needs to clearly articulate the objectives of the communication campaign. For example: 'To increase among 6 million men who are experiencing hair loss, the number of prospects who are persuaded that Sigma can stop their hair problem from 10% to 15% in one year.' In this example, the target has been clearly identified. The objective has been defined and quantified. A time limit has also been set to measure the results of the campaign.

Messages can be broken into different categories: What information, persuasive arguments, associations, reminders are we trying to convey? In delivering the message, a delicate balance must be found between the use of testimonials, humor, sensuality, comparison, fantasy or a 'slice-of-life'.

- *Testimonials:* Uses a well-known personality or an authority to present the product (for example Cindy Crawford and Michael Schumacher for Omega watches). The high profile of the personality is likely to attract the attention of potential consumers. However, research shows that they may not remember the product.
- *Humor:* Good humor can be very effective, poor humor can be devastating.

- *Sensuality:* Research shows that it is generally not very effective.
- *Comparative:* Risky as the competition can retaliate by pointing out the weaknesses of our own products.
- *Fantasy:* Implies that the use of the product will help the consumer reach an ideal (for example cosmetics).
- *Slice-of-Life:* Uses a popular song and/or images of the past to position the product (for example Levi 501s).

Media

'What vehicle should be used to most effectively communicate our message?' The answer to this question is very much related to the initial objective of the firm. One first dimension that needs to be considered is time frame: does the firm expect immediate or long-term results. If the marketer aims at increasing awareness for his or her product or the company over the long term, media such as advertising and public relations are usually the most effective vehicles. On the contrary, if the marketer expects short-term sales results, couponing and sales promotion are likely to be more effective vehicles. A second key dimension that needs to be considered is the amount of specific information that we want to communicate. Indeed, corporate sponsorship or public relations (such as Andersen Consulting sponsoring Formula One racing) are low information providers and more long-term communication tools. The use of these two media is specifically to reinforce brand awareness and is unlikely to provoke immediate sales. On the other hand, flyers and personal selling are stronger information vehicles to generate more short-term purchasing actions. Most companies actually use a combination of different media vehicles to reinforce the global effectiveness of each communicating technique.

Advantages and disadvantages of some major promotional tools

- *Advertising:* On the one hand, the main advantage of advertising is that this vehicle helps reach many consumers simultaneously. It offers a high degree of flexibility in terms of media to choose from (for example billboards, prints – magazines, newspapers –, radio and television) and great diversity regarding messages that can be conveyed. On the other hand, many customers reached are not potential purchasers and consumers tend to be over exposed with general advertising.
- *Personal selling:* This is a highly effective but costly tool as sales representatives can influence directly decision-makers. It allows two-way communications with the right customer target and is the most effective vehicle to promote technical products. As a disadvantage, personal selling implies a high cost per contact and often suffers from a poor image when it comes to door-to-door selling.
- *Sales promotion:* Be it at the trade or at the consumer level, sales promotion is an effective tool to stimulate demand and change buying behaviors. Its main drawbacks are its short-term impact and possible damage on brand image if over-used.

- *Direct marketing:* This form of communication is the fastest growing medium and a relatively cheap promotional tool. Customers are identifiable by name, address and purchase behavior. The marketers can control the product chain until delivery. On the negative side, some consumers feel a high-perceived risk since the product is bought unseen. Some forms of direct marketing techniques have been overused (for example 'junk mail') and have contributed to a poor image of this medium. However, new forms of direct marketing (e-commerce for example) are providing new opportunities for both consumers and manufacturers to trade with greater convenience.
- *Sponsoring:* This medium has evolved to form an integral part of brand management, strong enough for even the most conservative companies to recognize as an indispensable ingredient of their marketing mix. Sponsorship is an excellent way to build corporate prestige and brand awareness. However, it does not bring short-term effects and its impact on sales is more difficult to measure.

Push versus pull strategy

Marketers often rely on a combination of 'push' and 'pull' activities to promote their products. A **push strategy** (primarily through sales force and trade promotion) includes all activities aimed at getting products into the dealer pipeline and accelerating sales by offering different incentives to the channel members (distributors, retailers, salespeople). In contrast, a **pull strategy** (mainly through advertising and consumer promotion) encompasses all marketing activities directed at the consumer with the prospect that end-users will ask channel members for the product and thus induce the intermediaries to order the product from the manufacturer.

Money

'How much should we spend?' is often a difficult question to answer for marketers. If the firm spends too little, effects on sales will be minimal. If, on the contrary, too much is spent, some money will be wasted. Many companies determine how much to spend on communications by one of the following methods: 'the inspired guess', 'what can be afforded', 'what was spent last year', 'matching what competitors are spending', 'a fixed percentage of expected sales', 'what is needed to achieve marketing objectives'.

- *The inspired guess* is certainly the least appropriate method to define a communication budget, since it does not take any strategic consideration into account. The decision is left totally arbitrary and should therefore be avoided.
- *What can be afforded* is very much a production-orientated approach. After calculating all its production costs and defining a profit level, whatever is left is allocated to communication expenditure. This approach is not satisfactory either, as it neglects marketing as a strategic tool for the firm.
- *What was spent last year.* Many companies use historical data to work

out a communication budget from year to year. Unfortunately, it does not take into account any strategic consideration of where the product is in its life cycle or how the competition compares in terms of marketing expenditures.

■ *Matching the competition.* This approach uses competitors as a benchmark. Many companies and advertising firms track competitive marketing expenditures, comparing competitors' expenses in TV, radio, prints, billboards with their own spending. Some companies use this method on the principle that market share is related to the ratio between the communication expenditure of a particular firm over the total expenditure of all competitors for a particular product category ('share of voice'). Therefore, to potentially increase its market share, the firm needs to boost its advertising expenditure above the competition's level with the hope that its message will be better heard by its consumer target. However, this method should not be used by itself as competitors probably have different marketing objectives as well as different resources available that may not be comparable to others.

■ *A fixed percentage of expected sales.* This method is one that many firms practice. However, this approach has one major flaw. In case of declining sales, the amount spent on advertising will be reduced and may diminish sales further.

■ *What is needed to achieve the marketing objective.* This method is certainly the most logical approach when it takes into account the following factors:[7]

Product life cycle: A new product generally requires significant communication resources to create awareness and induce consumers to try the product.

Strategy objective of the firm: To gain extra market, for example, the firm will often need to spend more than the competition.

Competition intensity: The more competitive the market is, the more the firm will need to spend to be heard by its customer target.

Measurement

There are various ways to test the effectiveness of communications before, during and after the campaign. Advertising agencies and market research organizations such as Gallup or Nielsen have developed many different tools for this purpose.

However, the effectiveness of measuring communication campaigns depends very much on the objective of the firm. If a firm aims at measuring the level of awareness for a product or for the firm, the effectiveness of the campaign can be measured with pre-test and post-test tools. Such methods include **recognition tests, unaided** and **aided tests**. A **recognition test** uses actual advertising shown to individual subjects who are then asked whether they recognize it or not. In **unaided** or **spontaneous tests**, respondents are asked to identify advertisements seen

---

7. For more details see Donald E. Schultz, Dennis Martin and William P. Brown, *Strategic Advertising Campaigns*, Cairn Books, Chicago, 1984.

recently but are given no clues to help them remember. **Aided** or **prompted recall tests** refer to situations in which customers are asked to identify advertisements while being shown a list of products and corporate names to challenge their memory. The justification of these tests is that consumers are more likely to buy a product if they can remember an advertisement about it than if they cannot.

To pre-test a communication campaign, marketers may also use some **consumer focus groups**.[8] These tests are based on the assumption that consumers – rather than advertisers or the manufacturer – know best what will influence their buying behavior.

During and after the campaign, marketers may also use focus groups to judge whether advertising X is superior or advertising Y or Z. Changes in sales can also be monitored if the communication campaign aims at ensuring rapid purchasing actions. However, this is often a difficult task to complete: competition may advertise and/or promote their own products, government regulations may change as well as economic conditions. Consequently, it becomes much more difficult to isolate with precision the different factors that may influence consumer behavior. However, with experience and sophisticated computer models, advertisers may estimate grossly the effects of a communication campaign on both sales and market share evolution.

Conclusions

The marketing mix is the tactical toolkit used by marketers to implement the marketing plan and reach the consumer. The key tools of the marketing mix are the '5Ps': positioning, product, price, place and promotion need to be managed consistently for maximum effectiveness in the marketplace. Moreover, marketers should not forget that the implementation of these decisions has a direct impact on both customer and competition's behavior. Consequently, it is important to complete a regular audit of these two elements to estimate the effectiveness of the marketing actions before moving to the new round of marketing decisions.

Learning Points

The students can expect the following learning points from analyzing and discussing the cases in this section:

- Managing the marketing mix
- Managing products and services
- Managing price
- Managing communication
- Positioning and repositioning a product
- Managing brands
- Managing distribution
- Putting a marketing plan together

---

8. Focus groups are made up of a number of potential or actual buyers of a product.

Konica Corp.

This case was written by Professor Dominique Turpin. Some names have been disguised to respect confidentiality.

At the end of October 1987, Toshiyaki Iida, manager of the Photographic Film Division, was back in his Tokyo office after a series of meetings with several colleagues from Konica, the second largest photo film manufacturer in Japan. Mr Iida and his colleagues had shared their latest information about competitors in the (non-professional) photographic film market in Japan. Data suggested that throughout 1986, Fuji Photo Film, the leading domestic film manufacturer, had maintained its 67.5% market share for retail sales of photographic film in Japan. Also, Eastman Kodak had accelerated its Japan market offensive by increasing its market share from 10.1% to 11.2%, while Konica had lost one point of market share – moving from 22% to 21% during the same time period. At the end of the meeting, Mr Matsumura, General Manager of the Photographic Film Division, who was chairing the meeting, expressed concern about Kodak's dramatic performance and entrusted Mr Iida with the task of reviewing the segmentation of the photographic film industry in Japan.

Konica

Established in 1873, Konishiroku Photo Industry (which became Konica Corp.) got underway when Rokuemon Sugiura began selling photography and printing material in Tokyo. Since 1903, when Konica was the first to sell photographic print paper and cameras mass-produced in Japan, the company had steadily built up its resources in silver halide, optical and precision instrument technology, and brought out numerous well-known cameras. In 1934, it introduced the first X-ray film made in Japan and was first again in developing infrared, 16mm movie film and color film of domestic make.

In 1987, Konica was the second largest producer of photosensitive materials in Japan and the third in the world after Eastman Kodak and Fuji Photo Film. For several generations of Japanese, Konica's products were better known to the general public under its Sakura and Konica brand names. Sakura had been the trademark for all film made and sold by the company, while Konica had been the brand name for the cameras manufactured and distributed by the company. In July 1987, the company had officially changed its name from Konishiroku Photo Industry Co. to Konica and had united all product lines under the Konica brand. According to Mr Ide, President of the company at that time, this change had been decided to 'reflect both the company's continuing diversification throughout the information imaging industry and its increasingly international stature'.

For the fiscal year ending April 2 1987, Konishiroku Photo Industry (referred to hereafter as Konica) and its consolidated subsidiaries had registered a net profit of ¥5,128 million for sales of ¥298,893 million[1] (refer to **Exhibit 1**). In early 1987, the company and its consolidated subsidiaries comprised some 13,000 employees overseas and about 4,900 in Japan.

In recent years, a key policy of the company had been to expand its international marketing force with the establishment of direct sales agencies overseas, both in North America and Europe. A coordinate policy for international marketing was also to locate production facilities within or near user markets. A subsidiary which would manufacture its U-Bix photocopiers was to begin operations in October 1987, and the construction of a plant to produce photographic paper had just started. Plans were also underway to build a plant in Maryland (USA), which would produce consumables for photocopiers and computer terminal printers.

Konica's Product Line

In early 1987, Konica's chief product lines included: photographic film (26.9% of total sales); photographic paper (17.5%); photo-related industry equipment (14.2%); business machines (27.6%); cameras and optical products (9.5%); magnetic products (4.3%).

Mr Iida had decided to review some of the recent trends in the film industry, and so there were several piles of data and reports on his desk waiting to be examined.

The World Film Industry for Amateurs

The photo market for amateurs could be divided into three major segments: film, photofinishing, cameras and accessories.

The film industry in 1987 was expected to enjoy steady growth throughout the world. In 1986, there had been over 43 billion images shot worldwide, with more than 85% exposed on color negative film. Worldwide, three companies dominated the market for photographic film. Eastman Kodak was the world's top photo film producer, with close to 65% of the world market. Right behind Kodak was Fuji Photo Film Co. with an 18% share, followed by Konica with 12%. A fourth company, Agfa-Gevaert from West Germany, was credited with less than 10% of the world market by Mr Iida. Each company had its own geographic strengths. Kodak and Fuji had an almost dominant position in their respective home markets, but Konica was clearly the leader in such countries as India, Saudi Arabia and Scandinavia – either under the Konica name or through private brands.

---

1. Average exchange rate in 1987: US$ = 135 yen.

The Film Industry for Amateurs in Japan

With 7 billion images shot in 1986, Japan was the third largest market in the world for film for amateur photography, right after the US and Western Europe (refer to **Exhibits 2 and 3**). At the retail level, the value of the total amateur photography market in Japan was estimated at ¥814 billion in 1986 with photographic film representing nearly 20% of this market (refer to **Exhibit 4**).

Traditionally, the photography market was divided between two types of customers: professionals and amateurs. In number of units, amateurs accounted for 82% of the total film market in Japan. In terms of exposures, the Japanese amateur market had grown 3.6% in 1986. In Japan, the average number of exposures per capita in 1986 was 60.5 shots per person[2] (versus 61.5 in the US). This figure had doubled during the last 10 years. Color film represented 76% of the total amount of photographic film sold to amateurs in Japan. Color print film represented 73% of this total versus 3% for color slide film. Mr Iida estimated that, on average, Japanese consumers were spending ¥12,257 a month on photographic material (twice the 1976 figure). Of this number, ¥6,210 was spent on cameras and accessories, ¥1,146 on film and ¥4,901 for photofinishing.

The Japanese Photofinishing Industry

Within the amateur photography industry, photofinishing represented almost half the total retail value. In 1986, the total value of the Japanese photofinishing industry was estimated at ¥28 billion (refer to **Exhibit 5**). Photofinishing was a synonym for 'developing and printing' pictures. After being bought at a store and then exposed, a film would be dropped off for processing and printing at a film counter. Although most pictures were taken by men on weekdays, film was usually returned for processing on Mondays, with 70% being dropped off by women.

The photofinishing industry could be divided into two sub-segments: the 'retail level' and the 'finishing level' (refer to **Exhibit 6**). The 'finishing level' referred to the wholesale or 'macro' labs where film was processed, developed and printed. The 'retail level' referred to the network of retailers which served as intermediaries between the customers and the 'macro' labs.

In 1987, camera shops accounted for 58% of all film purchases by amateurs and for 61% of the photofinishing market for data processing and color printing. However, their market was being eroded by new competition which occurred with the recent development of convenience stores offering the same service.

The retail network for the film and the photofinishing industries comprised 214,000 outlets: 31,000 camera stores, 36,000 drug stores, and 17,000 supermarkets and convenience stores (refer to **Exhibit 7**). Many retail stores were also affiliated with film manufacturers. Fuji Photo Film had four affiliated chains with a total

---

2. In 1986, there were 121.67 million inhabitants in Japan.

of 12,500 stores. Konica and Kodak had 9,200 and 4,400 store members, respectively. Affiliated stores were either exclusive or selective distribututors for one, two or three film manufacturers for both film sales and photofinishing.

Competition on the price of photofinishing was intense. Both the average price of developing the film and the average price of color printing had been going down substantially during the last five years (refer to **Exhibit 8**). Mini-labs were also frequently being installed in camera stores and were charging comparable prices to those being charged by wholesale finishers ('macro' labs) – and even less in some cases. This price erosion had many Japanese wholesale finishers concerned about their future. In 1985, the number of 'macro' labs declined for the first time, and Mr Iida estimated that mini-labs would capture about 25% of the amateur photofinishing market by the end of 1989.

The Japanese Camera Industry

Since the late 1960s, the world camera industry had been clearly dominated by such Japanese manufacturers as Canon, Nikon, Minolta, and Asahi Pentax. In 1986, Japanese still camera manufacturers had exported 70% of their production overseas. However, since 1981, total shipments of Japanese still cameras were slowly decreasing in volume (both in units and value). In value terms, total shipments were down from ¥490 billion in 1980 to ¥470 in 1986. In the domestic market, the trend was identical. The Japanese camera market was mature; the household penetration rate was 87% (versus 65% in France and 77% in Germany). From 1981 to 1986, total camera sales in Japan were down from ¥105 to ¥104 billion, although trends differed from one segment to another (refer to **Exhibit 9**). For example, sales of 35mm SLR cameras were down from ¥44 billion in 1981 to ¥25 billion in 1986, while sales of 35mm LS cameras were up from ¥46 to ¥72 billion during the same time period.

To revitalize the market, Japanese camera manufacturers were launching a range of new products targeted at teenagers, women and semi-professionals, respectively. In 1986, teenagers accounted for 23% of all camera purchases (a 3-point growth over three years). In 1986, 31.5% of all cameras sold in Japan were bought by women (refer to **Exhibit 10**) and, increasingly, women were shifting from pocket cameras to more expensive 'still' cameras. As a result, women in the 25 to 34-year-old bracket were also buying more film than males in the 16 to 24-year-old group (refer to **Exhibit 11**).

A Canon executive had explained the trend to Mr Iida in these words:

New cameras are getting much easier to use. In our view, new features such as auto-exposure, built-in motors for self winding and rewinding systems, the quick-charging auto-flash, and multi-mode zoom lenses have been successful attempts by all Japanese manufacturers to make cameras more user-friendly. Moreover, introducing more sophisticated products through the use of new optico-electronics has also been a way to rejuvenate the market and gain market share. (Refer to **Exhibit 12**.)

Fuji Photo Film and Konica competed with each other in the lower end of the Japanese 35mm camera market. Konica had only a 5.5% share while Fuji commanded 9% of this market. Konica had always been active in developing new products. In 1986 alone, the company launched three different versions of its Konica MT-11, a fully automatic motorized camera with close-up capacity to 45cm with a 35mm f/2.8 lens. Four new models, including the Konica Jump/Manbow (a fashionable caseless, water resistant 35mm camera targeted at women), were scheduled to be launched in 1987. Moreover, Konica was also working on a filmless camera, the Konica Still Video Camera KC-400, to be introduced in the late part of 1987.

Recent Developments in the Camera Industry

Several Konica executives believed that a major threat to the traditional camera market was the growing sales of video cameras (also called camcorders). Mr Iida felt that sales of camcorders were contributing to an erosion of the camera market and could eventually emerge as the preferred way to capture memories of holidays and family events, particularly as camcorders were declining in price and households increasingly had a video recorder. Between 1983 and 1986, domestic sales of video cameras had grown from a few thousand to more than a million units by the end of 1986. In comparison, domestic sales of VCRs (videocassette recorders) in Japan had grown from 964,000 units in 1980 to 6.3 million in early 1987. The ownership ratio of VCRs in Japan was estimated in 1987 to be 53%, or 60.3 machines per 100 homes.

Consumer electronics firms like Sony Corporation, Toshiba and Matsushita Electric and so on had recently used their expertise in video equipment to introduce filmless cameras (also called electronic or floppy cameras). This new technology allowed up to 50 video stills to be recorded on a single reusable 2-inch floppy disk. Electronic cameras could be played back immediately on a standard TV with an adapter. Electronic pictures could also be printed by a special machine, but the cost of such a printer was much more expensive than a typical computer printer. Moreover, the quality of the printed electronic images was not as good as traditional color prints.

Although traditional camera manufacturers (including Konica) had also been pioneering this new product, in order to compete with the consumer electronics firms, so far film-less cameras had had only a limited impact on the market for traditional cameras. Prices, however, were dropping quickly, and Konica was now working on an electronic camera to be introduced in early 1988, which would be sold to the end-user for less than ¥100,000. Yet, Mr Iida considered that the average price of an electronic camera alone (excluding the price of both a TV adapter and a printer) was still too high (typically around ¥250,000) for most Japanese consumers. The most sophisticated systems in the market cost ¥1–10 million. As a result, sales of electronic camera systems were mainly restricted to professional users such as advertising or news agencies. Sales of film-less cameras were less than 20,000 units in 1986. However, industry experts estimated that the demand for electronic cameras would climb to 3.8 million units by 1995.

Another major recent development in the camera industry perceived by Mr Iida was the growing presence of Korean manufacturers in the Japanese market. Although Korean cameras still had only a small share of the camera market in Japan (less than 5%), they were attacking the lower end of this market, where most of Konica's cameras were positioned.

Disposable Cameras in Japan

During the past two years, the development of disposable cameras had been a novelty within the film industry. Disposable cameras were first launched in Japan in 1986. This product concept stemmed originally from Fuji Photo Film's awareness of an everyday situation – that sometimes people wanted to take pictures, but had forgotten to bring a camera. A disposable camera was actually a film that had a lens and shutter in a compact 35mm-film package using regular color negative film. When the pictures were taken, the package was dropped off for processing at a film counter. The film manufacturers (Fuji, Kodak and Konica) believed that this new product would generate increased picture-taking opportunities and make photography a more convenient pastime. Fuji was clearly the leader in Japan for this new type of film. In July 1987, Fuji Photo Film had launched a new disposable camera with lens/flash, which significantly boosted picture-taking possibilities. Konica, which had launched its first disposable cameras in September, was planning to launch another model with flash three months later.

During the previous two years, the disposable camera market had grown at a very rapid rate. More than 2 million disposable cameras had been sold in 1986. Mr Iida expected that this number would triple by the end of 1987 and projected a market of 30 million units by 1990 or 8–9% of total 35mm color film sold in Japan. In 1987, sales of disposable cameras represented less than 5% of total sales of film to amateurs in Japan, and Fuji had more than 70% of this market.

Competitors in the Japanese Film Industry

Three companies with market shares of 67.5%, 21% and 11.2% respectively – Fuji, Konica and Kodak – dominated the Japanese film market. Private brands accounted for the small remaining fraction of the market. Agfa-Gevaert, the German company, had pulled out of the Japanese color film market for amateurs in 1976.

Fuji Photo Film

Established in 1934, Fuji Photo Film, the world's second largest producer of photographic film, was trying hard to catch up with Eastman Kodak in world markets. Fuji Photo Film boasted steady management with no bank borrowing. In fiscal year 1986, Fuji Photo Film recorded a net profit of ¥54 billion from net sales of ¥644 billion (refer to **Exhibit 19**). The company had 11,100 employees and was diversified into various non-silver salt products such as cameras, magnetic tapes and 8mm videocameras. Consumer photography products sales (a category including film for both amateur and professional use, photographic paper, cameras, electronic imaging equipment and other related products) accounted for 49.4% of the company's total sales. The domestic market accounted for 66% of the company's total sales in 1986.

Kodak Japan Ltd

Based in Rochester, New York (US), Eastman Kodak was the largest photography company in the world, with total sales of $11.5 billion in 1986, of which 57% came from amateur, professional and commercial imaging equipment and supplies. In 1986, Eastman Kodak had 124,400 employees worldwide. The American company had been present in Japan for nearly 100 years. In the early 1920s, Kodak had signed an exclusive distribution agreement with Nagase Sangyo, a local trading company which had been the exclusive importer and distributor of Eastman Kodak products in Japan. The impetus for Kodak's decision to increase its penetration of the Japanese market began in 1983 when Kodak underwent a major personnel reorganization, and Colby Chandler was appointed Chairman of the Corporation.

Until 1983, Japan had been part of a much larger geographic zone which included Asia, Africa and Australia, referred to by Kodak executives as the 'Triple A'. In 1984, Kodak decided to open a branch office in Tokyo (Kodak Japan Ltd) through a 50-50 joint venture with Nagase Sangyo; its objective was to push Kodak into the number two position in Japan. Industry experts estimated that with the recent 30% re-evaluation of the yen against the US dollar, Kodak would gain a major price edge over its Japanese competitors.

Mr Iida believed that Kodak was now working on new product developments for the amateur market, partly in response to some criticism that its film tended to make Japanese look yellowish. Kodak was also working on increasing the number of its affiliated retail stores as well as the number of developing laboratories. In 1987, Fuji Photo Film had about 400 affiliated laboratories in Japan (versus 200 for Konica), which served a large number of retail store outlets. As one insider described Fuji's strength: 'No matter where you go, even in the most remote areas of Japan, you see the green Fuji film name everywhere.' In contrast, Kodak had established 28 developing laboratory companies to date. But, in the long term, Konica executives believed that boosting the number of its developing laboratory affiliates would be the key to Kodak's success in Japan. To achieve this goal, Eastman Kodak had established Kodak Imagika K.K. in 1987, through a joint venture with Imagika Corp., which had been processing Kodak film for years. Holding a 51% equity in the new company, Kodak was believed to be using this company as the basis for expanding its laboratory system.

Mr Iida also knew that another goal for Kodak was to develop its basic research in Japan. Besides a research center in Rochester, Eastman Kodak had research centers in the UK and France. Kodak was now completing a four-story, 4,000 m^2 R&D building in Yokohama which could accommodate as many as 250 researchers.

During the past three years, Kodak had also improved its marketing mix. Until recently, Kodak had been selling film in US packaging that was printed only in English. In 1984, Kodak decided to use a new packaging with the date and instructions written in Japanese. Kodak also installed neon signs in Ginza and Shinjuku stations, two of the busiest places in Tokyo. Kodak had been focusing on sales promotions in major department stores in central Tokyo and had started to advertise aggressively on television. Since 1984, Kodak had also become active in sponsoring local events, and national sports events like sumo and judo tournaments, to become better known by the Japanese public.

Using a different management style, sales of film, copiers, chemicals and other Kodak products in Japan had more than doubled between 1984 and 1986. While Kodak had yet to announce its sales figures for fiscal year 1986, management did state its goals in early 1987: to quadruple sales from 1985 to 1988; and reach a sales target of $1 billion in Japan by 1989.

The New Konica Color Film Line

For more than 50 years, Konishiroku Photo Industry had been selling color film for amateurs under the Sakura name[3] with its red and orange packaging. However, to reflect the recent management decision to unify all product lines under the new Konica name, every Sakura product was being redesigned and given new packaging with the Konica name. The variety of color photographic films offered by Fuji, Konica and Kodak was about the same. The three competitors offered about 20 different types of color negative film, with a range of different sizes (from 35mm to color reversal sizes) and different sensitivities (from ISO25 to ISO1600).[4]

Color 35mm negative film was the size that accounted for 94% of all film sold in Japan. ISO100 film was by far the most popular film speed and accounted for close to 90% of total film sales in Japan (refer to **Exhibit 13**). In July 1987, Konishiroku Photo Industry began marketing its new Konica series of color print film, including a completely new ISO3200 film speed for a segment in which Konica had a monopoly (refer to **Exhibit 14**).

---

3. Sakura was the Japanese word for cherry blossoms.
4. ISO was an international standard that defined the sensitivity of photographic film according to different light exposures.

In January 1987, Konishiroku Photo Industry also introduced a new film for color prints targeted at teenagers. The packaging of this new product featured Snoopy, the popular dog from the Peanuts cartoon (refer to **Exhibit 15**). At a retail price of ¥510 for 24 prints, sales of the Snoopy Color Prints line were quite successful in Japan, contributing to an extra 13% increase in total units sold. However, because royalties had to be paid for using the Snoopy character, Konishiroku Photo Industry's profits on this product were only modest.

Retail prices of photographic film were fixed by the manufacturers[5] (refer to **Exhibit 16**). However, some retailers offered discounts (of up to 15%). Film manufacturers were also competing aggressively through their retailers, using promotions offering packs of two, three or more films. Film packs often were accompanied by some promotional present like a small picture frame, pens, tissues, and so on.

Behavior of Film Consumers in Japan

Mr Iida believed that, because of the desire of the Japanese for more leisure and the recent appreciation of the yen against the US dollar, tourism was by far the most common reason for taking pictures. In 1986, 48% of all color prints were taken during a domestic (35%) or overseas trip (13%). Family pictures were the second most popular theme, followed by special events (19%), and then business pictures (16%). Reasons for taking photographs varied according to both age and sex (refer to **Exhibit 17**). Research commissioned by Mr Iida showed that 51.2% of women buying film and cameras were new mothers and grandmothers who wanted to take pictures of their first baby or grandchild from ages 0–4.

Seasonality affected picture-taking occasions (refer to **Exhibit 18**). Also, indoor pictures were on the increase. In 1972, indoor pictures had represented only 19% of all color pictures taken in Japan, but this figure had climbed to 38% by 1986. Family events represented 36% of all indoor pictures taken.

After having reviewed all the data he had in front of him, Mr Iida felt that re-segmenting the traditional photographic film industry could be a fruitful exercise. He knew that no magic formula existed. However, he believed that with all the information he had gathered and a bit of imagination, a new segmentation of the market could offer new business opportunities for Konica. Also, he had to determine what actions should be taken as soon as he had the new segmentation on paper.

---

5. Japanese legislation allowed retail price fixing for items under ¥1,000.

EXHIBIT 1

Konishiroku Photo Industry (Konica) Selected Data

Income (¥mn)	Sales	Operating Profit	Current Profit	Net Profit	Earnings per sh.	Dividend per sh.	Equity per sh.
April 1984	258,077	11,654	16,593	10,282	¥41.1	¥9.0	¥462.4
April 1985	272,906	13,145	18,688	9,828	36.0	9.5	500.4
April 1986	313,612	16,988	15,909	7,102	23.0	10.0	499.4
April 1987	298,893	11,729	11,566	5,128	16.1	10.0	509.1

Financial Data (¥mn)	April 1987
Total Assets	449,953
Fixed Assets	163,045
Current Assets	277,472
Current Liabilities	212,818
Working Capital	64,654
Bank Borrowing	98,532
Capital Stock	25,599
Capital Surplus	66,268
Shareholders' Equity	150,287
Equity Ratio (%)	33.4
Interest & Dividend Net	–

Sales Breakdown	(Oct. 1986, %)
Photosensitive Materials, Cameras, Copiers and Others	64
Business Machines	27
Optical Goods	9

EXHIBIT 1 (CONTINUED)

Prices	High	Low
1983	¥676	¥560
1984	780	529
1985	755	601
1986	811	580

Export Ratio	44%	
Facility Investment (¥mn)	16,100	
R&D Expenditures (¥mn)	16,900	
Employees (Av. Age)	4,938	(35)

Source: Company Records, 1987.

EXHIBIT 2

World Amateur Photographic Exposures (units in bns)

	1987 (est.)	1986	1985	1984	1983
US					
Conventional	17.7	15.9	15.1	14.3	13.6
Instant	0.9	0.8	1.0	1.0	1.2
Combined	18.6	16.7	16.1	15.3	14.8
Europe					
Conventional	9.0	8.6	8.2	7.9	7.6
Instant	0.4	0.4	0.4	0.4	0.5
Combined	9.4	9.0	8.6	8.3	8.1
Japan					
Conventional	7.4	7.0	6.8	6.5	6.1
Instant	0.2	0.2	0.2	0.2	0.1
Combined	7.6	7.2	7.0	6.7	6.2
Others					
Conventional	9.0	8.7	8.2	7.8	7.5
Instant	0.3	0.3	0.4	0.4	0.5
Combined	9.3	9.0	8.6	8.2	8.0
Worldwide					
Conventional	43.1	40.2	38.3	36.5	34.8
Instant	1.8	1.7	2.0	2.0	2.4
Combined	44.9	41.9	40.3	38.5	37.2

Source: Konica, 1987.

EXHIBIT 3

Japanese Photography Exposures (bn shots)

Year	Total	Color			B&W
		Total	Negative	Slide	
1987*	7.394	6.827 (92.3%)	87.4%	4.9%	0.567 (7.6%)
1986	7.030	6.399 (91.0%)	86.2%	4.8%	0.631 (9.0%)
1985	6.784	6.093 (89.8%)	85.2%	4.6%	0.691 (10.2%)
1984	6.531	5.784 (88.6%)	84.1%	4.5%	0.747 (11.4%)
1983	6.118	5.434 (88.8%)	84.1%	4.7%	0.684 (11.2%)
1982	5.444	4.937 (87.5%)	83.1%	4.4%	0.707 (12.5%)
1981	5.267	4.561 (86.6%)	82.2%	4.4%	0.706 (13.4%)

Note: The color exposures are shown as total, with share of overall exposures, and the breakdown of that share into color negative and color transparency.

* Estimated figures

Source: Konica, 1987.

EXHIBIT 4

Japanese Amateur Total Photographic Expenditures (¥100 mn)

	1987 (est.)	1986	1985	1984	1983
Photofinishing					
Color	4,045	3,812	3,642	3,490	3,323
B&W	187	201	223	237	250
Film					
Color	1,544	1,442	1,390	1,350	1216
B&W	62	69	77	84	79
Lenses & Cameras	2,036	1,949	1,844	1,721	1,823
Accessories	663	675	679	676	665
Total	8,537	8,148	7,855	7,558	7,356

Source: Konica, 1987.

EXHIBIT 5

The World Photofinishing Industry (US$100 mn)

	1983 1984	1985	1986
US			
Amateurs	32.95	35.50	38.10	41.40
Professionals	21.80	23.40	25.10	28.70
Total	54.75	58.90	63.20	70.10
Japan			
Amateurs	14.90	15.55	17.60	24.30
Professionals	2.25	2.40	2.75	3.80
Total	17.15	17.95	20.35	28.10
Europe			
Total	34.50	35.60	44.00	59.50
Others			
Total	24.25	25.05	26.05	28.45
World			
Total	130.65	137.50	153.60	186.15

Source: Konica, 1987.

EXHIBIT 6

Photofinishing Sales in Japan (¥ bn)

	1986	1985	1984	1983
Retail Level				
Total	401.3	386.5	372.7	357.3
Color	381.2	364.2	349.0	332.3
B&W	20.1	22.3	23.7	25.0
Finisher Level				
Total	259.2	261.0	258.5	247.0
Color Printing	210.2	210.0	208.3	199.5
Film Processing	49.0	51.0	50.2	47.5

Source: Konica, 1987.

EXHIBIT 7

Sales of Data Processing by Type of Outlet (% of total value)

Type of Outlet	1986	1985	1984	1983	Total of Outlets (1986)
Camera Store	61%	62%	62%	64%	31,000
Supermarket & Department Store	17%	16%	17%	17%	9,000
Convenience Store	4%	3%	2%	2%	13,000
Cooperative Association	2%	2%	3%	3%	10,500
Drugstore	5%	5%	5%	5%	36,000
Station Stand	1%	1%	1%	1%	5,500
Other	10%	11%	10%	8%	85,000
Total					190,000

Source: Konica, 1987.

EXHIBIT 8

Photofinishing Prices in Japan (¥)

	1987 (est.)	1986	1985	1984	1983
Color					
Developing					
(Price for 24-E Prints)	1123.4	1155.8	1165.2	1188.6	1209.0
Average Print	34.3	36.1	36.7	37.6	38.7
E-Size Print	29.1	30.7	31.3	32.4	33.5
B&W					
Developing	330.0	325.0	315.0	304.0	301.0
Average Print	36.0	35.0	34.8	34.4	33.0

Note: E-print (82.5x117mm) accounted for 76% of all regular picture sizes for photo printing in Japan.

Source: Konica, 1987.

EXHIBIT 9

Sales of Still Cameras in Japan (¥ mn)

Types of Cameras	1986	1985	1984	1983	1982
Domestic 35mm SLR*	25,143	23,752	20,863	28,885	34,887
35mm LS**	72,190	68,045	65,880	55,776	48,549
35mm Imports	910	410	735	400	452
Cartridge	579	1,549	1,948	3,171	5,239
Import Pocket	846	844	961	872	830
Import Folding	1,202	486	514	659	935
Import 60mm	897	2	3	3	3
Domestic Others	579	1,310	1,932	2,035	1,667
Import Others	2,016	2,387	2,236	2,873	5,808
Total: (in value)	104,362	98,785	95,072	94,674	98,370
(in units)	5,878,712	5,087,527	4,699,748	4,642,052	4,947,514

* SLR: Single-lens reflex cameras
** LS: Lens shutter cameras

Source: Konica, 1987.

EXHIBIT 10

Sales of Cameras in Japan by Sex and Age Group (%)

| Type of Camera | 35mm SLR* | | 35mm LS** | | Pocket Cameras | | Total | |
Year	1986	1985	1986	1985	1986	1985	1986	1985
Sex								
Male	94.1	94.5	64.7	67.3	37.7	41.5	68.5	70.1
Female	5.9	5.5	35.3	32.7	62.3	58.5	31.5	29.9
Age Group								
Under 19	6%	10%	13%	12%	40%	40%	13%	12%
20–29	23	25	26	26	23	22	26	25
30–39	28	25	21	21	17	18	21	22
40–49	16	17	14	14	8	7	15	14
Over 49	26	23	26	27	12	13	25	27

*SLR: Single-lens reflex cameras
**LS: Lens shutter cameras

Source: Konica, 1987.

EXHIBIT 11

Sales of Photographic Film in Japan by Sex and Age Group

Sex	Age Group	Number of rolls used per year
Men	15 and under	2.9
	16–24	3.1
	25–34	4.4
	35–44	3.6
	45–54	3.5
	55 and over	3.5
Women	15 and under	1.2
	16–24	2.2
	25–34	3.2
	35–44	2.8
	45–54	2.7
	55 and over	2.6

Source: Konica, 1987.

EXHIBIT 12

Market Shares in the 35mm SLR Camera Industry in Japan (1975–86)

1975		1980		1985		1986	
1. Nikon	26%	1. Canon	24%	1. Canon	41%	1. Minolta	25%
2. Asahi	22%	2. Nikon	22%	2. Nikon	25%	2. Canon	24%
3. Canon	18%	3. Asahi	21%	3. Asahi	13%	3. Nikon	16%
4. Minolta	14%	4. Minolta	8%	4. Minolta	4%	4. Asahi	10%
5. Others	20%	5. Others	25%	5. Others	17%	5. Others	25%

Others include: Olympus: 9.5%, Fuji: 9%, Konica: 5.5%, Kyocera, Ricoh and Kowa.

Source: Nikkei Business, 1987.

EXHIBIT 13

Sales of Color Negative Film in Japan by Size, Sensitivity and Prints (Film for Amateurs Only)

Sales by Size

Color Negative 35mm Size	92.4%
Color Negative Rolls	4.5%
Color Negatives 110	2.9%
Color Negatives 120	0.2%

Sales by Size and Sensitivity	35mm	110
ISO25	0.1%	–
ISO100	84.8%	94.4%
ISO160	–	–
ISO200	3.7%	3.0%
ISO400	9.1%	2.6%
ISO1000	0.1%	–
ISO1600	2.2%	–
ISO3200	0.1%	–

Sales by Size and No. of Prints	35mm	110
12 Prints	19.0%	16.0%
24 Prints	60.5%	84.0%
36 Prints	20.5%	–

Note: No significant differences between Fuji, Kodak and Konica.

Source: Photo Market, 1987.

EXHIBIT 14

Konishiroku Photo Industry Product Line for Color Print Film
(Film for Amateurs Only)

Color Films	ISO	Size and No. Exposures	Characteristics
Konica GX100	100	135mm-12,24,36 120mm-12 110mm-12,24	Most popular speed, ultra-fine grain, especially effective for scenery
Konica GX100 'Snoopy'	100	135mm-24	Same characteristics as Konica GX100 but targeted at teenagers
Konica GX200 Professional	200	135mm-12,24,36 120mm-12	Extra-fine grain, especially effective for portraits
Konica GX400	400	135mm-12,24,36 120mm-12 110mm-24	High speed especially effective for fast action
Konica-GX3200	3200	135mm-24,36 120mm-12	World's first color print film in its speed class. Best suited for action or poor light conditions

Source: Konica, 1987.

EXHIBIT 15

Konishiroku Photo Industry Product Line for Color Print Film
(Film for Amateurs Only)

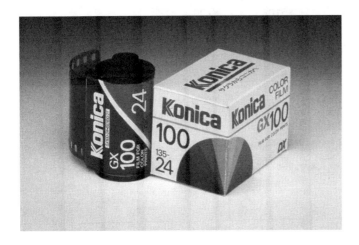

Source: Konica, 1987.

EXHIBIT 16

Comparative Retail Prices for Color Print Film in Japan 1987*

	12 prints	24 Prints	36 Prints
Konica ISO100	¥400	¥510	¥700
Fuji Super HRII ISO100	¥400	¥510	¥700
Kodak ISO100	¥400	¥510	¥700
Fuji Super HR100 ISO400	¥456	¥575	–

* Retail Prices at a Tokyo department store in Tokyo, 1987

Source: Photomarket, 1987.

EXHIBIT 17

Photographic Subjects for Color Prints by Sex and Age Group

Age Group:	Males (%)						Females (%)					
	Under 20	20–30	30–40	40–50	50–60	Over 60	Under 20	20–30	30–40	40–50	50–60	Over 60
Playtime	30	44	59	38	12	17	61	53	61	25	17	12
Drive	45	84	71	63	50	31	59	79	64	52	41	27
Picnic	20	27	38	38	24	23	32	36	50	35	25	20
Camp	14	13	9	10	1	1	11	5	14	8	2	1
Sports	3	5	12	8	1	1	6	7	17	6	1	-
Seaside	35	52	50	35	15	9	42	43	49	22	8	9
Zoo-Park	21	38	57	38	21	23	41	50	57	33	30	22
Exhibition	21	29	28	29	28	21	31	27	30	32	26	23
Travel (J)*	23	44	55	55	65	67	54	40	53	50	65	60
Travel (O)**	3	9	9	10	10	7	5	17	5	4	7	6
Photography as a Hobby:	7	13	14	13	17	18	7	10	8	4	3	5

* Domestic trips
** Overseas trips

Source: Photo Market, 1987.

EXHIBIT 18

Photographic Subjects for Color Prints by Season* (ISO100, Color Prints 1980–86)**

Year/Subjects	Winter (%)	Spring (%)	Summer (%)	Autumn (%)
1980				
Domestic Tourism	30	43	52	41
Overseas Tourism	3	4	7	5
Family Pictures	30	24	16	19
Event Pictures	20	17	10	22
Business Pictures	17	12	15	13
	100	100	100	100
1983				
Domestic Tourism	30	44	48	33
Overseas Tourism	8	4	7	5
Family Pictures	24	19	17	15
Event Pictures	20	19	13	29
Business Pictures	18	14	15	18
	100	100	100	100
1986				
Domestic Tourism	26	38	48	40
Overseas Tourism	8	6	12	7
Family Pictures	31	18	17	14
Event Pictures	18	22	10	25
Business Pictures	17	16	13	14
	100	100	100	100

* Winter: December to February, Spring: March to May, Summer: June to August
  Autumn: September to November
** Unit: % of total color prints as processed by laboratories

Source: Photo Market, 1987.

EXHIBIT 19

Fuji Photo Film Selected Data

Income (¥mn)	Sales	Operating Profit	Current Profit	Net Profit	Earnings per sh.	Dividend per sh.	Equity per sh.
Oct 1984	566,396	92,325	95,774	45,057	¥122.0	¥11.5	¥875
Oct 1985	646,212	114,288	122,566	54,652	147.9	13.5	1,010
Oct 1986	644,957	102,172	113,907	54,836	147.8	13.5	1,149
Oct 1987*	700,000	105,000	128,000	56,000	150.0		

Financial Data (¥mn)　　　October 1986

Total Assets	686,542
Fixed Assets	224,447
Current Assets	462,095
Current Liabilities	165,087
Working Capital	297,008
Bank Borrowing	0
Capital Stock	20,437
Capital Surplus	39,054
Shareholders' Equity	426,677
Equity Ratio (%)	62.1
Interest & Dividend Net	14,496

Sales Breakdown (Oct. 1986, %)

Cameras, Film	46
Business/Commercial Use Products	41
Magnetic Products	12

Prices	High	Low
1982	¥2130	¥ 60
1983	2490	1480
1984	2330	1440
1985	2210	1550
1986	3930	1720

Export Ratio (1986)	34%
Facility Investment (¥mn, 1986)	42,400
R&D Expenditures (¥mn)	42,700
Employees (Av. Age)	10,950　(39)

*Estimated

Source: Company Records, 1987.

CASE 2.2

Kirin Brewery Co. Ltd (A)

*This case was prepared
by Professor
Dominique Turpin,
with the assistance of
Research Associate
Joyce Miller.*

In late October 1987, Hideo Motoyama, President of Kirin Brewery, convened a meeting of the executives of the Beer Division in Tokyo. Given the recent competitive move by Asahi Breweries, Motoyama felt it was critical to review the market situation. Motoyama opened the meeting:

Asahi Breweries' launch of 'Super Dry' beer this spring put a kick in a market that has been quietly growing at 3% annually. By now, all of you have seen the figures that I circulated yesterday. In 1987, the market will have grown 7.5%, and next year's growth is expected to reach 8%. At the same time, our share has sagged from 60% to 57%, just as we're about to celebrate the 100th anniversary of the Kirin symbol. What is happening? We need to get a handle on the seriousness of this situation and make a decision about how to respond to Asahi's challenge.

Some History

Kirin Brewery Co. Ltd was the top brewer in Japan and the fourth largest in the world (refer to **Exhibit 1**) with profits of ¥31,047 million on sales of ¥1,210 billion[1] in 1986 (refer to **Exhibit 2**). Kirin traced its origins back to 1870 when W. Copeland, an American entrepreneur, established the Spring Valley Brewery in Yokohama, 40 kilometers south of Tokyo. In 1885, the operation was reorganized into the Japan Brewery Co. Ltd with the financial backing of Eiichi Shibusawa and Yanosuke Iwasaki, prominent figures in the Japanese business community. The connection with Iwasaki provided a close relationship with the powerful Mitsubishi Group, a bond that still existed in 1987. The Mitsubishi, Mitsui, and Sumitomo Groups represented the three largest industrial organizations ('keiretsu') in Japan. Yoshikazu Miyazaki, a professor at Kyoto University, defined keiretsu as 'a closely-tied complex of industrial and financial corporations'. Companies belonging to the keiretsu typically had access to significant intra-group financing.

Using German brewing expertise, Japan Brewery offered a German-style lager under the brand name Kirin Beer. One of the directors, Herr Baehr, designed the 'Kirin' logo, which was based on a benevolent creature from Chinese legend. In 1907, Kirin Brewery took over the operations of Japan Brewery and, building on its predecessor's philosophy, established the management tenets that still guided the

---

1. Average exchange rate in 1987: US$ = ¥135.

company 80 years later: 'Quality First' and 'Sound Management'. Kirin reached an important milestone in 1954, capturing the leading industry position away from Sapporo Breweries. Kirin, Sapporo, and Asahi continued to be close competitors with roughly a third of the market each (refer to **Exhibit 3**).

Since the early 1950s, in the public's eye, 'Beer meant Kirin'. By 1966, Kirin commanded over a 50% share of the market, and by 1979, the company had seized a 63% share of the beer market in Japan. At this point, the Fair Trade Commission, acting under the provisions of the Japanese Anti-Monopoly Law, threatened to break Kirin Brewery into two separate companies and prevent it from gaining a monopoly in the market. In the end, though, Kirin remained intact.

Kirin began diversifying its operations in 1971. Its first agreement was with Canadian-based J.E. Seagrams & Sons Inc. to import liquor produced overseas, including the company's flagship brand, Chivas Regal. Five years later, Kirin established K.B.B. Malting Co. Pty Ltd (currently Kirin Australia Pty Ltd) through a joint venture with Australia's BBA. As well, Kirin had entered a domestic venture with Koiwai, a respected name in the dairy industry, to market Koiwai's food products.

In 1977, Kirin advanced into the United States by forming KW Inc. to bottle and market Coca-Cola. In 1983, Kirin created Kirin USA, Inc., which aimed to use beer brewed in Canada by Molson Ltd to further expand its presence in the US market. At this time, Kirin also strengthened its European ties by establishing a representative office in Düsseldorf (West Germany) and associating with Heineken N.V., Europe's largest brewer.

Recently, Kirin had entered joint ventures with US-based Amgen, Inc. and Plant Genetics, both active in the field of biotechnology. In addition, the company had tied up with several Czech organizations to exchange information and technology. Despite the diversification into soft drinks, whisky, food products, and biotechnology, Kirin remained heavily dependent on beer. In 1987, 93% of the company's revenues would be generated from the sale of beer.

The Beer Industry in Japan

The Japanese beer industry was born in 1853 when a medical doctor 'test-brewed' some beer at his home in Edo (now Tokyo), based on a description he found in a Dutch book. Although Shozaburo Shibuya was said to have been the first to brew and sell beer as a business in 1872, it was not until the Sino–Japanese War (1937–41) that large numbers of people, mostly Japanese soldiers, enjoyed their first taste of beer.

By the time World War II broke out, the industry was dominated by two companies: Dai Nippon Breweries (which held two-thirds of the market) and Kirin. In 1945, the allied powers ordered the dissolution of the 'zaibatsu' (financial cliques). As a result, Dai Nippon was transformed into Asahi Breweries and Sapporo Breweries, which remained market share leaders with 38.6% and 36.1% respectively, ahead of Kirin with 25.3%. Over the subsequent three decades, however, Kirin managed to outrun its rivals.

By 1987, beer was a popular and widely preferred beverage, representing 67% of all alcoholic beverages consumed in Japan, followed by Japanese sake, 17.7%; shochu (a white spirit), 7%; and whisky and brandy, 4%. Between 1965 and 1987, per capita consumption of beer in Japan doubled from 20.2 liters to 43.8 liters, while per capita consumption of all alcoholic beverages during the same time period grew from 36.3 liters to 65.3 liters. Japan was the fourth largest beer market in the world, with an annual consumption of just under 500 million kiloliters. However, international comparative data on beer consumption ranked the Japanese as the 28th highest on a per capita basis, a level that was half the American figure and less than one-third that of Germany, Czechoslovakia, Denmark, and New Zealand.

Production

The production of beer in Japan was strictly controlled by the state through a license system, which made it difficult for newcomers to enter the market. In Japanese legislation, beer was defined as a brewed beverage obtained by fermenting malt, hops, and water. Rice, corn, starch, and saccharine substances could be used, provided that the total weight of these submaterials did not exceed half the weight of the malt. While each brewer imported raw materials from Europe, North America, or Australia, most brewers produced their own yeasts. Yeasts were essential to ferment the sugars contained in the raw materials. Kirin's Production Manager believed that the process of brewing beer was similar among competitors. However, economies of scale could be significant.

The production and sale of beer were heavily influenced by seasonality, with 36% of sales made between June and August. According to Kenji Yamamoto, Deputy General Manager of Kirin's Beer Division, 'Investment in production is still dictated by market share. Today, one market share point is worth ¥5 billion in terms of marginal profits.'

In 1987, beer was produced at 35 brewing plants in Japan, 14 of which belonged to Kirin, while Sapporo, Asahi, and Suntory Ltd operated 10, 6, and 3 plants respectively. Most of Kirin's breweries were located close to Japan's largest cities to ensure freshness, an element that had become a major selling point for many Japanese consumers. Yamamoto remarked, 'For beer lovers, the fresher, the better.' He estimated that Kirin's extensive network of production facilities gave the company a logistical cost advantage as well. Each brewery had an average production capacity of 250,000 kiloliters. Constructing a new brewery would represent a ¥50 billion investment (including the price of land) in 1987. However, around Tokyo real estate prices were much higher, and building a new brewery could require an investment of up to ¥80–90 billion.

Market Segmentation

The Japanese beer market could be divided into two major segments: 'lager' and 'draft'. The Japanese definition of lager beer was slightly different from the international definition. By international standards, lager was a beer with a long brewing process. However, in Japan, consumers regarded lager as a beer pasteurized by heat, while draft beer (also called 'nama') was unpasteurized and produced under strict microbiological control using a technique called microfiltration. While draft beer represented 9% of the total beer market in 1974 (versus 91% for lager), this segment had grown to 20% by 1980. Currently, the Japanese beer market was almost equally divided between pasteurized (lager) and unpasteurized (draft) beers. Kirin held 90% of the lager segment. Kirin's lager was by far the bestselling beer in Japan, and the company had built up its dominant position in the market over the past 40 years almost exclusively from this single product. The four major brewers shared the draft segment (refer to **Exhibit 4**).

Foreign beer accounted for about 3% of the total beer market. All major Japanese brewers had tied up with foreign companies to brew and distribute their brands in Japan. Budweiser (from the United States), brewed and distributed in Japan by Suntory, was the most popular foreign brand, selling the equivalent of 3.1 million cases[2] in 1987. Heineken (from the Netherlands) had a similar agreement with Kirin and was the second strongest brand in this segment, with one million cases sold in January–September 1987. During the same period, Asahi brewed and distributed Coors (an American beer) and Lowenbraü (a German beer), which had sold some 700,000 and 230,000 cases respectively. Beer imports, primarily from the United States, West Germany, France, and Denmark, were growing rapidly and had doubled in volume between 1984 and 1987, reaching 22.4 million liters.

Consumers

The total adult population in Japan (aged 20 years and over) had been increasing at an average rate of 1.2% per annum. The population of males aged 40 and over (regarded by Japanese brewers as the 'heavy user' segment) had grown even more rapidly, at an average rate of 1.4% per annum. Heavy users, Asahi's key target for Super Dry, were defined as people drinking more than the equivalent of 8 regular bottles (663ml) of beer each week. Heavy users represented 15% of the beer drinking population and accounted for 50% of the total volume of beer consumed in Japan. 'Middle users', representing another 15% of beer drinkers, were people who consumed more than 3 large bottles of beer but fewer than 8 bottles weekly. Finally, 'light users' (70% of beer drinkers) were people who consumed fewer than 3 bottles per week. Middle and light users each represented about 25% of the volume of beer consumed. In Japan, less than 10% of the total adult population never drank beer.

---

2. One case contained 20 bottles of 633ml each.

During the 1980s, more Japanese women began drinking beer. Women tended to be more health and weight conscious than men. To meet the needs of this segment, as well as generally increase the level of daytime consumption, Kirin introduced Kirin Beer Light in 1980 and Kirin Palm Can in 1985. Kirin Beer Light had a lower alcohol content (3.5%) than regular beer (4.5%). As well, Kirin Beer Light was attractively packaged and clearly differentiated from other Kirin products. In 1987, light beer represented 0.3% of Kirin's total beer sales, whereas lager accounted for 83% of the company's revenues.

In Japan, 70% of the beer volume sold was consumed at home versus 30% in bars and restaurants. The Japanese associated no class connotation with beer, and it was quaffed with equal enthusiasm everywhere from 4-stool diners to elite restaurants. However, Japanese consumption patterns were somewhat different from those in many Western countries. In Japan, beer was consumed primarily after 6 pm, before dinner, after the traditional 'ofuro' (Japanese bath), or after playing sports. An executive in Kirin's Beer Division explained:

> Drinking together after working hours is as much a part of Japanese business as coming to work on time. Many Japanese feel guilty drinking beer during the day on workdays. Because we Japanese have a different enzymology (enzymes in the human body), we tend to blush quickly after a drink or two. If employees have a beer during the day, their working colleagues would immediately notice, and this could be quite embarrassing.

Japanese consumers considered beer as a light, casual drink, while wine was perceived as light but more formal. Kirin's market research showed that beer was seen as a healthy, natural drink because it was brewed with no artificial additives. Shochu, a distilled spirit, was also considered a casual drink, but it was relatively strong and was losing its popularity. Although shochu had experienced an increase in consumption over the past five years, industry experts now believed this was a fad, and some predicted that the Super Dry boom could be the same.

Marketing

Marketing expenditures by the major brewers had almost doubled in recent years, from ¥65 billion in 1984 to ¥117 billion in 1987,[3] partly as a result of Asahi's launch of Super Dry (refer to **Exhibit 5**). Y. Matsui, General Manager of Asahi's marketing division, observed: 'Advertising is crucial in Japan's super competitive marketplace where neon is king and gimmickry is commonplace.' Matsui was referring to the 'packaging war' that had taken place between 1984 and 1986 when Japanese brewers had offered numerous 'gadget products', like the Suntory Penguins and the Kirin Beer Shuttle, designed to attract consumer attention. By 1987, Matsui felt that consumers had become bored with such sales tactics.

---

3. Typically, 80% of all marketing expenditures were made between January and May of each year.

Pricing

Although retail prices could be set freely, the National Tax Agency advised Japanese brewers on the appropriate prices for alcoholic beverages. Beer was the most heavily taxed alcoholic beverage at a rate of 46.9% (versus 36.3% for whiskies and brandies, and 17–20% for sakes and shochus). This meant that when a consumer paid ¥300 for a regular 633ml bottle of beer, ¥140.7 was collected by the state. Kirin executives estimated that corporate profits increased by ¥4 billion when the price on its beer line was increased by one yen.

Distribution

Brewers sold beer to the consumer through a group of primary wholesalers, who, in turn, sold to numerous sub-wholesalers. These sub-wholesalers distributed products to a large number of retail outlets. Wholesalers and retailers were licensed by the state, which strictly limited the issue of new licenses. Most distributors in the Kanto (Greater Tokyo area) dealt with all four major brewers, while exclusive distributors in the Kansai region (Western Japan) had a stronger position. The use of sub-wholesalers was declining, but developing personal relationships with wholesalers continued to be a key success factor for the brewers. In 1987, more than 1,800 wholesalers distributed beer and other alcoholic beverages in Japan. Kirin worked with 800 wholesalers, 70% of whom had an exclusive agreement with Kirin.

Retailers were liquor store owners who sold beer to consumers as well as to neighborhood bars and restaurants. Typically, retailers independently selected which beer to sell according to a brand's popularity. Each major brewer had a merchandising sales force that worked to ensure their company's products were effectively displayed in the stores.

Distribution was a major barrier for new entrants. An executive of a Danish brewery explained:

> It's difficult to distribute beer in a country with more than a million bars, pubs and restaurants, and hundreds of thousands of stores in huge cities with virtually no street names. Tying up with a local player is a prerequisite. Establishing our own distribution network through primary wholesalers, secondary wholesalers, and sometimes tertiary wholesalers would probably take us ten years.

The Competition

Since 1945, the Japanese beer market had evolved into an oligopoly of four companies, which accounted for over 99% of the total sales volume. Two smaller brewers, Hokkaido Asahi and Orion, operated on a local basis on the northern island of Hokkaido and in Okinawa in the southernmost part of Japan, respectively. Together, these brewers served less than 1% of the national market.

Sapporo Breweries Ltd

Established in September 1949 out of the former Dai Nippon Breweries, Sapporo was once the leading market player. Over time, however, the company had gradually lost ground. In 1987, Sapporo was the second largest brewer in Japan, holding a 20% share of the market. Sapporo dominated the 'draft' segment with a 40% share of this submarket (refer to **Exhibit 4**). Although Sapporo had diversified into soft drinks, wine, and imported liquors – such as J&B whisky – beer still accounted for 94% of the company's sales volume (refer to **Exhibit 6**).

Suntory Ltd

Suntory was founded in 1899 by Shinjiro Torii, the father of the company's current president. Suntory was the major producer of whisky in Japan and a large importer of Scotch whiskies, bourbons, cognacs, wines, liqueurs, beers, and so on. Suntory's dominance in the whisky market was comparable to Kirin's leading position in the beer market. In 1986, Suntory had total sales of ¥625,843 million and held a 63% share of the Japanese whisky market. Kirin-Seagram (Japan's third largest whisky company) had only a 7.6% share of this market, and Nikka Whisky (the second largest local whisky producer) had a 21% share.

Privately held, Suntory was headed by Keizo Saji, who had a reputation for an aggressive management style. In 1960, Saji turned his attention to beer making, since Suntory had reached a near monopoly position in whisky. Most of the beers available in Japan at this time were German-style lagers. Wondering whether this type of beer was entirely suited to Japanese tastes, Saji began searching for alternatives. After considerable research, he concluded that beer produced under strict microbiological control – similar to Danish-style beer – had a 'cleaner and milder' flavour, which was a better match for Japanese cuisine.

Suntory was a latecomer to the beer industry, introducing its first beer in 1963. Four years later, Suntory began producing only unpasteurized bottled and canned draft beer. Recently, Suntory had caught up to Asahi in terms of market share. The company had developed a strong position in the draft segment as well as in the 'all malts' sub-segment (refer to **Exhibit 4**). In addition to brewing its own beers, Suntory produced and marketed several foreign beers under license through agreements with US-based Anheuser-Busch Co. and Carlsberg, the famous Danish brewer. As well, since 1984 Suntory had brewed beer in China through China Jiangsu Suntory Foods Co. Ltd, the first joint venture in China to specialize in beer.

In 1987, Suntory expected to capture 9.6% of the Japanese beer market. In fiscal year 1986, beer represented 27% of Suntory's total sales.[4]

---

4. Because Suntory was a private company, detailed information was not available.

Asahi Breweries Ltd

Asahi, currently the third largest brewer in Japan, was established in 1949 after Dai Nippon was dissolved. Where Kirin was affiliated with the Mitsubishi Group, Asahi was related to the Sumitomo Group. Since the early 1970s, Asahi's board of directors had regularly appointed the company's president from within the Sumitomo Group. Japanese financial analysts pointed out that Sumitomo Bank was a secure financial backer for Asahi, and similarly, Kirin could count on the support of the Mitsubishi Group.

Over the years, Asahi had lost ground to Kirin, Sapporo, and Suntory, holding only 10% of the market in 1985. Although its sales had grown substantially between 1976 and 1986, net profits had declined from ¥2,130 million in 1976 to ¥1,510 million in 1986, although a recovery was forecasted in 1987 (refer to **Exhibit 7**). An Asahi manager elaborated:

> In the 1970s, our company was imprisoned in a vicious circle. Tastes were changing, and Asahi's sales decreased, resulting in high inventories which, in turn, affected our revenues. Also, since consumers did not have a high image of our products, retailers didn't push our products, no matter how much effort our salesmen put into the trade. The salesmen blamed the engineers for not turning out good products, and the engineers blamed the salesmen for not selling products that they thought were as good as the competition.

Employee morale in the company had suffered as a result of the poor performance. Between 1981 and 1985, the staff was decreased from 3,120 to 2,740, although the reductions were achieved mainly through attrition. Because data on market share and corporate performance was regularly published in the Japanese press, Masahiro Maeda, Vice President of the First Boston Corporation in Tokyo, believed that Asahi's sales decline had also affected the company's recruitment program. Top Japanese graduates preferred to join companies with the best track records.

In an effort to improve market share, Asahi management had pushed to reduce the dependence on beer and to expand sales of soft drinks, foods, and pharmaceuticals. By 1987, soft drinks represented 20% of the company's total sales.

In 1982, at the suggestion of Sumitomo Bank, the Asahi board of directors appointed Tsutomu Murai as the company's new president. Murai, an Executive Vice President of the bank, was credited with the turnaround of Toyo Kogyo when the automobile company had faced a major crisis after the 1973 oil shock. In 1987, Toyo Kogyo (now Mazda Motor Corporation) was the fourth largest manufacturer of cars in Japan.

After joining Asahi, Murai quickly surmised that the company had become too conservative. Moreover, Murai did not encounter a feeling of crisis as he had at Mazda when he was brought in to turn that company around. A 1980 report by the Tokyo office of McKinsey & Co. had concluded that Asahi had a weak presence in the marketplace and that efforts to improve its position had not been recognized by the public. The report also indicated that the company was not communicating effectively with its customers, stressing that the quality of Asahi products needed more emphasis. The McKinsey group recommended developing a new corporate identity and pressed the company to become more market driven. Murai's plan was to remobilize the entire organization and thus improve Asahi's competitiveness.

In 1984, Murai created two task forces of functional managers to work on developing a new Corporate Identity (CI) and a Total Quality Control (TQC) program. In its recommendations, the CI team suggested changing the Asahi logo to show that the company was moving in a new direction, that is, towards its customers. The traditional imperial rising sun had been Asahi's symbol for nearly a century. Although many employees and consumers were very attached to the logo, it tended to be perceived as somewhat old-fashioned.

Over the years, little market research had been conducted to monitor changing customer needs, and too few new products had been launched to meet those needs relative to the competition. Murai promptly commissioned a marketing survey to re-examine consumer attitudes towards beer. In 1984, in both Tokyo and Osaka, data were collected from 5,000 adult males and females regarding new Asahi beers as well as competitive products. The researchers discovered that consumers highly valued 'body' and 'sharpness' in a beer. 'Thirst quenching', 'long-lasting feeling', 'less sweet', and 'no aftertaste' were found to be important attributes as well. Additional research confirmed that consumers associated 'cork' and 'mellowness' with 'richness', and associated 'clarity' with 'sharpness'.

The marketing data also revealed that consumer preference was shifting from the bitter, richer taste of Kirin's Lager beer to a sharper draft taste. On the basis of this research, Asahi's marketing department proposed changing the taste of its draft beer. The production engineers were quick to denounce the inconsistency between sharpness and richness. However, Murai was convinced that a new Asahi Draft could be an intermediary product between traditional draft beer and the sharper 'dry' beer, which had recently been defined by the marketing team. Launched in early 1986, the new Asahi Draft, 'koku-kire' (rich and sharp), got off to a smooth start. However, Asahi's share of the total beer market continued to drop, and the number of retailers carrying the Asahi brand was also on the decline.

A New President

In 1986, when Tsutomu Murai turned 69, he asked Sumitomo Bank to appoint Hirotaro Higuchi as Asahi's new President. Born in 1930, Higuchi had entered Sumitomo Bank in 1949 after graduating from the Faculty of Economics at Kyoto University. Higuchi had worked for the bank for 37 years and was the youngest executive to reach the position of Vice President of International Affairs.

In the spring of 1986, Higuchi took over the presidency of Asahi Breweries and Murai became the company's Chairman. Higuchi intended to pursue Murai's objective to turn Asahi into a truly customer-orientated company. His ultimate goal was to restore Asahi's market share to the level it had enjoyed previously, when the company had competed neck-and-neck with Sapporo and Kirin.

At the outset, Higuchi observed that, over the past 30 years, a corporate culture had developed where everyone blamed someone else in the company for the annual loss of market share. Higuchi's initial course of action involved a corporate identity campaign aimed at modifying Asahi's internal and external image. A booklet containing '10 commandments' was handed out to all employees as a guide to daily behavior. These commandments were also read aloud every morning so that each employee would understand the new direction in which Asahi was proceeding. The new corporate philosophy emphasized quality first, followed by customer orientation, mutual respect, labor-management conciliation, cooperation with the trade, and social responsibility.

To change Asahi's image, Higuchi decided to develop new packaging for all Asahi products. As part of this plan, all beers carrying the old-fashioned imperial flag were recalled from the retail shelves, at a high cost financially. Higuchi aimed to send the trade, the public, and the competition a clear message that Asahi had changed significantly. As well, Higuchi implemented a 'Quality First' policy and instructed the Purchasing Department to use only the best raw materials, even if this entailed higher costs. Finally, Higuchi decided to increase the company's advertising and promotional expenditures to the highest possible levels, even at the risk of eating up all the net profits.

Preparing for Super Dry

When, in the fall of 1986, Higuchi discussed the 'dry beer' concept for the first time with 12 Asahi executives, not one person really supported the idea. Higuchi recalled that the director who was in charge of production went so far as to say: 'We can't produce a dry beer, this is nonsense to me.' A marketing manager explained that the meaning of the word 'dry' was important:

> Dry suggests something new, decisive, and bold. We have found that a 'wet' person is very strongly attached to family, the company and friends, while a 'dry' type is more individualistic.

Higuchi was aware that the company had often been criticized for launching many products and quickly giving up on them when they did not fulfill management's expectations. Consequently, Higuchi felt that he should postpone the launch of a new 'dry' beer until the new Asahi Draft had established a stronger position in the market. Eiji Kobayashi, a young Asahi executive, countered that other young managers in the Marketing, R&D, and Production departments were quite comfortable with the 'dry' concept and were pushing to place such a product on the market. Asahi's production engineers indicated that brewing dry beer would not require a major breakthrough in terms of production technology. One of the marketing people offered his view:

> I think that the 'dry' concept is viable, but I can't tell you how much we can expect to sell.

Since Higuchi had been appointed to turn Asahi around, he felt that he should not discourage young managers with fresh ideas. 'After all,' Higuchi said, 'Asahi has little to lose.'

The Launch of Super Dry

By early 1987, the R&D Department had managed to develop a 'dry' beer. Meanwhile, the Marketing Department used 'hands-on' test markets to gather additional data to assess consumer attitudes. A comprehensive marketing plan was developed, setting a sales target of 800,000 cases for the first year. Asahi's Super Dry beer was officially launched on March 17, 1987.

Junichi Nakamura, a 54-year-old retailer in Shinagawa and one of the 130,000 liquor store owners in Japan, wondered how successful Asahi's Super Dry would be in the long run. Nakamura was used to seeing some 40 kinds of new beer packaging arrive on his shelves each year, then disappear after a few months. Nakamura also wondered if consumers could really tell the difference between Asahi Dry and other regular beers. He remarked:

> For non-connoisseurs, Japanese beers tend to taste more or less the same. Japanese brewers do not yet offer the wide spectrum of tastes that Europeans can enjoy, for example. In bars and restaurants, some customers may ask for a specific brand, and many people especially want to try Asahi's Super Dry. But generally, people simply order beer and the waiters serve them the major brand they carry. When customers come to my store, it's the same. Connoisseurs will ask for Kirin, Asahi, Sapporo, or Suntory because they can differentiate the taste, or they will choose between draft and lager. But the connoisseurs are a minority. Many people drink Kirin because it has been the leading brand for so many years. As for Super Dry, I'm not sure if it's another fad or a revolution.

Super Dry was designed as a draft beer and targeted at heavy drinkers. It was made using less residual sugar, which produced a beer that was less sweet. Super Dry contained 0.5% more alcohol than the 4.5% regular draft beers. Super Dry was positioned as much sharper and softer than traditional draft beers (refer to **Exhibit 8**). Super Dry was made using the best hops from Czechoslovakia and West Germany, as well as malt from the United States, Canada, and Australia. Asahi's production engineers had also shortened the time from production to consumption by 20% – to an average of 20 days, while other brewers operated on a 23–25 day cycle. The Super Dry silver label with Asahi's new logo and modern lettering reinforced the image of a truly different product (refer to **Exhibit 9**).

In 1987, Asahi had a marketing budget of ¥38.1 billion, a 33% increase over the previous year, ¥4.2 billion of which would be used solely to promote Super Dry (refer to **Exhibit 5**). Shigeo Sakurai, a Planning Manager in Kirin's Beer Division, observed:

To launch Super Dry, Asahi ran full-page advertisements in all five major dailies. The ads were spread over three weeks: a 'coming soon' preview, a 'debuts today' announcement, and a 'have you tried it yet?' follow-up. Television commercials, a key element of the introduction, were double the usual frequency for a new product campaign.

Asahi also distributed free product samples to a million people throughout Japan. In addition to its 500 salespeople (versus Kirin's sales force of 520), Asahi established sales teams with a total of 1,000 'field ladies' to promote and merchandise Super Dry at the retail level. These teams also collected additional qualitative marketing data from customers regarding preference, consumption levels, and so on. By October 1987, while the Japanese beer market had grown by 7%, Asahi's revenues had increased by 34%, primarily through sales of Super Dry.

Kirin's Response

Asahi's impressive performance had the effect of a small earthquake within the Kirin organization, and several teams were put to work to meet the competitive challenge. In late October 1987, Kirin's President, Hideo Motoyama, called a special meeting with the executives from the Beer Division to discuss the alternatives for action and to develop a strategy for the 1988 beer season.

The Alternatives

1. Cut the Price

Izumi Nakane, a Marketing Manager, suggested that one option was to reduce the price (by ¥10) on the 500ml can, one of Kirin's major products. This would be the first price cut in 26 years. Nakane believed that this action would help Kirin restore its share position, as well as lessen the impact of Asahi's new dry beer in the marketplace. Cutting prices could be offset by the less expensive raw material costs that had resulted from the recent appreciation of the yen. Nakane pointed out that Kirin had long been viewed as the price setter in the industry, and he argued that consumers would appreciate a price cut. Recently, many Japanese firms had come under fire for not passing on the effects of cheaper raw material imports. The benefit for the consumer would be a reduction in the retail price of a 500ml can of beer from ¥280 to ¥270.

In Nakane's view, Suntory was in the most vulnerable position with regard to a price cut. While sales of 500ml cans accounted for only 6% of Kirin's total revenues, the same product accounted for as much as 12% of Suntory's total beer sales. At Asahi, this figure was close to 9%. Nakane continued:

In other words, we will lower prices on the products which least affect Kirin's own sales and competitiveness. Relative to the competition, we sell far fewer 500ml cans. The impact of a price cut on Kirin would be minimal, while Sapporo and Asahi would each suffer damage in the range of ¥300 million if they chose to follow us down in price.

2. Launch Kirin's Dry Beer

Jinichiro Kuroda, an executive in the Marketing Department, favored launching Kirin's own dry beer. He believed that Kirin had the distribution capability and the financial resources to support a major advertising campaign. A few months earlier, Kirin's R&D Department had developed a product that was similar to Asahi's Super Dry. If necessary, production could begin within a month.

Kuroda's proposal fueled a long and heated ongoing discussion within the company. One executive, Yoshio Suzuki, wanted to take a 'wait-and-see' approach. Another wanted to first assess the reactions of Suntory and Sapporo, while a third suggested that Kirin should immediately launch its own dry beer. Shuji Ogawa, also in the Marketing Department, disagreed:

If we launch a me-too product, we will give legitimacy to the very same dry segment we want to minimize.

3. Reinforce Kirin's Lager

Matsumi Kohara, a brand manager for pasteurized beer, suggested:

Dry beer may be a fad. We should make stronger efforts to convey the good aspects of our lager beer. Why don't we emphasize the good taste of lager beer and have 'lager' clearly displayed on our bottles. Look, lager is only a subtitle on our products right now. The only thing you see on our bottles today is Kirin (refer to **Exhibit 10**).

4. Launch Other Products

After patiently listening to his colleagues, Dr Hideo Matsuda, who worked in the Research Department, suddenly broke into the conversation with the following proposal:

We are all concerned about the impact of Asahi's Super Dry. Indeed, this is one of the most successful products Asahi has ever introduced in all the years I can remember. But we also have many good products in reserve that could be backed by strong advertising and kicked off either separately or simultaneously. And we have much better distribution capabilities and stronger financial resources than Asahi. We have been working on several good products that could be launched immediately.

Dr Matsuda described two of these products:

Kirin Fine Malt: This is a totally new delightful draft beer with a 4.5% alcohol content. It is 100% malt, made from a variety of selected fine malt and aromatic hops. This product would reinforce our presence in the draft segment and be the base to effectively compete against Asahi's Super Dry.

Kirin Fine Pilsner: This is another product that we could launch quickly. It's a beer of traditional Pilsner stock, rich and smooth, made from fine malt and superior hops. Our R&D team has found that its rich velvety taste brings the consumer great refreshment. Moreover, its alcohol content (5%) is similar to Asahi's Super Dry.

Matsuda believed that both these products could be put onto the market within a matter of weeks. On average, launching a new brand cost about ¥900 million.

After listening to the various proposals, Motoyama, Kirin's President, paused for a moment, looked around the table at his executives, and asked:

I wonder what will happen to our market position if Suntory and Sapporo also decide to launch dry beers. Moreover, if we should decide to launch a dry beer, will this be enough to restore our market share to 60%?

EXHIBIT 1

The World Beer Industry (1987)

Rank	Company (country)	Sales Volume (10,000 Kl)	Domestic Market Share	Export Ratio	Beer Sales (¥100 mn)	Net Profits (¥100 mn)
1.	Anheuser Bush (USA)	901	41.9%	1.5%	13,045	890
2.	Miller (USA)	472	21.0%	2.8%	4,381	–
3.	Heineken (Netherlands)	430	51.0%	85.0%	4,755	205
4.	Kirin (Japan)	303	56.4%	0.4%	13,567	354
5.	Bond (Australia)	299	45.0%	73.0%	13,370	565
6.	Stroh (USA)	258	11.7%	0.5%	–	–
7.	Brahma (Brazil)	215	49.0%	0.2%	1,085	54
8.	Elders (Australia)	210	45.0%	62.0%	31,676	1,414
9.	Coors (USA)	192	8.4%	2.0%	2,156	69
10.	BSN (France)	188	48.1%	44.7%	1,343	–

Source: Kirin Brewery Co. Ltd, 1987.

EXHIBIT 2

Selected Financial Data

Income (¥mn)	Sales	Operating Profit	Current Profit	Net Profit	Net Earnings	Dividends (*)	Equity (*)
Jan 1985	1,151,762	60,682	66,576	25,106	28.5	7.5	267.8
Jan 1986	1,210,857	65,534	73,324	31,047	35.0	7.5	295.8
Jan 1987	1,221,847	72,127	79,301	33,340	37.1	9.5	328.2
Dec 1988**	1,270,000	71,000	81,000	34,500	38.2	7.5	–

Operating Margins:	5.9%
P/E Ratio:	69.5

Financial Data (¥mn)	July 1987
Total Assets	835,504
Fixed Assets	314,768
Current Assets	520,735
Current Liabilities	379,251
Working Capital	141,484
Bank Borrowings	9,663
Capital Stock	51,929
Capital Surplus	20,756
Shareholders' Equity	307,730
Equity Ratio (%)	36.8
Interest & Dividend Net	6,194

Sales Breakdown in January 1987 in %	
Beer	93
Soft Drinks	6
Others	1
Export Ratio	0

Facility Investment (¥mn)	
1987:	23,900

R&D Expenditures (¥mn)	
1987:	13,400

Employees	7,656	(*) Per share
Average Age	39	** Forecasted

Source: Kirin Brewery Co. Ltd.

EXHIBIT 3

Comparative Market Shares in the Japanese Beer Industry (1949–87*)

Year	Brewers:	Asahi (%)	Kirin (%)	Sapporo (%)	Suntory (%)	Takara (%)
1949		36.1	25.3	38.6	–	–
1950		33.5	29.5	37.0	–	–
1951		34.5	29.5	36.0	–	–
1952		32.5	33.0	34.5	–	–
1953		33.3	33.2	33.5	–	–
1954		31.5	37.1	31.4	–	–
1955		31.7	36.9	31.4	–	–
1956		31.1	41.7	27.2	–	–
1957		30.7	42.1	26.2	–	1.0
1958		30.9	39.9	27.5	–	1.7
1959		29.3	42.4	26.5	–	1.8
1960		27.2	44.7	26.0	–	2.1
1961		28.0	41.6	27.8	–	2.6
1962		26.4	45.0	26.4	–	2.2
1963		24.3	46.5	26.3	0.9	2.0
1964		25.5	46.2	25.2	1.2	1.9
1965		23.2	47.7	25.3	1.9	1.9
1966		22.2	50.8	23.8	1.7	1.5
1967		22.0	49.4	25.0	3.2	0.4
1968		20.2	51.2	24.4	4.2	–
1969		19.0	53.3	23.2	4.5	–
1970		17.3	55.4	23.0	4.3	–
1971		14.9	58.9	22.0	4.2	–
1972		14.1	60.1	21.3	4.5	–
1973		13.6	61.4	20.3	4.7	–
1974		13.1	62.6	19.5	4.8	–
1975		13.5	60.8	20.2	5.5	–
1976		11.8	63.8	18.4	6.0	–
1977		12.1	61.9	19.5	6.5	–
1978		11.6	62.1	19.6	6.7	–
1979		11.1	62.9	19.2	6.8	–
1980		11.0	62.2	19.7	7.1	–
1981		10.3	62.6	20.1	7.0	–
1982		10.0	62.3	19.9	7.8	–
1983		10.1	61.3	20.0	8.6	–
1984		9.9	61.7	19.5	8.9	–
1985		9.6	61.4	19.8	9.2	–
1986		10.4	59.6	20.4	9.4	–
1987		12.9	57.0	20.5	9.6	–

*1982–87: Casewriter's estimates.

Sources: Figures up to 1981: estimated by the Brewers Association of Japan.

EXHIBIT 4

Segmentation of the Beer Market in Japan by Product Categories and Brewers in 1987 ($\times$ 10,000 kiloliters)

Brewers	Segments							
	Lager*	Draft	All Malts	Light	Dry	Foreign Brands	Others	Total
Kirin	250.3 Kirin Lager	48.0 Kirin Draft	1.7 Heartland Export	1.0 Kirin Light	–	0.7 Heineken	0.3 Black Stout Mainbraü	302
Sapporo	17.0	91.2	2.2 Ours Classic Quality	0.3 Next one	–	0.3 Miller Guinness	–	111
Asahi	6.0	43.2	0.1 100% Malt	–	17.0 Super Dry	0.5 Löwenbrau Coors	0.2 Black	67
Suntory	–	40.8	10.3 Malts	0.1 Penguin's Bar	–	2.0 Budweiser Carlsberg	–	53
Total:	273.3	223.2	14.3	1.5	17.0	3.2	0.5	533

Notes: * pasteurized
The major brands by brewer and by segment are in italics.
Beer as a percentage of total sales is as follows:
Kirin 93%, Asahi 79%, Sapporo 94%, Suntory 28%

Source: Casewriter's estimates.

EXHIBIT 5

Comparative Marketing Expenditures of the Major Japanese Brewers 1983–87 (¥ bn)

	Advertising Expenses	Promotion Expenses	Total Marketing Expenses	As % of Beer Sales
Kirin				
1983	10.5	16.0	26.5	2.5
1984	11.4	18.1	29.5	2.7
1985	15.9	21.7	37.6	3.2
1986	13.9	21.4	35.3	2.9
1987*	15.9	28.1	44.0	3.5
Asahi				
1983	6.8	6.8	13.6	6.3
1984	7.9	7.5	15.4	7.1
1985	8.9	10.0	18.9	8.0
1986	7.9	10.9	18.8	7.9
1987*	11.7	13.8	25.5	9.8
Sapporo				
1983	7.5	4.0	11.5	3.2
1984	8.6	4.9	13.5	3.7
1985	11.0	5.5	16.5	4.3
1986	12.1	6.0	18.1	4.5
1987*	13.3	7.8	21.1	4.8
Suntory				
1983	25.7	36.6	62.3	7.0*
1984	27.9	39.6	67.5	7.9
1985	26.7	39.8	66.5	8.7
1986	22.8	39.6	62.4	8.1
1987*	22.9	46.6	69.5	9.2

* Estimated

Source: Dentsu Inc., 1987.

EXHIBIT 5 (CONTINUED)

Comparative Advertising Expenditures per Media, 1987 (in %)

Product Lines	Newspapers	Magazines	MEDIA TV Programs	TV Spots	Radio Programs	Radio Spots	Media Total
Kirin Beers:							
Export	100	–	–	–	–	–	<1
Can Beer	26.8	15.3	7.2	49.9	5.3	<1	14.6
Classic	94.4	5.6	–	–	–	–	2.6
Lager	64.4	6.0	6.1	21.4	<1	<1	59.1
Lights	56.7	43.3	–	–	–	–	<1
Heartland	36.4	2.5	<1	61.0	–	–	15.1
Heineken	8.8	38.5	7.8	42.0	2.8	–	7.3
							100
Asahi Beers:							
Black draft	36.7	63.3	–	–	–	–	2.0
Draft	86.8	13.2	–	–	–	–	9.8
100% Malts	45.5	<1	4.5	42.3	–	7.4	7.1
Super Dry	58.4	3.5	3.7	29.0	1.1	4.3	58.1
Big Boy	100	–	–	–	–	–	<1
Coors	17.3	6.4	1.9	70.8	1.5	2.0	19.1
Lowenbräu	<1	17.3	7.4	67.5	7.4	<1	3.4
							100

Note: These figures exclude creative fees from the advertising agencies as well as corporate advertising expenditures and promotion for social events (sports, concerts, etc.).

Source: Dentsu Inc., 1987.

EXHIBIT 6

Sapporo Breweries' Selected Financial Data

Income (¥mn)	Sales	Operating Profit	Current Profit	Net Profit	Net Earnings (*)	Dividends (*)	Equity (*)
Dec 1985	402,552	12,178	10,691	4,505	15.9	5.0	178.2
Dec 1986	436,046	15,057	12,399	4,725	15.6	6.5	252.3
Dec 1987**	467,046	14,514	13,050	5,250	15.8	6.5	326.4
Dec 1988**	510,000	10,000	13,500	5,400	16.2	5.0	–
Dec 1989**	550,000	11,000	14,000	5,600	7.6	2.5	–

Operating Margins:	3.1%		Sales Breakdown in July 1987 in %	
			Beer	94
P/E Ratio:	118.9		Soft Drinks	3
			Others	3
Financial Data (¥mn)	July 1987		Export Ratio	0
Total Assets	365,830			
Fixed Assets	164,502			
Current Assets	201,327			
Current Liabilities	164,931		Facility Investment (¥mn)	
Working Capital	36,396		1987:**	60,000
Bank Borrowings	7,997			
Capital Stock	39,955			
Capital Surplus	28,274			
Shareholders' Equity	108,557		R&D Expenditures (¥mn)	
Equity Ratio (%)	29.7		1987:**	2,700
Interest & Dividend Net	(–)300			

(*) Per share
** Forecasted

Employees   3,791

Source: Japan Company Handbook, 1987.

EXHIBIT 7

Asahi Breweries' Selected Financial Data

Income (¥mn)	Sales	Operating Profit	Current Profit	Net Profit (*)	Net Earnings	Dividends (*)	Equity (*)
Dec 1985	236,383	4,398	3,270	1,364	6.1	5.0	147.0
Dec 1986	259,357	2,646	5,321	1,510	6.8	5.0	148.7
Dec 1987**	345,112	3,507	9,388	2,509	9.3	5.0	295.3
Dec 1988**	530,000	9,000	12,000	4,000	14.3	7-8	–
Dec 1989**	670,000	15,000	14,000	4,500	16.5	5-6	–

Operating Margin:	1.0%	Sales Breakdown in July 1987 in %	
P/E Ratio:	168.3	Beer	79
		Soft Drinks	20
Financial Data (¥mn)	July 1987	Others	1
Total Assets	266,235	Export Ratio	0
Fixed Assets	91,208	Facility Investment (¥ mn)	
Current Assets	175,027	1987:**	62,000
Current Liabilities	162,681		
Working Capital	12,346	R&D Expenditures (¥ mn)	
Bank Borrowings	30,618	1987:**	1,500
Capital Stock	34,315	Employees	2,944
Capital Surplus	26,969	Average Age	41
Shareholders' Equity	79,851		
Equity Ratio (%)	30.0		
Interest & Dividend Net	7,820		

(*) Per share

** Forecasted

Source: Japan Company Handbook, 1987.

EXHIBIT 8

Positioning Map for Beer Products

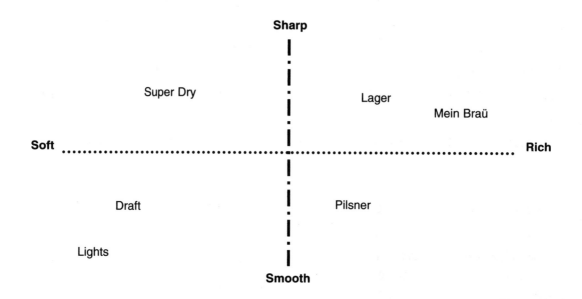

Source: Kirin Brewery Co. Ltd, 1987.

EXHIBIT 9

Asahi's Super Dry Label

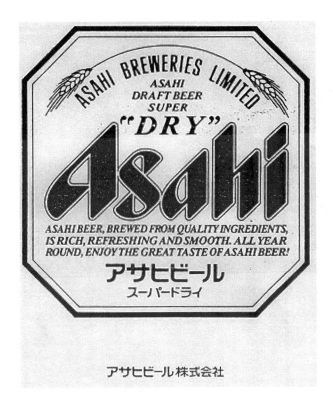

Source: Company Records.

EXHIBIT 10

Kirin's Lager Beer Label

Source: Company Records.

CLASS HANDOUT

Consumer Opinions on Dry Beer in Japan

Survey Design   *Area:* Tokyo   *Sample:* 504 people (all beer drinkers)

QUESTIONS

1   **What is your favourite type of beer?**

Responses by Sex

	Men	Women	Total
Lager	15.8%	6.0%	12.1%
Draft	20.9%	20.2%	20.6%
Dry	55.6%	65.6%	59.3%
All Malts	4.9%	4.9%	4.9%
Light	1.3%	2.2%	1.6%

Responses by Age Bracket

	20s	30s	40s	50s
Lager	6.2%	9.2%	17.0%	27.3%
Draft	21.2%	20.9%	20.6%	18.2%
Dry	61.6%	63.8%	54.6%	50.0%
All Malts	7.5%	3.7%	4.3%	2.3%
Light	2.7%	1.2%	0.7%	2.3%

2   **What made you drink dry beer?**

I saw some commercials on TV	64.0%
I read an article about it	37.7%
I saw it in a store	14.3%
I read some comparative studies	36.2%
It's available at home	34.2%
People around me drink it	36.2%

CLASS HANDOUT (continued)

 What made you drink...?

	Asahi Super Dry	Kirin Dry	Sapporo Dry	Suntory Dry
I saw some commercials on TV	63.4%	62.8%	72.0%	76.2%
I read an article about it	38.8%	35.9%	38.0%	33.3%
I saw it in a store	14.6%	12.8%	12.0%	28.6%
I read some comparative studies	34.8%	37.2%	38.0%	42.9%
It's available at home	35.1%	30.8%	32.0%	38.4%
People around me drink it	34.8%	37.2%	38.0%	42.9%

 Why do you think beer drinking attitudes changed?

Preferences have changed	12.7%
New products have been introduced	68.8%
People make comparisons	18.5%
Newspapers and magazines reported on it	30.2%
Lifestyles have changed	16.0%

5 **What were your impressions when you first tasted a dry beer?**

It tastes different	28.0%
It has good body	30.8%
It has a sharp taste	38.1%
It has a smooth taste	35.6%
It has more alcohol	20.3%
It tastes like other beers	17.8%
It is trendy	15.1%
It has a good label and a good name	15.3%
Others	2.9%

CLASS HANDOUT (continued)

6 **What do you mean by 'beer with good body'?**

A sharp beer	22.9%
A thick beer	52.2%
A bitter beer	30.4%
A sweet beer	18.8%
A good feeling in the throat	19.0%
It smells good	17.0%
A stronger beer	14.4%
The real beer	57.5%
Others	2.4%

7 **What type of beer do you associate most with this concept of good body?**

Lager	14.0%
Draft	17.8%
Dry	28.5%
All Malts	20.6%
Light	0.2%
Black	11.7%
Others	1.6%

8 **What do you mean by 'a sharp beer'?**

A good feeling in the throat	60.1%
A pure taste	38.5%
Bitterness disappears rapidly	51.6%
No bitterness	20.0%
A beer with a higher degree of fermentation	24.3%
A stronger beer	14.6%

CLASS HANDOUT (continued)

9   **What kind of beer do you associate most with this concept of sharpness?**

Lager	5.5%
Draft	21.9%
Dry	55.1%
All Malts	4.7%
Light	3.8%
Black	0.2%
Others	1.6%

10   **Do you think that your consumption of dry beer will increase or decrease?**

Will decrease	23.2%
Will remain stable	48.7%
Will increase	25.2%

11   **Why will your consumption of dry beer decrease?**

It is not my taste	44.6%
I don't see any difference from other beers	8.0%
I don't drink it because it is a fad	4.5%
People around me don't drink it	8.9%
It does not taste good	28.6%
I'm getting tired of it	28.6%
That's the way it is	25.0%
Other reasons	10.7%

CLASS HANDOUT (continued)

Why will your consumption of dry beer increase?

I like the taste	52.2%
People around me drink it	17.6%
It's trendy	21.3%
I'd like to try other beers	19.1%
It tastes good	63.2%
It's available at home	25.7%
I'm tired of other beers	5.1%
Other reasons	8.1%

Source: Mitsubishi Research Institute.

CASE 2.3

Daewoo Motor Company UK (A)

This case was prepared by Research Associate Debra Riley under the supervision of Professor Sean Meehan. Some data are disguised.

Pat Farrell had joined Daewoo from Rover, having previously served as Marketing Director for both UK and European operations. Shortly after joining the company, he was asked by Daewoo's Chairman to determine what it would take to achieve 1% market share as quickly as possible.

He and Les Woodcock, the Managing Director, agreed as to the enormity of the challenge. Pat's experience at Rover suggested that Daewoo could sell around 7,000 cars in the first year, given a reasonable promotion budget and dealer network. But to do so they would have to overcome concerns about the cars' performance and reliability – the Nexia and Espero – which were viewed as re-bodied, old versions of Vauxhall Astras and Cavaliers sold much cheaper than the originals.

Accordingly, they met with other members of the original management team, Peter Ellis, Ray Battersby and David Gerrans as well as Gary Duckworth, from their newly appointed advertising agency, to determine how to launch successfully in the UK market by the end of February 1995. Emotions were mixed that Friday evening the previous August as they drove to a Berkshire retreat for a weekend of heavy brainstorming. Les was upbeat:

> This is probably one of the biggest challenges of my career. Never before has a new car company entered this market and gained a 1% share in three years. But this is what they want and we have a free hand to do whatever it takes to achieve that target.

Daewoo Group: From Korea to the World

Daewoo Group, a South Korean industrial giant, or 'chaebol' was ranked the 33rd largest company in the world by Fortune in 1993, with sales of over $33 billion. In 1994, the group comprised 31 companies in Korea and more than 450 subsidiaries and branches worldwide. It was engaged in diverse activities such as trading, construction (both domestic and overseas), shipbuilding, automobiles (encompassing passenger cars, commercial vehicles and auto components), heavy equipment, machine tools, telecommunications equipment, consumer electronics, home appliances, textiles and financial services.

Daewoo's globalization strategy was based on a broad portfolio and a vision driven by Chairman Kim Woo Chung. In 1990, Daewoo launched its global management plan, 'Vision 2000', which facilitated an aggressive program of international expansion around electronics and passenger cars, established core areas. The objectives of the strategy were to secure additional world markets through global buying power and localized production. Other Korean giants such as Hyundai, LG and Samsung had grown enormously through similar strategies.

'Vision 2000' called for the production of more than two million cars a year, half of these outside Korea. It had embarked on joint venture vehicle production projects in five countries, including Uzbekhistan, Iran and the Philippines. The company was aiming to become the tenth largest car producer in the world by the end of the century. In 1993, Daewoo had sold over 300,000 cars worldwide. These ambitions meant it had to be successful in the high volume European market. Daewoo was planning a simultaneous launch for the Nexia and Espero in seven Western European countries with plans to roll out in a further seven a few months later. Its target was 100,000 sales in the first year, with 1% of the new-car market in each country it entered by 1998. Daewoo's European assault would be decentralized, with each market having its own promotional campaign and distribution program. The company had also embarked on an extensive product development program to come up with its own designs. In 1993, Daewoo had acquired British-based IAD, one of Europe's biggest automobile design agencies, whose staff of 400 were already hard at work developing cars for launch in 1997.

The UK Car Market

UK car production had grown by 15% over the previous three years, with most of the increase accounted for by Japanese manufacturers Honda, Nissan and Toyota, and by the Rover Group. The UK car market had been hurt by the recent recession, and new car registrations had yet to recover their 1989 peak. Ford, Vauxhall and Rover dominated the market with over 50% market share between them (refer to **Exhibit 1**). This was due largely to the mass appeal of their models aimed at the so-called lower- and upper-medium segments of the market (refer to **Exhibits 2A and 2B**).

The Nexia and Espero would be aimed at the mainstream sector: the lower-medium and upper-medium segments. The available market was actually a smaller subset of these, as 22% of all UK cars were now diesel, and the cars would only be available in petrol versions. The Nexia and Espero would be very competitively priced, capitalizing on Korea's low manufacturing costs (as compared to Japan, Europe, and the US). However, they knew that fleet car sales were a substantial portion of overall sales in these sectors, 40% of the lower-medium and 80% of the upper-medium segment. The upper-medium sector saw particularly aggressive competition between the principal volume manufacturers, Ford and Vauxhall, for sales to the daily rental companies, leasing companies and other fleet operators.

Fleet sales (defined as sales to operators with more than 25 vehicles) and business sales had surpassed private sales, growing from 22% of the market in 1984 to 48%

of total sales for the first five months of 1994. Fleet sales were of particular concern in Daewoo's strategy development as most UK fleet car purchasers had a 'Buy UK' or 'Buy European' policy that precluded models that were not manufactured locally. As a result, Asian share of the fleet sales was only 0.5%.

Private Car Buyers

In May 1994, Pat Farrell had commissioned market research to profile private purchasers of medium-sized vehicles. This study found private buyers to be cost conscious, with over half of all cars (new and used) in use by households costing £6,000 or less. For lower-medium and upper-medium segment purchases, the average UK buyer was male, 35–54 years old, with a household income of £25–30 thousand. However, buyers of the 'emergent marques', the new Asian and East European brands, tended to be older, with a lower average household income of around £15,000. The principal source of finance for private car purchasing was family personal savings, accounting for over 60% of all cars bought.

The research highlighted three distinct sets of desires that individuals looked for when buying a new car: 'rational needs', such as reliability and fuel economy; 'emotional wants', such as anti-lock braking systems and electric windows; and 'badge value', the status or group membership associated with a brand.

However, Daewoo's research had stressed that purchasers of the 'emergent marques' – the South East Asian manufacturers such as Hyundai and Proton – considered price and value for money their top considerations in buying a car. The mechanical details of a car were increasingly considered a commodity, so functionality (such as roominess and storage), style and price had increased in importance. Customer needs varied somewhat by the product sector, but previous experience with a manufacturer was the strongest indicator of future purchasing patterns. New car buyers tended to buy the same model again, or buy a model higher in the range. Most visited local dealers, often making repeat visits, with a brief comparison shop for the sake of thoroughness. The dealer locations visited were usually ones the buyer had spotted when driving past.

There was a general level of mistrust and dislike for the entire car purchasing exercise. As Farrell explained: 'Most buyers dislike the haggling process of purchasing a car, feel that car salesmen are too pushy, and that the level of post-sales service is too low.' Customers did not understand dealer mark-ups. Recently, manufacturers and dealers had tried to counter this by focusing on simplified buying procedures and improving customer service. Ford offered 30-day unconditional guarantees, Vauxhall, Citroen and Nissan offered a year's free insurance for certain models, and Renault had started providing two years' free servicing on certain models. During his tenure at Rover, Farrell had been involved in a number of initiatives to make dealers more customer-focused. One common method was to offer an extra rebate of approximately 2% margin to dealers for meeting target standards of customer care and service. At Daewoo, he recognized the potential value of building a company image from scratch around customer value and service. He envisioned an aggressive pre-launch campaign of advertising and PR that would build brand awareness and position Daewoo as the most caring and customer-focused brand in the market. Such a media campaign would typically kick-off at the annual Motor Show in Birmingham in October, where discussions with potential dealers could commence.

Dealers

The management team understood they would need to move quickly in order to establish a dealer network for the February launch. There were 7,300 franchised dealer outlets in the UK operating around 5,500 retail sites. Around 25% of dealers operated multiple franchises. Many dealerships had been taken over by large groups that handled a large number of marques (refer to **Exhibit 3**). The core business of car dealers was to sell new and used cars, and to provide 'after market' services, such as repairs and sales of parts. There were two kinds of car dealers: franchised dealers, who were appointed by the car manufacturers to sell their new cars, and independent dealers, who sold used cars. Industry sources claimed that 40% of the average franchised dealer's sales were derived from new cars, 30% from used cars and the rest from repairs and servicing. The corresponding profit was 10%, 40% and 50% respectively.

New cars were supplied to dealers direct from manufacturers or importers ('one-tier' distribution) or indirectly through a 'main dealer' appointed by the car manufacturer as a wholesaler for a local area ('two-tier' distribution). The latter had all but disappeared and was now mainly practiced only by Ford and Rover. Cars remained one of the few product groups in the EU in which the supplier was allowed to grant or withhold supplies from a dealer. Increasingly, manufacturers were demanding much higher standards from dealers and their premises, to the extent that the cost to open a new site had reached £1–2 million. Thus, many small dealers were being driven out of business or taken over by larger groups.

Large groups tended to be diversified into businesses other than car retailing and servicing. Common commercial activities included leasing and contract hire, petrol forecourt activities, and commercial vehicles. Of the core car retailing and servicing activities, selling new cars was the least profitable activity – after-market sales were the essential ingredient for profitability. New car dealers had seen profit margins decrease in recent years, from 15% to 20% of list price down to 5% to 12%, with 10% typical for major makes. Additional bonuses and rebates were frequently offered; these were usually tactical promotions to concentrate dealer energy on stock the manufacturer wanted to move quickly. Such bonuses ranged from £500 to £2,000 per car sold and gave the dealers more leeway for negotiation with their customers. Other sources of dealer profits on new cars were manufacturer service rebates, delivery charges, sales of accessories, and finance and insurance commission. Delivery charges were a particular source of resentment for car buyers. Typically set at £400–£500, the real cost of delivery and pre-delivery inspection was nearer to half this amount. Some manufacturers had started quoting 'on-the-road' prices, but the dealers still received their share of this delivery fee.

Daewoo management knew that individual car buyers tend to have little loyalty towards a particular dealer. New car buyers were likely to look for the car of their choice within a 25-mile radius of their homes. An urbanized area of this radius in England could contain around 300 franchised and independent car dealers, all in competition with each other, including dealerships belonging to the same group.

Servicing

Another issue to resolve was how the Daewoo cars would be serviced. In 1994, there were around 18,000 independent garages in the UK, with most occupying one site and over half retailing used cars. Nearly all independent garages offered servicing, repairs and the sale of car parts. Local specialists were considered vastly more experienced, honest and older by consumers. In contrast, dealer servicing was viewed as pricey and sometimes less skilled, but was considered necessary during the car's warranty period. Given this poor image, both Farrell and Woodcock were skeptical about relying solely on dealer servicing for problems that fell outside the warranty period. Given Daewoo's newness in the market, Woodcock was particularly concerned that an independent network of specialists familiar with the Nexia and Espero would develop too slowly to meet the company's growth needs. One consideration was to develop a network of wholly-owned service centers that would service Daewoo cars only. Woodcock strongly favored this approach, but was unsure about the implications for cost and market coverage. Another possibility was to contract with an established organization that could service the cars and could offer sufficient coverage.

Competition

Daewoo would face stiff competition from the 30 or so manufacturers offering over 40 small or medium-sized cars. Seven had manufacturing sites in the UK, and the majority had production facilities somewhere in Western Europe. In both the lower-medium and upper-medium segments, the top ten marques captured a share of 85% or more. Only six companies saw their segment market share increase.

Emergent Marques: South East Asia

The team felt their best opportunities to gain share would be from the emergent marques. During the 1990s, South East Asian car companies had begun to aggressively pursue the competitive European markets, and several manufacturers had already entered the UK.

Hyundai was Korea's leading car maker. In 1993, it had made over one million cars; within four years, it aimed to double that, boasting an ambition to become one of the world's top ten car manufacturers. In 1994, Hyundai expected to sell 10,000 new cars in the UK and around 95,000 across Europe Its new model, the Accent, an Escort-sized family car, would launch at the same time as Daewoo, with a price of £6,000 to £9,000. Hyundai was building three new factories in Korea and doubling its engineering resources.

Kia was the second Korean entrant. Launched in 1991, it had originally been set up in cooperation with Ford and Mazda to make models based on Mazda's designs. Kia's range was founded on a little hatchback called Pride (priced £5,699 to £7,099), which had been joined in August 1994 by a larger car, the Ford Escort-sized Mentor. The current level of UK sales was around 3,500 cars a year.

The Malaysian company, Proton, had successfully created a comfortable niche with a simple proposition: 'we're cheap'. Although Daewoo could undercut significantly the established majors (Korean labor costs were half those of Japan's), it could not afford Proton's price positioning.

Advertising

Despite a sizeable launch, budget advertising costs would have to be managed carefully. Automobiles are a heavily advertised product (refer to **Exhibit 4**). In 1993, 35 car manufacturers spent £407 million on 50 car campaigns, of which 80% went in roughly equal amounts to TV and newspaper advertising, with the remaining spend devoted primarily to magazines and posters. In the year to August 1994, the average consumer could conceivably have seen over 150 car commercials. Media advertising inflation was running at 10% per annum. The split between brand advertising and retail advertising (for specific models or deals) varied dramatically by manufacturer. Brand advertising was highest among the established British manufacturers, while the emergent marques focused their more modest ad spends on retail advertising. It was typical for 15% of a manufacturer's advertising budget to be spent on dealer support materials and cooperative advertising.

At the Tylney Hotel

As the team reviewed the market data, Farrell was mindful of the aggressive sales targets and short development window. Daewoo's overall proposition was to 'take all the concern and hassle out of buying and maintaining a car'. Positioning Daewoo as a leader in customer service and value was a natural extension of this, but the most effective strategy and tactics necessary to achieve this were unclear. Farrell was particularly worried that dealers he could sign up at short notice might not meet the appropriate standard of quality service. Was there any way he wondered, that they could come up with a winning strategy and implement it in time for the planned launch date of end-February 1995. The team settled down to a long weekend of serious brainstorming.

EXHIBIT 1

New Car Market Shares and Distribution Structure by Manufacturer: 1992–94

Make	1992 Registrations	%	1993 Registrations	%	1994 Jan–Jun Registrations	%	No. of Dealers
Audi	18,093	1.11	19,725	1.11	12,890	1.35	220
BMW	40,672	2.55	40,921	2.30	21,761	2.28	157
Citroen	64,415	4.04	80,826	4.54	42,038	4.40	245
Daihatsu	5,178	0.32	6,375	0.36	2,378	0.25	105
Fiat	31,006	1.95	42,841	2.41	27,848	2.91	250
Ford	353,339	22.17	381,671	21.46	211,365	22.11	1,066
Honda	26,786	1.68	30,902	1.74	16,522	1.73	172
Hyundai	9,337	0.58	9,189	0.52	5,902	0.62	185
Isuzu	4,391	0.27	4,187	0.24	1,168	0.12	132
Jaguar	5,607	0.35	6,224	0.35	3,409	0.36	94
Kia	3,619	0.23	4,445	0.25	1,690	0.18	155
Lada	11,907	0.75	10,071	0.57	4,143	0.43	187
Mazda	19,057	1.2	17,482	0.98	8,203	0.86	155
Mercedes-Benz	22,425	1.41	21,186	1.19	14,937	1.56	135
Mitsubishi	11,077	0.7	10,726	0.6	4,287	0.45	116
Nissan	74,188	4.66	89,209	5.02	43,644	4.57	267
Peugeot	124,019	7.78	142,714	8.02	75,148	7.86	402
Proton	14,957	0.94	141,96	0.8	7,133	0.75	235
Renault	73,165	4.59	93,200	5.24	55,980	5.86	270
Rolls Royce	382	0.02	362	0.02	225	0.02	37
Rover Group	215,257	13.5	238,003	13.4	122,483	12.81	700
Saab	9,874	0.62	9,156	0.51	4,819	0.50	105
Seat	8,198	0.51	8,658	0.49	6,126	0.64	170
Skoda	9,365	0.59	8,620	0.48	6,067	0.63	230
Subaru	4,561	0.29	4,217	0.24	4,560	0.48	145
Suzuki	8,384	0.53	10,140	0.57	4,910	0.51	143
Toyota	42,213	2.65	50,835	2.86	25,463	2.66	268
Vauxhall	266,072	16.7	303,926	17.09	162,291	16.98	534
Volkswagen	65,150	4.09	64,299	3.62	37,467	3.92	320
Volvo	43,141	2.71	43,740	2.46	20,933	2.19	220
Total	1,630,000	100	1,777,027	100	954,815	100	

Sources: Motor Industry of Great Britain – World Automotive Statistics, 1994 SMMT (Society of Motor Manufacturers and Traders); Daewoo Corporation.

EXHIBIT 2A

Overview of Segmentation of the UK Car Market

Segment	Description	Percentage of Market			Representative Models
		1992	1993	1994	
Mini	<1.0 liter Length less than 10 ft	0.9	1.1	1.0	RoverMini
Small or Supermini	< 1.4 liter 2 door Length <12.5 ft	25	25.3	26	Nissan Micra Peugeot 106
Lower medium	1.3–2.0 liter 2 doors Length < 14 ft	37	36.2	33.6	Volkswagen Golf Toyota Corolla Ford Escort
Upper medium	1.2–2.8 liter 4 doors Length < 14 ft 9 in	23.7	23.7	26.5	Ford Mondeo Vauxhall Cavalier
Executive	2.0–3.5 liter luxury appointments Length < 16 ft	8.1	7.7	6.3	Volvo 800 series
Luxury Sedan	3.5 liter More luxurious appointments than Executive	0.6	0.6	0.6	Jaguar XJ6, Rolls Royce
Specialist Sports (includes sports sedans, coupes and roadsters)		1.6	1.3	1.5	Mazda MX5 Toyota Celica
Dual purpose vehicles	4WD with off-road capability	2.5	3.3	3.7	Land Rover Discovery
Multi-person Vehicles	2WD/4WD estates with seating capacity of up to 8 people	0.5	0.7	0.8	Renault Espace Toyota Previa

Source: Daewoo Corporation.

EXHIBIT 2B

Market Share by Model: Lower- and Upper-medium Segments (1993)

LOWER-MEDIUM SEGMENT	%	UPPER-MEDIUM SEGMENT	%
Ford Escort/Orion	23.62	Ford Mondeo/Sierra	23.35
Vauxhall Astra	17.74	Vauxhall Cavalier	22.22
Rover 200 series	11.67	Peugeot 405	11.14
Volkswagen Golf	5.93	Nissan Primera	4.81
Citroen ZX	5.50	Toyota Carina E/Carina	4.63
Rover 400 Series	5.48	BMW Series 3	4.39
Peugeot 306/309	5.04	Volvo 440	4.16
Renault 19	4.29	Citroen Xantia	3.48
Nissan Sunny	3.37	Rover 600 series	3.09
Toyota Corolla	3.13	Audi 80	3.02
Honda Civic	2.64	Rover Montego	1.76
Proton NPI/Aeroback/Saloon	2.26	Mercedes C Class/Series 201	1.74
Fiat Tipo	1.57	Volkswagen Passat	1.49
Skoda Favorit	1.42	Renault Savannah/21	1.42
Mazda 323	1.04	Mazda 626	1.34
Lada Samara	0.98	Honda Accord	1.34
Rover Maestro	0.72	Volvo 460	1.05
Hyundai X2/Accent	0.69	Fiat Tempra	0.87
Seat Ibiza	0.60	Citroen BX	0.87
Honda Concerto	0.57	Seat Toledo	0.77
Lada Riva	0.57	Hyundai Lantra	0.71
Volkswagen Vento	0.47	Saab 900	0.50
Mitsubishi Colt	0.28	Volvo 240	0.44
Mitsubishi Lancer	0.13	Subaru Legacy	0.42
Subaru Impreza	0.13	Mitsubishi Galant	0.41
Alfa Romeo 33	0.08	Mazda Xedos 6	0.25
Daihatsu Applause	0.06	Alfa Romeo 155	0.14
		Proton Persona	0.11
		Lancia Dedra	0.07

Source: Daewoo Corporation.

EXHIBIT 2C

Private Buyers – Main Reasons for Purchase

Lower-medium Sector	%	Upper-medium Sector	%	Emergent Marques	%
Good Previous Experience	2	Good previous Experience	34	Price	42
Exterior Style	28	Exterior Style	26	Value for Money	26
Quality/Reliability	21	Quality/Reliability	22	Same model	24
Price	16	Equipment Level	17	Exterior Style	13

Source: Daewoo Corporation.

EXHIBIT 2D

Price Ranges of Competing Models: August 1994

Make	Model	From £	To £
Citroen	Xantia	12,310	13,240
	ZX	10,155	12,010
Ford	Escort	10,015	12,440
	Mondeo	12,535	15,320
Hyundai	Accent	8,422	10,322
	Lantra	12,535	15,320
Kia	Mentor	9,360	10,260
	Pride	5,699	7,099
Nissan	Almera	9,750	11,450
	Primera	11,420	13,250
	Sunny	8,244	11,330
Peugeot	306	10,235	11,410
Proton	MPI	9,365	9,405
	Persona	8,910	11,865
Renault	Laguna	11,769	14,440
Seat	Cordoba	9,220	10,422
	Toledo	11,320	12,420
Toyota	Carina E	11,778	13,178
Vauxhall	Cavalier	11,400	13,525
	Astra	9,945	12,345
VW	Golf	10,419	10,890

Source: Daewoo Corporation.

EXHIBIT 3

Largest UK Franchised Dealer Groups

Dealership	No. of Sites	Staff	New Cars Sold in 1993	Franchises
Lex Service	122	6,500	63,000	30 marques including Hyundai (exclusive), Ford, Vauxhall, Rover
Inchcape	72	N/A	24,000	Toyota (75% share), Chrysler Jeep, Ferrari
Evans Halshaw	58	1,900	20,600	22 marques including Ford, Vauxhall, Rover, Mercedes, Honda, Nissan
Appleyard	79	2,750	20,000	28 brands including Rover, VW, Audi, Vauxhall
Hartwell	59	3,327	30,000	25 marques including Ford
Pendragon	42	1,364	not available	29 marques, specialist in luxury brands, for example BMW, Jaguar, Land Rover, Mercedes
Lookers	49	2,200	not available	16 marques including Vauxhall, Rover, Audi, Renault
Reg Vardy	28	1,450	10,313	13 marques including Ford, BMW, Fiat, Alfa Romeo, Vauxhall, VW
Cowie	40	3,676	not available	12 marques including Ford, Vauxhall, Toyota, Peugeot, Rover
Sanderson	35	1,800	not available	11 marques including Ford, Audi, VW, Toyota, Mazda, Citroen
Henlys	33	1,445	16,600	17 marques including Vauxhall, VW, Rover, BMW
AFG	74	2,120	15,000	Nissan
A Clark	33	1,578	14,168	10 marques including Vauxhall and Ford

Sources: Industry sources.

EXHIBIT 4

Brand and Retail Advertising for Top Car Manufacturers

Manufacturer	Advertising Spend (millions) 12 Months to June 1993	Manufacturer	Advertising Spend (millions) 12 Months to June 1993
Ford	£55.2	Mazda	£16.7
Vauxhall	£38.2	Honda	£11.2
Rover	£32.3	Proton	£10.4
Peugeot	£34.8	Hyundai	£ 7.9
Nissan	£21.3		

Source: Daewoo Corporation.

CASE 2.3

This case was prepared by Research Associate Debra Riley under the supervision of Professor Sean Meehan.

Daewoo Motor Company UK (B)

On Tuesday morning, June 10, 1997, Pat Farrell and his marketing team were finalizing the details of the simultaneous launch of three new car ranges in September. The new cars were family cars and were expected to replace the Nexia and Espero. The advertising budget for the 1997 launch had been severely cut, and it looked as though little TV advertising would be possible. But the decisions facing Farrell were not simply about advertising spend and the creative use of small budgets. Since 1996, the staff numbers at Daewoo had doubled as the company built its network of retail outlets and service centers. The 'laid-back' approach of the Daewoo sales staff, which had earned plaudits in industry and consumer magazines, was in direct conflict with the increasing pressures to sell cars. The success of the initial launch had heightened the market's expectations as well as those of head office and staff. Farrell needed to decide how best to build on the success of the 1995 launch.

The 1995 Launch

The Daewoo Offer

Daewoo's research indicated that private individuals' experience of buying and owning a car was not ideal. Aggressive salesmen, hidden costs, poor after-sales service and advertising that focused on performance and/or fantasy portrayals of the driving experience did not appeal to a substantial portion of the car buying public. Research indicated that over a third of car buyers regarded their car primarily as a way to get from A to B, and were more concerned with the day-to-day practicalities of owning a car than with the car performance and engineering.

Daewoo decided to sell car ownership as a service, not cars as products. Farrell recalled:

> We decided car prices would be fixed, with no haggling required. We would focus on offering outstanding customer service, which meant we would need to have complete control of the interface with the customer.

Daewoo's Nexia and Espero were reworked latter-day versions of old Vauxhall designs from a decade earlier. The Nexia was based on the old model Astra, and the Espero on an obsolete Cavalier. Priced from £8,295 for the Nexia and £10,695 to £12,195 for the Espero, Daewoo's prices were roughly 10% below average in the relevant market sectors, but were not positioned at the bottom of each sector. The price included delivery to the buyer's home, tax for the first year, number plates, a full tank of petrol, a three-year/60,000 miles warranty, three years' membership of the AA, including European cover, free servicing for the first three years, including labor and parts, and a 30-day money back/exchange guarantee.

Building Awareness

Daewoo began a £10 million TV, radio and print advertising campaign in October 1994 aimed at building brand awareness, credibility and conveying the company's customer focus intentions. The campaign, tagged 'The biggest car company you never heard of', sought to cultivate confidence in the brand from UK car buyers by playing on Daewoo's reputation as one of the world's largest industrial companies. In order to build awareness quickly prior to launch, Daewoo ran their TV ads at twice the normal industry frequency. By Christmas 1994, prompted awareness of the Daewoo brand was 50%. Launch advertising was highly creative with four key messages: Deawoo Deal DIRECT; HASSLE FREE buying; PEACE OF MIND package; and COURTESY SERVICING (refer to **Exhibit 1**).

Distribution

Daewoo decided to build a direct marketing and service structure. This gave Daewoo complete control over the selling process and after-sales servicing. On launching with four showrooms on April 1, 1995, Farrell commented:

> We weren't certain that four sites would be sufficient to meet the immediate sales targets, and the quality and reliability of the cars was still an unknown.

Over the next 12 months, Daewoo rolled out the launch to include 18 retail stores and 100 smaller used car and servicing depots at a cost of £150 million. To provide the national presence it needed to service buyers' cars, the company formed a joint initiative with Halfords, the automotive parts retailers and servicing chain. Two Daewoo staff and three courtesy cars were placed at each of the 136 Halfords stores involved. Daewoo worked in conjunction with Halfords to run a hassle-free servicing operation; cars were collected from and returned to any location the customer required, with a free courtesy car left if requested.

The company estimated that 400,000 people visited its showrooms in the first 12 months, representing around 20% of the two million new car buyers each year. Daewoo designed its showrooms to cater for the whole family. Showroom staff were not allowed to approach unless invited, and they earned bonuses based on customer approval of how well they were treated, not how much they spent. Each showroom had a 'greeter' to welcome any one who entered and to advise them of the facilities available. Junior showroom staff did not typically have car industry experience, and were hired based on fitting desired personality profiles. A free café, supervised crèche and interactive video units enhanced the 'shopping experience'.

The Market Response

It was the most successful marque launch since 1975, the earliest year for which data were available. Daewoo sold 1,500 cars in the first month, and 18,000 cars in the first year – 0.92% market share. Nine months earlier, Daewoo had been unknown in the UK, with only 4% of car buyers having ever heard of the company. The company captured 1% share of the April 1995 market and outsold a string of long-established marques (refer to **Exhibit 2**). Further, this performance was sustained throughout the first 12 months. Daewoo received much media attention. Despite the cars' limitations, public response was enthusiastic.

Autocar (January 1996) rated both Daewoo's Nexia and Espero worst product in their sectors.

Top Gear (March 1996) rated Daewoo Espero 12th out of the 12 family cars it reviewed.

Daewoo's revolutionary approach to car retailing feels like a gale of fresh air blowing through the motor trade. (*Observer*, 9 April 1995)

Competitive Response

The entry of Daewoo into the market did little to upset the major car manufacturers. Ford, Vauxhall, and Rover, with their large manufacturing facilities in the UK, were not fazed by a new entrant targeting 1% market share. At the dealer level, the story was different. Daewoo's advertising portrayed car salesmen as sharks, great play was made of hidden costs, and to cap it all, Daewoo published a survey of potential customers which highlighted how many disliked the whole car buying process. Daewoo was expelled from one trade show, and newspapers were contacted by the dealer networks and asked to pull Daewoo ads. Overall, the effect was negligible. Those dealers or manufacturers in a position to respond to Daewoo's aggressive entry strategy found it difficult because of their traditional manufacturer/dealer network structure that squeezed profit margins through the distribution chain. Only Renault, who had 20 company-owned sites out of 300, responded with Daewoo-type offers.

Post Launch Performance

Daewoo's strong performance continued through 1995. By December, prompted awareness was 90%, and research showed it to be the third most 'customer focused' car company, after Vauxhall and Nissan. The consistent investment in brand positioning continued in 1996, with the communications strategy focused on providing more details about the cars' appearance, pricing and specification, and re-emphasizing the Daewoo offer.

In February, Daewoo was forced to issue a safety recall on all 8,000 Nexias sold to date, due to a potential fire risk with engine bay wiring. Despite this setback, by May 1996 Daewoo total sales outstripped Hyundai, Suzuki, Saab and Mitsubishi. Continuing research showed that Daewoo was perceived as the best 'value for money' marque and second only to Vauxhall for customer care. Sales performance remained unaffected through two price rises, in September 1995 and March 1996. Although Daewoo was targeting the individual buyer, it did manage to secure some fleet customers, mainly rental.

In September 1996, Daewoo cut its advertising budget in order to achieve annual profit targets. The company's objective was to reach breakeven within three years. This would mean maintaining sales without the heavy advertising support required in the first 18 months. Marketing efforts began focusing on achieving short-term volume targets through tactical incentives. Despite the reduced support, sales performance remained strong through 1996.

1997: A Challenging Year

The Daewoo marketing team faced increasing pressure in 1997. Sales declined 19% over 1996, as the public became less interested in cars that could not offer the performance and styling of competitive offerings. All measures for the Daewoo brand were at their lowest since summer 1995. Internal retail targets were up 77% versus the same period in 1996. Translating these goals to the retail centers was proving difficult, as they were not measured on sales targets, but customer service. Farrell had recognized the potential conflict in Daewoo's approach early on – the customer-driven, 'demand-pull' strategy – was in direct conflict with the 'supply-push' philosophy adopted by all car manufacturers with high fixed costs and excess capacity. Improving the conversion rate from store visit to actual sales was proving difficult, as the staff had been trained to take a very low key approach with customers. The relaxed culture at the retail centers was also damaging efforts to build its direct marketing database. Frequently, customer questionnaires were sent to head office incomplete or had been completed by Daewoo staff rather than the customer.

In addition, concerns over the residual values of the used cars had become apparent. In 1995, Daewoo's embryonic sales network did not have much retail space for used cars. As sales to rental companies typically return to the manufacturer within six months, Daewoo found it had more used cars than could be promoted through its own retail structure. Rather than push these vehicles to other potentially hostile dealer networks, a decision was made to hold the cars. This temporary policy was extended into 1996 and resulted in insufficient used cars coming onto the market for the industry to assess an accurate residual value. By early 1997, this issue was being highlighted in the press. According to *Motor Trader*, the car trade magazine, 80% of new and used car dealers in Britain would not take a Daewoo as part exchange for another vehicle, citing concerns over residual values. At the same time, *Glass's Guide*, one the two 'bibles' used by the trade to work out used values, slashed 10% off the prices of used Daewoos. A Nexia worth £11,000 today was estimated to be worth no more than £4,450 after two years and 30,000 miles. Recognizing the negative impact this would have on new car sales, Farrell had promoted a change in strategy that pushed used Daewoos on to other manufacturer's retail networks.

Despite the general downturn in the market, other Asian manufacturers were also gaining share, particularly Hyundai. The company had over 150 showrooms nationwide, and benefited from the 'Korean-ness' brand associations that had been established by Daewoo. Other manufacturers were also looking at ways of bypassing the traditional salesman. In 1997, Daihatsu announced the launch of 'virtual showrooms', where teams of mobile salespeople would deliver a new, licensed and insured vehicle to your home for a test drive.

The New Car Launch

Farrell and his team hoped that the launch of the Lanos, Nubira, and Leganza would resolve the performance and price issues associated with the existing models (refer to **Exhibit 3**). New car buyers would be offered the same extensive service and warranty package offered with the Nexia and Espero. Test marketing gave the new models a more favorable rating than the Nexia and Espero, but highlighted continuing issues such as the engine design (carried over from the previous models) and poor interior details. Farrell was keen to build on the success of the market entry and develop the Daewoo brand further. The impending launch was critical, he needed all the input he could get and looked forward to Charlie's input.

EXHIBIT 1

Daewoo Launch Advertising

The following four pages provide a representative sample of Daewoo's launch print advertising.

EXHIBIT 1 (CONTINUED)

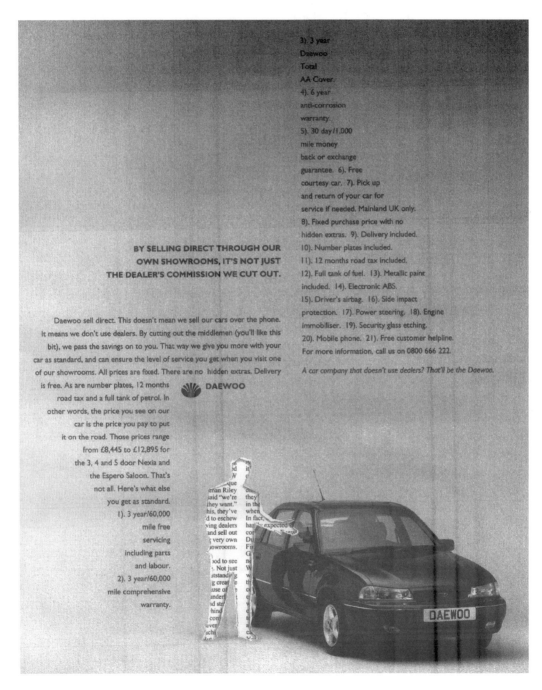

Source: Daewoo advertisement.

EXHIBIT 1 (CONTINUED)

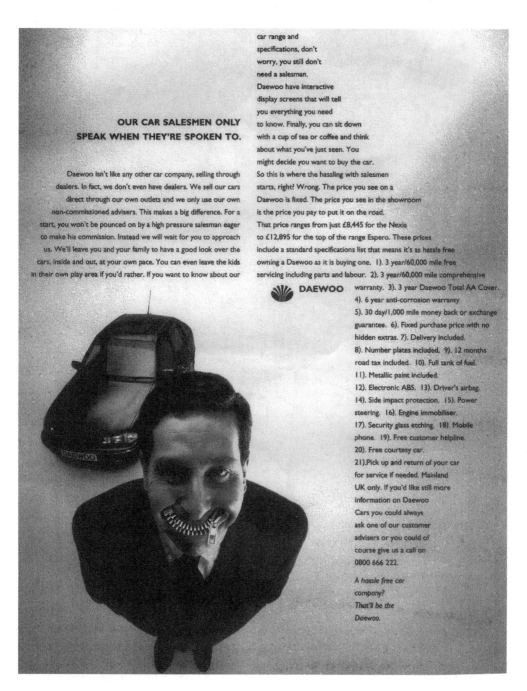

OUR CAR SALESMEN ONLY SPEAK WHEN THEY'RE SPOKEN TO.

Daewoo isn't like any other car company, selling through dealers. In fact, we don't even have dealers. We sell our cars direct through our own outlets and we only use our own non-commissioned advisers. This makes a big difference. For a start, you won't be pounced on by a high pressure salesman eager to make his commission. Instead we will wait for you to approach us. We'll leave you and your family to have a good look over the cars, inside and out, at your own pace. You can even leave the kids in their own play area if you'd rather. If you want to know about our car range and specifications, don't worry, you still don't need a salesman. Daewoo have interactive display screens that will tell you everything you need to know. Finally, you can sit down with a cup of tea or coffee and think about what you've just seen. You might decide you want to buy the car. So this is where the hassling with salesmen starts, right? Wrong. The price you see on a Daewoo is fixed. The price you see in the showroom is the price you pay to put it on the road. That price ranges from just £8,445 for the Nexia to £12,895 for the top of the range Espero. These prices include a standard specifications list that means it's as hassle free owning a Daewoo as it is buying one. 1). 3 year/60,000 mile free servicing including parts and labour. 2). 3 year/60,000 mile comprehensive

DAEWOO warranty. 3). 3 year Daewoo Total AA Cover. 4). 6 year anti-corrosion warranty. 5). 30 day/1,000 mile money back or exchange guarantee. 6). Fixed purchase price with no hidden extras. 7). Delivery included. 8). Number plates included. 9). 12 months road tax included. 10). Full tank of fuel. 11). Metallic paint included. 12). Electronic ABS. 13). Driver's airbag. 14). Side impact protection. 15). Power steering. 16). Engine immobiliser. 17). Security glass etching. 18). Mobile phone. 19). Free customer helpline. 20). Free courtesy car. 21).Pick up and return of your car for service if needed. Mainland UK only. If you'd like still more information on Daewoo Cars you could always ask one of our customer advisers or you could of course give us a call on 0800 666 222.

A hassle free car company? That'll be the Daewoo.

Source: Daewoo advertisement.

EXHIBIT 1 (CONTINUED)

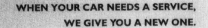

**WHEN YOUR CAR NEEDS A SERVICE,
WE GIVE YOU A NEW ONE.**

How would you like a courtesy car every time yours is in for a service? How would you like the option of having it delivered to your doorstep (or wherever you want for that matter), and yours picked up at the same time? You wouldn't say no, would you? What about a phone call to tell you when your Daewoo is due for a service? Or a phone call from the technician before the service to make sure any minor details are not forgotten? And, after your car is brought back, another call to make sure everything's okay? Well you can. And this is the best bit. None of it will cost you a penny, you pay for the car and that's it. (Even that's not a lot. The prices start at £8,295 for the Nexia, to £12,195 for the top of the range Espero.) How come? Firstly, we sell direct through Daewoo Motor Shows, Car Centres and Support Centres, cutting out the middlemen. This means we don't use commissioned salesmen. It also means we can afford to give you more as standard. Just read the list.

1). Free courtesy car.
2). Pick up and return of your car for service if needed. Mainland UK only.
3). Direct contact with the technician who services your car.
4). 3 year/60,000 mile free servicing including parts and labour.
5). 3 year/60,000 mile comprehensive warranty.
6). 3 year Daewoo Total AA Cover.
7). 6 year anti-corrosion warranty.
8). 30 day/1,000 mile money back or exchange guarantee.
9). Fixed purchase price with no hidden extras.
10). Delivery included.
11). Number plates included.
12). 12 months road tax included.
13). Full tank of fuel.
14). Metallic paint included.
15). Electronic ABS.
16). Driver's airbag.
17). Side impact protection.
18). Power steering.
19). Engine immobiliser.
20). Security glass etching.
21). Mobile phone.
22). Free customer helpline.

All in all, quite a number of reasons to choose Daewoo. For more information, call us free on 0800 666 222.

*A free courtesy car?
That'll be the
Daewoo.*

Source: Daewoo advertisement.

EXHIBIT 1 (CONTINUED)

EVERY NEW DAEWOO COMES WITH A RATHER ATTRACTIVE EXTRA.

Tempted? So you should be because all our models come with three years free servicing. No small print, no disclaimers, just free servicing including all labour and parts. (Apart from the tyres that is, they come with their own guarantee.) Unlike other car manufacturers this offer isn't for a limited period, nor is it an extra, hidden in the hiked up cost of the car. Our offer is the same right across the Daewoo range and is included in the fixed price you see on the cars in the showroom. Those prices range from £8,445 to £12,895 for the 3, 4 and 5 door Nexia and the Espero saloon. As if this isn't enough of an offer, we'll even telephone and arrange your car's service, then collect it from your doorstep leaving you with a courtesy car until yours is returned, if you wish. But what happens in between servicing? That's covered too. Every new Daewoo comes with a three year comprehensive warranty, three years Daewoo Total AA Cover and a six year anti-corrosion warranty. In fact, the only thing you do pay for is insurance and petrol. Take a look at the list and see for yourself. 1). 3 year/60,000 mile free servicing including parts and labour. 2). 3 year/60,000 mile comprehensive warranty. 3). 3 year Total AA Cover. 4). 6 year anti-corrosion warranty.

5). 30 day/ 1,000 mile money back or exchange guarantee. 6). Free courtesy car. 7). Pick up and return of your car for service if needed. Mainland UK only. 8). Fixed purchase price with no hidden extras. 9). Delivery included. 10). Number plates included. 11). 12 months road tax included. 12). Full tank of fuel. 13). Metallic paint included. 14). Electronic ABS. 15). Driver's airbag. 16). Side impact protection. 17). Power steering. 18). Engine immobiliser. 19). Security glass etching. 20). Mobile phone. 21). Free customer helpline. If you were glad to hear all this we'd be glad to tell you more, so please call us on 0800 666 222.

A car where the extras aren't extra? That'll be the Daewoo.

DAEWOO

Source: Daewoo advertisement.

EXHIBIT 2

New Car Registrations in UK by Marque: 1994–97

	1994 #	%	1995 #	%	1996 #	%	H1 1997 #	%
Ford	418,657	22.2	410,722	21.4	396,988	19.7	195,793	18.9
Vauxhall	310,617	16.4	294,131	15.3	283,989	14.1	143,437	13.9
Rover	245,250	13.0	240,007	12.5	221,658	11.0	100,317	9.7
Peugeot	146,551	7.8	143,321	7.5	153,242	7.6	80,123	7.7
Renault	112,663	6.0	120,485	6.3	132,374	6.6	77,169	7.5
VW	74,548	3.9	81,656	4.3	114,084	5.7	59,711	5.8
Fiat	58,703	3.1	70,828	3.7	85,948	4.3	42,768	4.1
Citroën	84,522	4.5	80,241	4.2	76,485	3.8	41,016	4.0
Nissan	91,955	4.9	91,972	4.8	93,408	4.6	36,443	3.5
Toyota	51,939	2.8	54,384	2.8	58,491	2.9	34,402	3.3
BMW	45,574	2.4	55,034	2.9	56,840	2.8	30,426	2.9
Honda	38,187	2.0	45,772	2.4	50,075	2.5	25,978	2.5
Mercedes	29,186	1.5	32,694	1.7	35,813	1.8	20,795	2.0
Volvo	41,599	2.2	39,654	2.1	33,737	1.7	20,285	2.0
Audi	22,978	1.2	25,555	1.3	30,327	1.5	18,078	1.7
Mazda	16,741	0.9	16,291	0.8	24,273	1.2	14,957	1.4
Hyundai	12,247	0.6	13,984	0.7	18,959	0.9	11,668	1.1
Mitsubishi	9,227	0.5	10,823	0.6	16,383	0.8	10,845	1.0
SAAB	9,339	0.5	11,534	0.6	14,886	0.7	9,280	0.9
Daewoo	0	0	13,169	0.7	21,438	1.1	9,200	0.9
SEAT	12,921	0.7	11,049	0.6	13,530	0.7	7,884	0.8
Chrysler Jeep					11,624	0.6	7,870	0.8
Skoda					13,017	0.7	7,459	0.7

EXHIBIT 2 (CONTINUED)

	1994 #	%	1995 #	%	1996 #	%	H1 1997 #	%
Suzuki	10,380	0.5	13,817	0.7	14,195	0.7	6,199	0.6
Jaguar	6,659	0.4	8,727	0.5	8,401	0.4	4,855	0.5
Proton	12,452	0.7	9,800	0.5	9,555	0.5	4,683	0.5
Subaru	4,995	0.3	4,616	0.2	5,753	0.3	3,579	0.3
Daihatsu	4,869	0.3	3,378	0.2	3,536	0.2	3,161	0.3
KIA	3,939	0.2	4,004	0.2	4,919	0.2	2,619	0.2
Lada	9,398	0.5	8,259	0.4	4,762	0.2	1,595	0.1
Isuzu	2,165	0.1	1,938	0.1	2,419	0.1	1,350	0.1
Lexus					2,012	0.1	1,132	0.1
Total	1888251	100	1917809	100	2013121	100	1035077	100

Sources: Motor Industry of Great Britain – World Automotive Statistics, 1997 SMMT (Society of Motor Manufacturers and Traders); Daewoo Corporation.

EXHIBIT 3

Daewoo New Model Pricing

Model	Description	Price	Rivals
Lanos	3,4, 5 doors 1.3/1.6 liter	£8,795 -£10,695	Ford Escort Peugeot 306
Nubira	4 door saloon estate (later)	£10,495 – £12,995 £12,995 – £13,995	Vauxhall Vectra Ford Escort
Leganza	4 door saloon 2.0 liter	£13,795-£14,995	Ford Mondeo, Toyota Carina, Hyundai Sonata VW Passat

Source: Daewoo Corporation.

CASE 2.4ᴿ **Interdrinks**

This case was prepared by Research Associates Srinivasa Rangan and Janet Shaner, under the supervision of Professor Kamran Kashani. Some facts and figures have been disguised.

One afternoon early in February 1998, Helmut Fehring, the Managing Director of Interdrinks Company (IDC), held a meeting with his national sales manager, Antoine Jeanneau, to discuss IDC's sales force performance. The two executives disagreed in that meeting as to whether there was a problem of productivity with the company's sales force. Fehring was of the opinion that the field force (of 31 people) was underproductive and, at any rate, too costly for the revenues it generated. Jeanneau, on the other hand, maintained that his people were performing at the upper limits of their potential and were one of the best performing forces in the industry.

Fehring, who had recently returned to his family-owned bottling company after a year's leave to attend an intensive executive education program, was not convinced by Jeanneau's arguments. He thought that IDC's sales force was simply not producing enough sales, and that current management policies and practices were partly responsible. He also thought that the recent changes in the industry made it necessary for IDC to re-examine its current marketing strategy, including its product line and distribution policy. Fehring was convinced that a viable strategy, aided by a well-motivated sales force, was what his small company needed to survive the increasing industry competition.

But, as the meeting with the national sales manager indicated, Fehring's concerns with IDC's marketing and sales problems were not necessarily shared by the other executives. Nevertheless, he was determined to press for the changes which he believed were needed to turn his company's declining fortunes around.

Company Background

IDC was founded in 1933 by Paul Fehring, Helmut's father, in the city of Zug, Switzerland. Initially, the company had bottled mineral water sourced from the springs of the nearby resort town of Berg. The water was thought to have therapeutic value, but had never before been bottled for sales outside the town.

In the ensuing years, the company grew rapidly, adding flavored drinks which combined fruit-based extracts with mineral water. The company's Berg lemon, orange and grapefruit drinks were pioneers in their category in Switzerland. In 1954, the company began bottling Schweppes, an international brand of carbonated soft drinks. IDC purchased the concentrate from a well-known British company which marketed the brand internationally through franchising contracts. In 1962, IDC added Pepsi-Cola to its line under a similar agreement with the international seller of the concentrate, Pepsico International. Before that date, Coca-Cola had been the sole contender in the Swiss cola-flavored market. IDC marketed both its own Berg brand and the international brands in the central German-speaking part of Switzerland. (Refer to **Exhibit 1** for a map of the geographic area covered by IDC and background information about Switzerland.)

Helmut Fehring took over the management of IDC in 1988 when his father retired. At that time he was 30 years old, had a degree in business from a Swiss university and, for several years, had held various positions in the company. In 1997, Fehring left his job for one year to take part in a general management executive training program. He later explained: 'Our profits were going down the drain and we needed to learn new ways to run the business. So I decided to start at the top, with myself.' In his absence, the company was managed by the chairman of the board of directors. (**Exhibit 2** gives a partial organization chart depicting the management structure as of early 1998.)

IDC produced and sold 55.5 million bottles of soft drinks and mineral water in 1997, a total volume of 32 million liters. The company's modern facilities were capable of producing 83 million bottles, working two shifts daily. Capacity utilization had improved since 1995, when the company had been operating at only about 50% of its bottling capacity. (Highlights of the recent financial statements of IDC appear in **Exhibits 3 and 4**.) The company's poor earnings were attributed by Fehring to 'deteriorating profit margins in an increasingly competitive environment'.

Marketing at IDC

According to Muller, IDC's marketing manager, the company's products could be divided for marketing purposes into four distinct categories: Schweppes, Pepsi-Cola, the flavored soft drinks, and mineral water. The latter two categories were further broken down into IDC's own brand, Berg, and private labels produced for retail chains. (The product line is described in **Exhibit 5**.)

In 1997, more than 50% of IDC's sales volume in Swiss Francs was made up of branded products which were distributed through some 400 small and large wholesalers in the central part of Switzerland. Of this volume, slightly more than half was resold to grocery stores, with the rest going to hotels, restaurants and cafés (often referred to by the trade as the HORECA outlets). The private labels produced for Coop and Denner, two large food chains with a total of about 2,200 stores nationally, were distributed directly to the chains' warehouses as well as through a number of wholesalers to individual outlets.[1] The company began

---

1. Private label bottles displayed the chain's name prominently on the label and identified IDC as the bottler in smaller print.

bottling private labels in 1997. (Refer to **Exhibits 6 and 7** for a breakdown of sales by different outlets.)

In recent years, the company's 50 largest wholesalers had accounted for approximately two-thirds of its sales of branded products. Management considered the wholesale network indispensable to its distribution. Fehring explained, 'How else can you reach 22,000 potential outlets?'[2]

Product prices and profit margins varied by brand and container size. The international brands were premium priced and, as such, enjoyed higher unit contribution margins than the other brands. The private labels, on the other hand, were priced competitively and were the least profitable. The small single-serving bottles produced exclusively for the HORECA outlets were generally more profitable than the larger bottles. (**Exhibit 8** gives ex-factory prices for different products and container sizes. **Exhibit 9** provides data on the variable manufacturing costs.)

In recent years, IDC had spent close to 14% of its sales on the advertising and promotion of branded products. In the case of international brands, the total expenditure was shared between IDC and the brands' international franchisers, with the latter contributing 50% for Schweppes and 30% for Pepsi-Cola. For the company's own Berg brand, however, the entire advertising and promotion costs were borne internally. (**Exhibit 10** gives levels of advertising and promotion expenditures by product for 1996 and 1997.)

IDC's advertising themes varied by brand. Schweppes was advertised as a product used by 'sophisticated' people for 'intimate' occasions. Pepsi-Cola, whose advertising was coordinated by Pepsico International, followed what Muller called a 'me too' positioning to that of Coca-Cola, the leader in the cola-flavored market. In the case of fruit flavored drinks, which were advertised to mothers of young children, the emphasis was placed on the mineral water base of the soft drinks and their 'health promoting' benefits. Among IDC's various products, Muller identified Schweppes as the brand that was most popular with consumers. 'It has a different taste and enjoys a unique positioning. All others are "me too" products; they don't have a unique selling point.'

The wholesale and retail prices of IDC's Berg products followed the general pricing practices of Swiss bottlers. The company did not attempt to compete on price. For the international brands, prices were set according to the recommendations of the international concentrate companies. IDC published a suggested trade and consumer price list for all its products. However, the company had no control on the final prices charged by retailers.

IDC's periodic trade promotions took the form of wholesale price discounts. Consumer promotions were limited-time discounted price offers. Typically, the company absorbed the full cost of consumer promotions by reimbursing the trade for lost margins.

---

2. There were about 650 wholesalers, 4,000 grocery shops and 18,000 HORECA outlets in the Swiss German area served by IDC. The corresponding figures for the whole of Switzerland were 825, 8,000 and 27,000 respectively. These figures excluded chain outlets.

IDC's field sales force was the company's primary link with the wholesale and retail trade. The 31-member force sold directly to the wholesalers, and called on the independent stores and HORECA outlets to promote the company's branded products at the retail level.

Fehring himself was responsible for the private label sales, handling all the negotiations related to the annual supply contracts. The field sales force did not call on the outlets of the two chains the company supplied with private labels. Fehring pointed out:

> Our marketing has evolved over the years to what it is today with much improvisation and little analysis of the industry and our position in it. But our environment is changing. It is becoming more competitive and less charitable towards smaller regional bottlers like us. The recent developments in the industry, particularly among our distributors and competitors, force us to take a hard look at our strategy to see if it is going to stay viable – to see if we can survive the new rules of the game.

The Swiss Soft Drink and Mineral Water Industry

In 1997, an estimated 590 million liters of bottled soft drinks, worth Sfr475 million in ex-factory prices, were consumed in Switzerland. For mineral water, the corresponding figures were 580 million liters and Sfr350 million in ex-factory prices. (The trends in industry sales of soft drinks and mineral water from 1992 to 1997 are shown in **Exhibit 11**.)

The consumption of soft drinks and mineral water took place at home and on premise at HORECA. It was estimated that home consumption accounted for slightly more than 80% of total soft drink and mineral water consumption. These ratios had not changed significantly in recent years.

Altogether 63 bottlers served the Swiss soft drink and mineral water market. Some bottlers operated several bottling plants located near major cities. They tended to serve the entire Swiss market with nationally known brands. Others, operating one or two bottling plants each, served limited geographic areas. The high cost of transportation prevented the regional bottlers from serving distant markets.

In 1997, the four largest national soft drink bottling companies together accounted for 55% of the Swiss soft drink market, up from 46% five years earlier. For mineral water, the concentration was higher with the top four accounting for 71% of the market, up from 60% five years earlier. Most bottlers produced both soft drinks and mineral water. (**Exhibit 12** gives the market shares of major bottling companies.)

Substantial overcapacity characterized the Swiss soft drink and mineral water industry. Estimated at about one-third of the installed capacity, the excess capacity was attributed by industry observers to plant expansions based on over-optimistic forecasts of consumption growth rates. This condition had led to increased competition among bottlers along price and advertising expenditures.

The regional brands tended to compete on the basis of price alone. The national and international brands, on the other hand, were premium priced but also heavily advertised. The financial assistance, provided by international suppliers of concentrates to their franchisers, as well as the generally greater financial strengths of the national bottling companies, were given as reasons for the proportionately larger sums spent on advertising these brands.

It was estimated that close to 60% of the soft drinks, and nearly 100% of the mineral water, consumed on premise were the premium priced brands. At home, on the other hand, the premium priced brands accounted for only 30% of consumption in the case of soft drinks and 63% in the case of mineral water.

The growth of private labels was a key development in the Swiss industry. Major food chains had introduced soft drink and mineral water products under their own 'house' brands. The private labels, produced either by the chains' own bottling facilities or under contract by an independent bottler, had brought more pressure on prices.[3] (**Exhibit 13** shows representative consumer prices for selected international, regional and private brands.)

Increasingly, the national, international and private brands accounted for a large share of soft drink and mineral water sales in Switzerland. In 1997, four brands (Sinalco, Rivella, Coca-Cola and Aproz) accounted for 64% of all soft drink sales.[4] Similarly, four national brands (Aproz, Valser, Henniez and Passugger) accounted for 71% of all mineral water sales.

Distribution of Soft Drinks and Mineral Water

The retail distribution of soft drinks and mineral water in Switzerland took place through small independent shops as well as retail chain outlets. The small shop, typically a neighborhood store, stocked most of the daily food requirements of its nearby clientele. Industry analysts estimated that mineral water and soft drinks comprised 3–8% of the turnover of such food stores. The margins on these items ranged from 20% to 50%. Retailers generally stocked the more popular brands. They normally carried an inventory of about one week of sales and received their stocks from one or more beverage wholesalers in the area.

In recent years, with the growth of major food chain stores, the small retailers had declined in numbers and importance. Between 1987 and 1997, the number of independent food retail outlets declined from 20,000 to about 8,000. At the same time, the dominance of chains in food retailing had grown. The three largest chains in the country accounted for nearly 78% of all food and 54% of all non-alcoholic beverages in the country (refer to **Exhibit 14**).

---

3. Contracts with independents were typically oral agreements between the chains and the bottlers. The excess capacity in the industry gave bargaining power to the chains and enabled them to avoid binding written contracts.
4. Sinalco and Coca-Cola were international brands; Rivella was a national brand and Aproz was a 'house' brand promoted by Migros, the country's largest food chain.

Mineral water and soft drinks represented 1% and 2% of the chains' total turnover. On branded products, they enjoyed margins ranging from 25% to 50%; the margins on private labels were 20% to 40%, owing to their lower prices. The chains normally carried an inventory of three days of sales at the outlets and an equal amount at their warehouses.

Migros, the dominant food chain store with about 581 outlets throughout Switzerland, carried only its own private label soft drinks and mineral water under the Aproz brand name. Few other brands were represented in the chain's stores. However, other chain retailers – such as Coop and Denner – carried both branded products and their own private labels. These chains received their deliveries either directly from the bottler or through each outlet's local beverage wholesaler. Unlike the other chains, Migros owned and operated its own bottling and distribution facilities.

In 1997, there were approximately 27,000 HORECA outlets in Switzerland. Analysts segmented the outlets according to the size of their workforce. Small outlets (less than five employees) accounted for 74% of all HORECA establishments, and 44% of the total HORECA mineral water and soft drinks sales. In these smaller outlets, non-alcoholic beverages accounted for 20–40% of total sales. At the larger outlets, the corresponding range was 10–20%. A typical HORECA establishment was served by one or two local beverage wholesalers who restocked its inventory on a weekly or bi-weekly basis. Normal HORECA retail margins ranged from 75% on mineral water and soft drinks to 50% on food.

A number of Swiss breweries had diversified into the ownership of restaurants. It was believed that close to 10% of total HORECA volume of soft drinks and mineral water was channelled through brewery-owned restaurants.

The wholesalers, also called distributors, were an important link in the distribution chain from the bottler to the consumer. They stocked various alcoholic and non-alcoholic beverages and delivered them to their customers, the retailers and HORECA outlets located within a given geographical area. Many distributors also made deliveries door-to-door, directly to consumers' homes when orders were large enough. In each geographic market, wholesalers tended to avoid competitive price cutting and respected each other's customer list. Few distributors maintained a sales force.

Generally, distributors carried a full line, including competing brands. Their normal inventory of 20–30 days of sales was mostly financed through the bottlers' trade credits. Mineral water and soft drinks represented 40–50% of a distributor's turnover. Margins on these sales averaged around 30%.

The beverage wholesaling industry in Switzerland was becoming increasingly concentrated as small family-owned wholesalers were gradually giving way to larger operations. The industry concentration was also aided by mergers of smaller distributors and acquisitions by the larger ones. As a result, between 1965 and 1997, the number of beverage distributors in Switzerland had declined from a total of about 1,100 to approximately 800. The resulting wholesaling structure was one of domination of each major geographic market by one or two large distributors. In 1997, 10% of beverage distributors accounted for nearly 80% of the wholesale beverage trade.

Another and more recent development in the wholesaling industry was the entry of breweries into beverage distribution, primarily through acquisition. As of 1997, it was estimated that the share of industry sales going through brewery-owned distributors was about 40%, as compared to only 10% in 1992.

IDC's Competition

In central Switzerland, where IDC marketed its products, the four main competitors were: The Coca-Cola Company, Feldschlösschen, Eptingen and Henniez. The Coca-Cola Company bottled soft drinks; Feldschlösschen bottled soft drinks, mineral water, and beer; Eptingen bottled both mineral water and soft drinks; and Henniez supplied IDC's region with only mineral water. The Coca-Cola Company, Feldschlösschen and Henniez were national bottlers; Eptingen, like IDC, was a regional bottler.

The Coca-Cola Company, which was a fully owned subsidiary of the international company, bottled the parent's three house brands: Sprite (citrus based), Fanta (orange flavored) and Coca-Cola. Unifontes, which was owned by Feldschlösschen brewery, marketed Elmer (citrus based), Orangina (orange flavored) and Queen's (bitter lemon flavored). Eptingen sold its mineral water under its own name and its soft drinks under Pepita (fruit flavored). Henniez's mineral water was marketed under the same name.

IDC's management was unable to establish the precise size and market shares of its competitors. (The marketing manager's 'rough guesses' are shown in **Exhibit 15**.) Muller considered The Coca-Cola Company and Feldschlösschen his company's toughest competitors.

The pressure on bottler prices and margins had intensified in recent years. Trade margins were augmented indirectly through various volume discounts and year-end cash rebates based on total purchases. No accurate information was available, however, on the actual levels of discounts and rebates offered by IDC's competitors.

Also unavailable to IDC's management was the amount spent on media advertising. Muller estimated that The Coca-Cola Company spent proportionately twice as much on Coca-Cola as IDC spent on Pepsi, using a variety of media including the cinema, TV and billboards. Henniez was also thought to be spending heavily on advertising. Little else was known, however, about the advertising practices of the other two companies. The Coca-Cola Company did not seem to engage heavily in either trade or consumer price promotions. But the other three companies were believed to be offering promotions similar to IDC's.

All competitors, except Henniez, employed a field sales force in the region. It was estimated that The Coca-Cola Company, which relied on its own direct distribution network, employed 55 driver-salesmen in central Switzerland. IDC's national sales manager estimated that there were 20–30 salesmen for Unifontes in IDC's region and 20 for Eptingen. Henniez did not have any salesmen in the territory, although its three sales managers were said to be frequently calling on local wholesalers.

According to Jeanneau, the sales force activities of the other companies were similar to those of IDC.

Alhough little was known about the sales force management practices of competitors, Jeanneau believed that all their salesmen were being compensated with fixed salaries. He thought The Coca-Cola Company's salaries were less than IDC's and those of Unifontes and Eptingen were more. In addition, he believed that The Coca-Cola Company practised an incentive bonus scheme but had no other information about it.

IDC's Sales Force

IDC's sales force was composed of 31 field salesmen, three district sales managers and a national sales manager. Through the force the company sold its branded products to approximately 400 distributors who in turn covered about 9,000 HORECA outlets and some 3,000 grocery stores. In 1997, sales force expenditures amounted to Sfr5.4 million. (A breakdown of expenses is given in **Exhibit 16**.)

Profile

The average age of IDC's field sales force was 43; the actual ages ranged from 25 to 65. With a few exceptions, the salesmen had at least one full-time job and some selling experience before joining the company. (**Exhibit 17** provides a breakdown of age and length of service of the sales force.) Jeanneau described the turnover among the salesmen as 'low by most standards'.

Organization

The area in which IDC marketed its products was organized into three districts: West, Central and East. Each district was headed by a manager who reported to the national sales manager, with 9–11 salesmen assigned to each district. Each salesman covered an exclusive geographic territory which varied in size, with the smallest being about a 20 kilometer radius and the largest about 100 kilometers.

Activities

As the job description formally stated, IDC's salesmen were responsible for 'producing profitable sales' within their assigned territories. They called on both the wholesale and retail trade, with the major accounts being visited once every two to three weeks. A salesman typically made eight retail and one or two distributor calls per day. A strong personal relationship was considered important in selling to the retail trade. Price promotions, free gifts and promotional items, as well as partial financing of refrigeration equipment, were some of the ways that salesmen could influence clients' loyalty.

Retail calls to independent grocery shops and HORECA outlets gave salesmen a chance to check on inventory, ensure that IDC's products and promotional items were being prominently displayed, and take orders. When orders were taken, they were passed on to each outlet's wholesaler for delivery. Often, however, the client preferred to place his orders directly to the wholesaler by phone or mail. According to IDC's sales management, salesmen were able to actually write an order during a call only 5% of the time.

Although visited often by the salesmen and district managers, the distributors preferred to place their orders directly by phone to the clerks in the sales department. On an average summer day, for example, 50–60 wholesalers' orders were received by the department in this manner. This practice was presumed to be industry-wide and reflected the distributors' preference to control their own inventory and maintain a balance among different suppliers.

Compensation

IDC's field salesmen and their managers were compensated by fixed salaries. In addition, they were reimbursed for travel and social expenses. It was the policy to raise the salaries annually, at least by the percentage increase in the Swiss Retail Price Index. An additional raise was awarded yearly to salesmen whose performances were judged superior. (A copy of the evaluation form used for this purpose is shown in **Exhibit 18**.) Performance-related raises were proposed by the district managers to Jeanneau for approval; they were typically 3–10% of the base salary.

In 1997, the monthly salary for salesmen ranged from Sfr8,400 for the oldest member of the force to Sfr6,400 for the youngest. In that year, seven salesmen received performance-related raises ranging from 7% to 10%; another 18 received raises ranging from 3% to 6%.

In management's opinion, the salesmen were generally satisfied with the company's compensation plan. Jeanneau, however, believed improvements could still be made. He explained:

> Personally, I'd like to see a sales-related bonus scheme, but I realize it would not be easy to administer. We have no accurate records for each salesman because the distributors don't have clearly defined sales territories. Also, since our sales records show only our sales to the distributors, we can't tell for sure how much each salesman actually sells at the retail level.

Supervision

The salesmen enjoyed a fair degree of freedom in organizing their routine activities. The call schedules were prepared by the salesmen themselves, with the district managers being informed of each week's plans ahead of time. Also, the district managers received a weekly report on the actual visits made, the orders written, and any sales expenses incurred. The managers were expected to spend part of their time traveling with the salesmen, making calls jointly. Jeanneau described IDC's supervisory system as one in which good wages and personal trust played important roles.

Planning, Measurement and Evaluation

The sales planning process at IDC was a simple one. Each year the marketing and national sales managers jointly projected the unit sales volume in bottles for each product for the following year. These forecasts were generally based on past trends. Inputs from the district sales managers were also included at this stage. The projected total unit sales volume was then converted into district and territory sales quotas for the following year. The quotas were allocated based on the territories' past performance and management's assessment of salesmen's abilities. A salesman's annual quota was usually expressed in total number of bottles, regardless of size or brand.

Achieving unit quotas was one of the factors considered in measuring performance and determining annual salary raises for the salesmen. Other factors taken into account in annual performance evaluations included the salesman's relationship with the distributors, his knowledge of business and selling skills. Achieving district quotas entitled the district managers to sales awards. One recent prize was two free tickets to a European city chosen by the winner.

Sales and Marketing Management's Appraisal

Both Jeanneau and Muller thought highly of IDC's sales force and its effectiveness in the field. Jeanneau commented:

> In this business, price and advertising are the keys for success. Given these conditions the sales force is doing well. The good thing about our salesmen is that they think of the company's interests first. They put in, on average, nine hours of extra work per week. Of course, there is always room for improvement. For instance, they are more likely to sell products that are easy to sell than those that are profitable to the company. I believe in time they will improve in these areas, too.

Muller agreed with Jeanneau's views that IDC's sales force was probably one of the best in the industry:

> Our salesmen are well trained and have lots of experience in the field. I think there are two things we can still do better. One is a more systematic prospecting for new accounts and the other is a higher number of sales calls per salesman.

Fehring's Concerns

Soon after returning to IDC, Fehring identified a number of areas that deserved immediate management attention. Among them were the changes taking place in the industry, IDC's marketing strategy, and the sales force's productivity. On the changes in industry he commented:

> Our problems come from a number of directions. Take the brewers, for example. They have lots of money they don't know what to do with. They are buying themselves into the industry by acquiring bottlers and distributors. They can introduce new products, advertise them heavily and in the early years sustain substantial losses. We are witnessing this in the case of Sibra (a division of Feldschlösschen) which has recently introduced an exotic flavor drink called 'CAP'. I hear they are going for market share and are willing to wait for five years if necessary before they make any money.

Fehring was similarly concerned about the developments among distributors and chains. He said:

> On the other side, the distributors are getting larger and greedier. They seem to think that they can demand ever higher margins from us as a matter of right. And the retail chains all want to become another Migros. Since Migros *sells* at low prices, they want to *buy* at low prices.

Fehring believed the changes in the industry were forcing IDC to take a fresh look at its marketing strategy:

> So far our salesmen have received no direction as to which products to push and which outlets to emphasize. That strategic direction has been missing simply because we never had one. But now, I am beginning to see the longer-term marketing issues along two dimensions, products and channels. Basically, we have three product groups, and two different channels. The product groups are the private labels, the international brands, and our own Berg products. The channels are the chains, on the one hand, and the HORECA and small shops on the other. I think IDC needs to look at its broader strategy in terms of specific product-channel strategies.

Fehring saw different sales force roles for IDC's different products and channels:

> Pepsi and Schweppes sell easily. The main battleground, as far as these products are concerned, is advertising. The other products, however, need the sales force push; otherwise we will have to compete purely on the basis of price alone. As for channels, the chains need to be catered to separately by the head office because of their overall impact on our sales and profitability. The HORECA outlets and small shops are where our field selling effort can make a difference. Perhaps we should push our international brands in

one type of outlet and Berg in another. Whatever product-channel strategies we come up with will be an improvement over the past when the selling effort was diffused.

In examining the strategic alternatives open to IDC, Fehring did not want to prematurely exclude any options:

I think we should keep an open mind and consider all possible directions for our company. Among these, I believe, are strategies of specialization along products or channels. For example, we could seriously look at the viability of a strategy that takes us out of branded products altogether and makes us exclusively a private label contract bottler for chains. Of course, this is only one option; there are others including staying in the existing products and channels.

Along with searching for a viable strategy, Fehring was looking for ways to upgrade the overall productivity of selling activities:

It is my strong suspicion that we have a lower productivity per salesman than our competitors. Our salesmen are costing us a fortune for what they generate; I am convinced we should and can do better.

Fehring believed that one factor contributing to low productivity was a lack of motivation on the part of salesmen. He explained:

It didn't take very long after I returned from the management school to realize that we have a real problem with sales force motivation. Basically, I don't see any fire in them. On the other hand, my national sales manager tells me that our type of selling is a 'missionary' one where the sales force doesn't sell directly but facilitates sales through distributors. Frankly, I am now beginning to understand why they all work and act like missionaries! They're a peaceful, calm, and easy-going bunch. I'd like to see considerable changes in the whole compensation system which currently neither rewards a good performance, nor punishes a poor one.

Fehring was aware of the difficulties of designing a strongly performance related compensation system:

A problem we face is how to measure individual performance. My managers have long argued that sales to distributors, which we maintain records for, do not accurately represent sales within our sales force's geographic territories. Some distributors, especially in large cities like Zürich, spread over two or more of our territories. I am aware of this problem, but I also think we can come up with a reasonable solution. One that I have been thinking about is restructuring our territories to match those of our distributors. But, being realistic, I would expect strong sales force resistance to any changes to the territories or the compensation system.

Conclusion

As the early-February meeting between Fehring and Jeanneau had proved inconclusive, the two executives agreed to hold another session a week later on the issues of sales force productivity and priorities for management action. Muller, the marketing manager, would also be joining them at that meeting.

As Fehring pondered the specific items to be placed on the next meeting's agenda, he talked about his longer-term goals and the price he was willing to pay to achieve them:

> Our environment doesn't allow any slack in our performance. We have to move, and move fast, if we are to survive. So I am pushing for more productivity from our sales force. I mean 50% or more output from our existing force. To achieve this, we need people who can adapt to the changing requirements of a performance-orientated company. I am willing to wait two years, maybe even three. I am prepared for that. In the process, I expect some casualties – up to 30% of the force at all levels. But then, life is like that. You can't achieve anything without some pain.

EXHIBIT 1

Switzerland and IDC's Geographic Coverage*

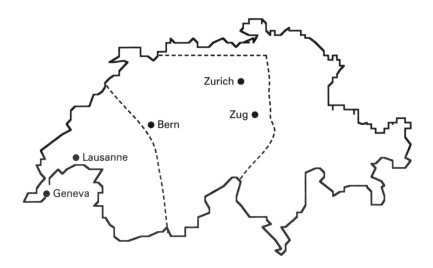

* IDC's coverage in central Switzerland is shown with dotted lines.

Switzerland

Total Population:	7.1 million
Languages:	75% German 21% French 4% Italian and others
Age Groups:	0–19 23% 20–64 62% 65+ 15%
GDP Per Capita:	$35,445

Sources: Annuaire Statistique de la Suisse, 1998; World Competitiveness Yearbook, 1998.

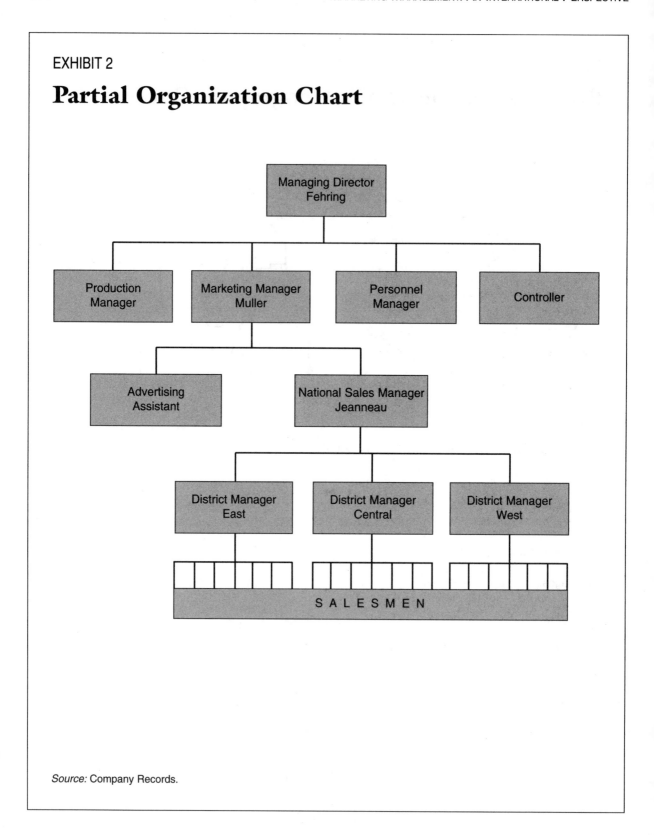

EXHIBIT 2

Partial Organization Chart

Source: Company Records.

EXHIBIT 3

Income Statement (in thousand Sfrs)

	1993	1994	1995	1996	1997
Net Sales*	35,744	32,918	33,192	35,918	38,688
Less: Total Manufacturing Costs	19,544	16,306	17,784	19,502	22,190
Gross Profit from Bottling	16,200	16,612	15,408	16,416	16,498
Add: Net Profit from Trading**	998	966	3,636	5,400	4,200
Total Gross Profit	17,198	17,578	19,044	21,816	20,698
Other Expenses (Bottling):					
Salaries/Employee Benefits	5,910	6,392	6,900	7,368	8,218
Selling Expenses	4,270	4,308	4,806	5,414	5,414
Advertising and Promotion	4,040	4,358	4,304	4,020	4,760
Other General Expenses	4,128	3,002	3,210	4,216	3,714
Total Other Expenses	18,348	18,060	19,220	21,018	22,106
Miscellaneous Income	1,300	1,648	1,268	1,200	1,410
Investment Write-off	–	(4,890)	–	–	–
Net Profit	150	(3,724)	1,092	1,998	2

* After discounts and year-end rebates.
** IDC had a trading operation in flavors unrelated to its bottling activities.

Source: Company Records.

EXHIBIT 4

Balance Sheet (in thousand Sfrs)

	1993	1994	1995	1996	1997
ASSETS					
Current	8,236	7,482	8,234	9,204	9,734
Fixed	28,936	26,478	24,556	23,836	26,360
Miscellaneous (Securities, Overdue Receivables)	14,084	11,798	11,508	9,260	8,390
Total Assets	51,256	45,758	44,298	42,300	44,484
LIABILITIES and EQUITY					
Current	8,258	9,566	9,678	7,814	11,754
Long Term	29,540	25,976	23,312	21,180	19,422
Shareholders' Equity	13,458	10,216	11,308	13,306	13,308
Total Liabilities & Equity	51,256	45,758	44,298	42,300	44,484

Source: Company Records.

EXHIBIT 5

IDC's Product Line

Products	Flavors	Bottle Sizes (Liters)
Soft Drinks		
Schweppes	Tonic Water	0.18
	Bitter Orange	0.18
	Bitter Lemon	0.18
	Ginger Ale	0.18
	Soda Water	0.18
Pepsi-Cola	Cola	0.3, 1.0
Berg	Citron	0.3, 1.0
	Orange	0.3, 1.0
	Grapefruit	0.3, 1.0
	Himbo	0.3, 1.0
	Simbo	0.3, 1.0
Private Label	(same as for Berg Brand)	1.0
Mineral Water		
Berg	–	0.3, 1.0
Private Label	–	1.0

Source: Company Records.

EXHIBIT 6

1997 Sales by Outlet (in thousand Sfrs)

	Shops	HORECA	Chain	Total
Soft Drinks				
Schweppes	4,632	7,488	2,178	14,298
Pepsi-Cola	2,754	2,408	654	5,816
Berg	9,410	1,298	–	10,708
Private Label	–	–	4,778	4,778
Mineral Water				
Berg	804	468	–	1,272
Private Label	–	–	1,816	1,816
Total	17,600	11,662	9,426	38,688

Source: Company Records.

EXHIBIT 7

1997 Sales by Outlet (in thousands of bottles)

	Shops	HORECA	Chain	Total
Soft Drinks				
Schweppes	7,721	11,013	3,632	22,366
Pepsi-Cola	4,008*	2,315	629	6,952
Berg	9,047	2,027	–	11,074
Private Label	–	–	6,288	6,288
Mineral Water				
Berg	2,012	1,116	–	3,128
Private Label	–	–	5,673	5,673
Total	22,788	16,471	16,222	55,481

* The split between 0.3L and 1.0L containers was 5:3.

Source: Company Records.

EXHIBIT 8

Average Ex-factory Prices by Outlet* in 1997 (Sfrs)

	Container Size (liters)	Shops	HORECA	Chains
Soft Drinks				
Schweppes	0.18	0.60	0.68	0.60
Pepsi-Cola	0.30	0.50	1.04	–
	1.00	1.04	–	1.04
Berg	0.30	–	0.64	–
	1.00	1.04	–	–
Private Label	1.00	–	–	0.70
Mineral Water				
Berg	0.30	–	0.42	–
	1.00	0.40	–	–
Private Label	1.00	–	–	0.32

* The company could distinguish among bottles of similar sizes destined for different outlets as the containers were dissimilar.

Source: Company Records.

EXHIBIT 9

Variable Manufacturing Costs* (in Sfrs)

Product/Bottle Size	18cl	0.3L	1 liter
Soft Drinks			
Schweppes	0.22	–	–
Pepsi-Cola	–	0.12	0.36
Berg	–	0.12	0.32
Private Label	–	–	0.44
Mineral Water			
Berg	–	0.04	0.06
Private Label	–	–	0.10

* Includes sugar, the raw materials, and packaging (non-returnable bottles, caps, and labels).

Source: Company Records.

EXHIBIT 10

Advertising and Promotion Expenditures (in thousand Sfrs)

	1996		1997	
	Advertising	Promotion	Advertising	Promotion
Schweppes	414	320	244	280
Pepsi-Cola	500	400	528	520
Berg Soft Drinks	1,290	876	1,760	1,144
Berg Mineral Water	–	220	–	284
Total	2,204	1,816	2,532	2,228

Source: Company Records.

EXHIBIT 11

Swiss Soft Drink and Mineral Water Consumption (millions of liters)

	Soft Drinks	Mineral Water
1992	535	495
1993	560	510
1994	545	515
1995	585	560
1996	580	570
1997	590	580

Source: Company Records.

EXHIBIT 12

National Market Shares of Top Bottling Companies (1997, liters)

Soft Drinks Bottler *	Estimated Market Share %
Feldschlösschen	21
The Coca-Cola Company	21
Refresca	12
Rivella	12
Aproz (Migros)	10
Henniez	6
IDC	3
Others	15
Total	100

Mineral Water Bottlers	Estimated Market Share %
Henniez	30
Aproz (Migros)	15
Valser	16
Feldschlösschen	10
Others (Including IDC)	29
Total	100

* International, national, and regional brands.

Source: Trade Sources.

EXHIBIT 13

Representative Consumer Prices (in Sfrs)

	Container Size (liters)	Shops	Horeca	Chains
Soft Drinks				
Schweppes	0.18	1.30	3.90	0.96
Queens	0.18	1.10	3.90	0.80
Pepsi-Cola	0.3	1.10	6.00	–
	1.0	2.30	–	1.70
Coca-Cola	0.3	1.50	6.00	–
	1.0	2.70	–	2.10
Berg	0.3	–	3.70	–
	1.0	2.30	–	–
Coop/Denner Private Label	1.0	–	–	1.20
Mineral Water				
Passugger	0.3	–	2.40	–
	1.0	1.80	–	–
Henniez	0.3	–	2.40	–
	1.0	1.40	–	–
Berg	0.3	–	2.40	–
	1.0	0.90	–	–
Coop/Denner Private Label	1.0	–	–	0.80

Source: Company Records.

EXHIBIT 14

Share of Food Chains in Total Consumer Purchases (%)

	Food	Beverages*
Migros	48	24
Coop	24	24
Denner	6	6
Total	78	54

* All categories.

Source: Company Records.

EXHIBIT 15

Estimated Sales of Competitors Within IDC's Region

	Bottles (millions)	Swiss Francs (millions)
The Coca-Cola Company	200	200
Feldschlösschen	80	70
Eptingen	60	48
Henniez	100	70

Source: Marketing Manager, IDC.

EXHIBIT 16

Breakdown of Selling Expenses (Sfrs 000s)

	1995	%	1997	%
Compensation	2,208	46	2,604	48
Car	1,302	27	1,398	26
Travel	768	16	872	16
Entertainment	528	11	540	10
Total	4,806	100	5,414	100

Source: Company Records.

EXHIBIT 17

Age and Service Profile of Salesmen

Age	20–30	30–40	40–50	50–60	60+	Total
West	4	1	3	2	1	11
Central	–	3	5	2	1	11
East	1	3	2	2	1	9
Total	5	7	10	6	3	31

Years of Service	1	2	3	4	5	6–10	11–15	15+	Total
West	1	6	–	–	–	1	2	1	11
Central	1	1	–	3	–	4	1	1	11
East	2	–	1	1	1	1	2	1	9
Total	4	7	1	4	1	6	5	3	31

Source: Company Records.

EXHIBIT 18

Performance Evaluation Form

Name:. . . . .

Date of the evaluation:. . . . . By:. . . . .

	Very Good	Good to Satisfactory	Unsatisfactory
Number of orders			
Number of bottles sold			
Relations with distributors			
Knowledge/skills			
Call planning			
Sales promotion			
Appearance			
Sales expenses			
General impression (for example car, administration, etc.)			
Total points *			

Comments :

* The company followed the system of allocating points ranging from (10) (very good) to (1) (unsatisfactory). These points, for each of the criteria, were then added to arrive at total points.

Source: Company Records.

CASE 2.5

Salomon: The Monocoque Ski

This case was prepared by Professor Francis Bidault.

Yes, it's excellent... I really love this prototype. You have all done a truly superb job! But, we are still only half way into this venture. There is a lot more work to do... I would say you will probably need another four years before we can see Salomon skis, as well as boots and bindings, on the slopes. But, it *is* time to discuss an action plan and I would like to present it at next month's New Product Committee meeting! So, I'd appreciate it if you could let us have *your* plan a few days beforehand.

Georges Salomon, the 62-year-old President of Salomon S.A., was stroking, with visible excitement, the new prototype that the development team had just presented during one of his regular meetings with them. It was November 15, 1987 and he was glad to see the progress made by the team on this truly strategic project which he had initiated in July 1984: to design a Salomon ski as an addition to the company's successful product portfolio.

As Georges Salomon was making his concluding comments, the project team had mixed feelings. They were happy that their work had gained such positive recognition from the President, but they also felt under pressure, knowing what remained to be done. Until now, the development of the first Salomon ski had been a very exciting adventure: unlimited creativity, daring solutions and generous support. That was the easy part. Now, the time had come to try and make the 'dream' come true: they would have to work hard to complete the development and prepare a commercial launch. The real challenge was still ahead.

As they were leaving the meeting room, each member of the team was recollecting the key events that had led to this development and considering the significance of this project for the company and for the overall ski market.

Salomon S.A.

Salomon, a fast-growing company with headquarters in Annecy in the French Rhône-Alpes region, was proud of being the world leader (based on its sales) in winter sports equipment (refer to **Exhibit 1**). The company, always aiming for the top, had regularly improved its position in each of its market areas: Number 1 in ski bindings with a 46% market share; Number 1 in cross-country ski boot-bindings with a 30% market share; and Number 2 in alpine ski boots where it was just a few percentage points behind Nordica. A line of accessories – clothes, bags, caps, and so on ('Club-Line') – completed its winter sports offerings. In addition, Salomon owned Taylor-Made, a successful firm in the golf equipment business (clubs and accessories).

Salomon's sales were distributed around the globe: 30% in North America, 22% in Japan, 40% in Europe and 8% in the rest of the world. Salomon had fully owned subsidiaries in 12 countries including Japan, which was the largest in terms of sales.

The company was seriously involved in competition, in winter sports as well as in golf. Success in competition was considered very important for establishing the credibility and reputation of its products. Consequently, Salomon invested a significant amount of money in these particular activities (some FF50 million annually).

Salomon's management philosophy followed three basic principles:

- Partnership with employees
- Cooperation with suppliers and distributors
- Innovation for customers.

The partnership with the company's workforce was founded on the premise that success could only come if the employees were competent and felt associated with the future of the firm. Therefore, training was regarded as a key driver in the company's effectiveness, with over 5% of the payroll 'invested' in this activity. In addition, employees benefited from the company's success by receiving bonuses, based on annual results, and a regular distribution of shares. The 1986–87 annual report[1] mentioned that 3% of the company's equity was held by its employees.

Salomon recognized that cooperation with suppliers and distributors was needed in order to have effective high-quality support for delivering its products. The company relied on numerous subcontractors to manufacture up to 60% of its production of bindings and boots, and all of its 'Club-Line' products. There was also a worldwide network of retailers offering the necessary service to the customer (advice, testing, adjustments, and so on). For both the subcontractors and the retailers, Salomon provided continuous information and training to ensure the quality of their contribution. Recently, the company had taken a further step by introducing the concept of the 'Salomon Authorized Dealer', whereby the rights and duties of retailers *vis-à-vis* the company were specified.

The third principle was no less essential: ongoing innovation and investment in new technology that would serve the needs of the sportsman in increasingly better ways! Salomon spent some 4% of its consolidated sales on research and development, and registered around 100 patents worldwide every year. From the very beginning, innovation had always been a key word at Salomon.

---

1. Salomon's annual report covered the time period from April 1 to March 31 of the following year.

Salomon: The First Forty Years

In 1947, François Salomon and his wife, Jeanne, set up a small firm that performed metal processing activities. Initially, it made saw blades and steel edges for skis, a technology for which François owned a patent. At that time, the edges were attached to the wooden skis by the retailers.

The Salomons' son Georges decided to give up his job as a schoolmaster and to join the family firm. Soon afterward, Georges invented a machine to improve the processing of steel for ski edges.[2] However, in only a few years, the Salomons realized that the ski manufacturers were integrating this process and that they needed to look for other activities to prepare for the future.

In the early 1950s, Georges was approached by a Parisian inventor with a new type of ski binding that no manufacturer was interested in. Georges immediately saw its potential and decided to buy the technology. This innovative device filled a real need at a time when the market was developing quickly. Orders came soon and sales grew fast, particularly in North America. Thus, the firm was able to benefit from the post-World War II growth of skiing as a major leisure activity, at an international level right from the beginning. In 1962, Georges realized that the growth of his company needed to address the world market. From then on, the commercial development of Salomon S.A. was based on two pillars: new products and international presence.

Georges, however, did not become complacent with success and systematically continued to look for ways to improve the protection of skiers against accidents. In 1967, he introduced the first ski binding without a cable. This innovation was a real breakthrough, one that radically changed skiing safety and comfort, and also resulted in a profound restructuring of the bindings industry. Such an accomplishment had only occurred because Georges was determined to concentrate on product innovation, devoting much of his time to it – as he preferred that activity to administrative tasks.

By 1972, Salomon had gained a real presence in foreign markets, surpassing Tyrolia and Marker to become the world leader in bindings – a position the company continued to keep thereafter.

In the early 1970s, Salomon began to look for new products beyond ski bindings. Several options were studied, among them the markets for ski boots and skis. In 1974, the decision was made to pursue the former. Georges Salomon had a clear objective: to come up with a boot that was not only better but would also offer a significant and visible improvement. In 1979, Salomon introduced a truly innovative boot design – the rear-entry boot – which addressed a key frustration for skiers: lack of comfort. This 'revolutionary' ski boot concept was reasonably well accepted. However, in spite of this success the industry (racers, journalists, ski instructors, and so on) gave it a lukewarm welcome. They claimed that it was not tight enough on the foot and gave it the uncomplimentary nickname, *'la*

---

2. *Salomon S.A.*, Case Study, Jim Whyte, Department of Management, Napier College, Edinburgh, 1986.

pantoufle'.[3] Even though sales were significant, they did not develop as quickly as expected. Salomon gradually adapted its design, keeping rear-entry for only one part of the line and, in this way, eventually was able to gain a steady market share. By 1987, the company held second place, close behind Nordica (of Italy).

During this same time period, starting in 1978, Salomon undertook to enter the cross-country ski market. Again, the ambition was to offer a clearly superior product. In 1980, Salomon made the headlines when it introduced a unique system: a cross-country boot and binding combination. This was definitely a superior concept, which took off very quickly and put Salomon at the top with an amazing 30% of the market in 1987.

Meanwhile, being dependent on winter sports had become a major concern for Salomon's management: it considered several activities that could provide a counterbalance. One option was windsurfing, which was turned down because it did not offer enough potential and was already suffering from a huge over-capacity. Eventually, the golfing business was chosen, an industry worth about twice as much as winter sports: about FF12 billion. In 1984, Salomon purchased the entire shareholdings of the American company Taylor-Made, which manufactured and sold upmarket golf clubs. The choice of Taylor-Made was based on its similarity to Salomon: the philosophy of providing excellence through innovation.

Over the years, Salomon's progressive product diversification reflected ambitious goals for each market entry, which had its roots in the corporate culture and, especially, in the personality of the President.

Management, Structure and Culture

In the mid-1980s, Salomon had become a mini-multinational with subsidiaries in 12 countries. The headquarters in the suburb of Annecy also had a definite international feeling, with managers coming from around the world (Canada, Norway, the US). Like Philips and Bosch, Salomon had a matrix organization that was structured around its products (bindings, shoes, cross-country equipment, and so on) and their respective markets (using national sales organizations). The company had come a long way from the little workshop that made ski edges to become a multi-line sports equipment firm.

At Salomon S.A., recruitment was considered a particularly important task. The company was very demanding and therefore selective, and could afford to be so because its sporty and dynamic image made it a very attractive employer. Early on, it had recruited engineers and technicians from the best schools. It also was able to attract the most senior managers from top companies. The majority of the people working at Salomon had a double profile: highly skilled in their discipline and expert in a sport. Indeed, several of them were former ski champions. Consequently, Salomon was managed with state-of-the-art technology and highly skilled, motivated teams who, literally, 'loved' their products.

---

3. 'the slipper'.

The personality of Georges Salomon as an individual had a big impact on the culture of the company. Even though he did not have a technical education, he spent a lot of his time looking for ways that new technology could bring value to products. He had personally developed several products, which gave him credibility with his team. He was the one mainly responsible for the goal to launch only products that were clearly and visibly superior. Also essential to the company's successful product development record was its impeccable use of extreme caution in all decision-making. This prudence came, in large part, from Georges's anxiety about the outcome of each company project. Everyone who managed a major project knew that he must be thoroughly prepared with an answer for all of Georges's concerns. Above all, Georges was a mountaineer and a careful climber who was aware that 'rushing tends to be dangerous'.

Georges Salomon's daily behavior also carried some messages to his organization; he made no secret about where his priorities were. Even though he had received countless awards in Paris for the company's performance (in design, innovation, exports), Georges avoided personal publicity. He did not care much about pleasing the establishment, either. He much preferred walking around the company's workshops discussing new products, contributing ideas, even occasionally drawing a quick sketch. When he had to meet with bankers or high-ranking officials, he would insist on inviting them to the company canteen.

Georges's personal lifestyle reflected his passion for his job and dedication to the company. In his dress, he was informal and casual – preferring mountaineering clothing. For a long time, he drove a rusty Renault 5, which was a frequent topic of discussion. His chalet, on a slope overlooking Annecy, was considered spacious but not luxurious.

He played a central role in company strategy, particularly when it came to market-entry decisions. Georges was very demanding, systematically wanting to ensure that every product would really make a difference and that the strategy concerning its development and launch was optimal. He often reminded the project team that he would 'pull the plug' at any time if he had any doubts about the project's success. And he meant it; indeed, he had actually cancelled some projects a few weeks before their official launch.

The Decision to Enter the Ski Market

By 1984, Georges Salomon had come to the conclusion that it was time to enter the ski market. In his view, Salomon, the world's largest company in the winter sports industry, could no longer ignore such an essential piece of equipment for skiers.

Skis, as a product, had several characteristics that made them attractive to Salomon. First, they were the most visible piece of equipment. In practical terms, in a photograph of a skier in action, it was the skis that one could see most clearly; the boot and the binding were usually not so easily distinguishable. Hence, from a communication point of view, skis offered better support to the brand name. Second, skis had the highest value, because they were the most expensive item bought by skiers and, therefore, the market size was bigger (about twice the amount of the bindings market). Finally, skis were the piece of equipment most talked about by skiers, the focus of an enthusiast's passion, in a way that boots and bindings could not equal. Consequently, skis were a powerful contributor to brand awareness. As Georges Salomon explained to his staff: 'Ski companies that are much smaller than Salomon in terms of sales enjoy a greater brand recognition by the public... which is why this ski development challenge is so important for our firm.'

Salomon's management felt that it had the capability to enter the ski market successfully. The company had adequate experience, it was argued, to take on this new activity, given its track record and current situation. For example, Salomon had:

- *A mastery of innovation:* thanks to the most advanced design tools, and databases on skiers' needs and desires, and on the behavior and reaction of various materials
- *A know-how in automation:* which allowed it to achieve higher quality levels and competitive production costs
- *A financially healthy situation:* which made it possible for the corporation to afford the high R&D expenditures and the necessary financial investment at the manufacturing stage
- *A strong brand image and distribution network:* which could quickly promote sales of this new ski and generate economies of scale at the same time.

In a survey conducted in 1984 to learn about Salomon's brand image, it appeared that the market was definitely anticipating such a move: in fact, a significant proportion of interviewees believed that Salomon was already making skis! This surprising piece of information provided even more motivation to enter this market, in spite of the risks.

Salomon's management was conscious that moving into skis was not a risk-free operation. After all, the company's bindings were being mounted on other manufacturers' skis. Even though the ski-binding assembly was done at the retail level, some feared that large ski competitors might try to retaliate by joining forces with other bindings producers – for example 'ski X prefers bindings Y'. Also, this move could prompt a countermove into Salomon's own territory, with other ski manufacturers deciding to compete in bindings and boots. Finally, the issue of branding was also raised. Salomon was planning to offer all three products (skis, bindings and boots) under its own brand name. It would be the first company to make such an offering. Clearly, there were some risks associated with this strategy, that is, if a customer had a bad experience with one of the products, the other products could be affected as well.

These concerns, however, did not prevent the company from going ahead with the diversification. By 1985, Salomon's top management had set up ambitious objectives for the ski business:

1. To become a world leader, in 5 or 6 years, in the medium to top segments of the market.

2. To reach, at 'cruising speed', a net profitability of the same order of magnitude as bindings and boots (around 9% of sales).

In order to pursue these demanding objectives, the following strategic principles were established:

- To give skiers a piece of equipment with a 'plus', based on some visible innovation that would be identified through market surveys and technical research
- To emphasize partnership with distributors in order to provide optimal quality service
- To gain recognition through success in competition, with the Winter Olympics in Albertville (Winter 1992) being used to enhance the impact.

The Ski Market in 1987

There were some 55 million skiers in the world in 1987. Most of them were in Western Europe (around 30 million), North America (9 million) and Japan (the single largest national market with over 12 million skiers). There were also some minor markets in Eastern Europe (particularly Yugoslavia, Poland, Czechoslovakia and the USSR) and in Australia. The proportion of skiers to the total population varied tremendously from country to country and was partly a function of local skiing possibilities. Switzerland was clearly the highest (with a ratio of 30.4%), followed by Austria (27.7%) and Sweden (23.8%), then Germany, Italy and France (in the 10–12% range). The USA, although a large market of 5.4 million skiers, had a very low ratio (2.2%) compared to Japan (9.9%).

Skiing as a sport was being influenced by several important trends. First, skiing had become affordable and accessible to an increasing number of consumers, but the relative time spent participating in winter sports had been diminishing. Second, skiers tended to be less 'fanatic' than in the past, especially as the competitive pressure of other leisure activities (golfing, cruising, tourism in exotic countries...) grew stronger. Third, skiing had become an increasingly diversified sport – with 'off-piste' (off the official groomed trails), mogul, freestyle, acrobatic and speed skiing, as well as the introduction of new types of equipment (monoskis and surfboards). The final factor was fashion: colors in equipment and clothing were becoming brighter and more dramatic, and styles and shapes were ever changing.

The Market

The international ski market was already mature. It was expected to plateau at around 6.5 million pairs (refer to **Exhibit 4**) with possible ups and downs following business cycles and the amount of snowfall. The world market was estimated at FF4.5 billion, compared to FF3.5 billion for ski boots and FF2 billion for bindings. The largest national markets were (in rank order) Japan, the USA, Germany and

France (refer to **Exhibit 5**). Some markets still seemed to be growing (North America), while others were flattening (Japan, Western Europe) or even declining (Scandinavia) over the short to medium term.

The price structure of the market was somewhat peculiar. In most markets, the distribution of sales along the price range could be seen as a pyramid, with sales of the most expensive segment being the smallest. The ski market, however, presented a different pattern, as the most expensive products sold more than the medium-priced ones (refer to **Exhibit 6**).

The traditional market segmentation made a first distinction between rental (10% of the volume), junior (another 20%) and adult (the remainder). Within the adult segment, there were three types of users: leisure (55% of the volume), sport (20%) and performance (25%). Leisure skiers tended to be people who skied for recreation and to have fun, not for 'records'. The second segment included skiers that were more 'aggressive' on the slopes, but not competing in any way. The last segment were those skiers who were involved in some form of competition. The last two segments (sport and performance), sometimes called 'medium' and 'top', represented around 2 million pairs of skis.

The Competitors

The number of competitors was much higher in skis than in bindings or boots. Some 80 different brands were competing worldwide (21 in Japan, 15 in the USA, 12 in Austria, 6 in France and 20 more in other countries). Most companies owned one brand, except large players like the world leader Rossignol (France) which controlled Dynastar (also in France). On average, the number of brands present in each country was about twice as large as in bindings.

In addition, skis were sold under private label. The estimate was that, worldwide, this represented around 50% of volume, with the proportion varying considerably from country to country.

The market was dominated by Rossignol (France), Atomic (Austria), Elan (Yugoslavia), Head (USA), Dynastar (France), and Blizzard (Austria), which all sold more than half a million pairs every year (refer to **Exhibit 7**). Most Japanese manufacturers were relatively small (100 to 150,000 pairs), except for Yamaha which barely passed the 200,000 pair threshold. While the Western brands were present in Europe, the Japanese producers were virtually nonexistent outside Japan.

Competitors differed in their approach to the ski market in many ways. A few strategic dimensions seemed to be critical in discriminating among industry players. The first dimension was the overall product positioning. Some companies, such as Rossignol and Atomic, offered skis for all levels – from beginners to racers, while others focused on a specific market niche (the upmarket: Völkl, Fischer, K2; the low to medium end: Head, Elan). Participation in ski competition also affected a company's positioning. Brands that addressed the top end of the market (Rossignol, Völkl, K2) sponsored ski racers in an effort to enhance the visibility of their products, while companies focusing on the lower niches did not pursue this activity. Another important dimension was the scope of market presence. Most of the 80 ski manufacturers around the world were only local players that marketed their products in their own country. This situation was particularly true for the Japanese brands. Among the companies that had 'gone international', the scope of market coverage differed. The leaders (Rossignol, Atomic, Elan, Head, Dynastar) were present in all significant markets; other companies (like Blizzard) had substantial international sales, but were not represented in all national markets.

The Manufacturing of Skis

Skis, which had been in existence for at least 5,000 years, only were considered 'sports equipment' at the beginning of the 20th century, when they were brought to Switzerland by British tourists. The first skis were very simple, made out of ordinary wood. In order to achieve a more solidly constructed ski, one of the first innovations was to use laminates of wood that were glued together, thus gaining greater flexibility and a longer ski. Metal edges were introduced later in order to reduce deterioration of the sole of the ski and provide a better grip. After World War II, plastic soles were added to enhance the ski's sliding capability. In 1950, Head introduced the metal sandwich ski, which irreversibly changed ski technology. Metal was later replaced by the various plastic and composite materials which dominated the market in the 1980s.

At this time, several types of design were used in the construction of skis. The most common structures were the sandwich ski and the torsion box ski (refer to **Exhibit 8**). A sandwich ski was essentially made of various materials arranged in layers, with the more rigid and resistant layers on the top and the bottom of the ski. This technology, which increased resistance to flexion and shock absorption, was the most widely used (75% of skis). In a torsion box ski, the resistance was obtained from a box located in the core of the ski. It gave a better grip in the snow, as well as a quicker reaction. Together, the sandwich and torsion box technologies represented 90% of the skis manufactured. There were a few other technologies, for example the 'omega' structure, but most of them had only a very limited production.

The Production Cycle

The production of skis started a full year before the winter season, in November. For instance, skis sold by retailers between November 1985 and March 1986 had been produced between November 1984 and November 1985. This production phase had been preceded by development work on shape, materials and art work. The duration of the development phase depended on the importance of the work involved, from four years for a major ski innovation to a few months for a cosmetic change, which was being done every year in recent years (colors and art work).

The production plan, initially made during the preceding summer, could be adjusted at three points. The first occasion was ISPO, the annual sports industry exhibition in Munich, in the second part of February every year when distributors started to order. Later, in May, when the number of orders was better known, a second adjustment would be made. Lastly, in September–October, as orders were being completed, it was possible to fine-tune production to market demand (volume and mix).

Over time, manufacturing had become a complex process. In the 1980s, it involved the assembly of several kinds of material (steel, fibers, resins, plastic sheets and so on) which represented around 13% of the retail price. Each material was carefully selected as it played a role in the performance of the ski. Production workers would typically put together the different materials needed (the sole, the edges, the various layers, polyester resin, the upper platform and so on) into a mold, which would then be put into a press with warm plates. Because of the material and equipment involved, which generated both heat and odor, working conditions were difficult. Manufacturing costs represented 19.5% of the retail price.

Distribution

Skis were sold through a network of wholesalers and retailers, which was organized by the manufacturers. Small brands tended to rely on local independent distributors (one per country), while large manufacturers often had their own sales organization for major countries. It was estimated that the cost of the wholesale function amounted to 17.5% of the retail price.

Retailing was shared between independent outlets and distribution chains. In ski resorts, independent retailers – usually also managing a large rental activity – were dominant. In major towns and cities, large retail chains (such as Intersport in Germany and Decathlon in France) represented the major portion of the market. Non-specialized chains (hypermarkets) had a limited participation, mostly selling inexpensive products. On average, the retailers' margin was 50% of the final price, including sales tax.

Depending on the country, retailers offered 5–10 different brands,[4] with 4–5 models in each one. There were some real technical differences, in terms of materials, structure and shape that needed to be evaluated in the selection process, along with more superficial considerations. Consumers thus had an enormous choice. The selection of a ski was often made through the recommendation of a salesperson, on the basis of physical characteristics, skiing style, ability and budget (refer to **Exhibit 9**).

Therefore, the sales process required having capable, often technical, explanations by the retail staff, a situation which called for training. Although large brands made a genuine effort to provide technical information to their network, communication with the retailers was not always appropriate. It tended to be

---

4. Except in Japan where retailers typically stored 25 different brands.

unclear with an over-emphasis on jargon. As well, ill-founded rumors and myths were not uncommon.

Communication with the consumer was thus very important. It was done through advertising in specialized magazines and point-of-sale material (catalogues, leaflets). As well, magazines published articles appraising new products coming onto the market and were another channel of information, mostly for the high end of the market.

The Monocoque Project

The origin of the monocoque project could be traced to early 1984 when Georges Salomon entered the office of Roger Pascal, the Director of the Bindings Division, and said: 'Pascal, you have to make me a ski!'

Roger Pascal, then 46 years old, had worked with Salomon since 1969. He was an engineer by training (INSA, Lyon), but he was also an expert skier, having been a ski instructor (Ecole du Ski Français) while he was a student. He had started in the engineering department and eventually had become manager, before heading the ski boot engineering department.

Initial Steps

Georges Salomon and Roger Pascal agreed that there could be no meaningful entry into the ski business without an in-depth knowledge of the ski market and industry. They reckoned that, even though Salomon was selling in related markets, its information on consumers' needs, technological solutions and marketing processes was not sufficient to make a difference in the ski market.

The ski project got underway with the appointment of Jean-Luc Diard in July 1984. Jean-Luc had just completed his studies at the ESC Paris, one of the top business schools in France. He was also an excellent skier, having won the annual French student ski championship. Recruited as a special kind of trainee,[5] he was sent to Salomon's Austrian subsidiary to study the ski market and industry. He focused on making an international study of the best products available at the time, and traveled extensively to meet and interview the world's experts. The information he gathered was encouraging for Salomon: there were still ways to improve on existing ski technologies.

At the same time, a series of market surveys were launched in order to appraise the level of satisfaction among skiers. The first results came as a surprise. While Salomon had detected significant frustration with ski boots in earlier surveys, it seemed that consumers were generally satisfied with skis. These results renewed Georges Salomon's conviction that the new ski must be radically better if it were to make a

---

5. A program which allowed graduates to be a trainee in a French firm or public organization outside of France, as a replacement for military service.

difference in the marketplace. In order to have a specific goal and objective for the team, Georges and Roger agreed that the ski should be able to sell at a 15% premium above the market price.

The Project Team

In the summer of 1985, Georges Salomon was able to convince two technology experts – Maurice Legrand and Yves Gagneux – to join the ski development team. Maurice Legrand, the former head of Rossignol's engineering department, was in charge of product technology. Yves Gagneux, the former head of manufacturing at Dynamic, was made responsible for process technology.

The team – Roger, Jean-Luc, Maurice and Yves – functioned like a 'commando operation', that is, a group of highly skilled volunteers who were totally devoted to their 'secret mission'. The team was maintained out of the normal organization, in an effort to preserve confidentiality as long as possible. Their work was kept secret, even to insiders, as Salomon did not want its competitors to know about it. Also, like a commando group, there was a sense of close community among the members, with each one knowing what the others were doing. Indeed, the competence of all the team members was truly exceptional: each individual was outstanding in his field and all were excellent skiers as well. In addition, the interaction was so interconnected that their disciplinary boundaries were blurred. Thus, Jean-Luc, in charge of marketing, also contributed technical solutions, while Maurice came up with marketing ideas.

Project Management

The activity of the ski development team was characterized by a high energy level, thanks to the enthusiasm and the sense of challenge that surrounded their mission. This project, however, was not a 'skunk works' operation.[6] Quite the contrary. Yves Gagneux explained: 'Maurice Legrand and myself were able to bring the technical knowledge that Salomon was lacking. But, Salomon provided us with a superb project management approach without which our expertise, as good as it was, would have been a lot less effective. Clearly, that was a strong point at Salomon!'

The management of the project actually used the whole gamut of modern techniques. At the very beginning, Georges Salomon had set the goal: to introduce a ski in 5 or 6 years, with excellent and visible advantages over existing products. The team translated this objective into a very detailed action plan, specifying the milestones, the resources needed, the tools used – Quality Function Deployment, Design to Manufacturing, Consumer Clinics. Early on, the team had worked on a business plan that outlined expenditures and income on a yearly basis, from the project's inception to the 'cruising speed' period in the mid-1990s.

---

6. A 'skunk works' project typically operated with a minimum budget and no real facilities.

The team reported regularly to the Executive Committee for major investment or expenditure decisions. It also presented a progress report to the New Model Committee on implementation issues. However, more important than the formal reporting were the team's meetings which Georges Salomon personally attended. In summing up his style, one individual commented: 'Georges Salomon isn't usually found behind his desk... he is more likely to be in the product-development lab... clomping around in ski boots and baggy sweater... doing what he likes best... devising ways to frustrate his competition.'[7] In order to answer all the probing questions that an anxious Georges Salomon inevitably asked, the team always had to be well prepared – an exercise which obviously took time. 'Se hâter lentement'[8] could have been the motto for this project.

The Concept Development

Between July 1985 and January 1987, Roger Pascal asked the team, which over time had progressively been enlarged, to systematically study all aspects of ski technology: measurements, the core, the sole, printing techniques, the spatula, edges, polishing, wax and so on. The mandate was for each team member to come up with 2 or 3 ideas for improving every aspect studied. The team leaders would meet regularly to review these ideas and seek ways to incorporate them into a concept. In fact, they succeeded in producing the first plaster model by the second semester of 1985.

The shape of the ski gradually emerged as a result of these systematic experiments. The team realized early on that little could be done to the shape of the sole, which had been already optimized over time to the point where skiers were accustomed to it. However, alternatives for the walls on both sides and for the surface of the ski could be considered. The team started to challenge the verticality of the side walls. Were they optimum? Could other settings be better? In a very creative fashion, they explored the various options: from being slanted outward to slanted inward. A closer examination revealed that the best solution was actually a progressive profile, with nearly vertical walls under the ski boots to provide an optimum grip where it was most needed, and side walls slanted inward to ensure optimum cutting into the snow at both extremes. These changes, in addition, had the required characteristics of being visible, one of the conditions set clearly by Georges Salomon (refer to **Exhibit 10**).

This initial idea naturally led to another important discovery: the side walls and surface of the ski should be made of a unique shell that would carry a major part of the stress. In conventional skis, the action of the skier passed from the steel edges through a succession of layers, particularly in the sandwich ski. This method of transmission was more indirect and resulted in less precision. The monocoque structure (the unique piece linking the surface to the edges) would thus provide a better control of the ski.

---

7. *Business Week*, April 19, 1989.
8. A French saying which means 'rushing slowly'.

The team was supplied with the best CAD system available in the industry at the time (ComputerVision and SUN Microsystems). The ideas were quickly converted into drawings in the engineering lab. Molds for prototypes were machined directly from the CAD system, which allowed them to create a large number of shapes for testing. By the middle of 1986, the first prototypes were available. They were tested in labs as well as on the snow, with test engineers and expert skiers, hired as consultants with a confidentiality agreement. The team at that time comprised around 35 people.

Several ideas for improving the manufacturing process were conceived. While most ski manufacturers applied composite material in a tacky state, the team found a new way to handle this step more satisfactorily. Yves Gagneux explored the 'dry process', which consisted of using fibers that had already been impregnated with resin and dried, which were therefore not only much easier to manipulate but had the additional advantage of not smelling strongly, as the 'wet process' did. It was expected that these enhanced working conditions would produce a much higher level of quality as well.

By November 1987, the engineering studies were providing interesting results. The team had developed a detailed understanding of the ski market. It knew the strengths and weaknesses of the best competitors. It had identified a long list of possible improvement areas. It had even singled out the particular areas where it wanted the new ski to make a difference. The prototypes that had been developed, through numerous trials and tests, were showing very promising potential.

The Decision

There were, of course, still a number of issues that needed to be clarified. In one sense, it was obvious that the team had done a good job, considering that the project had started from scratch in 1984. They had gone a long way towards the development of a radically new ski. Some of the detailed engineering still needed for the ski's final development was clearly going to be even more demanding. In order to proceed, the New Product Committee would have to release a budget for engineering work, testing and for the construction of a new plant. Given the technology required, some of it actually calling for custom-made equipment, the budget would amount to some FF300 million. As well, using a full-time team that would be expanded to 50 people would increase the operating costs.

The team's next challenge was to prepare a clear action plan for finalizing the development of Salomon's monocoque ski and launching it into the already crowded and mature ski market.

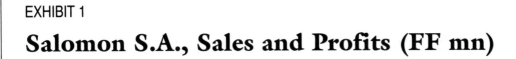

EXHIBIT 1

Salomon S.A., Sales and Profits (FF mn)

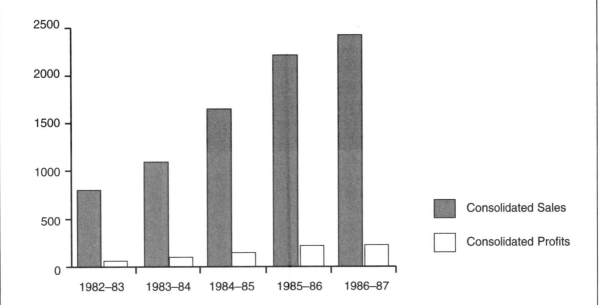

Source: Salomon S.A.

EXHIBIT 2

Growth of Sales and R&D Expenditures Index (1983–84 = 100)

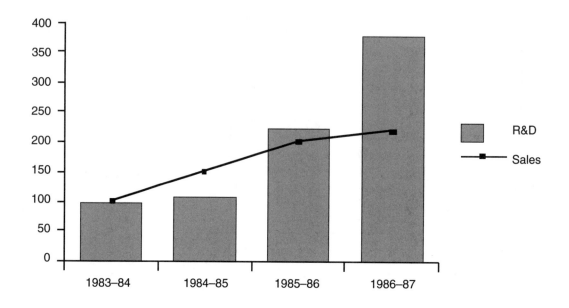

Source: Salomon S.A.

EXHIBIT 3

Salomon S.A., Five-Year Financial Summary

Financial Position	(Thousands of French Francs)				
Year ended March 31	1982/83	1983/84	1984/85	1985/86	1986/87
Net sales	817,170	1,109,263	1,666,277	2,220,686	2,241,770
Other revenues	8,656	22,182	19,462	25,200	21,307
Total revenues	825,826	1,131,445	1,685,739	2,245,886	2,443,077
Cost of sales-materials	(271,272)	(351,540)	(578,712)	(772,247)	(869,233)
Payroll expenses	(165,757)	(209,256)	(250,565)	(303,253)	(346,977)
Depreciation charge	(33,870)	(49,553)	(66,354)	(108,338)	(128,585)
Other operating expenses	(188,466)	(274,867)	(379,315)	526,268)	(569,116)
Operating profit	166,461	246,229	410,793	535,780	529,166
Interest expenses, net	(36,965)	(38,385)	(47,368)	(84,361)	(90,959)
Non-operating items	(10,383)	(10,487)	(38,124)	(36,759)	(79,407)
Pre-tax net income	119,113	197,357	325,301	414,660	358,800
Provision for income taxes	(53,700)	(96,651)	(156,655)	(197,625)	(135,637)
Net income	65,143	100,706	168,646	217,035	223,163
Cash and marketable securities	169,037	263,258	363,854	830,126	656,544
Accounts receivable	174,527	185,191	279,927	350,293	414,537
Inventories	158,951	260,536	381,093	562,221	601,505
Other current assets	37,382	157,758	58,414	77,719	195,184
Total current assets	539,897	866,743	1,083,288	1,820,359	1,877,770

EXHIBIT 3 (CONTINUED)

Financial Position	(Thousands of French Francs)				
Year ended March 31	1982/83	1983/84	1984/85	1985/86	1986/87
Property, plant and equipment, net	94,666	145,575	197,614	364,432	445,694
Other non-current assets	5,993	5,493	47,100	13,645	12,134
Total assets	640,556	1,017,811	1,328,002	2,198,436	2,325,598
Loans payable	108,893	300,230	302,329	646,597*	532,222*
Accounts payable and accrued expenses	326,462	300,943	381,830	498,495	568,546
Other liabilities	13,055	4,231	49,144	55,634	42,067
Shareholders' equity	192,146	412,407	594,699	997,710	1,182,763
Total liabilities and shareholders' equity	640,556	1,017,811	1,328,002	2,198,436	2,325,598

* Including capital lease obligations.

Source: Salomon Financial Annual Report 1987.

EXHIBIT 4

Ski Sales in the 1980s (millions of pairs)

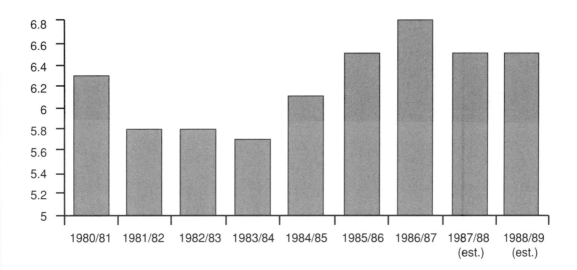

Source: Salomon S.A.

EXHIBIT 5

1986–87 Sales by Country (thousands of pairs)

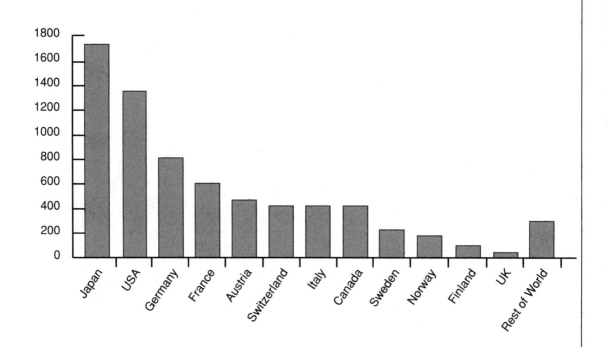

Source: Salomon S.A.

EXHIBIT 6

The Market Price Structure in the Ski Market

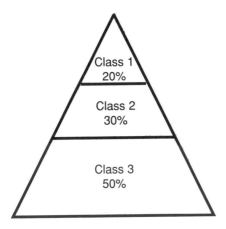

Conventional Market Price Structure

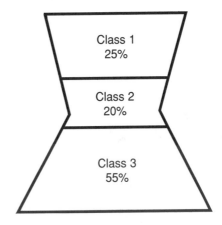

Ski Market in the late 1980s

Salomon Winter Sports Marketing Department defined three price-based segments: class 3 was the least expensive skis (roughly less than FF1,000), class 2 was medium-priced skis (1,000 to 2,000) and class 1 included the most expensive skis (2,000 to 3,000). FF3,000 or US$800 was considered the upper limit.

Source: Salomon S.A.

EXHIBIT 7

Sales by Manufacturers (thousands of pairs)

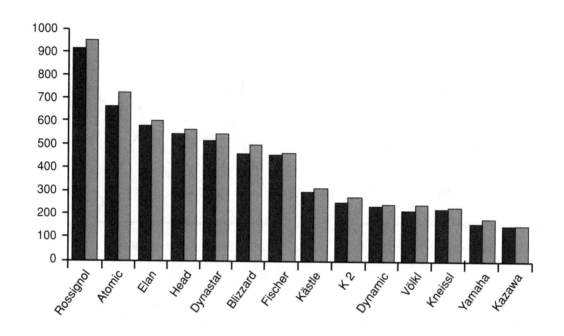

Source: Salomon S.A.

EXHIBIT 8

Types of Ski Structure

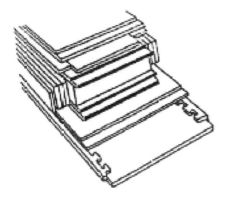

Sandwich Structure

Torsion Box Structure

Source: Salomon S.A.

EXHIBIT 9

The Ski Purchasing Process

The following table presents the distribution of answers to the question below asked to a sample of ski buyers:

What do you think is the best way to choose skis when buying them?

	Total	France	Germany	USA	Japan
1. Pick a brand with a good reputation	26	27	21	31	25
2. Select a brand you have already used	17	16	27	15	9
3. Listen to other people's advice	44	35	45	39	56
4. Be guided by a ski salesman	26	31	30	15	28
5. It is a personal decision. Choose the ski you like	16	12	5	19	26
6. Gather information, read reviews, study technical tests	20	14	23	23	18
7. Follow advice from ski instructors	8	12	8	4	7
8. Rent a ski and test it before buying	16	16	23	18	6
9. Pick the brand a champion uses	2	*	2	5	*
	1444	350	373	361	360

* Negligible

Source: Salomon S.A.

EXHIBIT 10

The Ski Concept: Progressive Profile

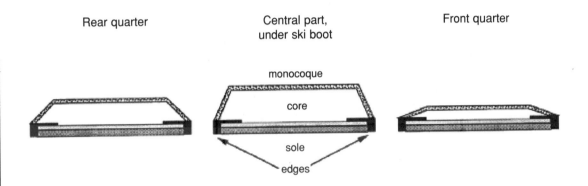

Rear quarter   Central part, under ski boot   Front quarter

monocoque

core

sole

edges

Note: Measurements are approximate.

Source: Salomon S.A.

CASE 2.6 Hong Kong & Shenzhen Bank (A)

This case was prepared by Professor Dominique Turpin of IMD and Giana Klaas of MSR. Names and data have been disguised to protect confidentiality.

On a rainy day in January 1993, Jian Cheng was sitting in her office on the 35th floor of one of the newly built towers facing the bay of Hong Kong. Jian had called a meeting with the management team of the International Trade Division of the Hong Kong & Shenzhen Bank to discuss what steps should be taken to improve the employees' motivation.

A report lying on Jian's desk gave the results of an internal survey, showing that 30% of the bank employees were unclear about their work objectives. Jian felt that if she could reduce this number, the gain for the bank could be substantial. During the last two weeks, Jian had visited several customers, Hong Kong Chinese as well as Western manufacturers who were struggling with similar issues. Several of her clients had turned to total quality programs. Others had started customer satisfaction campaigns as a way to enhance employee satisfaction. Jian had been struck by their enthusiasm. In one factory that she had visited recently, Jian had been surprised to see creative posters on the walls emphasizing customer satisfaction and the importance of the customer. After talking to colleagues both inside and outside the bank, Jian had been surprised to find out that their definition of customer service remained vague. Every employee and manager within the Hong Kong & Shenzhen Bank seemed to have a different definition of what an optimum level of customer service should be. While almost every manager was complaining about the increasing toughness of competition, Jian felt that improving employee satisfaction could help the bank in its search for new sustainable competitive advantages.

The Hong Kong & Shenzhen Bank

Hong Kong & Shenzhen Bank was a major Chinese commercial bank with headquarters in Hong Kong, and 162 subsidiaries in Hong Kong and other Asian countries. In 1992, the bank had 9,000 employees and had made a profit of US$272 million from a turnover of US$1.9 billion. The bank was organized around five divisions:

- **The Private Banking Division** managed the investment portfolio of wealthy Hong Kong residents and foreign customers.
- The **Business Banking Division** was in charge of loans to business firms.

- The **International Trade Division** took care of all banking operations dealing with foreign exchange, international credit and overseas businesses.
- The **Subsidiaries Division** managed all subsidiaries in charge of savings, loans and credits to the general public.
- The **Logistics Division** managed all the general services of the bank administration.

Jian Cheng

Jian Cheng, 42, had been in banking since graduating in Finance from the Chinese University of Hong Kong in 1973. Jian had joined the Hong Kong & Shenzhen Bank six years earlier and had had various experiences working in the different divisions of the bank in Hong Kong as well as in New York, London and Singapore. Six months previously, she had been transferred from the Hong Kong & Shenzhen Bank in Tokyo (Japan) to her new job in Hong Kong as general manager of the International Trade Division.

The Hong Kong & Shenzhen Bank's International Trade Division

The International Trade Division was divided into four departments:

- International Trade
- International Clients
- Letters of Credit
- Foreign Currency

The International Trade Department

This department was in charge of financing exports from Hong Kong as well as providing credit to Hong Kong firms with international activities. The head of this department, Bernard Chang, was responsible for evaluating financial risks, managing customers' files and approving letters of credit. His department was organized by cells. Each of the eight cells was run by a manager and his or her assistant. Each manager looked personally after the business of his or her assigned clients, ensuring follow-up on all business transactions and interfaces with the Letters of Credit and Foreign Currency departments.

The International Trade Department dealt with about 300 customers. The majority of customers in this department were small and medium-sized companies, engaged in international trade. Most of these firms were financially weak. Because of the risks involved with this type of activity, Jian Cheng kept a close eye on this department. Customers of the International Trade Department were of different cultures and nationalities: Chinese, British, American, and so on. The bank made contacts and followed them up mostly by phone. Each manager received an average of 12 calls per day and two or three calls per week from the same customer.

According to Bernard Chang, the definition of good service quality for the customers of his department was speed, friendliness and competence. Customers would visit the bank, ask for information and expect immediate answers to their problems, whether positive or negative. Customers also expected extra services such as obtaining privileged information – for example, locations where goods could be warehoused at a cheaper price. They would also expect to be put in touch with potential business partners.

In order to serve customers promptly, Mr Chang believed that the key success factors for customer service were:

- Smooth communication between the different departments of the Division and the Logistics Division of the bank
- Flexibility within the Foreign Currency Department. (Indeed, it was common that customers would call the bank for immediate transactions rather than make payments at a fixed date. Customers also often called outside the regular business hours.)
- State-of-the-art computers that could provide customers with instant information about their accounts and help the bank make a quick decision about whether or not to give credit
- An understanding of the customer's ethnic culture and needs.

The International Clients Department

This department dealt mainly with special credit conditions for private customers overseas. It also dealt with firms and accounts in fiscal paradises (such as Panama, the Cayman Islands, and so on) and credit services for banks with low liquid assets.

This department, headed by Annie Wong, worked closely with the Foreign Currency Department, the Letters of Credit, Leasing Services and the Accounting Departments. Much like the International Trade Department, the International Clients Department employees complained about the many operations they had to handle and the errors that resulted because of understaffing and overwork. Employees in this department worked mainly on the phone and rarely met customers.

The customers of this department were big multinational corporations that typically made 50% or more of their turnover overseas. These customers were more 'sophisticated' than those of the International Trade Department. The International Clients Department had about 50 customers. They tended to be extremely demanding clients who would not hesitate to call the bank to check at what time a fax had been sent. In Annie Wong's view, the key success factors for customer service were: speed and precision in information delivery.

The largest customers needed a careful follow-up on all their operations. They wanted better deals (typically lower commissions) and expected the bank to follow their orders blindly. They were also less loyal. As a result, Annie Wong's subordinates felt that these customers were less interesting for the bank. Consequently, the employee turnover in this department had traditionally been higher than in other departments.

The Letters of Credit Department

This department issued letters of credit, managed project financing for all kinds of firms, regardless of their size. The department was organized into two cells: the 'regular business cell' and the 'special affairs cell'. The first cell issued letters of credit for export businesses. The second dealt with letters of credit in which foreign manufacturers were involved. This department was managed by Ying-Ming Yeh and Charlie Wang. Their offices were next to each other, one floor above their 16 subordinates. The 'special affairs cell' was organized differently from the 'regular business cell'. In the former, new customers' files would arrive in a box located at the entrance to the office. In the morning, employees in the 'special affairs cell' would pick up a file (either at random or they would take one that looked interesting). Charlie Wang felt that this process could be handled differently so that employees would be more motivated and flexible.

The Foreign Currency Department

This department had two main activities. First, it dealt with currency arbitrations for the bank; and second, it fulfilled customers' orders. The first activity was managed by a team of four young managers, each specializing in a particular currency. One key requirement for doing this job was being fast and using efficient computer systems. Six brokers were responsible for the second activity. These two teams were in touch with customers almost exclusively by phone. Since exchange rates changed by the minute, speed was the key success factor in this business. The employees in this department worked independently and, in Jian's view, lacked team spirit.

The Next Steps

Jian Cheng was managing one of the bank's highest performing divisions. Jian's division was also perceived internally as one of the most customer-orientated divisions. However, Jian believed in the philosophy that 'Good can always be made better'. She was wondering how she could increase her staff's motivation while, at the same time, turn the International Trade Division into a customer-driven organization. Should she start with the employees or the customers? Jian was particularly concerned about any potentially negative reaction from the staff. At all costs, she wanted to avoid such comments as: 'Here comes another "great idea" from the boss.' 'We have gone through quality service issues before and they didn't work. Why should it work this time?' Jian knew that she could count on the support of Harry Lee, Executive Vice-President of the Bank, but what about her own staff?

A week before, Jian Cheng had attended a board meeting of the bank. The President of the bank, Kenneth Tan, had emphasized his goals for the next three years. He particularly emphasized that he wanted the bank to become the industry leader in customer service. Each subsidiary had been given 'carte blanche' to achieve this objective. The only constraint imposed by Mr Tan was that each subsidiary must focus first on internal quality – namely, improve the motivation of its staff. Harry Lee, the Vice-President to whom Jian Cheng reported, asked Mr Tan to set up a Quality Committee to improve customer service. The team consisted of Peter Lim, manager in charge of training, Chuck Li, a trainer, David Chan, head of personnel, Paul Jiao, assistant manager and Jian Cheng herself. The team had to decide on the following key issues:

- What steps should be taken to improve employees' motivation?
- How could the division become more quality-orientated?
- Should the team work exclusively inside the Division or include members of other divisions?
- Should the team be extended to include other members of the organization?
- When should the quality program start?

EXHIBIT 1

Organization Chart of the Hong Kong & Shenzhen Bank

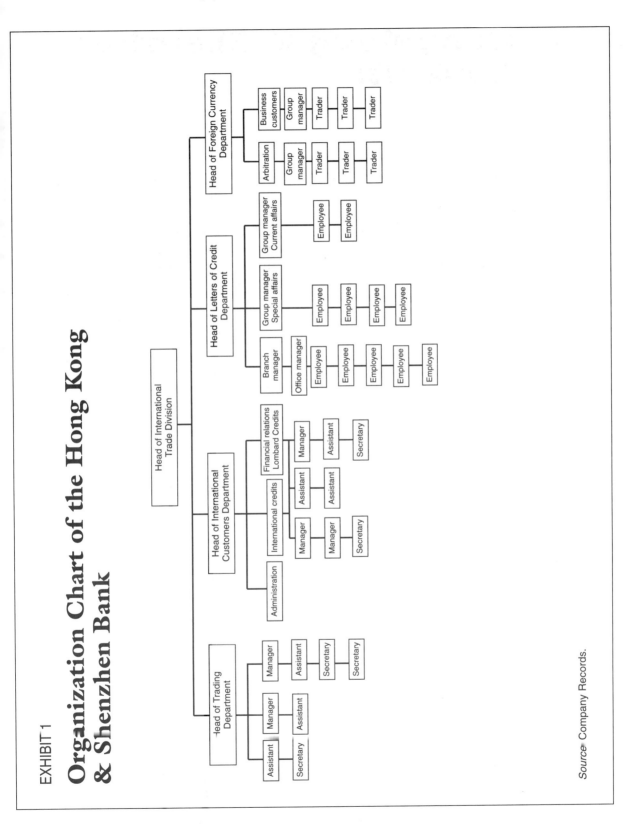

Source: Company Records.

CASE 2.6 Hong Kong & Shenzhen Bank (B)

This case was prepared by Professor Dominique Turpin of IMD and Giana Klaas of MSR. Names and data have been disguised to protect confidentiality.

Following the initiatives taken by Jian Cheng in January 1993, the Hong Kong & Shenzhen Bank decided that the International Trade Division would serve as the test ground for its quality movement. In the meantime, the Quality Committee members met on a monthly basis after work to discuss quality issues, employees' motivation and customer service. After four months of internal debate on how to proceed, very little action had taken place. Jian felt the reason was linked to a lack of experience in quality control management. The committee decided to call in an external consultant, Charlie Yu, for advice on how results could be achieved. Mr Yu was part of MSR, a leading consulting firm specializing in customer service with offices in London, Paris, New York, Tokyo, Singapore and Hong Kong. In November 1993, Charlie Yu made an initial presentation to the members of the bank's quality committee. He suggested that the quality movement start by looking at the customers' needs. It was essential, he stated, to understand the customers' expectations in order to work on the gap between expectations and actual delivery of the bank's services.

Following Mr Yu's presentation, a heated discussion took place. This approach was not what Jian Cheng had had in mind. She was convinced that the quality program should start by improving the motivation of the employees. Jian Cheng immediately referred to a recent internal survey which clearly indicated that morale among the staff was low:

> Employees in the different departments of this division are too independent. There is no team spirit. Look at the conclusions of this survey: 25–30% of our employees are unclear about their work objectives. If we can reduce this amount to 10%, it would be a major achievement. A more highly motivated spirit among the staff will result in better work output and thus greater customer satisfaction.

Mr Yu counter-argued that motivated people would certainly try to do a better job but not necessarily the job customers wanted. Jian was puzzled. Mr Yu persisted in asking the same questions again and again:

- Who are your customers?
- Why are they using the services of your bank?

Copyright © 1995 by **IMD** – International Institute for Management Development, Lausanne, Switzerland. Not to be used or reproduced without written permission from **IMD**.

222

- How do you differentiate yourself from the competition?
- What's unique about this bank?
- Do you know your customers?
- Do they get consistent service every time they set foot into one of your branches, whether in Hong Kong or Macao?

For Jian, the answers to these questions were so obvious. 'Of course, we know our customers! Of course, they get what they want!' Mr Yu was not convinced; he wanted to hear some real facts. Tension between Jian Cheng and Charlie Yu reached a high peak, but Mr Yu would not give up. He continued to elicit more specific arguments from Jian, but then always returned to the same conclusion – that motivated employees would certainly do a better job but would they be able to deliver what the customer really wanted? The meeting ended there. Over the next two weeks, Charlie Yu did not hear from Jian Cheng.

Therefore, Charlie Yu was rather surprised when Jian Cheng called him a few weeks later to announce, 'I have thought about what you were saying the other day. Let's give it a try. Let's put the customer at the center of our concern.'

Meeting with the Staff

A week later, Mr Yu was back at the Hong Kong & Shenzhen Bank to make a second presentation on customer service to all the employees of the International Trade Division. In the meantime, Jian Cheng had allocated the equivalent of US$350,000 to a fund called the 'Customer Care Project' – a pioneer project being sponsored by the bank in her division. Since employees at the front desk probably handled less than 30% of the services to the bank's customers, Jian Cheng also invited all the employees working in the back-office to attend Mr Yu's presentation. Employees of the Logistics Division had also been invited to join. To Jian's surprise, almost everybody working in this division came to the meeting. Employees in this division were flattered to receive Jian's invitation. As one of them told Jian, staff members felt that it meant that they were considered as not mere 'accessories' but key players in the customer–supplier chain. However, the feedback received informally after Mr Yu's presentation to the staff was rather mixed. Many employees were skeptical about the idea of putting the customer at the center of the bank's concerns. They needed to be convinced about the benefits that this project could produce. In the last three years, other quality projects had been launched without much success. The comments that Jian Cheng had not wanted to hear were already beginning to spread: 'This is just another "great idea" from the boss... time will kill it.'

Analyzing the market

Having come to an agreement with Jian Cheng and the other members of the Quality Committee, Mr Yu prepared the first steps of the quality program: an analysis of the bank's customers. He proceeded to take the following steps:

1. Research and analyze customers' expectations regarding the bank's services (quality perceived by the customers).
2. Measure the satisfaction level of the clients of the International Trade Division.
3. Measure staff's sensitivity to customer service.

The aim of the first survey was to generate customers' input on what services were needed (not reflecting specifically on the Hong Kong & Shenzhen Bank's present offering). In-depth interviews with customers were non-directed. Mr Yu scheduled 15 interviews – of about one hour each – to gather qualitative input from customers.

The purpose of the second survey was to measure the satisfaction level of the clients of the International Trade Division – based on a representative sample of customers. This survey was conducted by mailing a questionnaire to every Division customer. A letter signed by Jian Cheng explaining the objective of the survey was included with the questionnaire. A reminder letter was also prepared by Jian Cheng to be sent two weeks later – in order to increase the response rate.

The third survey intended to measure the staff's sensitivity to customer service and identify the essential components of service quality to the clients. Interviews conducted with the staff focused on the employee's definition of:

- his or her particular job
- his or her concept of quality
- customers and client segmentation
- customers' expectations
- the essential elements required to ensure customer service
- what was actually being done to satisfy present customers
- reasons for errors, the significance of the delays to correct them and do the job right.

The surveys would indicate what services the bank's customers were currently receiving and would contrast them with the customers' expectations, so that steps could be taken to fill the potential gap between the two.

Before launching the surveys, Mr Yu suggested communicating the objective of the project to the staff in a totally transparent manner. Posters explaining the different steps of the project were placed on the walls. The mission statement was visible everywhere: 'Our goal is to achieve the highest customer service level in the industry.' As well, memos were distributed regularly to explain the different steps of the project and their execution.

CASE 2.6 **Hong Kong and Shenzhen Bank (C)**

This case was prepared by Professor Dominique Turpin of IMD and Giana Klaas of MSR. Names and data have been disguised to protect confidentiality.

The following summarizes the findings of the surveys undertaken by the consulting company MSR on behalf of the International Trade Division of the Hong Kong & Shenzhen Bank.

Steps of the International Trade Division Quality Project

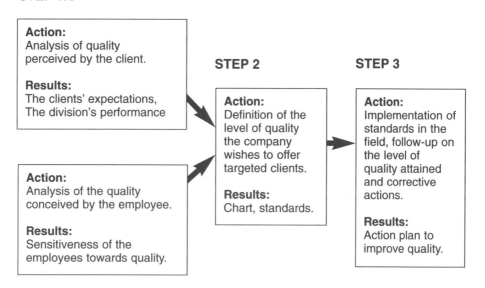

STEP 1A

Action:
Analysis of quality perceived by the client.

Results:
The clients' expectations,
The division's performance

STEP 2

Action:
Definition of the level of quality the company wishes to offer targeted clients.

Results:
Chart, standards.

STEP 3

Action:
Implementation of standards in the field, follow-up on the level of quality attained and corrective actions.

Results:
Action plan to improve quality.

Action:
Analysis of the quality conceived by the employee.

Results:
Sensitiveness of the employees towards quality.

STEP 1B

EXHIBIT 1

Step 1a: Summary of Clients' Expectations

This survey indicated that customers could be segmented into four categories – each with a different profile:

The 'Negotiators'

'Negotiators' were typically Chinese businessmen. To them, giving their word meant a strong moral obligation. They dealt with other business people throughout the world. To be accepted by the 'Negotiators', the bank had to understand their particular business and their needs. These customers expected the bank managers to pay a visit to their firm occasionally and even become part of the 'family'. 'Negotiators' personally took care of most transactions and wanted a smooth operation without last-minute 'surprises'. They were not interested in technical details. They preferred to delegate these functions to their banker – someone they could fully trust. 'Negotiators' expected their banker to:

- trust them and be trustworthy
- talk their language and understand their business
- be honest and practice fair play
- be a stable and unique contact
- take initiative
- be present when needed
- be flexible
- be discreet
- know their job and not waste the client's time.

The 'Entrepreneurs'

'Entrepreneurs' had a strong sense of 'financial opportunism'. They took a position quickly and wanted to be in control in any business situation. They knew the value of every HK dollar. Therefore, they needed constantly updated information about the dollar's performance in order to take decisions. 'Entrepreneurs' also needed flexibility and to have confidence in their suppliers. They considered their banker as a technical partner. In short, 'Entrepreneurs' expected:

- fast and reliable information in real time
- an open relationship with the bank
- audacity
- quick response time
- flexibility
- good prices and conditions.

EXHIBIT 1 (CONTINUED)

The 'Managers'

'Managers' loved systems, budgets and plans. They worked for a manufacturing company or the subsidiary of a large corporation. For them, good organization and trouble-free services were essential. They worked with suppliers they could trust. 'Managers' were less sensitive to price, provided that new services helped them increase productivity as well as the company's bottom line. 'Managers' were proud of their company, and so they wanted partners who would ensure that their identity was retained. What 'Managers' expected from their banker:

- optimal use of resources
- quick, trouble-free services
- competence
- honesty, confidence
- a single, stable contact at the bank
- a well-informed team
- speedy transactions
- information.

The 'Financiers'

'Financiers' worked in companies of sizable importance. They were well versed in financial management. For them, financial instruments were the critical elements of corporate success. 'Financiers' wished to participate directly in financial markets with or without the support of their bank. They wanted to be able to act fast. 'Financiers' were looking for partners who could take decisions and react very quickly. Simultaneously, they needed enough time to think and put things in perspective. 'Financiers' looked for advisors with a vision of where their markets were going. They strongly believed that banks offered a lot of pre-digested information with too much focus on the very short term. 'Financiers' needed analyzed information. They were also very interested in the latest developments in information technology and data systems. 'Financiers' expected the bank to provide:

- information with added value
- in real time
- a good knowledge of international business
- audacity
- good and flexible prices
- permanent mobilization
- a personal relationship with a team
- technological innovation and state-of-the-art financial products.

Source: Company Records.

EXHIBIT 2A

Step 1a: Division's Performance

Appraisal of the service quality of the International Trade Division departments by its external customers

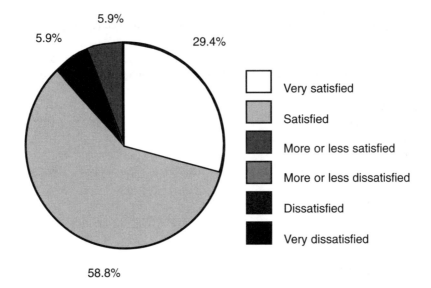

Level of external clients' satisfaction with the service performed by the International Trade Division compared to the competition

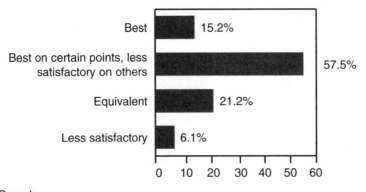

Source: Company Records.

EXHIBIT 2B

Step 1a: Division's Performance

External clients' satisfaction level with the service dimensions of the International Division

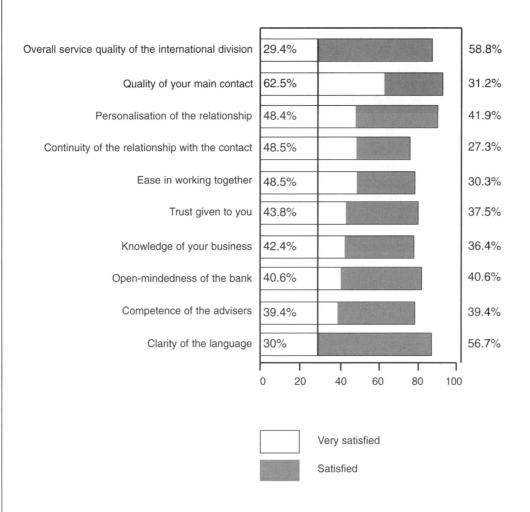

	Very satisfied	Satisfied
Overall service quality of the international division	29.4%	58.8%
Quality of your main contact	62.5%	31.2%
Personalisation of the relationship	48.4%	41.9%
Continuity of the relationship with the contact	48.5%	27.3%
Ease in working together	48.5%	30.3%
Trust given to you	43.8%	37.5%
Knowledge of your business	42.4%	36.4%
Open-mindedness of the bank	40.6%	40.6%
Competence of the advisers	39.4%	39.4%
Clarity of the language	30%	56.7%

Source: Company Records.

EXHIBIT 2C

Step 1a: Division's Performance

Appraisal of the service quality of the International Trade Division department by its external customers

Product quality	37%	3.7%
Employee initiative	38.7%	3.2%
Product diversity	42.3%	3.8%
Supply of market information	37%	14.8%
Boldness, imagination	37%	7.4%/7.4%
Product innovation	44%	8%
Possibility of training in the bank	33.3%	16.7%/4.2%
Pricing	40%	16.7%/10%/3.3%

☐ More or less satisfied

▨ More or less dissatisfied

▨ Dissatisfied

■ Very dissatisfied

Source: Company Records.

EXHIBIT 2D

Step 1a: Division's Performance

Appraisal of the service quality of the Hong Kong & Shenzhen Bank by its external customers

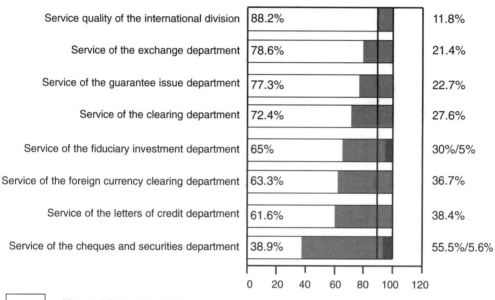

Service quality of the international division	88.2% ... 11.8%
Service of the exchange department	78.6% ... 21.4%
Service of the guarantee issue department	77.3% ... 22.7%
Service of the clearing department	72.4% ... 27.6%
Service of the fiduciary investment department	65% ... 30%/5%
Service of the foreign currency clearing department	63.3% ... 36.7%
Service of the letters of credit department	61.6% ... 38.4%
Service of the cheques and securities department	38.9% ... 55.5%/5.6%

0   20   40   60   80   100   120

☐ Very satisfied and satisfied

▨ More or less satisfied and more or less dissatisfied

■ Dissatisfied and very dissatisfied

External clients' reactions when dissatisfied

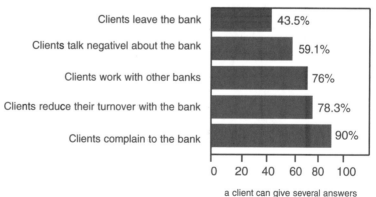

Clients leave the bank	43.5%
Clients talk negativel about the bank	59.1%
Clients work with other banks	76%
Clients reduce their turnover with the bank	78.3%
Clients complain to the bank	90%

0   20   40   60   80   100

a client can give several answers

Source: Company Records.

EXHIBIT 3A

Step 1b: Sensitiveness of the Employees Towards Quality

Summary of the internal qualitative study and survey

1. Employees see service quality for their clients as part of internal procedures, in order to give greater satisfaction.

   Satisfying the clients takes priority, with each one doing his best, however…

   - Employees confuse 'quality of work' with 'quality of service to clients'.
   - Work well done is perceived as conformity with the internal procedures rather than results for the client.
   - Employees think they understand the clients' needs, but frequently they do not. As well, they are satisfied to merely fulfill the needs expressed by the client, without looking further.
   - Taking initiative is important for a service leader, but most of them stay within the framework they have learned.
   - Employees in the back-office often feel isolated and that they are not participating in serving the client.

2. Employees see quality as accepting differences and working as a team.

   - Employees think that being a service leader means working as a team, while developing individual competences – being autonomous within a team framework.
   - Employees find their work interesting and motivating for the time being.
   - There is a good team spirit within each department but it is non-existent at the International Division level.
   - Everyone looks out for himself and blames the errors on others – the back-office is a convenient excuse for non-quality.
   - At all levels, employees feel a sort of internal segregation (the 'nobles', those in the bank, in the front and back-offices, and so on)
   - Education programs are perceived as too general and not related to either the service chain or attitudes and service behavior.
   - The existing management tools are not known and not mastered.

Source: Company Records.

EXHIBIT 3B

Step 1b: Sensitiveness of the Employees Towards Quality

Employees' satisfaction survey: reasons of satisfaction and dissatisfaction at work

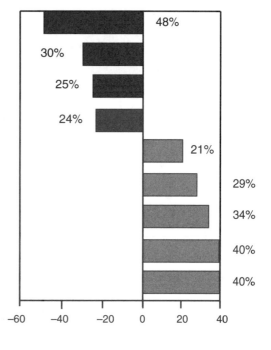

Very dissatisfied

Very satisfied

Source: Company Records.

EXHIBIT 3C

Step 1b: Sensitiveness of the Employees Towards Quality

Appraisal of the service quality of the International Trade Division departments by the different members of the Department

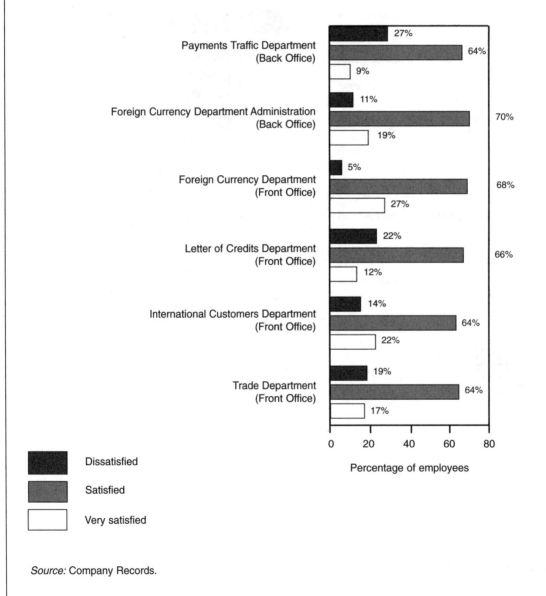

Source: Company Records.

EXHIBIT 3D

Step 1b: Sensitiveness of the Employees Towards Quality

Appraisal of the service quality of the International Trade Division departments by the Trade Department

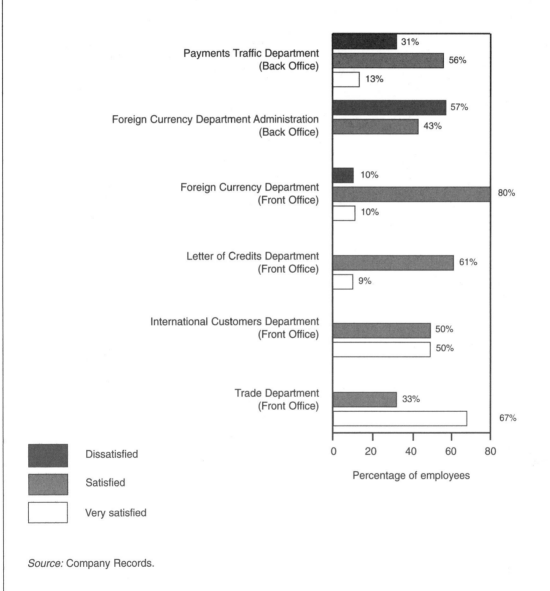

Source: Company Records.

EXHIBIT 3E

Step 1b: Sensitiveness of the Employees Towards Quality

Appraisal of the service quality of the International Trade Division departments by the International Customers Department

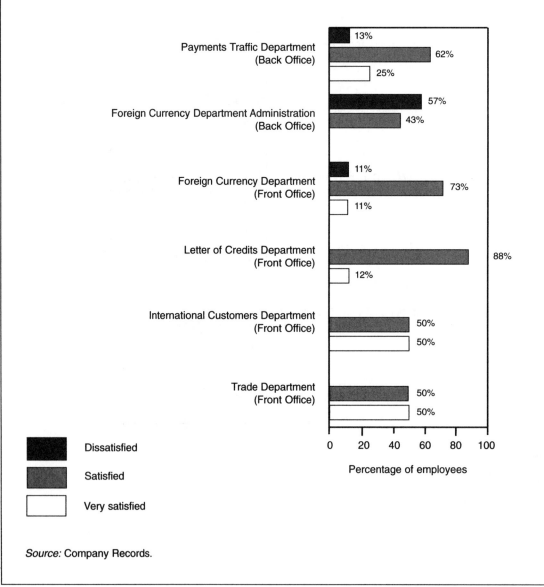

Source: Company Records.

EXHIBIT 3F

Step 1b: Sensitiveness of the Employees Towards Quality

Appraisal of the service quality of the International Trade Division departments by the Letters of Credit Department

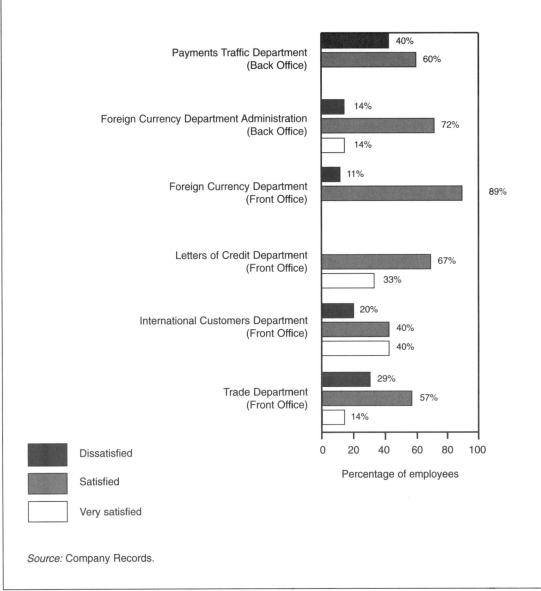

Source: Company Records.

EXHIBIT 3G

Step 1b: Sensitiveness of the Employees Towards Quality

Appraisal of the service quality of the International Trade Division departments by the Foreign Currency Department

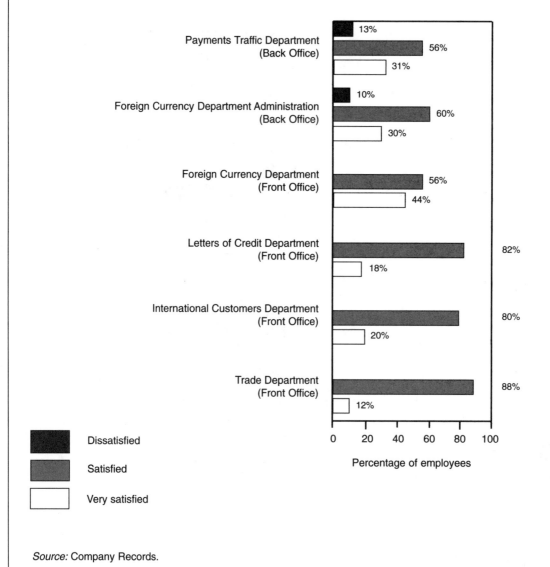

Source: Company Records.

EXHIBIT 3H

Step 1b: Sensitiveness of the Employees Towards Quality

Appraisal of the service quality of the International Trade Division departments by the Foreign Currency Administration Department

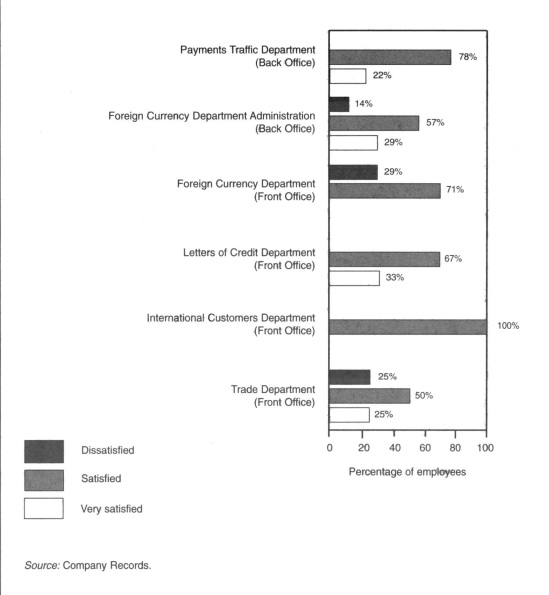

Source: Company Records.

EXHIBIT 3I

Step 1b: Sensitiveness of the Employees Towards Quality

Appraisal of the service quality of the International Trade Division departments by the Payments Traffic Department

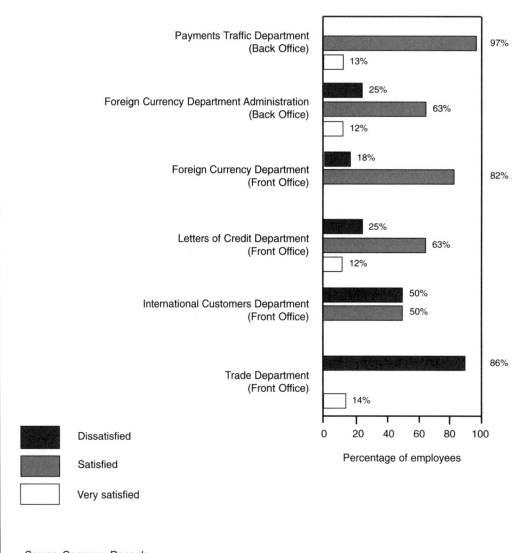

Source: Company Records.

CASE 2.6 **Hong Kong & Shenzhen Bank (D)**

This case was prepared by Professor Dominique Turpin of IMD and Giana Klaas of MSR. Names and data have been disguised to protect confidentiality.

In January 1994, Jian Cheng was invited to present the results of the progress made by the International Trade Division to the top management of the Hong Kong & Shenzhen Bank. Jian's presentation of the internal and external surveys generated mixed reactions. Jian explained that the next steps for the International Trade Division were: first, to communicate the results of the survey to all internal staff; second, to establish teams to analyze the survey and provide recommendations along with a calendar for implementation; and third, to establish a charter for customer service as well as working norms. 'Oh, that's too technical!' one senior Vice President complained. 'What you have to do is change the mentalities.' Another executive commented, 'In five years, we'll have great people but no more customers.' A third senior executive made it clear that he thought it had been a mistake to ask an outside consultant to work on this problem. 'We have all the expertise inside,' he said. 'There's no need to have outsiders looking into our problems.' Kenneth Tan, the President of the bank, had remained silent during the whole presentation. He had listened to the different arguments around the table without showing any emotion. Finally, Mr Tan spoke up: 'I think that we should support Jian's initiative. Other divisions have been working on this same issue, but none of them has set priorities, the way Jian has.'

Jian Cheng was also wondering how to proceed with the quality charter. The charter had to be unique and inspiring for the staff. According to Mr Yu, the charter was the expression of the bank's will to offer uncompromising service to customers. The charter had to give direction and define the bank's strategy. It should also help the bank differentiate itself from the competition. In order to see some examples, Mr Yu gave Jian Cheng copies of charters containing quality statements from several leading international firms (refer to **Exhibit 1**). Then, Jian Cheng and her team were ready to meet the challenge of preparing a quality charter that would reflect the bank's values and commitment to its customers. In March 1994, Jian Cheng and the heads of the International Trade Division Departments defined the service strategy or chart of the International Trade Division, based on customers' expectations. They had defined the chart after three workshops. Jian Cheng was happy with the result (refer to **Exhibit 2**). Customers who were consulted about the validity of the chart had provided the team with very positive feedback.

The next step was to translate the strategy or chart into operational terms: the norms. Four groups of employees from the International Trade Division began fixing quality norms. The groups worked once a week, from 6 to 8 pm over a period of four weeks. However, after two weeks, the two workshops had made very little progress. The four groups had been unable to reach a consensus. In Jian Cheng's mind, the problem was that the staff did not understand the purpose of the workshops. A member of the team had confessed to Jian Chen that he did not consider the procedure 'real', but rather considered it 'a nice intellectual exercise'. However, Jian Cheng felt that the bank's strategy must be established in a charter and then translated into operational terms. As well, the level of service rendered would have to be measured if it were to be improved. 'This is the same technique used in industry to measure the number of defective pieces,' Jian Cheng explained.

A whole year had passed since Jian Cheng had decided to improve employees' motivations. Although the groups had lost confidence when the other employees could not see any real results, Jian Cheng remained convinced that improved customer service was the key to success for the bank.

EXHIBIT 1

Examples of Company Charters

British Telecom (UK)

We put our customers first.
We are professionals.
We respect each other.
We work as a team.
We are committed to continuous improvement.

Kao (Japan)

Consumer trust is Kao's most valued asset.
We believe that Kao is unique in that our primary emphasis is neither profit nor competitive positioning. Instead our goal is to increase consumer satisfaction through useful, innovative products that meet real market needs. A commitment to consumers will continue to guide all our corporate decisions.

Source: Company Records.

EXHIBIT 2

The Hong Kong & Shenzhen Bank's Quality Chart

- We aim to be our customers' favorite banking partner.
- We deal with our customers in their own language.
- We welcome all new business.
- We give our customers a direct answer or propose a satisfactory solution.
- We share our excellent know-how in banking with all our customers.
- We handle customers' orders promptly.
- We provide our customers with an original and viable approach to banking.
- We maintain a relationship of mutual confidence with our customers that is lasting and trouble-free.

Source: Company Records.

Hong Kong and Shenzhen Bank (E)

This case was prepared by Professor Dominique Turpin of IMD and Giana Klaas of MSR. Names and data have been disguised to protect confidentiality.

Mr Yu of MSR suggested that Jian Cheng herself take over the work of the four groups and define the norms, using only the department chiefs. According to the consultant, having conviction and believing in the visible implications was what the project needed to succeed.

It was then decided that Jian Cheng would proceed as Mr Yu proposed. Several norms were defined. It was thus appropriate that Jian Cheng should continue to manage the following workshop on quality norms – with Mr Yu and MSR working behind the scenes with her. Six months later, the working groups had produced the quality norms. For example:

1. Clients are assured that the bank's handling of their business will be faultless.
2. Clients are always offered a service adapted to their individual needs.
3. Clients always feel that the Division is interested in their affairs and are sure that the bank will defend their interests.
4. Clients always deal with a counsellor who is well informed about their business affairs.
5. Clients can always express themselves (and be understood) in one of the world's major commercial languages.

Once the norms were defined, real measures then had to be implemented – namely, to improve the services so that they met the level fixed by the norms. Decisions had to be made about how to put these norms in place and what procedure should be adopted. The staff decided to implement the norms at the rate of one per month: each head of department had to present the norm to his staff, solicit ideas for improving the service and reach the level of quality fixed by the norms. Then, Jian Cheng and the heads of the International Trade Division Departments met once a month to decide on which idea to implement. Jian Cheng felt that soliciting ideas from the staff was a huge success – 120 different suggestions were given for the first norm. The collection process was accompanied by a communication campaign that included graphic illustrations of the norm being implemented as well as information about the suggestions received and put in practice. The intent was to demonstrate to the staff that the management was actually using their ideas and rapidly putting them into practice.

For Norm 5, 'Clients can always express themselves (and be understood) in one of the world's major commercial languages', it soon became evident that one barrier to implementation was the staff's lack of fluency in foreign languages. Therefore, lessons were provided which successfully improved language capability, a fact that was noted and appreciated by several clients.

For other issues, interdepartmental or even interdivisional working groups were set up. For Norm 4, 'Clients always deal with a counsellor who is well informed about their business affairs', follow-up tended to be poor whenever the counsellor was changed. Consequently, a group was set up to find ways to ensure a smooth transition between counsellors.

The last stage was to establish indicators for each norm that measured the quality level and observed the progress being made. They also had to determine the method to be used for collecting and centralizing the data, as well as communicating it. To address this issue, a preliminary analysis of all the existing data and statistics in-house was conducted. The objective of this task was to avoid unnecessary duplication.

For Norm 1, 'Clients are assured that the bank's handling of their business will be faultless', Jian Cheng felt that it was relatively easy to define indicators and corrective steps – the first indicator chosen was the percentage of badly executed orders. They began by preparing a list of existing customer complaints. Managers then wrote down a short report each time a client had a problem. Complaints concerning badly handled orders were added to those particular statistics and then were submitted to the Foreign Currency department for correction. This system enabled them to learn, based on the number of customer complaints received after the norms were established, that the majority of the problems concerned the Foreign Currency department. Thus, the Foreign Currency department was ordered to centralize all data in order to intercept and correct errors more easily, and to show them once a month to the division chief.

Jian Cheng felt that it was more difficult to address Norm 2, 'Clients are always offered a service adapted to their individual needs'. After giving it some thought, it was decided to measure this norm by appraising the clients' satisfaction through monthly surveys.

CASE 2.6 Hong Kong and Shenzhen Bank (F)

This case was prepared by Professor Dominique Turpin of IMD and Giana Klaas of MSR. Names and data have been disguised to protect confidentiality.

In September 1994, Jian Cheng was proud of the results achieved. Profits per client had increased substantially, poor quality had diminished, and morale was up! Two years after implementing the program on quality service, the badly handled orders had decreased by more than half. Clients were regularly congratulating employees for the improvements (listening more, greater attention and stronger efforts to resolve their problems). Team spirit among employees of the International Trade Division was greatly enhanced, and the turnover was lower. After creating the inter-departmental working groups, cooperation among the different departments also improved considerably.

A few months later, Jian Cheng was promoted to a new job at the bank headquarters, and Kenneth Tan, the President, decided to follow up by extending the experience to the other divisions of the group.

However, Jian Cheng was somewhat concerned about the future of the International Trade Division. Would her successor have the interest and the motivation to keep the customer satisfaction momentum going? Would her successor have her same commitment? Was she being overly emotional or committed about her success?

Computron Inc., 1994

This case has been revised by Professor Dominique Turpin. The original version, entitled Computron Inc., was written by Professor Ralph Z. Sorenson. The names of all individuals and companies have been disguised

In January 1994, Mr Thomas Zimmermann, manager of the East European Sales Division of Computron Inc., was preparing his bid to sell a 1000X computer to Slavisky & Cie., Poland's largest chemical company. The decision facing him was deciding how to determine the appropriate price for this computer. If Mr Zimmermann were to follow Computron's standard pricing policy of adding a 33⅓% mark-up to factory costs, and then including transportation costs and import duty, the bid he would submit would amount to US$155,600. Mr Zimmermann was afraid that a bid of this magnitude would not be low enough to win the contract for Computron.

Four other computer manufacturers had been invited by Slavisky to submit bids for the contract. Mr Zimmermann had received information from what he considered to be a 'reliable trade source', indicating that at least one of these four competitors was planning to name a price around $109,000. Computron's usual price of $155,600 would be $46,600 – that is, 43% – higher than the competitor's price. In conversations with Salvisky's vice-president of purchasing, Mr Zimmermann had been led to believe that Computron's chances of winning the contract depended on its bid being no more than 20% higher than that of the lowest competitor. As Slavisky was Computron's most important Polish customer, Mr Zimmermann was particularly concerned about this contract and was wondering what strategy to use in pricing his bid. The deadline for submitting bids was February 1, 1994.

Background on Computron and Its Products

Computron Inc. was an American firm which had, in the summer of 1988, opened a sales office in Vienna, Austria, with Mr Zimmermann as its manager. The company's main product, both in Western and Eastern Europe, was the 1000X computer.

Although it could be considered a general purpose computer, the Computron 1000X – which sold in the medium price range – was designed primarily for solving specific engineering problems. Ordinarily, it found its basic applications in chemical companies, public utilities, and areas of nuclear engineering. In these fields, it was typically used to solve problems of chemical process control, and design and control of power plants and nuclear reactor stations.

During the first six months after its opening, the Austrian sales office did only about $550,000 worth of business. In 1993, however, sales increased sharply, to reach a total for the year of $2,500,000. Computron's total worldwide sales for that same year were roughly $22,000,000. Of the Eastern European countries, Poland constituted one of Computron's most important markets, having contributed $600,000 – or 24% – of the Eastern European sales total in 1993. Hungary and the Czech Republic were likewise important markets, having contributed 22% and 18%, respectively, to the 1993 total. The remaining 36% of sales was spread over the rest of Europe.

The Computron computers sold to European customers were manufactured and assembled in Austria, then shipped to Eastern Europe for installation. Because of their external manufacture, these computers were subject to an import duty. The amount of this tariff varied from country to country. The Polish tariff on computers of the type sold by Computron was 17½% of the imported sales price.

Prompted primarily by a desire to reduce this import duty, Computron was constructing a plant near Warsaw, Poland. This plant, which would serve all the Eastern European Common Market, was scheduled for opening on March 15, 1994. Initially, it was to be used only for the assembly of 1000X computers. Assembly in Poland would lower the import duty from 17½% to 15%. Ultimately, the company planned to used the plant for the fabrication of component parts as well.

The new plant was to occupy 10,000 square feet and would employ 20–30 people in the first year. The initial yearly overhead for this plant was expected to be approximately $150,000. As of January 1994, the Eastern European sales office still had no contracts for the new plant to work on, although it was anticipated that training the employees and assembling/installing a pilot model 1000X computer in the new plant could keep the plant busy for two or three months after it opened. Mr Zimmermann was somewhat concerned about the possible risk that the new plant might have to sit idle after these first two or three months unless Computron could win the present Slavisky contract.

Company Pricing Policy

Computron had always concentrated on being the quality 'preferred' company in its segment of the process control computer industry. The company prided itself on manufacturing what it considered to be the best all-around computer of its kind in terms of precision, dependability, flexibility, and ease of operation.

Computron did not try to sell the 1000X on the basis of price. The price charged by Computron was very often higher than that being charged for competing equipment. In spite of this fact, the superior quality of Computron's computers had, to date, enabled the company to compete successfully both in Western and Eastern Europe.

The Austrian price for the 1000X computer was normally figured as follows:

Austria 'cost'   (Includes factory cost and factory overhead)

plus

Mark-up of 33⅓% on 'cost'   (To cover profit, research and development

                                                 allowances, and selling expenses)

Transportation and installation costs

plus

Importation duty

_____

Total Eastern European price

Prices calculated by the above method tended to vary slightly because of the country-to-country difference in tariffs and the difference in components between specific computers.[1] In the case of the present Slavisky application, Mr Zimmermann had calculated that the 'normal' price for the 1000X computer would be $155,600. (**Exhibit 1** shows these calculations.)

The 33⅓% mark-up on cost used by the company was designed to provide a before-tax profit margin of 15%, a research and development allowance of 10%, and a selling and administrative expense allowance of 8%. The stated policy of top management was clearly against cutting this mark-up in order to obtain sales. Management felt that the practice of cutting prices 'not only reduced profits, but also reflected unfavorably on the company's quality image'. Mr Zimmermann knew that Computron's president was especially eager not to cut prices at this particular moment, as Computron's overall profit before taxes had been only 6% of sales in 1993 (compared to 17% in 1992). Consequently, the president had stated that he not only wanted to try to maintain the 33⅓% mark-up on cost, he was in fact eager to raise it.

In spite of Computron's policy of maintaining prices, Mr Zimmermann was aware of a few isolated instances when the mark-up on cost had been dropped to around 25% in order to obtain important orders in the UK. He was, for example, aware of one instance in France when the mark-up had been cut to 20%. In the Eastern European market, however, Computron had never yet deviated from the policy of maintaining a 33⅓% mark-up on cost.

The Customer

Slavisky and Cie. was one of the largest manufacturers and processors of basic chemicals and chemical products in Poland. It operated a number of chemical plants located throughout the country. To date, it had purchased three digital computer systems, all from Computron. The three systems had been bought during 1993 and

_____

1. Depending on the specific application in question, the components of the 1000X varied slightly so that each machine was somewhat different from the rest.

had represented $500,000 worth of business for Computron. Thus, Slavisky was Computron's largest customer and had alone constituted over 80% of Computron's 1993 sales to Poland.

Mr Zimmermann felt that the primary reason Slavisky had purchased Computron computer systems in the past was because of their proven reputation for flexibility, accuracy, and overall high quality. So far, Slavisky officials seemed very pleased with the performance of their Computron computers.

Looking ahead, Mr Zimmermann felt that Slavisky would continue to represent more potential future business than any other single Polish customer. He estimated that, during the next year or two, Slavisky would have a need for another $500,000 worth of digital computer equipment.

The computer for Slavisky currently being bid on was to be used for training the operators of a new chemical plant. The training program would last approximately four to five years. At the end of the program, the computer would either be scrapped or converted for other uses. The calculations which the computer would need to perform were highly specialized and would therefore not require much machine flexibility. In the specifications, which had been published with the invitation to bid, Slavisky management had stated that their primary interest in selecting a computer would be dependability and a reasonable price. Machine flexibility and pinpoint accuracy were listed as being of very minor importance, since the machine would mostly be used for training purposes rather than design work.

Competition

In the Polish market, approximately nine companies were competing with Computron in the sale of medium-priced computers designed to perform scientific and engineering work. Four companies accounted for 80% of industry-wide sales in 1993. (**Exhibit 2** shows a breakdown of sales for these companies over one year.) Mr Zimmermann was primarily concerned about the competition offered by the following companies:

Ruhr Maschinenfabrik A.G.

This very aggressive Austrian company was trying hard to expand its share of the market in Poland. Ruhr sold a medium quality, general purpose machine at a price which was roughly 22½% lower than Computron charged for its 1000X computer. Of this price differential, 17½% was because there was no import duty on the Ruhr machine, which was entirely manufactured in Poland. Although, to date, Ruhr had sold only general purpose computers, reliable trade sources indicated that the company was currently developing a special computer in an effort to win the Slavisky bid. The price that Ruhr intended for this special purpose computer was reported to be around $109,000.

Elektronische Datenverarbeitungsanlagen A.G.

This German company had recently developed a general purpose computer that was comparable in quality to Computron's 1000X. Mr Zimmermann felt that Elektronische Datenverarbeitungsanlagen presented a real long-range threat to Computron's position in the industry. In order to gain a foothold in the industry, the company had sold its first computer 'almost at cost'. Since that time, however, it had undersold Computron only by an amount equal to the import duty on Computron's computers.

Digitex

This local firm had complete manufacturing facilities in Poland which could produce a wide line of computer equipment. The quality of the Digitex computer that competed with the Computron 1000X was only fair. Digitex often engaged in price-cutting tactics; in fact, the price of its computer had sometimes been even 50% lower than what Computron charged for its 1000X. Despite this difference, Computron had usually been able to compete successfully against Digitex because of the technical superiority of the 1000X.

Mr Zimmermann was not overly concerned about the remaining competitors, as he did not consider them to be significant in Computron's segment of the computer industry.

The Polish Market for Medium-priced Computers

The total estimated Polish market for medium-priced computers of the type manufactured by Computron was currently around $2,000,000 per year. Mr Zimmermann thought that this market could be expected to increase at an annual rate of about 25% for the next several years. For 1994, he was already aware of confirmed specific new business worth about $650,000 (broken down as follows):

Slavisky & Cie.

Warsaw plant	US$150,000
Pruszkow plant	125,000
Gdansk plant	75,000
Central Power Commission	220,000
Polish Autowerk	80,000
Total	**US$650,000**

This business was in addition to the computer for Slavisky's new experimental pilot plant. None of the business already confirmed was expected to materialize until late spring or early summer.

Deadline for Bids

In light of these various facts and considerations, Mr Zimmermann was wondering what price to place on the bid for the Slavisky contract. The deadline for submitting bids to Slavisky was February 1, 1994. Since this date was less than two weeks away, he knew he would have to reach a decision some time within the next few days.

EXHIBIT 1

Estimated Price for the 1000X Computer for the Slavisky Experimental Pilot Plant based on 'Usual' Calculations

Factory Cost	$96,000
33⅓% Mark-up on Cost	32,000
Austrian List Price	128,000
Import Duty (15% of Austrian List Price)	19,200
Transportation and Installation	8,400
Total 'Usual' Price	$155,600

Source: Company Records.

EXHIBIT 2

1993 Market Share for Companies Selling Medium-priced Computers to the Polish Market (US$)

Estimated Sales Volume		
Computron Inc.	$600,000	30.0%
Ruhr Maschinenfabrik A.G.	400,000	20.0%
Elektronische Datenverarbeitungsanlagen A.G.	250,000	12.5%
Digitex	350,000	17.5%
Six Other Companies (combined)	400,000	20.0%
Total	$2,000,000	100.0%

Source: Company Records.

CASE 2.8ᴿ Pharma Swede: Gastirup

This case was prepared by Professor Kamran Kashani, with the assistance of Research Associates Robert C. Howard and Janet Shaner. This case was developed with the cooperation of a company that wishes to remain anonymous. As a result, certain names, figures and facts have been modified.

Bjorn Larsson, advisor to the president and the head of Product Pricing and Government Relations for Pharma Swede, in Stockholm, Sweden, was reviewing the expected consequences of future European Union (EU) regulatory changes on Gastirup in Italy. Gastirup was a drug for the treatment of ulcers. Since its introduction in Italy six years ago, this innovative product had achieved considerable success in its category of gastrointestinal drugs. However, the success had come as a result of pricing the drug at a significant discount below the prevailing prices for the same product in the rest of Europe. Higher prices would have disqualified Gastirup from the government reimbursement scheme, the system by which the state health insurance agency reimbursed patients for pharmaceutical expenditures. The government-negotiated prices for Gastirup in Italy were 46% below the average European price.

Bjorn Larsson was concerned that, with the anticipated future removal of all trade barriers in Europe, Gastirup would fall victim to massive parallel trading from Italy to the higher-priced countries in the region. Furthermore, with the increased coordination among government health insurance agencies, also foreseen in future years, price differences among EU countries were expected to narrow. This likely development highlighted the need for a consistent pricing policy throughout Europe.

As head of Product Pricing and Government Relations, it was Bjorn Larsson's responsibility to recommend the actions that top corporate and local Italian management should take to avert potential annual losses for Gastirup, projected in the US$20–30 million range. Among alternatives being considered, the most extreme was to forego the large and growing Italian market altogether and concentrate the product's sales elsewhere in Europe. The Italian market for Gastirup had grown to $27 million in recent years and accounted for 22% of European sales. Another option was to remove Gastirup from the Italian government reimbursement scheme by raising the prices to levels close to those prevailing in the higher-priced countries. This action would most likely reduce the drug's sales in Italy by as much as 80%. Still another alternative was to take legal action in the European Court of Justice against the Italian government's reimbursement scheme and the related price negotiations as barriers to free trade. Finally, the company could take a 'wait and see' attitude, postponing any definitive action to a time when the impact of future EU regulatory changes was better known.

Company Background

Pharma Swede was formed in 1948 in Stockholm, Sweden; it concentrated solely in pharmaceuticals. The company employed over 2,000 people and earned $50 million on sales of $750 million, distributed among its three product lines: Hormones (20%), Gastrointestinal (50%), and Vitamins (30%). Gastirup belonged to the gastrointestinal product category and accounted for roughly $120 million of Pharma Swede's sales. (See **Exhibit 1** for a breakdown of Pharma Swede's sales.)

International Activities and Organization

Pharma Swede had wholly-owned subsidiaries in 11 countries in Western Europe, where it generated 90% of its sales. The balance of sales came from small operations in the United States, Australia and Japan.

Due to high research and development costs as well as stringent quality controls, Pharma Swede centralized all R&D and production of active substances in Stockholm. Partly as a result of these headquarters functions, 60% of the company's expenditures were in Sweden, a country that represented only 15% of sales. However, the politics of national health care often required the company to have some local production. Consequently, a number of Pharma Swede's subsidiaries blended active substances produced in Sweden with additional compounds and packaged the finished product.

Pharma Swede had a product management organization for drugs on the market (refer to **Exhibit 2**). For newly developed drugs, product management did not begin until the second phase of clinical trials, when decisions were made as to where the new products would be introduced and how. (Refer to **Exhibit 3** for the different phases of a new product's development.) Besides country selection, product management at headquarters examined different positioning and price scenarios, and determined drug dosages and forms. It had the final say on branding and pricing decisions, as well as basic drug information, including the package leaflet that described a drug's usage and possible side effects. As one product manager explained, the marketing department in Stockholm developed a drug's initial profile and estimated its potential market share worldwide. However, it was up to local management to adapt that profile to their own market.

As an example, headquarters management positioned Gastirup against the leading anti-ulcer remedy, Tomidil, by emphasizing a better quality of life and 24-hour protection from a single tablet. To adapt the product to their market, the Italian management, with the approval of Stockholm, changed the name to Gastiros and developed a local campaign stressing the drug's advantages over Tomidil, the oral tablet which had to be taken 2 or 3 times a day.

As a rule, headquarters limited its involvement in local markets. It saw its role as one of providing technical or managerial assistance to country management who were responsible for profit and loss.

Product Pricing and Government Relations

The Product Pricing and Government Relations department, located at the headquarters, was a recently established function within the company. It prepared guidelines for subsidiary management to use in negotiating drug pricing and patient reimbursement policies with local government agencies. The department was divided into Government Relations and Product Pricing. Those in Government Relations followed ongoing political events and prepared negotiating positions on such issues as employment creation through local production.

The role of Product Pricing, headed by Bjorn Larsson, was to determine the 'optimum' price for new products. An optimum price, Bjorn explained, was not necessarily a high price, but a function of price–volume relationships in each market. An optimum price also reflected the cost of alternatives, including competitive products and alternative treatments like surgery, and the direct and indirect costs of non-treatment to society and the government. Each of these criteria helped to quantify a product's cost-effectiveness or, as government authorities saw it, its 'treatment value-for-money'.

Using cost-effectiveness data in price negotiations was a recent development in the pharmaceutical industry and corresponded to the increasing cost consciousness among public health authorities. Economic exercises, which were initially performed in Stockholm to measure a drug's treatment and socioeconomic benefits, were repeated with local authorities during negotiations. In Bjorn Larsson's opinion, the latest measure of 'non-treatment cost' was becoming an important factor. He explained that a thorough understanding of the direct and indirect costs of an illness had come to play a key role in whether or not a government was willing to pay for a product by granting it reimbursement status, as well as the magnitude of that reimbursement. According to industry observers, the task of marketing to governmental agencies had become crucial in recent years as public agencies were scrutinizing drug prices more carefully. (Refer to **Exhibit 4** for an overview and further description of Product Pricing and Government Relations.)

The Pharmaceutical Industry

Approximately 10,000 companies worldwide competed in the $180 billion pharmaceutical industry. Industry sales were concentrated in North America, Western Europe and Japan, with the 100 largest companies in these areas accounting for nearly 80% of all revenues. Western Europe alone accounted for an estimated 25% of total volume.

The industry classified pharmaceutical products according to how they were sold and their therapeutic status. In the first instance, pharmaceutical sales were classified into two categories, ethical and over-the-counter (OTC). Ethical drugs, with four-fifths of all pharmaceutical sales worldwide and a 10% annual growth rate, could only be purchased with a doctor's prescription. These drugs were branded or were sold as a generic when original patents had expired. OTC drugs were purchased without a prescription; they included both branded and generic medicines such as aspirin, cough syrups and antacids. At Pharma Swede, ethical drugs accounted for more than 90% of total sales.

Ethical drugs were also classified into therapeutic categories, of which gastrointestinal was the second largest, representing 15% of industry sales. Within the gastrointestinal category there were a number of smaller segments, such as anti-ulcer drugs, used to control and treat digestive tract ulcers, anti-diarrhoeas and laxatives. The ethical anti-ulcer drug segment was valued at $7 billion worldwide and growing at 18% a year, faster than the total prescription market.

Trends in Europe

In parallel with worldwide trends, several factors were expected to play a role in shaping the future of the European pharmaceutical industry. Among these were an aging population, rising R&D and marketing costs, greater competition from generics, and government cost controls.

Aging Population

Europe's stagnating population was gradually aging. The segment of the population over 55 years old was forecast to grow and account for between 33% and 40% of the total by the year 2025 – up from below 25%. The segment below 30 years of age was forecast to drop from about 40% to 30%. The 'graying of Europe' was expected to have two lasting effects on drug consumption. First, low growth was projected in the sales of drugs normally used by children or young adults. Second, drug companies marketing products for age-related diseases, such as cancer, hypertension and heart ailments, could expect growing demand.

Rising R&D and Marketing Costs

Research and development expenses included the cost of identifying a new molecule and all the tests required for bringing that molecule to the market. Generally, for every 10,000 molecules synthesized and tested, only one made it through the clinical trials to appear in the market. Product development costs were estimated to average $200 million per drug, from preclinical research to market introduction. Industry estimates for research and development expenses averaged around 15% of sales, with some companies spending as much as 20% of sales on new drugs. Research in more complex diseases like cancer, as well as lengthy clinical trials and government registration processes, had raised these costs recently.

Marketing costs had also increased due to a general rise in the level of competition in the industry. Seven years ago, pharmaceutical firms spent, on average, 31% of sales on marketing and administrative costs. Now, the ratio had increased to 35% and was still rising. Some companies were reported to have spent unprecedented sums of $50–60 million on marketing to introduce a new drug.

Growth of Generics

Generic drugs were exact copies of existing branded products for which the original patent had expired. 'Generics', as these drugs were known, were priced substantially lower than their originals, and were usually marketed by a firm other than the inventor. Price differences between the branded and generics could be as large as 10-to-1. Depending on the drug categories, generics represented between 5% and 25% of the value of the total prescription drug market in Europe, and their share was expected to grow. For example, in the UK, sales of generic drugs had grown to represent an estimated 15% of the total National Health Budget and were forecast to reach 25% in the next five years. In line with efforts to contain costs, governments in many parts of Europe were putting increased pressure on physicians to prescribe generics instead of the more expensive branded drugs.

Government Role

Governments were one of the strongest forces influencing the pharmaceutical industry in Europe where, in conjunction with public and private insurance agencies, they paid an average of two-thirds of health care costs. In Italy, for example, 64% of all ethical pharmaceutical expenditures were covered by the public health care system. In Germany, France and the UK, the respective shares were 57%, 65%, and 75%. These ratios had risen considerably throughout the past 20 years.

European governments were facing two opposing pressures: to maintain high levels of medical care while trying to reduce the heavy burden placed on the budget for such expenditures. Influence on pharmaceutical pricing, according to industry experts, had become an increasingly political as well as economic issue.

Not surprisingly, government agencies seeking to reduce health insurance costs increasingly encouraged the use of generics. In fact, before the advent of generics and official interventions, well-known branded drugs which had lost their patents, such as Librium or Valium, often maintained up to 80% of their sales for several years. In contrast, in the current market, it was more likely that a drug would lose nearly 50% of its sales within two years after its patent expired.

Gastirup
Ulcers and Their Remedies

Under circumstances not completely understood, gastric juices – consisting of acid, pepsin and various forms of mucous – could irritate the membrane lining the stomach and small intestine, often producing acute ulcers. In serious cases, known as peptic ulcers, damage extended into the wall of the organ causing chronic inflammation and bleeding. Middle-aged men leading stressful lives were considered a high-risk group for ulcers.

Ulcers were treated by four types of remedies: antacids, H-2 inhibitors, anticholinergics, and surgery. Antacids, containing sodium bicarbonate or magnesium hydroxide, neutralized gastric acids and their associated discomfort. Some of the more common OTC antacid products were Rennie and Andursil. In contrast, H-2 inhibitors such as ranitidine reduced acid levels by blocking the action of the stomach's acid-secreting cells. Anticholinergics, on the other hand, functioned by delaying the stomach's emptying, thereby diminishing acid secretion and reducing the frequency and severity of ulcer pain. Finally, surgery was used only in the most severe cases, where ulceration had produced holes in the stomach and where ulcers were unresponsive to drug treatment.

The world market for non-surgical ulcer remedies was estimated at $8 billion, with most sales distributed in North America (30%), Europe (23%), and Japan (5%). Worldwide, H-2 inhibitors and OTC antacids held 61% and 12% of the market, respectively.

The Oral Osmotic Therapeutic System

Gastirup, introduced eight years ago as Pharma Swede's first product in the category of ulcer remedies, used ranitidine as its active ingredient. Ranitidine was available as a generic compound, after having lost its patent protection in that year. The US-based Almont Corporation was the original producer of ranitidine and its former patent holder.

What distinguished Gastirup from other H-2 inhibitors, including ranitidine tablets produced by Almont and others, was not its active ingredient, but the method of administration called the oral osmotic therapeutic system (OROS). In contrast to tablets or liquids taken several times a day, the Oral Osmotic Therapeutic System was taken once a day. Its tablet-like membrane was specially designed to release a constant level of medicine over time via a fine laser-made opening. By varying the surface, thickness and pore size of the membrane, the rate of drug release could be modified and adapted to different treatment needs. Furthermore, the release of the drug could be programmed to take place at a certain point in time after swallowing the tablet. Consequently, drug release could be timed to coincide with when the tablet was in the ulcerated region of the upper or lower stomach. (Refer to **Exhibit 5** for a diagram and brief description of the OROS.)

Drugs supplied via OROS had certain advantages over the others. First, because of a steady release of the medicine, they prevented the 'high' and 'low' effects often observed with the usual tablets or liquids. Furthermore, the time-release feature also prevented over-functioning of the liver and kidneys. In addition, because drugs contained in an OROS had to be in the purest form, they were more stable and had a prolonged shelf life. Pharma Swede management believed that drugs administered by OROS could lead to fewer doctor calls, less hospitalization, and reduced health care costs for insurance agencies and governments.

Because OROS was not a drug *per se* but an alternative method of drug administration, it was sold in conjunction with a particular pharmaceutical substance. Pharma Swede was marketing three drugs using OROS. Gastirup was the company's only OROS product in the gastrointestinal category; the other two were in the hormones category. The management of Pharma Swede characterized the use of OROS as an attempt to introduce product improvements that did not necessarily rely on new molecules but on new 'software', leading to improved ease of use and patient comfort.

Ranitidine, the active ingredient in Gastirup, was not made by Pharma Swede, because of its complex manufacturing process and the fact that, as a generic, it was available from a number of suppliers both inside and outside Sweden. Gastirup OROS tablets were manufactured by the company in Sweden; final packaging, including insertion of the drug information sheet, was done in a number of European countries including Italy.

Patent Protection

OROS was developed and patented by the Anza Corporation, a US company that specialized in drug delivery systems. In Europe, Anza had applied for patents on a country-by-country basis. Patent protection was twofold: OROS as a drug delivery system, and its use with specific drugs. The more general patent on OROS was due to expire in all EU countries within the next year. The second, and more important patent for Gastirup, covered Oral Osmotic Therapeutic Systems containing ranitidine. This latter patent, exclusively licensed to Pharma Swede for Europe, would expire everywhere on the Continent in ten years.

Although Pharma Swede sold more than one OROS product, it had an exclusive license from Anza for only the ranitidine-OROS combination. Over the years, a number of companies had tried to develop similar systems without much success. To design a system that did not violate Anza's patents required an expert knowledge of membrane technology which only a few companies had.

Competition

Broadly speaking, all ulcer remedies competed with one another. But, Gastirup's primary competition came from the H-2 inhibitors in general, and from ranitidine in particular. Since ranitidine joined the ranks of generics, it was produced by a number of companies in Europe and the US. Despite increased competition, ranitidine's original producer, the US-based Almont Corporation, still held a significant market share worldwide.

Almont had first introduced its Tomidil brand 20 years ago in the US. After only two years, the product was being sold in 90 countries capturing shares ranging between 42% and 90% in every market. Tomidil's fast market acceptance, considered by many as the most successful for a new drug, was due to its high efficacy as an ulcer treatment and its few side effects. The drug had cut the need for surgery in an estimated two-thirds of cases. Pharma Swede attributed Tomidil's success also to centralized marketing planning and coordination worldwide, high marketing budgets and focused promotion on opinion leaders in each country. Although Almont was not previously known for its products in the ulcer market, and the company had little experience internationally, Tomidil's success helped the firm to grow into a major international firm in the field.

In the opinion of Pharma Swede management, Tomidil's pricing followed a 'skimming' strategy. It was initially set on a daily treatment cost basis of five times the average prices of antacids on the market. Over time, however, prices were reduced to a level three times those of antacids. Eight years ago, the prices were cut further to about two times those of antacids. Currently, competing tablets containing ranitidine were priced, on average, 20% below Tomidil for an equivalent dosage. Tomidil's European share of drugs containing ranitidine was 43%.

Pharma Swede management did not consider antacids and anticholinergics as direct competitors because the former category gave only temporary relief, and the latter had serious potential side effects.

Results

Gastirup's sales in Europe had reached $120 million last year, or 7% of the ethical anti-ulcer market. (Refer to **Exhibit 6** for a breakdown of sales and shares in major European markets.)

Pricing

Gastirup was premium priced. Its pricing followed the product's positioning as a preferred alternative to Tomidil and other ranitidine-containing tablets by improving the patient's quality of life and providing 24-hour protection in a single dosage. While competitive tablets had to be taken two or three time daily, the patient needed only one Gastirup tablet a day. The risk of forgetting to take the medicine was thus reduced as was the inconvenience of having to carry the drug around all the time. Because of these unique advantages, substantiated in a number of international clinical trials, management believed that using Gastirup ultimately resulted in faster treatment and reduced the need for surgery. Gastirup was priced to carry a significant premium over

Tomidil prices in Europe. The margin over the generics was even higher. (Refer to **Exhibit 7** for current retail prices of Gastirup and Tomidil across Europe.)

Pharmaceutical Pricing in the EU

Drug pricing was a negotiated process in most of the EU. Each of the member states had its own agency to regulate pharmaceutical prices for public insurance reimbursement schemes. From a government perspective, pharmaceuticals were to be priced in accordance with the benefits they provided. Although the pricing criteria most frequently cited were efficacy, product quality, safety and patient comfort, European governments were putting increasing emphasis on 'cost-effectiveness', or the relationship between price and therapeutic advantages. Among diverse criteria used by authorities, local production of a product was an important factor. As a result of individual country-specific pricing arrangements, there were inevitably widespread discrepancies in prices for the same product across Europe.

For new products, price negotiations with state agencies began after the drug was registered with the national health authorities. Negotiations could last for several years, eventually resulting in one of three outcomes: no price agreement, a partially reimbursed price, or a fully reimbursed price. In the event of no agreement, in most EU countries the company was free to introduce the drug and set the price, but the patient's cost for the product would not be covered by health insurance. In many EU countries, a drug that did not receive any reimbursement coverage was at a severe disadvantage. Partial or full reimbursement allowed the doctor to prescribe the drug without imposing the full cost on the patient. Any price adjustment for a product already on the market was subject to the same negotiation process.

Once agreement was reached on full or partial reimbursement, the product was put on a reimbursement scheme, also called a 'positive list' – a list from which doctors could prescribe. Germany and the Netherlands were the two exceptions within the EU employing a 'negative list', a register containing only those drugs which the government would not reimburse. Drugs on the reimbursement list were often viewed by the medical profession as possibly better than non-reimbursed products. (Refer to **Exhibit 8** for a summary of price setting and reimbursement practices within the EU.)

Pricing Gastirup in Italy

Pharmaceutical pricing was particularly difficult in Italy. Health care costs represented 8% of the country's gross domestic product and one-third of the state budget for social expenditures. Government efforts to contain health care costs resulted in strict price controls and a tightly managed reimbursement scheme. Italy was considered by Pharma Swede management as a 'cost-plus environment' where pricing was closely tied to the production cost of a drug rather than its therapeutic value.

Eight years ago, Pharma Swede Italy submitted its first application for reimbursement of Gastirup. The submitted retail price was $33 per pack of ten 400-milligram tablets. On a daily treatment cost basis, Gastirup's proposed price of $3.30 compared with Tomidil's $1.35. Although priced 25% lower than the average EU price for Gastirup, Italian authorities denied the product admission to the positive list. They argued that Gastirup's therapeutic benefits, including its one-a-day feature, did not justify the large premium over the local price of Tomidil, which was already on the reimbursement scheme. Tomidil and another generic ranitidine-containing brand were produced locally, while Gastirup was to be manufactured in Sweden and only packed in Italy.

Despite the rejection by authorities, Pharma Swede chose to launch Gastirup in Italy without the reimbursement coverage. Management hoped to establish an early foothold in one of Europe's largest markets. Hence, Gastirup was introduced in Italy at a retail price of $37 for a pack of 10 units, and under the brand name Gastiros. This price translated into a daily treatment cost of $3.70, or 16% below the EU average retail price of Gastirup and nearly three times that of Tomidil in Italy.

The response of the Italian market to Gastiros was better than management had expected. Following an intensive promotional campaign aimed at the general practitioners, sales reached $500,000 a month, or 2% of the market. Meanwhile, the number of requests for reimbursement received by the Italian health care authorities from patients and doctors was growing daily. Management believed that these requests were putting increased pressure on the authorities to admit the product to the positive list.

In a second round of negotiations, undertaken at the initiative of management nine months after the launch, Pharma Swede Italy reapplied for reimbursement status based on a price of $31 per pack of 10 units. This price represented a daily treatment cost of $3.10 and was 30% below the EU average. Once again, the price was judged too high and the request was rejected. Two years later, management initiated a third round of negotiations, and Gastiros was granted full reimbursement status at $24 per pack, a price which had not changed since.

Gastirup's Italian sales and market share among H-2 inhibitors grew substantially following its inclusion in the reimbursement scheme. Currently, factory sales were at $27 million, representing a dollar share of 7% of the market. Gastirup was Pharma Swede Italy's single most important product, accounting for nearly a quarter of its sales.

In Italy, as in other countries, Pharma Swede distributed its products through drug wholesalers to pharmacies. Typical trade margin on resale price for pharmacies was 30%. Gastiros' factory price to wholesalers of $15 per pack of 10 tablets had a contribution margin of $3 for the Italian company, which paid its parent $1 for every 400-milligram tablet imported from Sweden. The transfer price was the same across Europe. In turn, the parent earned $0.70 in contribution for every tablet exported to its local operations. The variable cost of producing the tablets included raw materials and the licensing fees paid to Anza.

Lifting the Trade Barriers

As the EU trade barriers continued to fall, Pharma Swede management believed that two important issues affecting the European pharmaceutical industry would be manufacturing location and drug pricing. In the past, many of the cost-constraint measures taken by authorities had, by design or coincidence, an element of protectionism and represented national trade barriers. For example, local authorities might refuse a certain price or reimbursement level unless the sponsoring company agreed to manufacture locally. Under current EU regulations, such actions were considered barriers to trade and illegal.

As a countermeasure to such barriers, companies could take legal action against local agencies at the European Court of Justice. With the support of the European Federation of Pharmaceutical Industries Associations (EFPIA), drug firms could sue the agencies for violating the EU regulations. Although the companies had won 12 cases over the preceding decade, litigation processes lasted sometimes up to seven years, and the results were often partial and temporary in value. Even as trade barriers had been lifted, the element of local production linked to price negotiation still existed for many products.

Under an EU regulation called the Transparency Directive, government pricing decisions were open to review by the pharmaceutical companies. The directive served to eliminate any interference with the free flow of pharmaceutical products within the community caused by price controls or reimbursement schemes. It required state agencies to explain how they set drug prices in general as well as in each case. If not satisfied, companies that believed they had been discriminated against could appeal a ruling on price, first to local courts, thereafter to the European Commission and, ultimately, to the European Court of Justice.

In addition, the new law required that agencies act quickly when a new drug was approved for sale or when a company asked for a price adjustment. On average, it had taken Pharma Swede one year to reach agreement on a price for a new product. Price adjustments for old products, on the other hand, had taken as long as two years because of delays by local authorities.

Another development related to the creation of a single European market was the expected harmonization in pharmaceutical prices and registration systems among member states. Bjorn Larsson and others in the industry believed that, across Europe, pharmaceutical price differences would narrow in a two-stage process: initially as a result of the transparency directive, and thereafter as part of a more comprehensive market harmonization. Bjorn thought that harmonization was a gradual process and that the completion of a single European market would occur within the next five years.

Aside from narrowing of the differences in drug prices, possible outcomes for the future EU environment included a pan-European registration system and harmonized health insurance. Some observers predicted that a harmonized drug registration system would be put in place within the next two to five years, although the exact form it might take remained open. Harmonization of national health insurance systems, a very complex and politically sensitive process, was not expected for at least five years. Industry analysts believed that, in the interim, the states would continue to press for cost containment on a national basis. Private pan-European insurance offerings, on the other hand, were expected to increase with deregulation and the completion of the internal market.

The Problem

Until recently, Europe's parallel trade in pharmaceutical products had been limited to less than 5% of industry sales. Each country had local language packaging and registration requirements that tended to restrict or prohibit a product's acceptance and distribution in neighboring markets. Furthermore, according to some Pharma Swede managers, products produced in certain countries, such as Italy or France, suffered a poor quality image in other markets, such as Germany and England. National sentiments aside, distributors seeking to capitalize on parallel imports had to have approval from local authorities which often implied repackaging to meet local requirements.

Where parallel imports had been a minor problem in the past, they posed a serious challenge to drug firms, including Pharma Swede, as EU harmonization progressed. Such trade was now protected by law. Hans Sahlberg, the company's product manager for gastrointestinal drugs, explained that government insurance agencies were already examining price and reimbursement issues on a European-wide basis. For drugs already on the market, it was only a matter of time before authorities reimbursed on the basis of the lowest priced parallel import. As an example, this implied that Gastirup, priced at $2.40 per tablet in Italy and $5.40 in Germany, would be reimbursed in Germany at the lower price of imports from Italy. If this proved true, German revenue losses from Gastirup alone could amount to $17 million on current sales. Furthermore, if a system mandating a single EU price was to emerge, Pharma Swede would have to revamp its entire price setting policy completely.

Management Options

With the anticipated changes in Europe, Gastirup's pricing discrepancies had become a source of major management concern. If not carefully managed, Bjorn and his colleagues believed that the company could lose money, reputation or both. (Refer to **Exhibit 9** for relative prices of Gastirup in Europe.)

In looking for options to recommend to top management at headquarters and at the Italian operation, Bjorn and his staff developed four alternatives. The first, and the most extreme option, was to completely remove Gastirup from the Italian market and concentrate sales elsewhere in Europe. This action would be in defence of prices in the more profitable markets. This alternative was not Bjorn's first choice as it implied sales revenue losses of $27 million. It also went counter to Pharma

Swede's policy of marketing all its products in every European country. Bjorn feared that such a move would lead to heated discussions between headquarters and local management in Italy. It could even seriously damage the company's public reputation. 'How,' asked Bjorn, 'could Pharma Swede, an ethical drug company, deal with public opinion aroused by the apparently unethical practice of denying Gastirup to the Italian market?'

As another alternative, Bjorn could suggest removing Gastirup from the reimbursement scheme by raising prices to levels closer to the EU average. Such action would place Gastirup in the non-reimbursed drug status and lead to an estimated 80% loss in sales. Since the magnitude of this loss was nearly as great as in the first option, headquarters did not believe the Italian management would be any more receptive. Moreover, if Gastirup were removed from the reimbursement scheme, both the product and the company might lose credibility with the medical profession in Italy. According to Bjorn, many doctors perceived the drugs on the reimbursement list as 'economical' and 'really needed'.

Nonetheless, shifting the drug to non-reimbursement status would shift the financing burden from the government to the patient, thus coinciding with the Italian government's view that patients should assume a greater financial role in managing their health. With an increased emphasis on cost containment, such a proposal was liable to appeal to Italian authorities. Bjorn expected full support for this proposal from managers in high-priced markets whose revenues were jeopardized by low-priced countries such as Italy.

There was, however, a possibility that changing the reimbursement status might backfire. Hans Sahlberg recalled a case in Denmark where, after removing a class of cough and cold drugs from reimbursement, Danish authorities came under pressure from a group of consumer advocates and were forced to reverse their decision. If Pharma Swede requested that Gastirup be removed from the Italian reimbursement scheme and the government were forced to reverse that position, the company's public image and its standing with local authorities might be damaged.

Still, a third option was to appeal to the European Commission and, if necessary, start legal action before the European Court of Justice. As Bjorn explained, the artificially-regulated low drug prices in Italy placed higher priced imported drugs at a disadvantage and, hence, acted as a barrier to the free movement of pharmaceutical products. Since the EFPIA had sued and won a similar case against Belgium, Bjorn believed that Pharma Swede might have a good case against the Italian government. But as much as Bjorn might want to pursue legal action, he recognized the risks inherent in using a legal mechanism with which Pharma Swede had no prior experience.

Headquarters management, on the other hand, looked favorably at this option as it provided the opportunity to settle 'once and for all' the conflict with the Italian government over pharmaceutical pricing. Local management, however, feared that any legal action would create resentment and sour the atmosphere of future negotiations. At any rate, legal action could take several years and might even jeopardize Gastiros' status in Italy as a reimbursed drug.

A fourth option entailed taking a 'wait and see' attitude until the full consequences of the European harmonization became better known. Bjorn explained that, for the next two to three years, governments would continue to concentrate on price controls. Pressure for harmonization would reduce differences in drug prices, though it was impossible to project the direction the prices might take. As an estimate, the Product Pricing and Government Relations staff had calculated that uniform pricing translated to an EU-wide general decrease of 10% in drug prices, although prices in Italy would probably rise by about 15%. Thus, for the next few years, management at Pharma Swede could monitor the changes within the EU and prepare as carefully as possible to minimize any long-term price erosion. Bjorn felt this option argued for vigilance and 'having all your ammunition ready'. But, he was not sure what specific preparatory actions were called for.

Conclusion

Top management was deeply concerned about the impact that the changing regulatory environment might have on Pharma Swede's operations. Gastirup was the first product to feel the effects of European harmonization, but it would not be the last. A decision on Gastirup could set the pace for the other products. In evaluating the alternative courses of action for Gastirup, Bjorn had to consider their likely impact on several stakeholders, including the country management in Italy, the management in high-priced countries and at headquarters, the Italian and EU authorities, and the medical profession at large. Bjorn was not sure if any course of action could possibly satisfy all the parties concerned. He wondered what criteria should guide his proposal to the company president, who was expecting his recommendations soon.

EXHIBIT 1

Pharma Swede (Sales in $ mn)

Product Line	Year 1	Year 2	Year 3 (last year)
Hormones	90	130	150
Vitamins	175	205	225
Gastrointestinal	200	290	375
Total	465	625	750

Source: Company Records.

EXHIBIT 2

Partial Organization Chart

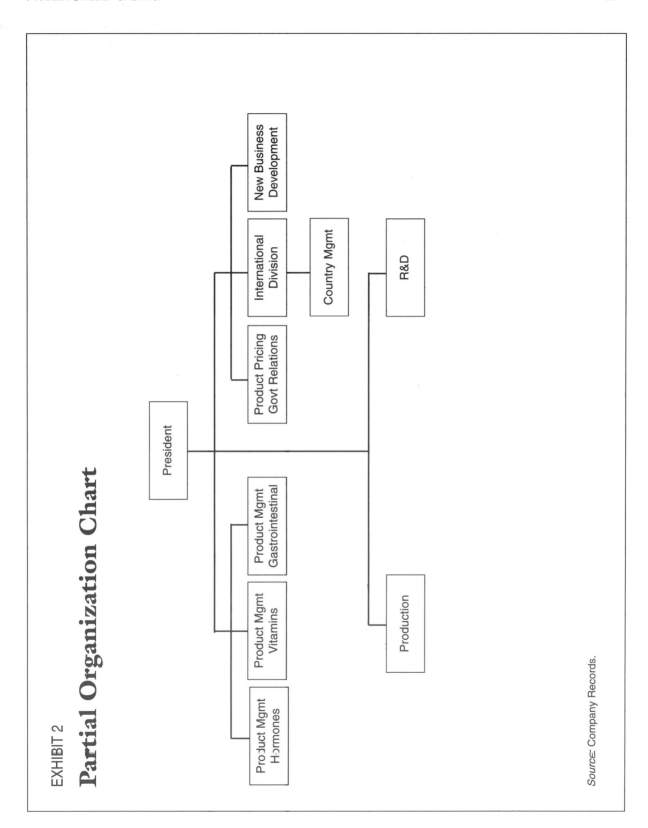

EXHIBIT 3

The Development of a New Drug

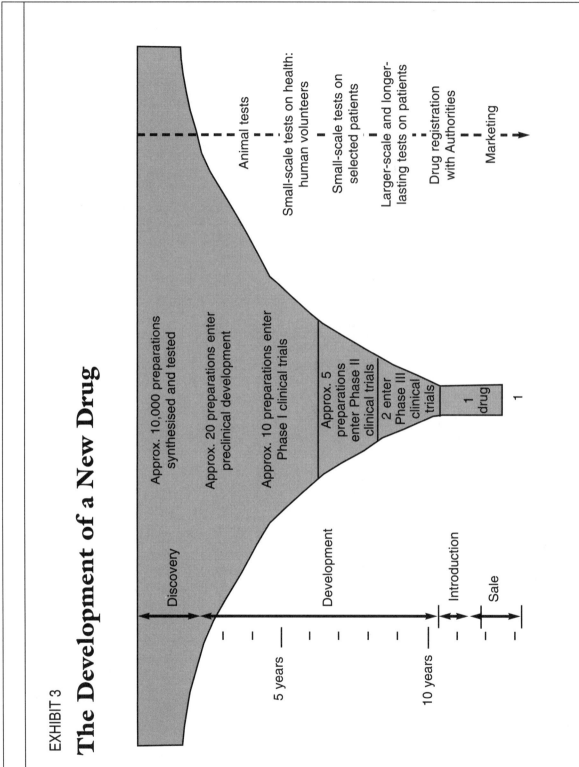

Source: Company Records.

EXHIBIT 4

Product Pricing and Government Relations

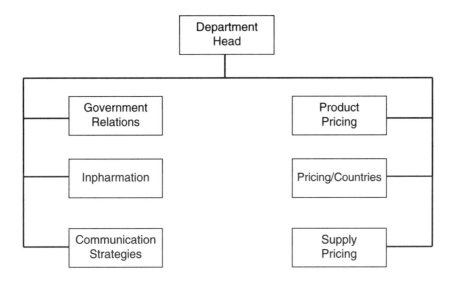

The Government Relations Group observed and recognized potential political problems for the divisions. When necessary, the group developed counterstrategies and oversaw their implementation.

Inpharmation gathered and made all pharmapolitical information on both a national and international basis.

The Communications Strategies Group advised the division on product strategies and proposed communications programs.

During drug development, the Product Pricing Group worked to secure drug registration, using economic and social data.

Pricing/Countries oversaw and helped build a favorable negotiating environment for pricing decisions.

Supply Pricing was responsible for administering prices and managing relationships with Pharma Swede's distributors.

Source: Company Records.

EXHIBIT 5

The Oral Osmotic Delivery System (OROS)

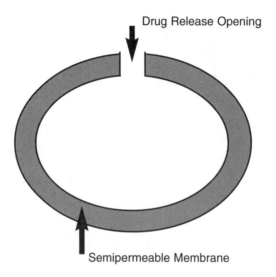

Although OROS looked like a normal tablet, the system used osmotic pressure as a source of energy for the controlled release of active substance. Water, present throughout the body, passed through the semipermeable membrane as long as the reservoir contained undissolved substance. An increase in reservoir pressure, caused by the influx of water, was relieved by releasing drug solution through the opening. Up to 80% of the drug was released at a constant rate; the remainder at a correspondingly declining rate. To guarantee the accuracy of the system, the opening had to comply with strict specifications. Hence, a laser was used to bore a hole through the membrane, in such a way that only membrane was removed, without damaging the reservoir.

Source: Company Records.

EXHIBIT 6

Sales and Market Shares in Major European Markets* (Sales in $ mn)

Countries	Total Market (100%)	Gastirup (% Share)	Tomidil (% Share)	Others** (% Share)
Belgium	41	2 (5)	16 (39)	23 (56)
France	198	15 (8)	61 (31)	122 (61)
Germany	318	30 (9)	51 (16)	237 (75)
Italy	394	27 (7)	110 (28)	257 (65)
Netherlands	81	8 (10)	25 (31)	48 (59)
Spain	124	5 (4)	11 (9)	108 (87)
Sweden	34	10 (29)	5 (15)	19 (56)
United Kingdom	335	18 (5)	97 (29)	220 (66)
ALL EUROPE	1,673	120 (7)	486 (29)	1,054 (63)

* All ethical anti-ulcer remedies
** Includes branded and generic drugs

Source: Company Records.

EXHIBIT 7

Retail Prices in Europe (Daily Treatment Cost)

Countries	Gastrirup	Tomidil	Gastirup % Tomidil
Belgium *	$3.86	$2.47	+56%
Denmark *	5.96	3.94	+51%
France *	3.69	2.12	+74%
Germany *	5.31	3.54	+50%
Greece *	3.43	2.36	+45%
Italy *	2.40	1.35	+78%
Netherlands *	5.66	3.11	+82%
Portugal *	3.13	2.24	+40%
Spain *	4.03	2.82	+43%
Sweden *	5.91	4.22	+40%
United Kingdom *	5.40	3.10	+74%

*Member of the EU

Source: Company Records.

EXHIBIT 8

Price Setting and Reimbursement in the EU

Countries	Price Setting	Reimbursement
Ireland	No price control for new introductions.	Positive list (prescription recommended). Inclusion criteria: ■ efficacy/safety profile ■ cost-effectiveness profile
	Prices of prescription drugs are controlled through PPRS (Pharmaceutical Price Regulation Scheme).	Positive list for NHS prescriptions (National Health Service).
	Control is exercised through regulation of profit levels.	Inclusion criteria: ■ therapeutic value ■ medical need
Belgium	Price control by the Ministry of Health on the basis of cost structure.	Positive list (Ministry of Health). Inclusion criteria: ■ therapeutic and social interest ■ duration of treatment ■ daily treatment costs ■ substitution possibilities ■ price comparison with similar drugs ■ co-payment: 4 categories (100%, 75%, 50%, 40%)
Greece	Price control by the Ministry of Health based on cost structure (support of local industry appears to be of importance).	Positive list (IKA, Social Security Ministry).
Portugal	Price and reimbursement negotiations with the Ministry of Health and Commerce based on: ■ local prices ■ lowest European prices ■ therapeutic value ■ cost-effectiveness	Positive list. Inclusion criteria: ■ therapeutic value ■ international price comparison ■ cost-effectiveness
Spain	Price control based on cost structure.	Positive list (Social Security System). Inclusion criteria: ■ efficacy/safety profile ■ cost-effectiveness

EXHIBIT 8 (CONTINUED)

Countries	Price Setting	Reimbursement
France	No control for non-reimbursable products. Price negotiations with the Ministry of Health.	Positive list (Transparence Commission and Directorate of Pharmacy and Pharmaceuticals, for reimbursed products, within the Ministry of Health). Inclusion criteria: ■ price ■ therapeutic value ■ potential market in France ■ local R&D Co-payment, 4 categories: ■ non-reimbursable ■ 40% of retail price ■ 70% of retail price ■ 100% of retail price
Luxembourg	Price control by the Ministry of Health. Prices must not be higher than in the country of origin.	Positive list. Inclusion criteria: ■ therapeutic value ■ cost-effectiveness
Italy	Price control for reimbursed drugs by CIP (Interministerial Price Committee), following guidelines of CIPE (Interministerial Committee for Economic Planning) based on cost structure.	Positive list (Prontuario Terapeutico Nazionale, National Health Council). Reimbursement criteria: ■ therapeutic efficacy and cost-effectiveness ■ innovation, risk-benefit ratio and local research also considered.
Germany	No direct price control by authorities.	Negative list. Reference price system. Principles: ■ drugs will only be reimbursed up to a reference price. ■ patient pays the difference between the reference and retail prices. ■ co-payment: DM3 per prescribed product: 15% of drug bill.
Netherlands	No price control by authorities.	Negative list. Reference price system.
Denmark	Price control based on: ■ cost structure ■ 'reasonable' profits	Positive list. Inclusion criteria: ■ efficacy/safety profile ■ cost-effectiveness profile

Source: Company Records.

EXHIBIT 9

Relative Retail Prices of Gastirup

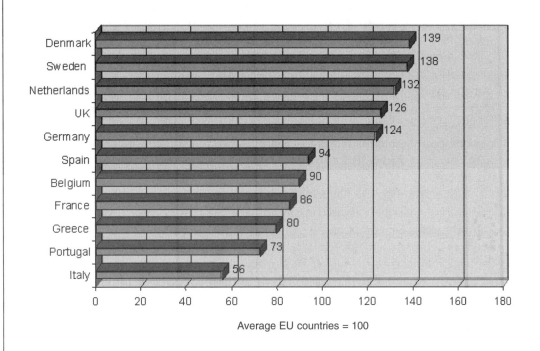

Average EU countries = 100

Source: Company Records.

CASE 2.9ᴿ Jordan A/S

This case was prepared by Research Associates David H. Hover and Janet Shaner, under the supervision of Professors Per V. Jenster and Kamran Kashani. The case is partially based on research by IMD Research Associates Dana Hyde and Mark E. Brazas and Peter O'Brien of the Industrial Development Authority of Ireland, and is part of IMD's Institutional Research Project: Managing Internationalization. Some facts and figures have been disguised.

Mr Knut Leversby, Managing Director of Jordan A/S, took a good deal of pride in the certificate on his office wall in Oslo. In Norwegian, it proclaimed Jordan 'Company of the Year' – as judged by a broadly composed jury and the journal *Næringsrevyen*. The jury had stressed Jordan's ability to conquer market positions, especially in an international context. Four years later, Mr Leversby remained proud of the award, but his internal compass guarded against pride turning into complacency. As Jordan's CEO, he knew better than anyone the strategic challenges that his company was facing. Jordan was a small company among multinational consumer goods giants like Unilever and Colgate Palmolive. And consumer goods was, more and more, a game that turned on volume, threatening to overwhelm smaller competitors.

Jordan had prospered by focusing its foreign strategy on 'mechanical oral hygiene products' – mainly non-electric toothbrushes, but also dental floss and dental sticks (toothpicks). By combining high product quality with an innovative distribution strategy, Jordan had successfully defined and defended its niche to become the number 1 toothbrush maker in Europe, and number 4 in the world. But, Mr Leversby was not sure that the tactics of the past would carry Jordan into the future. Increasingly, competition came from trade retailers and major multinationals, both of which had significantly greater resources than Jordan.

Jordan's retailers, mainly food-based mass retailers, were becoming increasingly concentrated to achieve economies of scale in purchasing and logistics. Larger scale also increased the bargaining power of retailers with suppliers on prices and trade terms. More and more, these trade terms included on-time delivery of increasingly smaller order lot sizes, as retailers implemented and refined just-in-time ('JIT') systems.

Retail chains had increased their cross-border activity, often via acquisitions or strategic alliances, to compete in the European Union. Consequently, they tended to favor pan-European brands for volume and ease of handling. Larger retailers could also contract production of 'own label' products to compete with manufacturers' brands. In fact, about 13% of Jordan's sales came from contract production of these private labels. Mr Leversby was concerned that Jordan's private label business might be cannibalizing name-brand sales and/or diluting the carefully built Jordan-brand image.

Concentration was also underway among European toiletries manufacturers, who performed contract distribution for Jordan. Mr Leversby was especially concerned about the recent acquisitions of some of these distributors by multinational consumer goods companies. For example, Procter & Gamble had acquired Richardson-Vicks, which distributed Jordan products in Italy and several other European countries. Quality distributors, like Richardson-Vicks, were difficult to replace.

Company Background

Jordan was founded by Wilhelm Jordan, a man familiar with hard times. Born in Copenhagen in 1809, he was the eldest of 11 children raised by his widowed mother. Leaving home at an early age, he apprenticed himself to one of the master combmakers of Hamburg. In 1837, Wilhelm Jordan moved to Christiania, Norway, with two fellow combmakers, starting a modest workshop destined to become the largest brush factory in Europe.

During the late 19th and early 20th centuries, the Jordan company distinguished itself as a social pioneer. Despite frequent labor unrest in Norway, the Jordan factory never experienced a strike. In 1910, the company set up a pension fund wholly financed by profits. Considering the conditions of the time, Jordan was a good place to work, a fact reflected in the long-term employment and loyalty of its workers. Throughout Jordan's history, advancement from the shop floor was common; Per Lindbo, Knut Leversby's predecessor as Managing Director, began his career with Jordan as a 15-year-old on the production line. A Jordan publication issued to commemorate 150 years of company history referred to the internal 'culture', strongly influenced by the founder's faith in the individual human being. For the employee with skill and the will to make the effort, the opportunity was there to accept the challenges, irrespective of formal education and qualifications.

Another continuous thread in Jordan's history was its commitment to product excellence. Brushmaking was a skilled worker's trade, and Jordan still produced handcrafted 'jewelry brushes' as nostalgia items. More importantly, the company continually invested in advanced technologies to maintain its competitive ability.

Jordan began producing toothbrushes in 1927 under the leadership of Hjalmar Jordan, grandson of the founder. By 1936, the company had captured half of the Norwegian market. In 1958, Jordan began to take a serious interest in exports, realizing that the oral hygiene field was largely underdeveloped. Jordan's subsequent success was evident. Last year, foreign sales of dental products provided over 60% of Jordan's revenues. (Financial information on Jordan is shown in **Exhibit 1**, and an organization chart in **Exhibit 2**.) The company's sales last year reached NKr330 million;[1] 44.6% of sales were made in Norway, 32.2% in the balance of Europe, and 10% in the rest of the world. The remaining 13.2% consisted of private label sales to other markets.

---

1. Exchange rates had fluctuated widely in recent years. Approximate values for the Norwegian kroner were: NKr1.00 = FF0.79 = US$0.13 = £0.08.

Management Challenges

Jordan had suffered a period of reduced earnings. The success that Jordan achieved in increasing exports led to over-emphasis on marketing and sales at the expense of financial performance. Steps were taken to re-emphasize the importance of financial results. Company-wide financial targets were set at 18% return on assets with 16% return on sales and were communicated directly to employees. In addition, efficiency measurements were established for the individual foremen to help them identify their contribution to the overall profitability objectives of the company. Monthly reports and annual reviews for production looked at labor hours per unit, scrap rates, absentee rates, energy usage and other measures of efficiency. Other reports for general distribution included weekly sales figures, profitability analysis, and accounts receivable.

The renewed emphasis on financial and efficiency measures made employees at all levels realize that the company was dependent on the successful interaction between production and marketing. This re-orientation of company values had a direct impact on performance. Sales more than doubled over the last ten years, while employment stayed flat at 450 after falling from 700. The workforce reduction resulted from Jordan's policy to increase productivity through mechanization. The reduction was, however, achieved without major employee displacement. With government aid, older workers were retired and approximately 80 workers pensioned. Manufacturing efforts achieved productivity improvements of 6–8% per year.

Downsizing remained a priority. The personnel department spent a considerable amount of time helping people leave the company. New people, however, were hired occasionally as needed, particularly in marketing. Jordan had achieved the reputation of being a good company for international marketing. A few individuals took advantage of Jordan, staying with the company only long enough to learn its methods and techniques before leaving and joining another company. Internationally minded employees were in high demand in Norway.

The Competitive Environment

Jordan's products were marketed in more than 85 countries worldwide; 1.4 billion toothbrushes were bought. Market size and toothbrush replacement rates varied considerably among countries (refer to **Exhibit 3**). Japan was the largest consumer of toothbrushes both in total volume and on a per capita basis. Whereas Japanese consumers purchased an average of 3.2 toothbrushes per year, Irish consumers, for example, replaced their toothbrushes about once every two years. (Jordan's market share in major markets is given in **Exhibit 4**. Information on major competitors is given in **Exhibit 5**. Key brands are listed in **Exhibit 6**.)

During the 1930s, Jordan had competed on quality, and its success had made Jordan-style quality an industry standard for toothbrushes. The company recognized that, as producing brushes was not a very difficult process, the battle of the future would not be about product development or production technology. As a result, Jordan shifted its focus towards product presentation and being responsive to end-user demands. Jordan concentrated its efforts on developing marketing techniques that reached the customer in the store, where most toothbrush purchase decisions were made. Through careful attention to point-of-sale promotions, packaging and product design, Jordan was able to establish and maintain a strong market presence.

In the increasingly competitive consumer product market, volume was a precondition for survival. Consequently, during the mid-1960s, Jordan considerably reduced its product lines (which included brushes, combs, toys and wooden soles for footwear). The slimmed-down product portfolio concentrated on products with volume-related potential. From that time onward, oral hygiene products became increasingly important to Jordan's success.

Jordan's cost structure was probably not typical for the industry, for two reasons. First, Norwegian labor costs were high. Hourly wages in Holland and Scotland, for example, were 70% and 30%, respectively, of the Norwegian rate. Manufacturing labor accounted for about 20% of the ex-factory sales price for toothbrushes. Second, as a small company with a niche strategy, Jordan did not have the financial or personnel resources for marketing and distribution that its large competitors had. Marketing expenses were generally allocated evenly between Jordan and the distributors in each country. Still, Jordan was limited in its ability to compete in some areas.

Jordan's experiences in the United Kingdom illustrated the problems Mr Leversby expected to see develop in the rest of Europe. Although the UK had been one of Jordan's first export markets, the company's success there had been uneven. Despite repeated attempts, Jordan had been unable to secure ongoing distribution in several of the large retail chains. It was a perplexing problem. Retailers demanded that manufacturers support their products with advertising, which Jordan management felt was unnecessary given the impulsive nature of toothbrush purchases. In one case, a retailer wanted Jordan to spend £2 million on advertising, almost twice the company's annual budget for promotions in the UK. The toothbrush advertising budgets in the UK for several of Jordan's competitors were estimated as follows: £2 million for Johnson & Johnson's 'Reach' brand; £1.5 million for Gillette's 'Oral B'; and £1 million for Unilever's 'Mentadent P Professional'.

Because Jordan would not meet their advertising demands, British retailers frequently placed Jordan products on lower shelves where the company's point-of-sales promotions were less effective. Under these conditions, sales could not meet expected levels, and so retailers would pull the line off the shelves entirely. Because of these difficulties, Jordan had only 4% of the UK market. (**Exhibit 7** shows a comparison of the leading brands and distributors in the UK.)

Some large retail chains increasingly demanded listing fees before they would stock a particular item.[2] For example, one large French chain required FF150 per store per variant for a similar product. The total listing fee for an initial introduction

---

2. Listing fees were a one-time fee, usually paid by the manufacturer or distributor at the time of new product introduction.

of 10 product variants in 1,200 stores would cost FF1,800,000. On the other hand, Jordan's relative scarcity of resources had led to the creative (and highly successful) use of marketing and distribution alliances, a key factor in the company's success.

By contractual agreement, most transactions between Jordan and its distributor and licensee partners were dominated in Norwegian kroner. The few exceptions included transactions with affiliates in developing countries and in Holland, which used US dollars and Dutch guilders respectively. The policy was a convenience. It was not Jordan's intention to push the foreign exchange risk onto its overseas partners. If its affiliates or distributors stopped making money due to exchange rate exposure (or any other reason), Jordan would soon lose them as partners. Jordan did not make currency denomination an issue in contract negotiations. Experience had shown that it was better to avoid involving the finance managers of the distributors, since 'they would start to make all kinds of funny arrangements'.

Retail Distribution

Toothbrush distribution varied from country to country. In France, for example, 83% of volume was accounted for by the grocery trade and 17% by pharmacists, while in the Netherlands the comparable figures were 62% and 38% respectively. Overall, however, pharmacists were losing ground to food-based retailers.

A second significant industry trend was the increasing concentration of the European grocery trade. Hypermarkets were getting a growing market share along with organized retail groups, which pooled their member stores' purchases and supply. European supermarkets were more likely to be chain members, and retail outlets were generally getting larger, although there continued to be some variation among countries, the share of food turnover by the top 10 food buying organizations in West Germany had reached 81%; in the UK, the figure was 66%; for France 62%, compared to only 36% in the US.

For the end-user, a larger sized retailer meant not only lower prices but a wider range of product choices. For the retailer, size meant more bargaining power with suppliers on prices, packaging and other product characteristics, as well as payment terms, order lot sizes and delivery times. The size of the new stores was a significant factor in managing distribution: one Euromarché hypermarket in France, for example, sold the same volume of toothbrushes as 260 Norwegian stores.

The retail price of toothbrushes also varied from country to country for a number of reasons, including distributor and retailer margins. For the product category, retailer margins across Europe averaged 35% of the final consumer price. Country differences, however, could be significant; margins in France were about 25% whereas UK retail margins reached 60% in some cases. Large retail chains and hypermarkets considered 30% the target margin in the product category. Wholesaler and distributor margins averaged 10–15% although country differences could also be substantial. In Spain, distributor margins ranged as much as 20–25%, while margins in the UK averaged about 10%. Manufacturers' coverage of sales, marketing and overhead expenses were approximately 30% of the final retail price.

After European integration, the European retail distribution trade concentrated further. As competition rose, closures, acquisitions and strategic alliances accelerated. Carrefour, the leading French hypermarket chain, had already allied with Castorama, the leading French do-it-yourself chain, normalizing relations after a previous Carrefour takeover attempt. Cross-border activity was also increasing in retail distribution, in contrast to the previous tendency of retail multiples to operate entirely within their domestic markets.

Coinciding with retail concentration was the increasing sophistication of retailers in obtaining and using market information. Retailers were highly aware of consumer preferences, competitive products and market opportunities. Processing this market information had been enhanced by point-of-sale scanner systems which evaluated product contribution per increment of shelf space. Armed with analytical data closely tied to their own bottom line, retailers were increasing their demands on suppliers' sales representatives for changes in packaging, pricing and other product attributes. As retailers became more aware of the changing market, product and package life cycles were getting shorter. Also, retailers were increasingly using JIT, which reduced their inventories but put a heavier logistical burden on suppliers to deliver smaller orders with less lead time.

Jordan's Export Development

Jordan began to take a serious interest in exports in 1958 when the EFTA and EC were in their formative stages. According to Leversby, the primary motivation for developing exports was that 'four million Norwegians did not consume enough toothbrushes to keep the company moving!' Jordan's initial exports, however, were vacuum cleaner brushes rather than toothbrushes. Choosing Great Britain as its first market because 'they spoke the language', Jordan was disappointed with the results. The company realized that building a profitable business as a subcontractor was a difficult task.

The company, however, saw toothbrushes as an underdeveloped market, characterized by low usage rates and an increasing awareness of dental hygiene, with clear volume-related potential. With toothbrushes, Jordan could also take advantage of its dominant domestic market position to support developing overseas operations.

The strategy adopted by Per Lindbo, who was then Managing Director, and Mr Leversby, was simple and inexpensive. Jordan asked distributors to cover product launch expenses in return for sharply discounted prices on toothbrushes. Because the toothbrushes were of good quality and supported by Jordan's marketing acumen, distributors found this offer attractive. It also allowed Jordan to enter new markets without substantial cash commitments.

Exports of toothbrushes were first made to Denmark, where Jordan entered into a distribution contract with the pharmaceutical company Astra. Denmark was chosen because of its physical proximity, cultural similarities and the small size of the market. Later, because of Danish import restrictions, a factory was established in Copenhagen. The Danish factory assembled parts supplied by the Oslo factory.

Jordan continued to diversify its export markets by expanding the Astra partnership to include Astra-Wallco in Sweden and Finland. Jordan toothbrushes were introduced in the Netherlands in 1963, with 240,000 units sold in two and a half months. In 1964, Switzerland, Belgium and France were added to the export map as Jordan became more confident in working with distributors and new markets.

A major boost to Jordan's initial export moves was a partnership with the large German consumer goods company Blendax Werke, started in 1961. A license contract allowed Blendax to produce and market Jordan-designed toothbrushes in West Germany under the Blend-A-Med name. This arrangement with Blendax was still operational, making Germany the only country in Europe where the Jordan brand name was not used. The relationship with Blendax was very important to Jordan in the competitive West German market. Mr Leversby did not relish the idea of having to go it alone if something should happen to Blendax.

Export Strategy

Jordan's international strategy had a number of key elements. First, the company consciously and persistently pursued a niche policy, sticking to mechanical oral hygiene products. Shortly after Jordan went international, it selected one product only – toothbrushes – for export. Since then, the company had enlarged its foreign product line to include dental floss and dental sticks (interdental cleaners made from wood), but mechanical dental care remained Jordan's export business focus. The company's sales budget estimated that 97% of dental product volume would be exported.

Jordan deliberately shunned the toothpaste market. Entering it would put Jordan into a larger and, therefore, more visible competitive arena, inhospitable to companies of Jordan's size. (About 80% of all oral hygiene sales were toothpaste.) Moreover, Jordan did not have either experience or any particular strength in this arena.

Second, international expansion was conducted step by step, one country at a time. Jordan's *modus operandi* involved getting to know the culture of a particular target country and making an assessment of the market. If conditions looked promising, the company would begin to search for a local distributor, possibly collaborating with a local advertising agency. This process could take between one and two years. Given the right 'chemistry' with a distributor, marketing would begin, with Jordan being introduced as an international rather than a Norwegian brand.

Third, Jordan fielded its own sales force only in the Norwegian market. Foreign sales were entirely handled by local distributors. There were several reasons for this policy. Overseas sales forces would overstretch Jordan's resources. Moreover, with only a limited product range to offer retailers, Jordan had no real distribution strength. Finally, an independent sales force would challenge well-developed distributors on their own ground. Instead, as Mr Leversby put it, 'Company management traditionally viewed limited marketing resources as an advantage. We continued to think small by gradually building all new export markets through distributorships and working arrangements with established, successful firms.' The development of local distributors as active partners was crucial to the success of this strategy.

Resources

Similarly, Jordan tried to conserve its resources by limiting its capital expenditures. Thirty percent of Jordan toothbrushes sold were produced by licensed subcontractors in eight different countries, including Venezuela, Thailand, and Syria. Relative to direct foreign investment, licensing was an efficient way for Jordan to avoid tariff barriers. Even the high perceived value of Jordan products did not allow the company to remain profitable when import duties were as high as 60–80%, as was the case in some countries.

Direct foreign investment was made only when market factors dictated it. Jordan opened a factory in Holland as a manufacturing bridgehead within the EU. The Dutch plant was also used to separate private brand production from Jordan brand. Private brand production ran in small lots, requiring many changeovers. To optimize the volume-based manufacturing technologies available at the Norwegian plants, private label production was done almost entirely in Holland. The proximity of the Dutch plant to the major private label customers also facilitated integration with the JIT requirements of these companies. The decision to manufacture in the Netherlands was heavily influenced by the Dutch government's offer to provide 35% of the plant cost. Other important factors included the sales volume available in the Dutch market as well as tax, culture and language issues.

Despite Jordan's successes, the company had not been able to enter markets at will. In Great Britain, the changing nature of the retail industry had disproportionately increased buyer power for the time being. High listing fees demanded by mass retailers exceeded the returns Jordan believed could be achieved. The situation in the US was different; in Leversby's words, it was 'a big black hole'. Despite the attractiveness of its size, the US market presented more risks than Jordan management was willing to undertake. Jordan, however, had not excluded the market and had actually begun working with an American company. In general, Jordan's managers believed that more attractive opportunities existed in countries with low toothbrush usage rates and limited penetration by competitors. Finance Director Erik Foyn emphasized, 'We cannot succeed in all markets, we must be selective.'

Private Label

Jordan management also faced the problem of how to balance the Jordan brand and private label parts of the company. Although the private label business provided only 13% of Jordan's sales, there was considerable debate about how this business fitted into the company's future.

The private label business was organized as a separate company, Sanodnet, under the leadership of Mr Juliussen, a member of the General Management team. To distinguish the two, toothbrush designs used for the private label were not the same as those used by the Jordan brand. The private label business had a diverse customer base, including Colgate-Palmolive and Safeway, the American retail chain.

Jordan's management was acutely aware of the problems associated with having two similar competing brands in one company. Cannibalization of the carefully built branded sales by the private label products was one such problem. It was possible to have two Jordan products next to each other on shelves, one Jordan brand and the other Jordan designed and manufactured, but private label. For retailers and distributors, this could cause a conflict of interest between Jordan-made private label products with their name and the Jordan brand. As one distributor commented, 'I don't mind Jordan's private label business, but why do they have to be so good at it?'

International Management Issues

Control over the operations of licensees was also a major issue for Jordan. Because the company operated under the Jordan brand name throughout the world, it was felt that quality had to be uniform. Engineers were dispatched from Norway annually to inspect licensee plants, and product samples were sent to Oslo on an ongoing basis to insure that standards were being met. Production volumes were controlled by supplying at least one part of the final product from Norway, usually the back of the package. Foreign accounts were relatively easy for Jordan to track as there was usually only one distributor per country.

Expansion into Greece

Greece was one of the few European countries where the Jordan brand name was not known. Management felt that entering the Greek market was a logical step towards consolidating the company's position in Europe.

Preliminary market research, using readily available sources such as government statistics, trade journals, country reports and Nielsen data, confirmed original suspicions that Greece was an attractive opportunity characterized by low usage rates and underdeveloped competition. More comprehensive research, including extensive discussions with various distributors, retailers and consumers, was carried out before securing a distributor. The interviews, besides giving Jordan management a first-hand account of local business practices, also allowed management to evaluate numerous potential in-country partners.

In Greece, as in many markets, it quickly became apparent that Jordan would have to work closely with the retail trade to create a new selling environment. Traditionally, Greek retailers kept toothbrushes behind the counter, forcing customers to ask for assistance, thus giving the store clerk a significant role in product selection. Jordan's competitive strategy relied on the impulsive nature of toothbrush purchases, which dictated that the products be readily visible to the customer.

To introduce the trade to Jordan's marketing concept, the company held two presentations for interested distributors. More than 250 representatives attended these meetings. The concept behind point-of-purchase displays was explained, samples were demonstrated, and results in similar countries were outlined.

After selecting a partner, Jordan made a successful launch in the Greek market. Jordan's first year target was for 5% of the market. The company's first shipment, (equal to 1.6% of total annual market sales volume) sold out in less than a month.

The Future

During its years of exporting, Jordan management had consistently relied on its knowledge of country markets and its ability to develop relations with experienced and qualified distributors. This had not always been easy. The changing European retail and economic environment implied that Jordan would face many more challenges in the future.

The consolidation of competitors in the industry, including the purchase of Jordan's local distributors by large multinationals, was straining the company's resources. The Jordan family, however, wanted to keep their company. Despite a number of attractive offers, the company was looked on as the family inheritance as well as a prestigious institution in Norway for well over 150 years. The greater financial and distribution power that would come from a merger would be beneficial, but 'after 12 months the spirit would be gone', Mr Leversby explained.

Despite the challenges facing his company, Mr Leversby was optimistic about the future: 'Fortunately, we have a long way to go.'

EXHIBIT 1

Selected Financial Results (millions of Norwegian kroner)

Income Statement	Year 1	Year 2	Last year
Operating revenues	265.0	307.0	321.0
Operating expenses:			
Depreciation		(14.0)	(15.6)
Other		(240.0)	(257.5)
Total op. expenses	(226.4)	(254.0)	(273.1)
Net op. revenues	38.6	53.0	47.9
Net financial income (cost)	(8.3)	(2.0)	1.2
Extraordinary items	1.3	(8.7)	2.2
Profit before allocations to funds and taxes	31.6	42.3	51.3
Allocations	(15.8)	(11.8)	(12.6)
Taxes	(7.4)	(15.4)	(21.2)
Net profit	8.4	15.1	17.5
Balance Sheet			
Cash	31.9	55.2	81.5
Accounts receivable	42.8	35.8	52.9
Inventory	23.6	24.4	28.3
Total current assets	98.3	115.4	162.7
Long-term investments	10.8	12.9	14.2
Property, plant and equipment	124.1	129.6	144.5
Total fixed assets	134.9	142.4	158.7
Total assets	233.2	257.9	321.4

EXHIBIT 1 (CONTINUED)

Income Statement	Year 1	Year 2	Last year
Current liabilities	71.1	75.0	98.4
Long-term liabilities	61.1	57.0	66.2
Untaxed reserves	79.7	91.5	106.7
Minority interests	-	-	0.8
Shareholders' equity	21.3	34.4	49.3
Total liabilities and shareholders' equity	233.2	257.9	321.4
Return on assets	18.0	23.4	18.2
Cash ratio	14.6	20.2	28.0
Equity ratio	43.3	48.8	48.5

Source: Jordan.

EXHIBIT 2

Sales Budget Total: 330 mn kroner

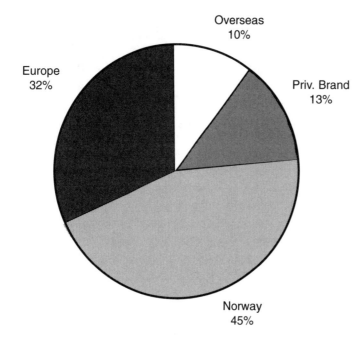

Source: Jordan.

EXHIBIT 3

The World Market for Toothbrushes (data unavailable for some countries)

Country	Unit sales	
	Total (millions)	Per capita
Japan	360.0	3.2
North America:		
US	300.0	1.4
Canada	25.0	1.1
Western Europe:		
*UK	53.0	0.9
*Italy	38.1	0.7
*France	36.0	0.7
*Spain	15.8	0.4
*Sweden	15.0	1.8
*Netherlands	12.4	0.9
Switzerland	11.0	1.7
*Denmark	7.2	1.4
Norway	5.8	1.4
*Finland	4.3	0.9
*Belgium	4.2	0.4
*Ireland	2.0	0.6
South America:		
Brazil	90.0	0.7
Colombia	21.0	0.7
Argentina	10.0	0.4
Venezuela	6.8	0.4
Chile	4.2	0.3
Australia	10.0	1.5

* Denotes member countries of the European Union.

Source: EIU/Trade sources.

EXHIBIT 4

Jordan Market Share by Country

Country	Market Share (%)
Norway	90
*Finland	70
*Netherlands	50
*Denmark	48
*Belgium	30
*Ireland	28
*Sweden	20
Iceland	20
*Spain	16
Canada	15
*France	15
*Portugal	13
*Italy	3
Switzerland	4
*UK	4

*Denotes member countries of the European Union.

Source: Company Records.

EXHIBIT 5

Major Competitors in Toothbrushes
Selected Financial and Operating Statistics
($ mn)

Company/Nationality	Sales Total	T/brush	Net Income	Return on Assets (%)*	Employees
Lion Corp. (Japan)	2,451	20.3%	41	4.8	4,892
Gillette (US)	3,167	4.0%	230	19.5	30,100
Unilever (NL/GB)	31,279	0.002%	1,407	7.6	294,000
Johnson & Johnson (US)	8,012	0.5%	833	19.2	78,200
Colgate-Palmolive (US)	5,648	1.6%	204	16.5	24,700
Anchor Brush Co. (US)	50	+50%	N/A	N/A	1,150
Jordan (N)	46	69.7%	2	23.4	475
Procter & Gamble (US)	17,163	0.01%	327	3.6	73,000

*Operating profit/total assets

Sources: Company records, *Advertising Age*, Annual Reports.

EXHIBIT 6

Major Competing Brands of Toothbrushes

Manufacturer	Major toothbrush brands
Lion	Lion
Gillette	Oral-B, Dr. West
Unilever	Gibbs, Signal, Mentadent, Pepsodent, DX, FSP
Johnson & Johnson	Micron, Reach, Prevent, Tek, Alcance
Colgate-Palmolive	Colgate, Dentagard, Defend, Tonigencyl
Anchor	Various private labels
Jordan	Jordan, private labels
Procter & Gamble	Blendax
Addis	Wisdom

Source: Jordan, Annual Reports.

EXHIBIT 7

British Toothbrush Market

Brand	Jordan	Wisdom	Mentadent	Oral B	Reach
Distributor	Alberto Culver	Addis/ Wisdom	Elida Gibbs	Oral B (Gillette)	Johnson & Johnson
Number of Salespeople	10	20	N/A	11	15
Market Share	2.5%	26.3%	1.9%	22.4%	7%
Average Consumer Price	99p	99p	£1.19	£1.09	99p

Source: Jordan.

CASE 2.10 GPS[1] One-hour Service (C): Moving Abroad

This case was prepared by Research Associate Els van Weering under the supervision of Professor Jacques Horovitz. The research for this case was done in 1996 by IMD MBA students Pierluigi DiTuri, Jim Hinds, Giles Houghton-Clarke, Jean-Francois Laborde, Allan Li, and Richard White.

As 1997 was unfolding, the GPS management team had to take a high risk, difficult decision. Would Grand Optical – the successful optics division of Groupe Photo Service (GPS) – go international? Or would trying to export a concept that was so well suited to the French market be asking for trouble?

Daniel Abittan and Michael Likierman, co-Presidents and founders of GPS, felt confident that the Grand Optical concept was strong enough to venture across the French borders into new territory. But they were not so sure which market they should enter first. Nor were they sure about the strategy to follow and the speed with which to go. Grand Optical had grown successful by adhering emphatically to its concept of customer focus, large open stores, one-hour service, quality, convenience, maximum choice, and highly professional staff. Would the transfer of Grand Optical skills to employees in another country be possible?

International competitors had already started expansion outside their home countries and it was likely that they would advance into France as well. Additionally, in some countries, one-hour service already existed. Daniel Abittan:

> We can see the limits of our development in France. By the year 2000, Grand Optical should have covered its natural territory in France. We must be ready for the new stage. Additionally, we must pre-empt others from conquering markets we would like to be in.

Although there was a sense of urgency, Likierman and Abittan were not going to jump in unprepared. In 1996, they had commissioned a group of IMD MBA students to research the opportunities for Grand Optical in seven countries around the globe.[2] The group had come up with descriptions of attractive markets as well as signals for caution. The management team was now ready to take decisions.

---

1. On December 22, 1997 GPS changed their name to GrandVision. 'Why GrandVision? Grand: like the world that is the future horizon of our development. Vision: only visionary enterprises do well in the long term. And also, the word belongs to our two professions, photo and optical. GrandVision: a name easily pronounced in French and English. It will be quickly adopted by all...' (GrandVision 1997 Annual Report).
2. Sources: *Retail Trade Monitor*, *Euromonitor*, EIU, *Retail Trade International,* 20/20 Europe, 20/20 Vision Asia, Eurostat, World Bank, Company Annual reports, *Yearbook of Statistics, World Competitiveness Yearbook,* Press, Stock Market reports, European Optical Society, AC Nielsen Market Research, *European Directory of Shopping Centers, National Associations of Opticians, Yearbook of Statistics,* OECD Economic surveys, Price Waterhouse, Healey & Baker, Internet Pages, Interviews, Site visits.

Grand Optical and Photo Service in France

By 1997 – 16 years after GPS was born – the company had evolved from a being a pioneer in mini-laboratory film development service to holding various companies in the amateur photo and optical industry (refer to **Exhibits 1A and 1B**). GPS had over 430 stores in France, sales (exc. VAT) of FF2,692 million and 3327 employees. All of the companies in the Group shared a drive to satisfy their clients' needs and exceed their expectations, which resulted in exceptional customer loyalty (refer to **Exhibit 2**). Another core competence of GPS was its ability to create and develop original retail concepts. Many of these concepts originated from constant benchmarking of new and successful concepts, both in France and abroad. GPS continually conducted both quantitative and qualitative research into customers' changing motivations, so that it could understand and respond to new client needs.

GPS in the Photo Market

GPS's first innovation was its one-hour photo film development service in shopping malls. Photo Service started in 1980 with the first development mini-laboratory in France. In 1996, the company had 188 stores. It was built up with a strong emphasis on one-hour service, quality and convenience. In 1995, 'Photo Station' was acquired. Photo Station had 106 stores and was positioned as a budget photo developer. Photo Station offered its clients photo developing services in less than 48 hours. The different designs of the two stores emphasized the difference in positioning (refer to **Exhibit 3**).

GPS in the Optical Market

Grand Optical

For an overview of the optical industry refer to **Exhibit 4**.

Grand Optical was launched in 1989. Likierman and Abittan made use of Photo Service's core competencies in the area of one-hour service. The new, one-hour concept for buying spectacles appealed to the French; by the end of 1996, Grand Optical had 58 outlets in France, sales were FF848 million and Grand Optical had a market share of 5%. Grand Optical's rapid growth was the result of its locations in regional shopping malls where customers could do their shopping while their glasses were being prepared. Of all eye correction equipment (spectacles and lenses), 93% could be ready within an hour. Recently, Grand Optical had also appeared in city centers. It had opened a flagship store on the Champs Elysées in Paris that posted sales of FF16 million in 1996 (it was Grand Optical's top selling store).

The HPV (high perceived value), one-stop shopping concept had required the management to work according to a set of typical, Grand Optical principles. The stores were in the best locations; they were open, with high quality shop fittings, and with 300m², they were large (typical, traditional optical stores were no more than 50m²). In contrast to its competitors, Grand Optical believed that its outlets – rather than advertisements – were the best medium for promotion, and they were treated as such (refer to **Exhibit 5**). In the stores, the customer was offered a large selection of frames (at least 3,500) and lenses. Purchasing was centralized, which entailed frequent deliveries and careful logistic planning. Marketing focused mostly on the stores that communicated a strong image of quality and superior – one-hour – service. Staff were selected carefully, trained extensively and motivated to provide the high, Grand Optical service levels.

La Générale d'Optique

Grand Optical was not the only optical activity of GPS. To be able to cater to the more price-conscious buyers, GPS created 'La Générale d'Optique' in 1993. By the end of 1996, it had 52 stores. It targeted consumers who were primarily motivated by price when buying medical products. The store offered a relatively large selection of frames (2,200 models) and sold them under its own brand label 'Selection La Générale'. In order to make its offer simple, it had created three collections with three all-inclusive prices (FF490, 690, 990). Price levels were approximately 30% under the prices of traditional outlets. This allowed the store to present models that would be almost totally reimbursed by the health system. La Générale d'Optique also offered customers the option to pay only the difference between the price of their spectacles and the reimbursement of complimentary insurance. To be able to do this, La Générale d'Optique had signed numerous agreements with mutual societies and insurance companies. Spectacles were finished in a central edging and mounting laboratory, which meant that customers would usually have their spectacles within two days.

For La Générale d'Optique, GPS partly followed the same big shopping-mall-location policy as for Grand Optical, but it also looked at convenience shopping centers (centers with a large hypermarket and a few stores) as rents were lower. La Générale had also started to open in city centers as rents were lower and opening hours shorter. La Générale d'Optique had a market share of 1.5% (refer to **Exhibit 6**).

The GPS Optical Home Market

The first step in the MBA students' research into the options for introducing Grand Optical in other countries was to make a benchmark of home country France. France had provided the resources and consumer profile to realize Grand Optical's growth to 51 shops in six years. One of the main reasons for success was the French one-stop shopping culture. Around 25% of all retail sales were made in hypermarkets. The market share of these stores gave an indication of the popularity of one-stop shopping habits. France counted 100 regional shopping malls and 600 convenience shopping centers or hypermarket galleries in 1996.

France had 27 million spectacle or lens wearers (nearly 50% of the total population) and represented a market value of FF15.7 billion. Over the last three years, the optical market had experienced slow growth in value (between 1% and 3% per year) The average French person purchased a new pair of glasses after 3.5 years, at an average price of FF1,500. The average price that was paid for a pair of glasses at Grand Optical was FF1,600.

The French could be regarded as brand and fashion conscious people. An indicator for this was their high rate of shoe buying. In France, people bought around six pairs of shoes a year. After Japan (8.2 pairs) and Singapore (6.8 pairs), this was the highest figure.

In contrast to many other countries, the French had to visit an ophthalmologist (outside the stores) to have their eyes tested if they were to be reimbursed, fully or partially, for their eyewear. Reimbursements in France were generally poor, although for 80% of the population, mutual society or insurance policies helped reimburse a further part of the costs.

Some 6,800 opticians were divided between independents (41% of the market and 59% of the outlets), multiple and voluntary chains (45% of the market with 36% of the outlets), and mutual society opticians (14% of the market and 5% of the outlets). Grand Optical and La Générale d'Optique were the major branch networks. The other chains were cooperatives or franchisees. As in the photo market, bipolarization was developing between the higher-priced, service-and-choice segment (branded frames and lenses crafted with the latest technologies – 'the best') and a low-price/low service segment based on the mutual societies ('the cheapest').

Driving Forces Behind Internationalization

Internationalization had become an opportunity as well as a need. Within a reasonable time, the Grand Optical concept would not gain much more market share. A Grand Optical store needed a catchment area of around 300,000 people to justify its investment in size and machinery. So, there was still an additional potential of only 30 to 50 stores for Grand Optical in France. A Générale d'Optique, however, needed 100,000 people in its catchment area, given its costs structure and target market, so its potential in France could still be as high as 250 new stores.

Grand Optical had inspired others to make frames accessible on the store's wall, to give the customers more choice and therefore to create larger stores (although Grand Optical still remained the biggest optical store in France). So far in France, no one had imitated the one-hour concept, but one-hour service had become common in other countries like the United Kingdom and had recently been launched in Spain. No doubt, other optical chains would be venturing into France and other countries outside their home markets. To pre-empt foreign competitors, Grand Optical would have to make a decision this year on which country – or countries – to enter first, and with what strategy. Marcel Cezar, General Manager for Grand Optical:

Going international is a necessity. Otherwize, we will have less and less growth; we will get old, and we will waste a lot of energy searching for minor locations.

Grand Optical would certainly not be the first international optical chain. The following competitors had already gone beyond their home country borders, or were planning to. Vision Express (United Kingdom) had opened in Belgium, Poland, Russia, Argentina, Malaysia and more recently in Germany and Luxembourg. Fielmann (Germany) had just bought a company in Switzerland. Dollond & Aitchison (United Kingdom) was already present in Italy and Spain (refer to **Exhibits 7 and 8**). In some countries, there was already a strong presence of local multiples such as Visilab (Switzerland) and Boots (United Kingdom). The independents were declining in importance, although this varied per country. In Germany, the independents retained only 23% of the market value as opposed to Italy, where they were nearly the only providers of optical services, with a 96% share of the market.

Going international had many attractions for Grand Optical: there would be scale economies in purchasing and in distribution. Grand Optical would gain access to cheaper supplies – in Italy for example, supplies would cost 25% less than in France. In addition to the benefits of economies of scale and international purchasing, Grand Optical acknowledged that its customers traveled and that finding Grand Optical abroad would re-enforce their choice of Grand Optical as a supplier of their glasses.

Scanning for Opportunities and Pitfalls in Seven Markets

The MBA students studied and visited the following countries to assess Grand Optical's chances: Germany, Italy, Portugal, Spain, Switzerland, Hong Kong and Singapore. This selection of countries came from a previous study that had looked into a wider selection of possible locations. Some were already regarded as too-late-destinations, as competitors had already taken the best spots in shopping centers and established themselves comfortably. In the seven prospective countries, the MBA project team made use of sources like opticians associations and local data banks. They also went to the local stores and shopping malls to get a feel for store formats, customer approaches, prices and assortments (refer to **Exhibits 9 and 10**).

Germany

Germany represented the largest market in Europe, with 36.8 million wearers who repurchased slightly more frequently than the French: every 3 years. In comparison to France, German shopping habits were still traditional. The Germans had many in-town shopping areas where most of the shopping took place. Until the rush of building after the re-unification in 1990, Germany had relatively few purpose-built shopping centers. As of 1993, more and more of these centers had been opened. In 1996, there were 180 in the country, totalling 6.2 million square meters of space, up from 67 centers in 1980 and 93 in 1990.[3]

With the increase of newly built shopping centers, there was a shift to out-of-town shopping. Shopping hours were being extended from the traditional nine-to-six to include evening shopping. The independent shops, especially (and 8,000 independent opticians), resented the new shopping hours regulations. It was forecast that the new regulations would favour sales in malls, with a 3% to 12% increase in sales.

Shopping for Eyewear in Germany

The fashion consciousness of the Germans was on the higher end of the 'shoe buying scale' (4.8 pairs a year). As for eyewear, the Germans put strong emphasis on both fashion and technical aspects; 70% of the lenses sold were anti-reflection coated (in France, only 35–40%). A drawback of anti-reflection lenses was that their preparation was more time-consuming, which made it impossible to keep the one-hour promise. The average price of eyewear was FF1,600. In addition to these fashion and technical conscious buyers, there was also a large budget-conscious group (20% of the eyewear units were priced below FF167). In fact, the leading discounter, Fielmann, had 33% of the volume and 16% of the value of spectacle sales.

Only 2% of the optical outlets were found in shopping malls; most were in the city centers. In 1996, there was only one store in Germany (a newly opened Vision Express outlet in a brand new shopping mall in Oberhausen) that offered one-hour optical service. It was too early to tell if the one-hour concept would prove successful. Chains represented 27% of the optical market value, buying groups 50%, and the independents 23%. Among the existing opticians, there was already fierce competition, which was intensified by the fact that the market volume was decreasing (4% for lenses, 8% for frames).

Fielmann: A Major Competitor

The strongest player among the chain stores was the German multiple 'Fielmann'. The rapidly growing world's number two in optical retailing had 33% market share in volume and 16% market share in value. Fielmann had positioned itself as the store for 'null Tarif' (zero priced) glasses, which meant DM20 (around FF60). This was the amount the social insurance reimbursed per frame. In 1997, this reimbursement would disappear, even though the reimbursement for lenses (DM80) would remain intact. Fielmann was the only optical chain in Europe that matched Grand Optical's

---

3. Source: 'Corporate Intelligence on Retailing', *The European Retail Handbook*, 1997, p. 123.

large branded assortment. It had 343 stores in Germany (and six in Switzerland), including some superstores, all of which had high in-store traffic. Fielmann even had 'greeters' at their doors who welcomed the customers and indicated where to go for specific needs. Daniel Abittan's opinion of Fielmann:

> It is good, it is cheap, there is choice. Fielmann is a great competitor. Their DM20 glasses are very fashionable. They are always put near more expensive branded products, so the consumer can compare. Fielmann's guarantee is also strong. If the customer finds any branded item for a lower price in another store, they will be reimbursed with the difference! When a competitor offers fashion, choice and price, it is not easy to beat him.

Fielmann differed from Grand Optical in that it emphasized price rather than the convenience of one-hour service. Fielmann glasses took five to six days from order to delivery.

Fielmann had been enjoying continuous growth in its home market, but the question was if it would be able to maintain such growth in the years to come. It would not be able to keep on capturing an increasing proportion of the German market indefinitely. Goldman Sachs Europe research indicates that Fielmann should reach saturation in Germany at 450 to 460 stores, beyond which the company would be moving into catchment areas that were too small or would cannibalize existing stores.

Legislation

In Germany, the measurement of eye corrections could be done in the stores, but it was heavily regulated by the 'Masters system'. The hiring, training and managing of opticians' staff was left to Masters, who ran the optics stores. Becoming a Master took five years of study and two years of apprenticeship. Each year, only 200 Masters were certified. In 1996, there was a shortage of Masters, which led to increases in their salaries. With the extension of shopping hours, the shortage of Masters would only grow; 40% of the prescriptions were made in-store, 60% were made by ophthalmologists outside the stores. The relationship between the two professional groups was tense.

Over time, Fielmann had been able to find a way around the restrictive Master practices by putting a growing number of its own employees through the training program. Fielmann master opticians received a higher remuneration by working in a Fielmann store than when they started up their own.

Pearle Came and Went

Fielmann had seen competition come and go. In 1981, Pearle had entered the German market by acquiring Bode, and a bitter fight for market share ensued. Pearle was an American optical chain with 875 stores worldwide, 183 in Europe, mainly in

The Netherlands and Belgium. Fielmann was able to draw on its reserves for price competitiveness, and won a price war. Pearle consequently left Germany in 1983. But in 1990, Pearle entered the market anew with superstores and a one-hour service, but Fielmann was again able to rely on its price competitiveness to parry the threat. Pearle withdrew in 1993.

Italy

In Italy, there were no restrictions on in-store testing; 65% of the prescriptions were done in-store. It had 24.5 million wearers, a number that was expected to increase due to an aging population. The Italians had flexible shopping hours. Only 3.5% of retail sales were realized in hypermarkets, and there was a trend towards more sophisticated retailing techniques. One-stop shopping was starting up, and since 1992, more and more shopping malls were appearing. As French mall developers had a strong presence, French retailers had the lead in the foreign entrants in Italian malls.

Optical chain stores had 2% of the optics sales value. The few that there were sold 2.5 times as much as the independents. Only 1% of the optical stores were found in malls, but a sevenfold increase was expected in the next three years owing to the number of new malls and their cheaper rents. Although the one-hour concept had just been introduced by others, none of the existing stores had a wide range of frames, and few shops had an area larger than 250m². Customers considered spectacles more a fashion item than a visual aid. Well-known, fashionable brands sold well. The National Health Service covered the expenses of only consumers with extreme sight deficiencies. Private insurance was gaining in importance.

One competitor – Poliedros, a small but aggressive chain – offered a one-year guarantee, in addition to excellent service with self service, a fidelity card, 'satisfied or reimbursed' policy, free sight tests and maintenance, and 90% of the spectacles in one hour. Poliedros could be expected to use its franchising strategy for rapid expansion.

Access to resources was difficult in Italy. Establishing relations, getting the right locations (key money and trading licenses were required in commercial centers as well as for occupied locations in city centers), and getting enough opticians were the most important issues to be tackled. Grand Optical had some talented Italian people in the company who could help make a possible move into Italy smoother.

Portugal

Portugal's retail sales had doubled to FF150 billion in the last six years. The population was shifting from the countryside to the towns. There was an explosive growth of shopping centers over the last ten years, mostly in and around Lisbon and Porto, where 38% of the population lived but where 74% of the retail sales were realized. This was attracting many foreign retailers such as Toys R Us, Marks & Spencer and

Carrefour. At least four of the new shopping centers would be attractive Grand Optical locations. One-stop shopping was still underdeveloped, although there had been a growth of 187% in the number of hypermarkets during the period of 1989 to 1993. In 1996, 24% of retail sales took place in super and hypermarkets. Opening hours in Portugal were flexible.

There were close to four million eyewear users. The young and urban Portuguese were highly fashion conscious and willing to pay a high price for their glasses, however, the average price for a pair of glasses in Portugal was about 30% lower than in France. Repeat purchase was once every 3.8 years on average.

Ninety percent of the market was served by independent opticians, and chains were small. By law, only ophthalmologists could prescribe corrective lenses. In practice, however, as consulting an ophthalmologist was expensive and not well reimbursed, most customers had their refraction done at optical outlets. The National Health Service reimbursed an average 10% of the costs of spectacles, depending on the type of lenses needed. Only a minority of the population had access to complementary insurance.

There was no other superoptical concept, and there were no apparent intentions of other players to enter the Portuguese market, except for Visionlab, the major, Spanish one-hour service competitor which was due to start in September 1997. Being the first in the best locations could create an advantage and keep other players out. Key money was required in the shopping centers. High street locations were more difficult to obtain due to antiquated tenure laws. Around the bigger cities, it would not be difficult to recruit qualified opticians. In the areas outside Lisbon and Porto, recruitment could become a problem as the rates of literacy and skills were much lower.

Spain

The Spanish market was fragmented, large and growing quickly. There were 17 million wearers who were used to renewing their glasses every 3.5 years. The shopping habits were shifting towards one-stop shopping in hypermarkets and shopping centers. In the period 1980 to 1992, the number of hypermarkets had grown from 15 to 110. Shopping centers also mushroomed (680% in the period 1980 to 1992). By 1996, they represented 8% of the retail sales. There were seven promising and two possible regions for Grand Optical stores in Spain. The Spanish were moderately fashion conscious (3.8 pairs of shoes per year). They saw spectacles mostly as a medical device. Opening hours in Spain were flexible.

In the optics sector, the independents and groups were losing out, although independents still had 55% of the outlets. Chains had 8% of the outlets, but 25% of the turnover. They consisted of four major national chains and a number of regional players. Spanish buyers had experienced one-hour service but not self service, as all opticians kept their frames in the drawer instead of on a self-service display. Most prescriptions were delivered in-store. There was no state health insurance. The Spaniards paid an average price of around FF1,000 for a pair of glasses.

'Ferri' (VisionLab) was a genuine competitor that offered one-hour service in its 20 big stores: each between 300 and 600m^2. Visionlab spent heavily on advertising. Compared to Grand Optical, it was cheaper, since it offered mostly unbranded frames from the Far East.

The prime locations in malls were taken by existing optical stores that usually had a loyal customer base. Key money had to be paid. Recent legislation had severely restricted new shopping center development. However, the new centers were outcompeting the older ones. Excess demand for space in the new centers was high (a waiting list of 50 was typical). The older centers were willing to accept rent as a percentage of turnover. Getting good locations on the high street was also difficult; the waiting lists were even higher than the ones in the shopping centers. Key money was high, and much of the good space changed hands without reaching the open market. French retailers were generally well accepted in Spain, and there was a proximity to French procurement.

Switzerland

Switzerland had 3.5 million spectacle wearers, the repurchase rate was 4 years, the average price for spectacles was the highest in Europe, a little over Germany's FF1,600. Shopping cultures varied by canton. In search for lower prices, the Swiss in many areas resorted to cross-border shopping and discounting. Shopping centers thrived in the big cities only (Zurich and Geneva). There were only eleven shopping centers of more than 20,000m^2. In contrast to other countries, key money was not always required in the Swiss shopping center locations. But the prices of real estate, especially in the prime locations, were among the highest in Europe.

Fifty percent of the retail sales was realized in city centers, 20% in villages, 15% in business quarters, 7% in suburbs and 8% in shopping malls. Superstores were just emerging. Opening hours in Switzerland were semi-flexible. Despite its still more traditional shopping habits, Switzerland was an attractive market due to the high disposable income of its inhabitants.

Most optical stores were located in main streets and city centers. Independents still had around 90% of the market. Chains had 5%, and the buying groups had 5% of the market value. Refraction was done in-store in 60% of the cases, normally in the shops that had a certified optician (Master). The other 40% of the customers had refraction done by an ophthalmologist. The one-hour concept had been established in the French-speaking part (Visilab) with a limited range of products. It was still undeveloped in the German speaking cantons, where two-thirds of the optical stores were located. Insurance reimbursed FF840 every three years, provided the customer had a prescription. Fifty percent of the spectacle wearers had additional insurance.

Fielmann from Germany had entered the market in 1995 by buying Pro Optic AG. They had six outlets in the German-speaking part of Switzerland and would be opening stores in three more locations in 1996. They were offering the Swiss a broad range of frames (over 3,000). Despite this, Grand Optical could still distinguish itself because it had both a broad range and one-hour service, a combination that none of the competitors offered (they did offer one of the two selling points).

The biggest barrier to entry was the access to Master opticians and their very high salaries. They were the only persons to do eye tests. There was only one school for Master opticians, which was controlled by Master opticians themselves. Another barrier was a law that prohibited advertising free eye tests. Competitors like Visilab and Fielmann were not to be underestimated for their power to react to new market entrants.

Hong Kong and Singapore

The people in Hong Kong had a shoe buying rate of 5.8 pairs per year. There were 2.5 million spectacle wearers, who repurchased every 2 years. The listed prices for glasses were very high, but usually a customer could get large discounts.

Singapore had 1.6 million wearers and a repurchase rate of 1.5 to 2 years. Their indicator for fashion consciousness was high, with 6.8 pairs of shoes a year.

Both markets had a trend towards fashion buying and a focus on professional services. The young age group was growing fast; they valued professional service and high quality product features. European brands had a stylish image. The shopping mall was developing in Hong Kong (there were around 20 malls in Hong Kong that would be able to carry a Grand Optical store), but it was already well established in Singapore. Most retailers in the malls were foreign.

In Hong Kong, fewer than 50% of the optical stores were found in malls. The optical shops in the malls were usually small. The chains owned around 25% of the optical stores.

In Singapore, more than 70% of the optical stores were in a mall. Seventeen percent of all optical stores were owned by a chain. In Singapore, most optical stores were small, and one-hour service was offered by many.

In both markets, the majority of the stores were owned by independents, although owing to pressure from chains that offered discounts, buying groups could develop. Even within the chain stores, the market was highly fragmented. They usually had a limited number of outlets and, often, there was no clear consistency among the outlets in shop plan, selection, service and even the names of the stores. Self service was limited, and there was a limited assortment of frames. Open shop plans were rare. Pushy sales techniques dominated customer service. Neither market offered government reimbursement or insurance benefit for customers.

Regulation in both countries used to be focused on contact lenses. Singapore had no formal regulatory body and no regulation of normal spectacles, but new regulation was likely to come in the near future. Singapore had no formal education program in optometry.

Hong Kong's official regulation of opticians came into effect in August 1996. As of that date, all shops needed to have a licensed optometrist. Hong Kong Polytechnic University offered an optometry degree and had 25 graduates per year.

Real estate was very expensive, especially in Hong Kong, and key money was often required. In Hong Kong rents were FF3,750–5,000 per m² per month. In Singapore, rents were FF300–600 per m² per month and typically FF10,000–15,000 per slot (30–50m²). Grand Optical would have to negotiate with several retailers in a center in order to get the right space and enough of it. Competition was strong, although the other opticians were not as clearly positioned as Grand Optical. Recruiting qualified opticians could pose a problem as there were not enough of them. There was economic growth in both countries – Singapore at 10% and Hong Kong at 5%. But the uncertainty of political stability in Hong Kong was a drawback for Grand Optical, as it was for many other businesses.

Grand Optical considered moving into Singapore or Hong Kong as a longer term option. There was no quick money to be made because of the high investments that were required, but one could see other reasons for opening up in Asia fast, as Michael Likierman said:

> Asia is the future; half of the world's trade is supposed to happen there in twenty years. By being there, we can also be ready when the Chinese market opens up. We know it is going to take long, so the sooner we start, the better off we will be when China opens up.

Strategy

After the MBA group presented their findings to the Grand Optical Management team, GPS managers would have to make up their minds about which country or countries to enter. After that, a strategy had to be formulated.

GPS had two choices for expanding abroad: either exporting the Grand Optical concept as it was, or adapting the French Grand Optical concept to the local market. Abittan and Likierman believed strongly in the first option as the concept was proven and they knew how to do it. On the other hand, strategies from France could have a totally different impact in another country and – after major investments – prove to be unsuitable. But then again, adapting to local markets also had its attraction; it could turn out cheaper, and there was an interesting learning potential in trying out new concepts in new markets, something that greatly appealed to the two pioneers. Daniel Abittan:

> We must show that in three or four years, the store brand can be developed abroad. Hence we must start now; the optical business differs in each and every country, and we need time to learn.

Some voices in the team suggested that GPS had also acquired competencies in the budget segment with La Générale d'Optique. Maybe it was not Grand Optical that should be seeing the world, but La Générale d'Optique. No matter which part of GPS would travel, many aspects had to be taken into account. Would the location strategy that GPS had followed in France be as effective in the new country? What about marketing, human resources and service? How would competitors react?

EXHIBIT 1A

Representation of the GPS Group

GPS companies are divided over the optical and the photo market (horizontal) and serve customers on the service and on the price axis (vertical).

Number of stores and employees are quoted at 31.12.1996. Sales are annualized for stores open at 31.12.1996. (The total figure for the optics market includes 16 Solaris stores. The total figure for the Photo market includes 12 Photo Points stores. The total headcount for GPS includes 25 employees at the head office.)

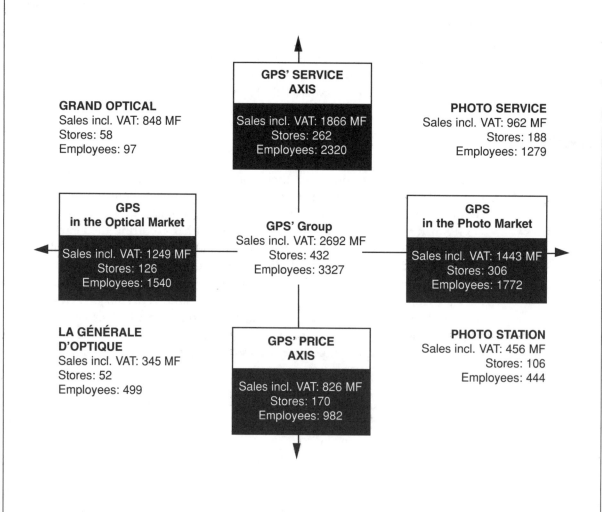

Source: Company Records.

EXHIBIT 1B

GPS Consolidated Profit & Loss 1992–96

FFMillion Year to December	1992	1993	1994	1995	1996
Net Sales Revenue	763	868	1040	1615	2012
% Growth		13.9	19.7	55.3	24.5
Gross Profit	500.9	586.6	742.3	1,210.4	1,493.0
% Gross Margin	64.9	66.8	70.3	73.9	72.2
Current Pre-tax Profit	56.4	75.4	95.7	124.8	229.6
Employee Profit Share	3.1	4.7	8.5	11.8	18.8
Net Profit After Tax	29.7	38.0	56.3	35.1	117.9
Net Profit as a % of Sales	3.8	4.3	5.3	2.1	5.8

Sources: Company Report and Goldman Sachs estimates.

EXHIBIT 2

The Spirit of GPS

The sharing of core values by all employees is at the heart of GPS and is the means of binding the Group together. Each new employee joining the Group receives a presentation of these values supported by examples of their application, so that everyone is aware of their rights and their responsibilities.

Our Core Values	The Rights of Our Employees	The Responsibilities of Our Employees	The Rights of Our Clients
Growing People ■ understanding why ■ clarity ■ empowering ■ sharing *Performing as a Team* ■ professional ■ alert ■ innovating ■ growing *Serving* ■ the client first ■ quality ■ reactive ■ ethical	■ The right to do everything necessary to satisfy a client ■ The right to take initiative and test ideas ■ The right to constructive criticism ■ The right to make mistakes ■ The right to understand ■ The right to be trained ■ The right to be clearly informed ■ The right to be recognized for one's achievements ■ The right to develop at one's own pace within the company ■ The right to be helped	■ The responsibility to do everything possible to satisfy each client ■ The responsibility to contribute to the performance of one's team ■ The responsibility to be a trainer and a mentor ■ The responsibility to communicate ■ The responsibility to set an example ■ The responsibility to be honest and loyal ■ The responsibility to respects one's obligations and those of the company ■ The responsibility to answer for one's actions ■ The responsibility to have ideas ■ The responsibility to constantly improve	We aim for the total satisfaction of our customers and recognize their rights: ■ The right to be loved ■ The right to be recognized ■ The right to services and products adapted to their real needs ■ The right to freedom to choose ■ The right to reliable products and services ■ The right to understand ■ The right to be treated as someone of good faith at all times ■ The right to have their interests defended ■ The right to make a mistake ■ The right to be ...amazed!

Source: Company Records.

EXHIBIT 3

Photos of GPS Stores

Source: Company Records.

EXHIBIT 3 (CONTINUED)

Source: Company Records.

EXHIBIT 4

Quick Look at the Optical Industry

The players in the optical industry included the manufacturers of frames, glasses and lenses, the central labs that put frames and lenses together according to a specific prescription for a customer and, of course, the different retail outlets where consumers bought glasses and contact lenses. It was a market of change in which the retail side, in particular, was going from a fragmented market with local players only, to a more organized market in which chain stores were gaining market share over independent opticians. These chain stores had begun expansion beyond their own borders, so the optical market was slowly becoming European or even global. The speed of these developments differed by country. Influential factors were legislation, consumer buying patterns in general and the development rate of shopping centers.

Manufacturing Frames

Eyewear frame manufacturers were mostly small, with the exception of some key players like Luxotica and Safilo in Italy and Rayban in the US.

The design of frames was playing a more and more important role as consumers no longer considered glasses a medical device. Many brands in fashion, cosmetics and leisure such as Armani, Dior or even Disney had created spectacle models under license. Retail prices ranged from FF100 to FF3,000 (not including couturier and 'jewellery-like' glasses that sold for FF20,000 or more). Selling spectacles under a brand name was a very good way for a high-profile consumer brand to reinforce its image and make some money on licensing fees.

However, except for a few designs, it was very difficult for the consumer to show that he was wearing branded goods, since the logo or brand name appeared on the side pieces of the frame in very small print only.

This made it very easy to imitate the brands' models. Fielmann in Germany – Europe's largest optical retailer – had pushed this opportunity to the extreme by asking manufacturers to make look-a-like models. Fielmann would then display the look-a-likes in the shop windows side by side with the much more expensive branded models. Sometimes the Fielmann model would cost DM20 and the brand DM200.

Depending on the country, the manufacturers sold either directly to retailers (usually the larger retailers only) or through distributors, of whom some had exclusivity for a particular brand.

Manufacturing and Mounting Lenses

In contrast to frames, lenses for spectacles and contact lenses were manufactured by only a few international competitors: Bausch & Lomb for contact lenses, Essilor, Zeiss, and Rosenstock for spectacle lenses. These companies had plants and sales offices in different countries. In highly automated laboratories, they cut, surfaced and mounted the lenses in frames for independent retailers.

Surfacing and mounting could also be done in independent laboratories or central labs. These labs bought lenses from the big manufacturers and would then cut, surface and mount them according to the specific shape of the spectacles. They would also add specific features chosen by the customer, such as anti-reflection coating or anti-scratch coating. Laboratories were owned by retailer chains or located in optical stores, as was the case of one one-hour service outlet. Next to taking care of mounting, the labs cut the lenses and applied an anti-reflection coating or other features. Typically, in a store, an optician could do about 15 to 20 pairs of glasses a day. In a centralized and automated lab, one person could do as many as 50 pairs a day.

EXHIBIT 4 (CONTINUED)

Retailers

There were five different kinds of retail outlets for the sale of spectacles and lenses.

Independent Opticians

Independent opticians took a traditional approach to business. They were usually located in the center of a small town or city and offered 600 frames. They catered especially to the elderly. In most European countries, a store needed to have at least one licensed (Master) optician. Studies for becoming a Master optician lasted from two years in France to eight years – including part-time study and apprenticeship – in Germany. Diplomas were not internationally recognized. The requirement of having a Master optician in the store made it difficult to start up in the optical business. As not many new competitors were opening up shop, the existing independent retailers had been surviving with high gross margin sales of more than 70%.

Buying Groups

Buying groups consisted of opticians who had formed associations or cooperations to buy in large quantities and perform other common tasks like advertising. In France, for instance, Krys and Optic 2000 comprised 500 stores under each name and did centralized buying and advertising. They had sites in shopping centers as well as in city centers.

Franchised Networks

Franchised networks were composed of stores with the same look and the same assortment. They had joint buying power, shared the same marketing policy and advertised heavily. Afflelou in France, for instance, had 500 stores under franchise and spent over FF100 million in advertising for a turnover of FF1,700 million.

Branch Stores

Branch stores were the true 'industrialists' in the business. Whether they provided one-hour service or had a service delivery of two to three days, they had uniform stores, marketing practices and assortments. Boots (300 stores), Dollond & Aitchison (450 stores) and Vision Express (100 stores) in the UK, GPS (Grand Optical 50 stores) in France, Fielmann (350 stores) and Apollo (177 stores) in Germany represented the new players. These stores relied heavily on advertising, except for Grand Optical, which did none.

Mail Order

Mail order was the most recent player in the optical industry. It was appearing only in Scandinavia and focused mostly on contact lenses.

Pricing Frames and Lenses

The classic independent store tended to price branded goods high. Buying groups, franchise operations and branch networks offered promotions (typically 'buy one, get one free') or a 40% discount on both brand and non-brand eyewear. They had cheap, non-brand eyewear made to their specifications by small manufacturers in Europe and the Far East. As for GPS, Grand Optical did not actively promote its branded goods, and La Générale

EXHIBIT 4 (CONTINUED)

d'Optique – another store chain started up by GPS in 1993 – focused on an everyday, low price policy for its non-brand glasses. As Grand Optical did not invest in advertising, it used the stores as its main communication medium.

Costs of Setting Up Stores

The costs for setting up a store varied per country, as one of the main variables was costs for space. In some countries, one only had the costs of the rent of the building; in others, one had to pay 'key money' to get in (Latin countries). If the location kept the same value, key money could be returned after leaving. In France, for example, key money usually amounted to around FF17,000 per m^2.

The Euro Consumer: Myth or Reality

When Likierman and Abittan started thinking about going abroad, the question arose as to the extent of adaptation needed to fit the needs and tastes of the consumers in the new country. No comparative study was available on the subject, but some points were the same for every country in the world. The first, most common feature was that about 40% to 50% of every country's population needed glasses (20% at age 20, 35% at age 40, 45% at age 65). Wearers needed to change these glasses every three to five years, depending on vision correction factors. Wearers over 55 needed to change them every two years. Only 10% to 20% preferred contact lenses and, at least at this point in time, surgery could not replace glasses (except maybe in 5% of the cases).

About 20% to 40% of the customers based their purchase on price, as they considered buying glasses a medical obligation. Of course, they preferred good design for a cheap price. About 20% to 25% of the buyers preferred branded goods. These people considered glasses a fashion item. In all countries, there was high loyalty to the optician that customers once started with.

Differences in consumer behaviour per country were caused by many factors, including legislation. In some countries, customers could not get glasses in a retail store without a prescription from an ophthalmologist (at least if they wanted compensation from the state insurance or private insurance). This was the case in France. In other countries, the prescription from the ophthalmologist was not compulsory. Lenses could be measured in the store by a licensed optometrist or optician (Germany, UK, Spain, Luxembourg). This did not mean that all consumers actually did that. In Germany, for instance, more than half still went to their doctor; in the UK, less than 20% did.

Reimbursement systems and levels also had an effect on the price consumers were willing to pay. In general, the local insurance system did not reimburse generously for eyewear (for example, in France the maximum was FF87.50). Sometimes, it was more generous for lenses. Consumers often had complementary insurance to compensate for the lack of state reimbursement. But to give an example from France: for a pair of branded glasses costing FF3,000, a typical client would get around FF150 from the state and FF1,500 from the insurance (about 50%). For spectacles priced FF1,000, one would get FF600.

Finally, more and more customers were alert to the dangers of ultraviolet radiation from the sun and, depending on where they lived, they increasingly wore sun glasses. Other differences in consumer behaviour with regard to eyewear had to do with the level of multi-possession, average price paid, add-ons for the lenses (an anti-reflection coating, for example), preferences for plastic versus metal or organic versus plastic, tastes for shapes and colors, and so on. With respect to both technical and quality factors, the most demanding customers in Europe were the Germans.

Source: Company Records.

EXHIBIT 5

Costs and Income of a Typical Grand Optical or La Générale d'Optique Store in France

	La Générale d'Optique Model	Grand Optical Model
Sales Per Store on Average in FF (ex. VAT)	6 mn	12 mn
Net Sales in %	100	100
Gross Margin in %	60	71
Store Costs in %:		
Staff	20	22
Space	11	12
External	3	3
Communication	4	3
Leasing m/c	–	3
Depreciation	3	5
Store Contribution %	19	23
Head Office Overhead %	10	12
Operating Result %	9	11
Financial Result %	2	2
Current Pre-tax Profit %	7	9

Source: Company Records.

EXHIBIT 6

Grand Optical Facts and Figures as per December 1996

Typical Profile of a Grand Optical Store	*Typical Profile of a La Générale d'Optique Store*
■ 300 m² of which 100 m² laboratory space	■ 200 m²
■ Catchment area: 300,000 inhabitants	■ Catchment area: 150,000 inhabitants
■ Sales (inc. VAT) per store: FF15 million	■ Sales (inc. VAT) per store: FF7 million
■ Investment: FF12 million	■ Investment: FF5 million
■ key money: FF5 million	■ key money: FF3 million
■ store design: FF5 million	■ store design FF2 million
■ equipment: FF2 million	■ equipment: 0
■ Frames on view: 3,500	■ Frames on view: 2,200
■ Stock of optical lenses: 9,000	■ Stock of optical lenses: 0
■ Stock of contact lenses: 600	■ Stock of contact lenses: 300
■ Number of staff: 14	■ Number of staff: 7
■ Sells about 8,000 equipment per year	■ Sells about 7,000 equipment per year
■ Average sale per equipment: FF1,600	■ Average sale per equipment: FF1,000
■ Store locations: 60% out of town shopping centers, 30% town center shopping centers, 10% high street locations	■ Store locations: 90% out of town shopping centers, 10% town center
■ No advertising, the store is the medium	■ Advertising: 5%
■ Pay back period: 5 years	■ Pay back period: 4 years

Source: Company Records.

EXHIBIT 7

Overview of International Competitors

Vision Express expanding rapidly but into less competitive markets

→ emphasis on one-hour service and promotion
→ started in the UK
→ heavy advertising (10% of sales)
→ smaller outlets, size is not essential
→ heavy advertising, just for mass media
→ expanding rapidly, formula easily implemented
→ opportunistic, no clear focus
→ present in: Philippines (1), Poland (9), Czech Republic (1), Belgium (9), Argentina (7 franchised), Latvia (6), Ireland (6), Russia (2, franchised), UK (100), Rest of the World (10)

Fielmann plans aggressive European expansion but no one-hour service

→ founded in Hamburg in 1972
→ largest optical retailer in Europe, large selection
→ positioned itself initially as the store for spectacles for free
→ accepts lower margin per pair of glasses
→ has high operating margin per square meter of shop
→ employees sell four pairs of glasses a day (industry average: 1.8)
→ does not believe in one-hour service
→ quality guarantee of three years on all spectacles
→ central labs for processing
→ varying store sizes, up to Superoptical size
→ consistent in merchandising to smallest detail in all stores
→ saturation of home market in 3–4 years, then growth by acquisition abroad
→ believe competitive advantage is price, quality, service, in that order
→ present in: Germany (350), Austria (2), Switzerland (9; 20 planned)
→ planned expansion in: United Kingdom, Spain, Italy, France?

EXHIBIT 7 (CONTINUED)

Dollond & Aitchison are international but undifferentiated

→   neither LDC (Low Delivered Value), or HPV (High Perceived Value)
→   covers regular and superoptical outlets
→   local management and local adaptation, not one formula across markets
→   present in: United Kingdom (469), Spain (70), Italy (90), Switzerland (15), Ireland (6)

Pearle Vision has problems

→   sometimes one-hour service
→   broad assortment of private label and middle market brands
→   heavy promotions, 'buy one get one free'
→   two attempts to enter the German market failed
→   financial problems?
→   present in United States (822), Belgium (60) Holland (147)
→   Grand Met is seeking to divest since 1990

Source: Company Records.

EXHIBIT 8

Positioning of the International Optical Chains

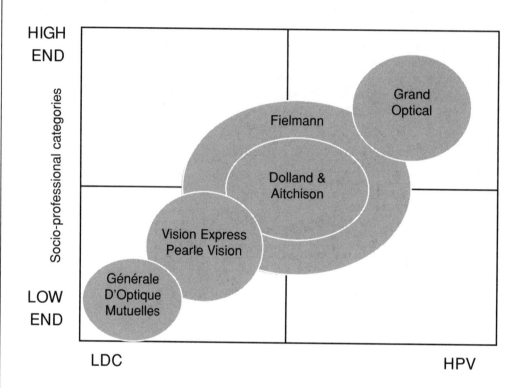

Source: Company Records.

EXHIBIT 9

Quantitative Market Data

	France	Germany	Italy	Portugal	Spain	Switzerland	Hong Kong	Singapore
Wearers in millions	27	36.8	24.5	3.8	17	3.5	3.5	1.7
Market value in FFbillion	15.7	18.4	10.4	0.5	6.0	2.9	1.7	0.4
Repurchase rate in years	3.5	3	3.5	N/A	3.5	4	2	1.5–2
Average price pair of glasses in FF 1,000–1,800	1,300	1,600	750	900	900–1,000	1,700	1,100–1550	
No. of shopping centers in 1995	614	180	300	30	326	45	est. 20 that would be suitable for Grand Optical	N/A
Square meters (in millions) of shopping centers	13.2	6.2	3.7	0.4	3.6	0.7		
Increase in number of hyper/ supermarkets in period 1989–93	27	21	69	187	91	N/A	N/A	N/A
Shopping hours	moderately flexible	were restrictive but were changing	flexible	flexible	flexible	moderately flexible	flexible?	flexible?
Wearers per outlet	3,978	4,300	2,400	3,040	3,272	3,700	2,040	2,667
Independents' share of market value in %	32	23	96	90	35	95	–	–
Chains' share of market value in %	N/A	27	2	N/A	17	17	N/A	N/A

Source: Company Records.

EXHIBIT 10

Competitors' Profiles per Market (as evaluated by the IMD MBA project team)

	Broad Range	1 Hour Service	Customer Service	Self Service	LDC/HPV*	Fashion/ Store Brands
GRAND OPTICAL **(market share 5%)**	**yes**	**yes**	**yes**	**yes**	**HPV**	**both**
FRANCE						
Mutual Insurance companies (19% market share)	no	no	no	no	LDC	store
Krys (14% market share)	yes	no	no	no	HPV	both
Afflelou (11% market share)	yes/no	no	no	yes/no	LDC	both
Optique 2000 (9% market share)	yes/no	no	yes	yes/no	HPV	both
GERMANY						
Fielmann (349 stores, $657m)	yes	no	yes	yes	LDC/HPV	both
Apollo (177 stores, $165m)	yes	no	yes	yes	LDC	store
Abele (51 stores, $50m)	no	no	yes	yes	HPV	both
Krane (72 stores, $63m)	yes	no	yes	no	HPV	both
Binder (34 stores, $41m)	no	no	yes	no	HPV	fashion
Family (10 stores)	yes	no	N/A	yes	HPV	–
Matt (41 stores)	no	no	yes	yes	LDC	store
Vision Express (1 store)	no	yes	yes	yes	LDC	both

EXHIBIT 10 (CONTINUED)

	Broad Range	1 Hour Service	Customer Service	Self Service	LDC/HPV*	Fashion/ Store Brands
GRAND OPTICAL (market share 5%)	**yes**	**yes**	**yes**	**yes**	**HPV**	**both**
Italy						
Salmoiraghi (102 stores, $48m)	no	no	no	no	HPV	both
Poliedros (30 stores, 12 one-hour)	no	yes	yes	yes	LDC	fashion
COI (166 stores, $49m)	no	no	yes	yes	HPV	fashion
Green Vision (105 stores, $43m)	no	no	yes	no	HPV	both
Portugal						
Pro Visao	no	yes	yes	no	HPV	fashion
Multiopticas	no	yes	yes	no	LDC	store
Spain						
General Optica (85 stores, $114m)	no	no	yes	no	HPV	both
Opticost (78 stores, $20m)	yes	yes	yes	no	LDC	store
Vision Lab (20 stores)	yes	yes	yes	no	HPV	both
Optica 2000	no	no	yes	no	HPV	both
Switzerland						
Visilab (17 stores, $55m)	no	yes	yes	yes	HPV	fashion
Fielmann	yes	no	yes?	yes	LDC/HPV	both
Delta Optik (16 stores, $15m)	no	no	yes	yes	HPV	fashion
Hong Kong and Singapore						
Optical 88** (HK 76 stores)	yes	yes	yes	no	HPV	fashion
The Optical shop** (HK 49 stores, Sin 8 stores)	yes	no	yes	some	HPV	fashion
Capitol Optique (Sin 20 stores)	yes	no	yes	no	HPV	fashion
Paris Miki (Sin 8 stores)	yes	no	yes	some	HPV	fashion

* LDC: Low Delivered Cost / HPV: High Perceived Value.   ** Heavy discounts on brands.
Source: Company Records.

CASE 2.11 Make Yourself Heard: Ericsson's Global Brand Campaign

This case was prepared by Professor Kamran Kashani.

In February 1998, Ericsson launched a major global communication campaign for its brand of mobile phones. This was the first time a leading telecommunications company had launched a brand campaign on such a scale. Inspired by 'the simple fact that personal contact is the most important and powerful element in mobile communication', the management of Ericsson's mobile phone and terminals division had decided to launch the massive advertising despite reservations expressed by others that the focus on brand building could take resources and attention away from the increasing number of new products Ericsson was bringing into the mobile phone market. But in the words of Jan Ahrenbring, vice president of marketing communication:

> The brand campaign is about Ericsson values, not just products. The brand platform is meant to convey a clear message about Ericsson's belief in the values of self-expression and ease of communication in relating to one another.

Company Background

Ericsson is a leading supplier of equipment and services for the telecommunications industry. The company produces advanced systems and products for wired and mobile telecommunications in both public and private networks, sold to customers in more than 130 countries.

In 1997, Ericsson had 100,774 employees and 168 billion Swedish kronor (SKr) in sales.[1] Close to 90% of its turnover was generated outside of Sweden, where it was founded more than 120 years ago.

Since early 1997, Ericsson's vast operations in virtually the entire telecommunications field had been organized into three business areas:

- *Radio Systems:* Mobile voice and data communication systems. 1997 sales: SKr78 billion.
- *Infocom Systems:* Multimedia communications solutions for transmission of voice, data and images to network operators, service providers and enterprises. 1997 sales: SKr48 billion.
- *Mobile Phones and Terminals:* End-user mobile phones and terminals, such as pagers. 1997 sales: SKr42 billion.

(Refer to **Exhibit 1** for a partial organization of Ericsson.)

In 1996, a large strategy study was completed. Entitled '2005: Entering the 21st Century', it constituted the basis for Ericsson's future strategy:

> Ericsson's mission is to understand our customers' opportunities and needs and to provide communications solutions better than any competitor. In doing this, Ericsson can offer its shareholders a competitive return on their investments.

1. In 1998: US$ = SKr7.9.

In recent years, Ericsson's R&D budget exceeded 20% of sales. More than 18,000 employees in 23 countries were active in research and development. The management estimated that with the fast pace of technological development, its entire product portfolio would be completely renewed within two years.

In 1997, Ericsson's mobile phone *systems* were estimated to have served 54 million subscribers in 92 countries. With 40% of the world market for such systems sold to network operators, the company was the leader in this area.

Ericsson entered the market for hand held mobile *phones* only in 1987. This was the first time the company marketed its products to consumers. The 1997 reorganization of Ericsson, which made mobile phones a separate division, was motivated by a recognition that, as an end-user market, mobile phones had their own 'different business logic'. The market share for Ericsson's mobile phones had strengthened recently compared with its two global rivals, Nokia and Motorola. (Refer to market share data in **Exhibit 2**.)

Past Advertising

Ericsson's advertising had been limited before it entered the mobile phone business. As a company targeting a few large telecommunication customers, typically large PTT organizations or business organizations, the management saw little need for advertising. Even after the introduction of its first mobile phone, the company abstained from heavy advertising. In the words of a senior mobile phone manager:

> In a hot market for mobile phones we sold whatever we produced, and the assumption at the time was simply that if we made good products, we didn't need advertising.

Most early mobile phone ads were initiated by Ericsson's local sales companies around the world. In each ad, a phone product was introduced under a communication strategy that was decided by Ericsson's country management.

In 1995, Ericsson successfully implemented its first pan-European advertising campaign for a new phone line, GH337. Under headlines all starting with 'It's about...' the ads introduced the new product's features. (Refer to **Exhibit 3** for samples of press advertising.)

Reflecting on the first pan-regional campaign, Goran Andersson, the marketing director for brand communications (reporting to Jan Ahrenbring), recalled:

> The local management were not used to supporting such an initiative and, naturally, they were not very happy with the idea at the beginning. But that campaign showed us all that together we can do very useful things.

Following the reorganization of the mobile phone into a separate division, the management embarked on its first global communication initiative. In 1997, Ericsson entered into an agreement with United Artists Pictures to place its mobile phones in the James Bond movie *Tomorrow Never Dies*. The division's management saw the product placement as an opportunity to show that 'Ericsson is the leading technological and style innovator... and to demonstrate its phones as part of everyday life.' For a period of 12 weeks the company used the James Bond film theme for tie-in tactical ads for new products around the world. (Refer to **Exhibit 4** for a copy of local James Bond advertising in Austria.)

It was estimated that in 1997 close to SKr2 billion was spent advertising Ericsson mobile phones worldwide. Of this total, 75% was spent by local organizations on product campaigns. The remainder was accounted for by pan-European or global product ads which appeared on such media as CNN, in-flight and business magazines.

Brand Building

The division management at mobile phones and terminals had closely monitored the forces that were fast changing the global mobile phone business. In the late 1990s, the market was growing faster than ever, but becoming increasingly competitive. While in early 1997 there were 137 million mobile phone subscribers worldwide, this number was expected to grow to 590 million by 2002. The growth was expected to be fastest in Asia-Pacific, followed by Latin America, Europe, and North America. Meanwhile, there were an estimated 20 producers of mobile phones, a number that was expected to grow significantly in the near future.

Management had come to believe that future leadership in the mobile phone business was the privilege of those few companies that could build strong brands with the end-users. For division management, the need for brands with differentiated consumer value was justified for a number of reasons:

1. Product differences among manufacturers were beginning to narrow down. Differentiation purely based on technology and features was becoming more difficult.
2. New products were witnessing ever-shrinking life cycles. While a new Ericsson mobile phone introduced in 1992 was in the market for three years before being replaced by more advanced, and lower cost, models, the recent launches were expected to have life cycles of 12–18 months. A proliferation of short-cycle models made product-specific communication expensive and possibly not effective.
3. The new generation of end-users was looking for different features in a phone than those who had entered the market early on. While the early adopters had been primarily business users who had looked for advanced features and small size, future growth was expected to come from non-business consumers who looked for different values in a mobile phone.

Furthermore, the management believed that in its competitive market, Ericsson could enjoy its traditional price premium (ranging for some models from 5% up to 30% over Nokia and Motorola) only if its reputation for technological leadership could be backed up with a strong brand. Goran Andersson commented:

While the network operators have tried to commoditize mobile phones by nearly giving them away to attract subscribers, we want the consumer to ask not just for a phone, but Ericsson's mobile phone – even if it costs more. Like the business buyers before them, we like the newcomers to the market to think of our products as something special, worth a premium.

While local market conditions differed widely, it was estimated that close to 60% of all mobile phones sold around the world was bought directly by consumers through a retail outlet. The rest was sold by network operators through their own promotional schemes. The share of retail sales was expected to grow.

Market Studies

In 1997, mobile phone division management commissioned a couple of studies the conclusions of which reinforced its own analysis of the trends in the mobile phone market, and the growing importance of brands in consumer choice. The first study, entitled 'Take Five', was a global segmentation effort aimed at better understanding the profiles of the mobile phone consumer. Researched in 24 countries in Europe, the Americas, and Asia, the study concluded that lifestyle and consumer values were better predictors of consumer behavior than traditional demographic factors. The study identified five global consumer segments, each with a different profile:

- *Pioneers:* Active individualists and explorers. Interested in and knowledgeable about technology. Motivated by innovation, they are impulsive buyers, attracted by strong brands and will pay for quality. Their loyalty is to technology, not brands.
- *Achievers:* Hard-working, competitive individualists. Willing to take risks, they are motivated by productivity, comfort, success and advance technology that is also useful, time-saving and visible. Care about appearance, but have limited brand loyalty.
- *Materialists:* Status seekers, they are attracted by well-known brands. Main motivations are recognition, status and sense of belonging. They want trendy products and are attracted to known brands.
- *Sociables:* Convivial and community-orientated, they are highly rational, well-informed and buy products that are easy to use and attractive. They are loyal to brands.
- *Traditionalists:* Attracted to social harmony rather than change, they are attracted to established products with basic features that offer ease and reliability. Low prices and well-known brands are important to them. They tend to be brand loyal.

The study proposed that the five segments are measurable by size, penetration and inclination to purchase. While in the early stages of market development in each country, the pioneers were by far the largest group of mobile phone buyers; over time other segments entered the market and grew in both absolute and relative terms. The management believed that the global segmentation had the capacity of guiding action along a wide range of activities, from strategic planning and product development to brand marketing and sales. Future products were to be conceived, designed and marketed with the values of different segments in mind.

The second international study, done in parallel with the first, was aimed at assessing Ericsson's current brand perceptions and defining directions for the future. The corporate 'soul searching', as some members of the management labeled the study, revealed that Ericsson was perceived differently in different countries and by different segments. Nevertheless, the brand was commonly perceived as 'cold, distant, conservative, and technology orientated'. The study also revealed that the brand awareness and recognition were low in most markets, especially among the growing numbers of non-business customers. For example, in the United Kingdom, which was typical of the more developed markets, spontaneous awareness among mobile phone users, and those who might purchase in the next 12 months, was 36%. This figure was at par with Motorola, but significantly below Nokia at 45%. In the United States, on the other hand, Ericsson's brand awareness was nil.

Among the second study's final conclusions, partly aimed at educating the management regarding the need for brand building, were the following statements:

1. For many people working in fast moving technological fields at Ericsson, branding may be a concept which is difficult to accept. They like things to be concrete, technologically different; branding, though, is a product of the 'mind and heart'. But it would be a mistake to believe that branding is unimportant because good brands outlive any passing technological breakthrough.

2. The ultimate goal in branding is to cement a relationship with our consumers. Capturing a share of his mind... his imagination... his emotions... It will generate sentiments like 'The Ericsson mobile phone brand really understands what I am about – my hopes, my dreams.' By creating a strong emotional and psychological bond, the Ericsson brand will give the consumers a reason to buy beyond price, features or rebates.

3. Ericsson must work on two fronts simultaneously: build a strong brand based on a consistent brand platform and pursue its traditional product innovation, which can quickly meet the ever-changing needs of consumers.

The study proposed a *brand platform* that was 'not about cold technology, but about human contact... the contact that comes through human conversation, through people talking and listening'. It defined Ericsson's *brand ambition* as 'to be recognized as the brand that makes personal contact the most important element in mobile telecommunication'.

Competition

The growing mobile phone market was dominated by three players: Nokia, Motorola and Ericsson. Others with well-recognized brand names, such as Sony and Philips, were also present but held smaller market shares. Nokia was known for a constant stream of advanced new products. Its latest model, Nokia 9000 Communicator, combined voice, fax, email and Internet functionality in a device that retailed at around $1,000. Nokia's international advertising, using the slogan 'Connecting People', had stressed these advanced features. Motorola, a leader in the field, had lost market share for lack of new models and poor marketing. After a recent reorganization, Motorola seemed to be fighting back. Its newest product, StarTAC, weighing 95 grams and selling at approximately $700, was the world's smallest phone, a claim stressed in the company's recent advertising. Before StarTAC, Ericsson's GH337, which sold to consumers for less than $200, had held the title of the world's smallest mobile phone.

Mobile phone prices had generally declined in recent years. In the United States, for example, the average consumer prices had dropped from $182 to $111 since 1994.

Global Brand Campaign

In 1996, with a view to launching a global brand campaign, the mobile phones and terminals division hired Young & Rubicam, an advertising agency with an extensive international network. To maintain a degree of consistency in communication, local Ericsson organizations, long accustomed to working with their own choice of agencies, were now required to work exclusively with Young & Rubicam.

In discussions that followed their appointment, the ad agency proposed two alternative platforms for a global brand campaign. Both platforms were seen by the agency as having the potential of fulfilling the brand ambition set out in the earlier study. The first proposal revolved around the slogan 'One Person, One Voice', but it was rejected for a number of reasons, including its political overtones, which limited its use in some countries.

The second platform was captured in the slogan 'Make yourself heard'. The agency and the management both believed that this platform was true to the goal of projecting Ericsson as a human and compassionate company, thus setting it apart from all the other feature-orientated mobile phone brands. In the words of Ericsson's group chairman, Lars Ramqvist, 'It is our belief that communication is between people – the rest is technology.' The management also believed that the platform empowered people to communicate what is on their minds, and showed respect for individuals and what they had to say.

For press advertising, the agency proposed a gallery of faces and a range of situations demonstrating shared thoughts, experiences and ideas that would capture the spirit of communication between people around the world. The pictures were to be of ordinary people in everyday situations. Each ad would carry a statement in smaller print at the bottom giving Ericsson's credentials, including the fact that the company's products were used in '40% of all mobile communications around the world'.[2] For TV, distinctive white-on-black TV commercials would feature a wordplay that would bring 'Make yourself heard' to life. (Refer to **Exhibits 5 and 6** for samples of campaign billboards and TV commercial storyboards.[3])

Unlike all previous Ericsson campaigns, the proposed ads did not show any mobile phone products. This unusual omission was thought to be the right approach, and for good reasons. First, the agency wanted to deflect attention away from specific products and their features towards the umbrella brand. Second, different models were being sold in different parts of the world, thereby limiting what could be shown in a standardized global campaign. Third, both the management and the agency wanted to leave the door open for the future use of Ericsson brand on non-phone products or services. Finally, in the words of Jan Hedqvist, Young & Rubicam account executive: 'The inclusion of a product would destroy the sense of intimacy we are trying to establish with the consumer. We would be seen as hawking something.'

To ensure that the company was betting on the right campaign, 'Make yourself heard' and its accompanying visual communication were pre-tested in 19 countries, representing 85% of total mobile phone sales. The key findings were:

- Ads generated unusually consistent reactions across countries. The slogan 'grew' on people, showing its long-term potential
- The slogan was found to have a universal appeal. It was seen to be intelligent
- Consumers found Ericsson as the brand that 'will help you say what you need/want to say'; 'cuts distance, mentally and physically, between people'; 'knows about and is interested in people'; and 'supports a global community'.

The research agency conducting the pre-test found the outcome so encouraging that it reported the following: 'These are the most positive and consistent results we have seen in advertising research.'

Early in 1998, a decision was made by the top management of mobile phones and terminals to launch the proposed global brand campaign, starting in Europe. The Americas and Asia-Pacific markets were to follow later in the year. The budget for the first leg of the campaign was not publicly announced, but it was estimated to be in the SKr250–300 million range. Of this expenditure, 20% was to be financed by the head office, and the rest by the regions (25%) and local markets (55%). The media spread was different in different markets, but generally 70% was targeted for press, and the rest for TV and outdoors.

---

2. The full body copy of press ads reads: 'Ericsson has been helping people share their thoughts for over 120 years. Today, Ericsson equipment is used in 40% of all mobile phone communications around the world. By mobile phone, data, pager or cordless phone – Ericsson gives you the power to be heard. Wherever you are, whenever you want.'

3. In some markets, such as Sweden and United Kingdom, the slogan 'Make yourself heard' was to appear in English. In other markets it would be translated into the local language. The copy was in local language.

To assess the campaign's results, tracking studies measuring consumer awareness and brand image for Ericsson and its rivals were to be conducted weekly in 20 countries.

Future Decisions

Barely a few weeks after its launch in mid-February 1998, the 'Make yourself heard' campaign was generating reactions and raising new issues. Some observers were wondering if the company was putting its resources in the right place. A commentary in the UK-based *Marketing Week* called the global campaign a 'courageous' move, but wondered if it 'detracts from product advertising and, even more pertinently, from sales'.[4]

Within the organization the campaign was raising other issues. One was whether the brand campaign should be coordinated with the product-orientated advertising sponsored by the regions and local operations. Goran Andersson explained:

> As a brand campaign 'Make yourself heard' isn't designed for any particular product or segment. It is about Ericsson and its values as a brand. On the other hand, more targeted product and segment ads are currently being run by the regional and local sales operations. The questions are whether or not the brand and the product campaigns should be coordinated and, if so, how.

Exhibit 7 shows a copy of a recent product advertising run by the European region for Ericsson's new GH688 model. Targeted at a segment the earlier research had identified as 'Achievers', the ad emphasized the product's features and carried the tag line 'Made for business. Good for life.' Product ads accounted for 80% of Ericsson's advertising budgeted for 1998; the rest was devoted to the brand campaign.

Andersson was aware of the fact that local and regional operations were jealously guarding their autonomy in deciding tactical product advertising. He also knew that the global campaign did not satisfy everyone in the local sales organizations. 'Eighty percent of the complaints I get from the field is about why we don't show a mobile phone in these ads', he noted.

Nevertheless, Andersson believed that the next phase of Ericsson's brand communication should address the growing number of new models that were coming out of development and which were targeting specific lifestyle segments. Five such models were expected to be launched in 1998 alone. 'The question is', Andersson commented, 'how to connect and link your global brand campaign with hundreds of local advertising and promotions which are by their very nature tactical, product-specific, and increasingly targeted at well-defined consumer segments.' **Exhibit 8** shows a copy of the press ad for the launch of GF788, a product targeted at the 'Sociables' segment.

Another related issue was the relationship between the mobile phone division's brand campaign and the communication strategies of other divisions. The recent

---

4. O'Sullivan, Tom. 'Ericsson strives to make itself heard', *Marketing Week*, February 5, 1998.

publicity around the global campaign had made some members of the corporate management wonder if the message 'Make yourself heard' was not equally appropriate for the other divisions of Ericsson. For Ahrenbring, vice president of marketing communication, a legitimate question was whether the brand campaign was an appropriate vehicle to promote a company dedicated to high technology.

Currently, Radio and Infocom Systems divisions were running limited press ads under different platforms. **Exhibit 9** shows a recent Radio Systems ad for a new line of base stations targeted at mobile phone network companies.

While flattered by the excitement the global brand campaign had generated in other business areas, Andersson was more concerned with the future of branding in his own division:

> If 'Make yourself heard' becomes a corporate brand platform, how can we in the mobile phone division communicate those values which are so intrinsic to our way of doing business? Doesn't that mean we would be condemned back to product advertising?

Latest News

On April 21, Andersson was to meet with the three regional heads of mobile phones and terminals to discuss the future of the global campaign. The issues of brand versus product advertising were very much on everybody's mind. Early campaign results from around Europe indicated increased awareness for the Ericsson brand among the general public; surveys also showed a trend towards positive and long lasting top-of-mind brand attributes. The first phase of the European campaign was supposed to wind down by the end of April.

Just a few days before the April meeting, Andersson came across a news item carried by the *Wall Street Journal Europe* under the banner 'Motorola Launches New Image Campaign'. The paper reported that Motorola was about to launch a $100 million-plus global advertising campaign, the largest in its history, to 'beat back rivals and change its image from sturdy to contemporary'.[5] The article explained that Motorola's new campaign, under the theme of 'Wings', was based on a year-long research that showed 'consumers were looking for an inspirational, uplifting, high-utility relationship with communication devices'. Against a background of Mick Jagger's music, the paper reported, the voice in TV commercials reassured the viewers that 'Motorola gives you wings. Wings sets you free.' An account executive for Motorola's ad agency, McCann-Erickson, was quoted as saying 'Motorola is known but not preferred… Consumers tend to say "good quality, durable", but there is no real affinity for who the company is, what the brand is. It lacks personality.' According to the paper, Motorola was trying to correct a situation in recent years in which it had lost market shares to both Nokia and Ericsson.

---

5. Beatty, Sally. 'Motorola Launches New Image Campaign', *Wall Street Journal Europe*, April 17–18, 1998.

EXHIBIT 1

Partial Organization Chart: Ericsson Group and Mobile Phones and Terminals

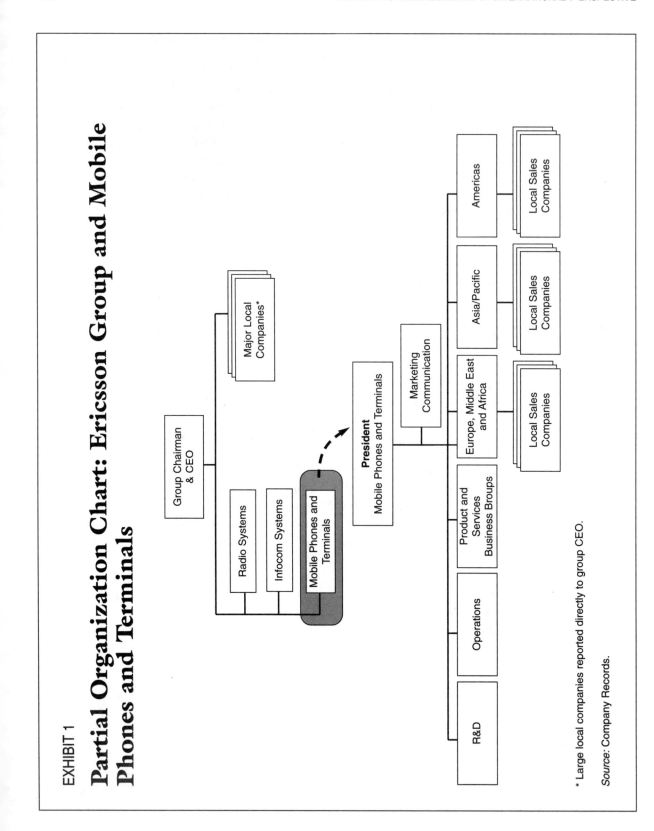

* Large local companies reported directly to group CEO.

Source: Company Records.

EXHIBIT 2

Mobile Phones: Global Market Shares

	1995	1996	1997
Nokia	23%	21%	21%
Motorola	31%	26%	22%
Ericsson	11%	12%	16%
All others *			
(Sony, Philips, Panasonic, etc.)	35%	41%	41%
Total	100%	100%	100%

* No single brand held a global share higher than 7%.

Source: Company Records.

EXHIBIT 3

Pan-European Press Advertising 1995

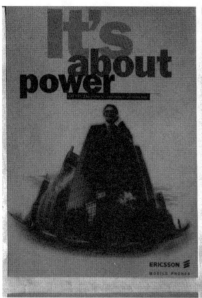

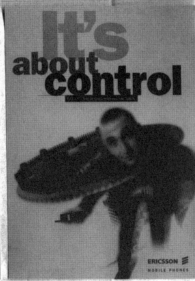

Source: Company Records.

EXHIBIT 4

James Bond Tie-in Advertising: Austria 1997

DIE HIGH-TECH REVOLUTION IM BUSINESS. ERICSSON GH688.

Wer Tag für Tag einen harten Job zu erledigen hat, braucht ein Handy, das ihn in allen Lebenslagen mit innovativer Technik unterstützt. Wie das revolutionäre GH688. Bei 130x49x23 mm und 160 g ist es so kompakt, dass man ihm die Leistungen, die in ihm stecken, fast nicht zutraut: GSM-Phase 2-Technologie, Rechner, Daten-Fax-Kommunikation, 99 Nummernspeicher, Alternate-Line-Service (ALS), SMS, Konferenzschaltung, Reisewecker, bis zu 4 h 20′ Sprechzeit und 100 h Stand-by (mit Hochleistungsakku) u.v.m. Sprachlos? Ihr Ericsson-Händler weiß mehr.

 *Ericsson Made / Bond Approved*

ERICSSON

Source: Company Records.

EXHIBIT 5

Global Brand Campaign Billboard Advertising 1998

Source: Company Records.

EXHIBIT 6

Global Brand Campaign TV Commercial Storyboards 1998

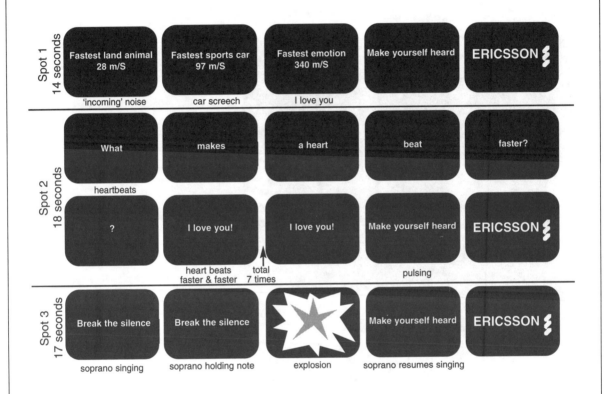

Source: Company Records.

EXHIBIT 7

European Region's Product Campaign Press Advertising 1998

Source: Company Records.

EXHIBIT 8

Local Product Campaign Press Advertising 1997

So small, it will change your perspective.

Forget those big mobile phones of the past. The Ericsson GF788 is
so small it hides in your hand. Forget poor sound quality, here is a phone that
lets you sound like you. Forget about having to keep your calls short,
with this phone you can talk for hours. The Ericsson GF788 is easy to use,
even though it is packed with features. And it comes in four discreet colours.
It will change the way you look at mobile phones.

Source: Company Records.

EXHIBIT 9

Radio Systems Press Advertising 1998

Nature has its own version of Ericsson's new Maxite™ base stations.

Like jackrabbits, Maxites are unobtrusive to the point of being invisible. But instead of those long, ultra-sensitive ears, they use active antennas to cover huge areas from a single box.

To GSM operators, this is great news: full macro-cell coverage from a micro base station. Making the job of finding, zoning and negotiating new sites a breeze.

Maxites will cut your site costs in half, and can be rolled out twice as fast as traditional macro base stations. Each is installed in an hour, and blends in with even the most sensitive environment.

The bottom line: you'll be building your new network (or enhancing coverage) faster than you ever imagined.

So Maxites aren't just hard to spot. Like jackrabbits they multiply – fast. **The Mobile Business Advantage.**

Out of sight,
but **never**
out of range

more information on GSM networks
visit our website at www.ericsson.se/gsm or fax us on +46 8 757 36 00.

Source: Company Records.

CASE 2.12^R **Mediquip S.A.**

This case was prepared by Professor Kamran Kashani. All names and financial data have been disguised.

On December 18, Kurt Thaldorf, a sales engineer for the German sales subsidiary of Mediquip S.A., was informed by Lohmann University Hospital in Stuttgart that it had decided to place an order with Sigma, a Dutch competitor, for a CT scanner. The hospital's decision came as disappointing news to Thaldorf, who had worked for nearly eight months on the account. The order, if obtained, would have meant a sale of DM2,370,000 for the sales engineer.[1] He was convinced that Mediquip's CT scanner was technologically superior to Sigma's and, overall, a better product.

Thaldorf began a review of his call reports in order to better understand the factors that had led to Lohmann University Hospital's decision. He wanted to apply the lessons from this experience to future sales situations.

Background

At the time, the computer tomography (CT) scanner was a relatively recent product in the field of diagnostic imaging. This medical device, used for diagnostic purposes, allowed examination of cross-sections of the human body through display of images. CT scanners combined sophisticated X-ray equipment with a computer to collect the necessary data and translate them into visual images.

When computer tomography was first introduced in the late 1960s, radiologists had hailed it as a major technological breakthrough. Commenting on the advantages of CT scanners, a product specialist with Mediquip said:

> The end product looks very much like an X-ray image. The only difference is that with scanners you can see sections of the body that were never seen before on a screen – like the pancreas. A radiologist, for example, can diagnose cancer of the pancreas in less than two weeks after it develops. This was not possible before CT scanners.

Mediquip was a subsidiary of Technologie Universelle, a French conglomerate. The company's product line included, in addition to CT scanners, X-ray, ultrasonic and nuclear diagnostic equipment. Mediquip enjoyed a worldwide reputation for advanced technology and competent after-sales service.

---

1. For the purposes of this case, use the following exchange rates for the Deutschmark (DM): DM1.00 = Sfr0.85, $0.60, Ecu 0.50, £0.35.

'Our competitors are mostly from other European countries', commented Mediquip's Sales Director for Europe. 'In some markets they have been there longer than we have, and they know the decision-makers better than we do. But we are learning fast.' Sigma, the subsidiary of a diversified Dutch company under the same name, was the company's most serious competitor. Other major contenders in the CT scanner market were FNC, Eldora, Magna, and Piper.

Mediquip executives estimated the European market for CT scanners to be around 200 units per year. They pointed out that prices ranged from DM1.5 to DM3.0 million per unit. The company's CT scanner sold in the upper end of the price range. 'Our equipment is at least two years ahead of our most advanced competition', explained a sales executive, 'and our price reflects this technological superiority.'

Mediquip's sales organization in Europe included eight country sales subsidiaries, each headed by a managing director. Within each country, sales engineers reported to regional sales managers who, in turn, reported to the managing director. Product specialists provided technical support to the sales force in each country.

Buyers of CT Scanners

A sales executive at Mediquip described the buyers of CT scanners as follows:

Most of our sales are to what we call the public sector, health agencies that are either government-owned or belong to non-profit support organizations such as universities and philanthropic institutions. They are the sorts of buyer that buy through formal tenders and have to budget their purchases at least one year in advance. Once the budget is allocated, it must then be spent before the end of the year. Only a minor share of our CT scanner sales goes to the private sector, profit-orientated organizations such as private hospitals or private radiologists.

Of the two markets, the public sector is much more complex. Typically, there are at least four groups that get involved in the purchase decision: radiologists, physicists, administrators and people from the supporting agency – usually the ones who approve the budget for purchasing a CT scanner.

Radiologists are the ones who use the equipment. They are doctors whose diagnostic services are sought by other doctors in the hospital or clinic. Patients remember their doctors, but not the radiologists. They never receive flowers from the patients! A CT scanner could really enhance their professional image among their colleagues.

Physicists are the scientists in residence. They write the technical specifications which competing CT scanners must meet; they should know the state of the art in X-ray technology. Their primary concern is the patient's safety.

The administrators are, well, administrators. They have the financial responsibility for their organizations. They are concerned with the cost of CT scanners, but also with what revenues they can generate. The administrators are extremely wary of purchasing an expensive technological toy that will become obsolete in a few years.

The people from the supporting agency are usually not directly involved with decisions as to which product to purchase. But, since they must approve the expenditures, they do play an indirect role. Their influence is mostly felt by the administrators.

The interplay among the four groups, as you can imagine, is rather complex. The power of each group in relationship to the others varies from organization to organization. The administrator, for example, is the top decision-maker in certain hospitals. In others, he is only a buyer. One of the key tasks of our sales engineers is to define for each potential account the relative power of the players. Only then can they set priorities and formulate selling strategies.

The European sales organization at Mediquip had recently started using a series of forms designed to help sales engineers in their account analysis and strategy formulation. (A sample of the forms, called Account Management Analysis, is reproduced in **Exhibit 1**.)

Lohmann University Hospital

Lohmann University Hospital (LUH) was a large general hospital serving Stuttgart, a city of one million residents. The hospital was part of the university's medical school. The university was a leading teaching center and enjoyed an excellent reputation. LUH's radiology department had a wide range of X-ray equipment from a number of European manufacturers, including Sigma and FNC. The radiology department had five staff members, headed by a senior and nationally known radiologist, Professor Steinborn.

Thaldorf's Sales Activities

From the records he had kept of his sales calls, Thaldorf reviewed the events for the period between May 5, when he learned of LUH's interest in purchasing a CT scanner and December 18, when he was informed that Mediquip had lost the order.

May 5
Office received a call from a Professor Steinborn from Lohmann University Hospital regarding a CT scanner. I was assigned to make the call on the professor. Looked through our files to find out if we had sold anything to the hospital before. We had not. Made an appointment to see the professor on May 9.

May 9
Called on Professor Steinborn who informed me of a recent decision by university directors to set aside funds next year for the purchase of the hospital's first CT scanner. The professor wanted to know what we had to offer. Described the general features of our CT system. Gave him some brochures. Asked a few questions which led me to believe other companies had come to see him before I did. Told me to

check with Dr Rufer, the hospital's physicist, regarding the specs. Made an appointment to see him again ten days later. Called on Dr Rufer who was not there. His secretary gave me a lengthy document on the scanner specs.

May 10

Read the specs last night. Looked like they had been copied straight from somebody's technical manual. Showed them to our Product Specialist who confirmed my own hunch that our system met and exceeded the specs. Made an appointment to see Dr Rufer next week.

May 15

Called on Dr Rufer. Told him about our system's features and the fact that we met all the specs set down on the document. He did not seem particularly impressed. Left him with technical documents about our system.

May 19

Called on Professor Steinborn. He had read the material I had left with him. Seemed rather pleased with the features. Asked about our upgrading scheme. Told him we would undertake to upgrade the system as new features became available. Explained that Mediquip, unlike other systems, can be made to accommodate the latest technology, with no risk of obsolescence for a long time. This impressed him. Also answered his questions regarding image manipulation, image processing speed and our service capability. Just before I left, he inquired about our price. Told him I would have an informative quote for him at our next meeting. Made an appointment to see him on June 23 after he returned from his vacation. Told me to get in touch with Carl Hartmann, the hospital's general director in the interim.

June 1

Called on Hartmann. It was difficult to get an appointment with him. Told him about our interest in supplying his hospital with our CT scanner which met all the specs as defined by Dr Rufer. Also informed him of our excellent service capability. He wanted to know which other hospitals in the country had purchased our system. Told him I would provide him with a list of buyers within a few days. He asked about the price. Gave him an informative quote of DM2,850,000 – a price my boss and I had determined after my visit to Professor Steinborn. He shook his head saying, 'Other scanners are cheaper by a wide margin.' I explained that our price reflected the fact that the latest technology was already built into our scanner. Also mentioned that the price differential was an investment that could pay for itself several times over through faster speed of operation. He was noncommittal. Before leaving his office, he instructed me not to talk to anybody else about the price. Asked him specifically if that included Professor Steinborn. He said it did. Left him with a lot of material about our system.

June 3

Went to Hartmann's office with a list of three hospitals similar in size to LUH that had installed our system. He was out. Left it with his secretary who recognized me. Learned from her that at least two other firms, Sigma and FNC, were competing for the order. She also volunteered the information that 'prices are so different, Mr Hartmann is confused'. She added that the final decision will be made by a committee made up of Hartmann, Professor Steinborn and one other person whom she could not recall.

June 20

Called on Dr Rufer. Asked him if he had read the material about our system. He had, but did not have much to say. I repeated some of the key operational advantages our product enjoyed over those produced by others, including Sigma and FNC. Left him some more technical documents.

   On the way out, stopped by Hartmann's office. His secretary told me that we had received favorable comments from the hospitals using our system.

June 23

Professor Steinborn was flabbergasted to hear that I could not discuss our price with him. Told him about the hospital administration's instructions to that effect. He could not believe this, especially when Sigma had already given him their quote of DM2,100,000. When he calmed down, he wanted to know if we were going to be at least competitive with the others. Told him our system was more advanced than Sigma's. Promised him we would do our best to come up with an attractive offer. Then we talked about his vacation and sailing experience in the Aegean Sea. He said he loved the Greek food.

July 15

Called to see if Hartmann had returned from his vacation. He had. While checking his calendar, his secretary told me that our system seemed to be the 'radiologists' choice', but that Hartmann had not yet made up his mind.

July 30

Visited Hartmann accompanied by the regional manager. Hartmann seemed to have a fixation about the price. He said, 'All the companies claim they have the latest technology.' So he could not understand why our offer was 'so much above the rest'. He concluded that only a 'very attractive price' could tip the balance in our favor. After repeating the operational advantages our system enjoyed over others, including those produced by Sigma and FNC, my boss indicated that we were willing to lower our price to DM2,610,000 if the equipment were ordered before the end of the current year. Hartmann said he would consider the offer and seek 'objective' expert opinion. He also said a decision would be made before Christmas.

August 14

Called on Professor Steinborn who was too busy to see me for more than ten minutes. He wanted to know if we had lowered our price since the last meeting with him. I said we had. He shook his head and said with a laugh, 'Maybe that was not your best offer.' He then wanted to know how fast we could make deliveries. Told him within six months. He did not say anything.

September 2

The regional manager and I discussed the desirability of inviting one or more people from the LUH to visit the Mediquip headquarter operations near Paris. The three-day trip would give the participants a chance to see the scope of the facilities and become better acquainted with CT scanner applications. This idea was finally rejected as inappropriate.

September 3

Dropped in to see Hartmann. He was busy but had time to ask for a formal 'final offer' from us by October 1. On the way out, his secretary told me there had been 'a lot of heated discussions' about which scanner seemed best suited for the hospital. She would not say more.

September 25

The question of price was raised in a meeting with the regional manager and the managing director. I had recommended a sizeable cut in our price to win the order. The regional manager seemed to agree with me, but the managing director was reluctant. His concern was that too big a drop in price looked 'unhealthy'. They finally agreed to a final offer of DM2,370,000.

Made an appointment to see Hartmann later that week.

September 29

Took our offer of DM2,370,000 in a sealed envelope to Hartmann. He did not open it, but he said he hoped the scanner question would soon be resolved to the 'satisfaction of all concerned'. Asked him how the decision was going to be made. He evaded the question but said he would notify us as soon as a decision was reached. Left his office feeling that our price had a good chance of being accepted.

October 20

Called on Professor Steinborn. He had nothing to tell me except that 'the CT scanner is the last thing I want to talk about'. Felt he was unhappy with the way things were going.

Tried to make an appointment with Hartmann in November, but he was too busy.

November 5

Called on Hartmann who told me that a decision would probably not be reached before next month. He indicated that our price was 'within the range', but that all the competing systems were being evaluated to see which seemed most appropriate for the hospital. He repeated that he would call us when a decision was reached.

December 18
Received a brief letter from Hartmann thanking Mediquip for participating in the bid for the CT scanner, along with the announcement that LUH had decided to place the order with Sigma.

EXHIBIT 1

Account Management Analysis Forms (condensed version)

Key Account: ....

ACCOUNT MANAGEMENT ANALYSIS

The enclosed forms are designed to facilitate your management of:

1. A key sales account
2. The Mediquip resources that can be applied to this key account

Completing the enclosed forms, you will:

- Identify installed equipment, and planned or potential new equipment
- Analyze purchase decision process and influence patterns, including:
  - Identify and prioritize all major sources of influence
  - Project probable sequence of events and timing of decision process
  - Assess position/interest of each major influence source
  - Identify major competition and probable strategies
  - Identify needed information/support
- Establish an account development strategy, including:
  - Select key contacts
  - Establish strategy and tactics for each key contact, identify appropriate Mediquip personnel
  - Assess plans for the most effective use of local team and headquarters resources

KEY ACCOUNT DATA

Original (Date: ....)   Account No:....................   Type of Institute: ....

Revisions (Date:............)   Sales Specialist: ....   Bed Size:.....................

County/Region/District:............   Telephone ....

1. CUSTOMER (HOSPITAL, CLINIC, PRIVATE INSTITUTE)

    Name:...

    Street Address: ....

    City, State:...

2. DECISION MAKERS – IMPORTANT CONTACTS

Individuals	Name	Specialty	Remarks
Medical Staff			
Administration			
Local Government			
State Government			

EXHIBIT 1 (CONTINUED)

3. INSTALLED EQUIPMENT

Type	Description	Supplied by	Installation date	Year to replace	Value of potential order
X-ray Nuclear Ultrasound RTP CT					

4. PLANNED NEW EQUIPMENT

Type	Quote		% Chance	Est. order date		Est. delivery		Quoted Price
	No	Date		1980	1981	1980	1981	

5. COMPETITION

Company product	Strategy/tactics	% chance	Strength	Weakness

6. SALES PLAN   Product: . . . .   Quote no: . . . .   Quoted price. . . . .

Key issues	Mediquip's plan	Support needed from:	Date of follow-up/Remarks

7. ACTIONS – IN SUPPORT OF PLAN

Specific action	Responsibility	Due dates			Results/Remarks
		Original	Revised	Completed	

8. ORDER STATUS REPORT

Revision date	Account name and location	Issues/Competitive strategy	Actions/ Strategy	Responsibility	% Chance	Expected order timing	Win/Lose

Source: Company Records.

International Marketing: Global Integration Strategy

International Marketing: Global Integration and Strategy

World markets enter the 21st century having been irreversibly changed in the final decades of the last millennium. While markets for goods and services have, since the beginning of commercial history, been primarily local in their scope, from production to consumption – with minor streams of trade in raw materials and finished goods all along – they have become increasingly integrated globally in the latter half of the 20th century. This process of 'globalization of markets'[1] has had far-reaching effects on the conduct of business in general, and practice of marketing in particular. For business, it has meant a tighter coordination and coordination of value-added activities around the world. The supply chains of many of today's major industries, from food to pharmaceuticals, and power generation to chemicals, circle the globe from sourcing of raw materials to production of finished products and their distribution to final customers. The historical national boundaries, and barriers, to the conduct of business have all but disappeared in developed markets. The developing world is fast joining the globalized markets.

To illustrate, in one of the world's most global markets, the automobile industry, Ford Motor Company has recently embarked on an integrated strategy that tries to link the company's far flung operations in the Americas, Europe and Asia in tight webs of product development, supply chain, and sales and marketing activities. Geography is no longer a major barrier to where the company designs its world cars or manufactures them. The head of new product development, for example, supervises an integrated web of five product centers in North America and Europe where, through electronic links, a given world design is worked on simultaneously by a multinational team of engineers located thousands of kilometers away from each other. Components are manufactured in different locations around the world, and crisscrossed in tight logistics programs for assembly of the finished vehicles which are, in turn, distributed for sale to distant corners of the globe.

---

1. The concept of 'globalization of markets' was first advanced in 1983 by Theodore Levitt in an article under the same title. While Levitt's ideas proved provocative and controversial at the time, since then, the experience of companies in many industries has only confirmed their validity. See: Theodore Levitt, 'Globalization of Markets', *Harvard Business Review* (May–June 1983): 92–102.

The implications of globalization for the practice of marketing are many. First, a narrow country-focused definition of markets is misleading. While consumption of products and services continues to take place in traditionally defined 'national' markets, consumers and their consumption are not necessarily bound by local traditions or habits. Consumer segments have emerged that cut across market boundaries historically confined to geography, language or ethnicity. Gillette, the world's largest maker of shaving products with an estimated 70% market share, believes in treating the world as if it were a single market. Gillette targets consumers, mostly male, who share in their desire for a comfortable shave, and who are willing to pay a premium price for the company's state-of-the art razors and blades. The company's successful track record with generations of shaving products confirms that there are indeed sufficient numbers of consumers with such a profile everywhere. Customers of industrial goods and services have similarly converged into identifiable international segments.

Second, as with consumers, competition has also taken on global dimensions. In many industries, a growing number of competitors have emerged as global rivals, confronting each other in local markets everywhere. In electricity generation and distribution, for example, the three players that seem to compete for every major order from anywhere in the world are: ABB of Switzerland, GE of the United States, and Siemens of Germany. In process foods, similarly, the world's largest marketer, Nestlé of Switzerland, faces a common list of

competitors in many of its more than 110 different country operations. These include Unilever of UK and Dutch origin, and three companies from the US: Mars, CPC International, and KGF (a division of Philip Morris). To view competition in such markets merely in local terms would miss the more significant competitive game which is played by the rivals on a much wider global stage.

Third, there are increasing international spill-overs of marketing strategies where actions taken in one local market have consequences in others. These apply to product launches, pricing, and brand communication, among others. Intel's mid-1990s problems with the design of its new Pentium microprocessor chip were not just a US development. Both the design issue and the subsequent recall of all defective chips were followed with great interest by PC buyers in every country where the company had previously campaigned for the 'Intel Inside' premium quality message. Such spill-over effects underscore the simple fact that markets are no longer isolated entities; globalization has rendered them increasingly interdependent.

Figure 3.1 shows broad-based trends in markets, from local (that is, nationally bound) to global. Together, these trends have redefined the scope and dynamics of markets.

This chapter sets the stage for a discussion of cases that deal with the management issues of global marketing. Here we define global marketing as a centrally inspired and directed marketing action that touches a number of national (that is, local) markets. Such action is in direct contrast to

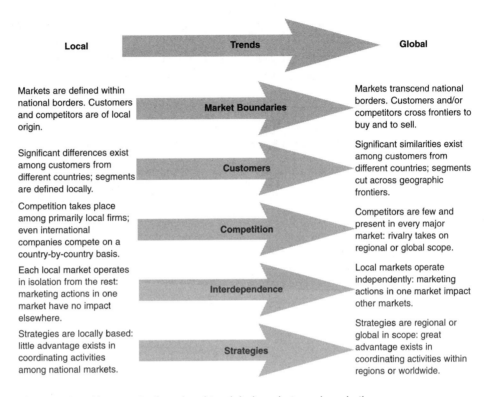

Figure 3.1 Key trends: from local to global markets and marketing

local marketing which takes place in individual markets, and is designed to cater to specific local market conditions – the context for many of the cases covered in Sections I and II. In this chapter, we will first examine the forces that have contributed to the irreversible effects of globalization in a large and growing number of markets. We will next look at how one company, Procter & Gamble, has been proactively taking advantage of these forces in detergents and personal care products, and redirecting its marketing towards global opportunities in these markets. Issues specific to global marketing strategy are reviewed next. Finally we will propose a framework for analysis as a tool for making informed global strategy decisions.

The application of the framework in the context of a computer company is demonstrated also.

Forces

Five forces have contributed to the globalization of markets and the emergence of ever-integrated global marketing strategies:

1. *Technology:* The fast pace of technology development, and the resulting drop in the life cycle of a new technology before it is displaced by another cycle, have contributed to the need to view markets globally. In the early part of the 1990s, for example, a new gen-

eration of fax machines incorporating the latest technology could be counted on to last at least two years before being made obsolete by the next generation. By the middle of the decade, however, this two-year cycle, already tight for major manufacturers such as NEC of Japan, had dropped down to a mere six months. The rapid pace was putting great pressure on the manufacturers to take their new products worldwide for maximum sales before the next cycle technologies came along.

2. *Investments:* Rising investments on product development and manufacturing are putting further pressure on companies to view their markets in the widest geographic terms. Ford's global car Mondeo cost the company nearly $7 billion to develop and gear up for production. With such high front-end expenditures, Ford looks at the world market for mid-sized cars as the only relevant geography to amortize its investments. Similarly, when molecule-to-market costs of drugs are approaching $300 million for each new compound, the pharmaceutical companies are increasingly orientating themselves to take advantage of opportunities around the globe to exploit their expensive investments.

3. *Communication:* The age-old barriers to communication of language and distance are falling, thereby creating a new force in globalization. Software is now being subcontracted and produced in Russia and India for Silicone Valley companies thanks to the new telecommunication technology, including the Internet, unavailable just a few years ago. Similarly, an increasing number of book lovers worldwide are electronically ordering books directly from US-based Amazon. com thanks to its informative web-site and easy ordering system. These examples, and many others from the growing number of global media, are bringing pressure on firms to think of their brand communication in world scale, instead of just in national or regional terms. The huge success of the 'Intel Inside' brand campaign is a testimony to the power of global branding in an increasingly interconnected world.

4. *Behavior:* Consumer behavior is converging worldwide, thereby creating huge segments that are more behavior-specific than geography. Increasing urbanization, rising disposable incomes, and access and exposure to international media (including satellite TV and movies) are some of the factors that have contributed to the growing similarities among world consumers. Companies that have taken advantage of the emergence of global segments in their sectors include IKEA in home furniture retailing, Body Shop in cosmetics, McDonald's in fast food, and Benetton in fashion. We have already seen in Section II how Ericsson's global brand campaign was inspired by the identification of five more-or-less homogeneous global consumer segments in the mobile phone market. Ericsson and others are focusing on segments of consumers who lead similar lifestyles, have convergent values, and are willing to spend their money on similar products

and services. See Figure 3.2 for a recent study of global consumer segments.

5. *Liberalization:* In recent years, world economies have taken major strides towards greater openness. NAFTA in North America and EU in Europe are clear examples of regional accords that aim at greater liberalization of previously protected economies. The World Trade Organization has a similar mandate: to press for increasing openness of local economies through inter-governmental agreements. With liberalization have come the opportunities of exploiting previously closed markets, but also rising international competition, and a recognition among companies that long-term success demands a per-

manent presence in markets around the world. Hence the spectacular growth of direct foreign investments in former Eastern Europe, as well as in Asia and Latin America. Liberalization has also contributed to the emergence of truly integrated business strategies. ABB's global business units, for example, view the world as a single arena for upstream activities of product creation and supply chain, as well as downstream marketing and sales operations.

P&G Goes Global

The above forces are a threat to those companies whose business practices remain out of step with the demands

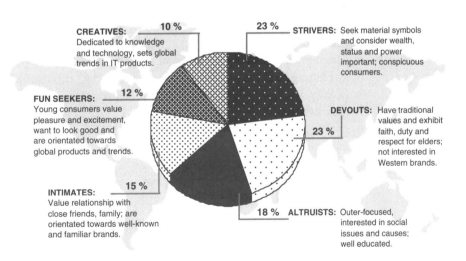

Figure 3.2 Global consumer hot buttons.* A study of global consumer value segments.

Source: Roper Starch Wordwide, as reported by Stuart Elliot, 'Global Consumers: Birds of a Feather', *International Herald Tribune*, June 26, 1998.

of their changing markets. For others, these forces are opportunities to be exploited for competitive advantage. Procter & Gamble is one such company.

The 1990s was the decade in which Procter & Gamble (P&G) transformed itself from a US-based company that sold its products around the world to a truly global enterprise. The company's best known brands include Tide and Ariel in detergents, Pampers in baby diapers, Crest in toothpaste, and Oil of Ulay in moisturizing creams. The impetus for change came in the early 1990s under a new top management team that was far more experienced in international markets than its predecessor. The management vision was articulated as making P&G 'a truly global company in the way we think, plan, and run the business'.[2] This vision, a pillar of the company's international growth for the decade, meant a number of specific goals and mandates:

- *Mission:* Management set the goal of leveraging P&G's strengths in technology to create world-class products that would outperform any of their rivals, anywhere in the world
- *Investments:* Priority was given to investments that would strengthen P&G's presence and performance internationally
- *R&D:* New product development was no longer the monopoly of any one geographic organization. New products would originate from the US (the traditional source), but

also from strengthened research centers in Europe and Japan
- *Learning:* Management was to proactively exploit the company's wide presence around the world – in about 140 countries – as a competitive weapon by learning from the best local practices and fast re-applying them elsewhere
- *Brands:* Creation of global brands was given the highest priority for product development and marketing. Global brands would be built on common technology platforms and positioning, but would be adapted to regional or local tastes in their form, packaging and marketing communication.

The payoffs from P&G's global strategy, at the core of it product innovation and brand marketing, have been many and significant. Technology development on liquid detergent, for example, was started in the US but was later perfected in Europe. This allowed the company to successfully launch Vizir and Ariel brands of liquid detergents in Europe, and Tide liquid in the US. The latter achieved unprecedented market shares for a new detergent. Similarly, borrowing an idea from its Japanese rival Kao, P&G further developed and marketed an improved compact detergent, a novel idea in Europe, North and South America. Another technological breakthrough, which allowed shampoo and conditioner to be presented in one product formula, was marketed globally under

---

2. Information on P&G is partly based on a company document 'Strategies for Global Growth', incorporating the text of a speech delivered by Edwin L. Artzt, Chairman and Chief Executive, in 1990.

the brand name Wash & Go.[3] Positioned uniquely for young and sportive women who seek the convenience of a two-in-one formula, the new shampoo's advertising in local languages followed similar executions everywhere. In less than two years Wash & Go was being sold in more than 30 countries, reaching the enviable position of the world's best-selling shampoo.

Global Marketing: The Issues

In a world characterized by isolated country markets, strategy-making is a relatively simple matter: each subsidiary management is responsible for developing a marketing strategy which reflects the peculiarities of its local market and which delivers the financial returns the parent expects from its investment in that country. As a relatively self-sufficient group, local managers decide what products to market, to whom and how. Typically, as long as the financial targets are met, headquarters stays out of the picture. The rationale is simple: only the local managers know what is best for their markets.

This oversimplified picture is no longer true for many firms operating internationally. Forces of globalization are changing the dynamics of many industries and complicating strategy-making. Country-by-country and decentralized decision-making are strategic liabilities for companies operating in markets with disappear-

ing national boundaries. For example, major computer firms are having to deal with an increasing number of global accounts who aim to buy from one vendor worldwide and who, in addition, demand special discounts on volume purchases, consistent level of service, and coordinated vendor contacts everywhere around the world. Nothing short of a central strategy for such global accounts, and a closely-knit network of local sales and service operations worldwide, can satisfy the needs of this segment.

As another illustration, many marketers have learned the hard way that uncoordinated local pricing can provoke trans-shipments of trade stocks from low-priced countries to the high-priced ones. This is true for many product categories where the cost of transportation relative to the price is small, and where information regarding local prices can be readily obtained. Such 'parallel trade' or the 'gray market', as the phenomenon is often called, is a persistent problem for a variety of firms in as diverse sectors as chemicals, photographic equipment and supplies, branded clothing, and even cars and tires. The rise in multinational wholesale establishments, central procurement by customers, and improved international communication are the engines behind the phenomenon.

What follows is a review of issues pertaining to global marketing strategy. It is organized along the five building blocks of a marketing strategy: Segmentation, Product Policy, Pricing, Distribution, and Communi-

---

3. In some markets the two-in-one product has been marketed under different brand names including: Pert Plus, Pantene Plus, Rejoy and Shamtu.

cation. Far from trying to be exhaustive, our aim here is to selectively highlight those questions that have a particular relevance to marketing decisions in global businesses.

Segmentation

The issues of segmentation have to do with grouping dispersed countries into meaningful clusters, and with the desirability or the practicality of targeting groups of customers in different country markets who have similar profiles and/or behavior:

- What specific criteria (such as economic growth, per capita income, market size, culture, political stability, and so on) should be used to group countries into meaningful clusters, or segments?
- What are the relevant dimensions for segmenting the market, within a country or across several countries?
- To what extent should these dimensions be country-specific, regional or even global?
- If country-specific, are the segments large enough to be viable economically?
- If regional or global, how practical or economical is it to carve out segments that cut across many country markets?

Product Policy

Issues in product policy deal with the opportunities that might exist in a unified approach to different country markets. The broad choices of global standardization versus local adaptation are at the core of these issues:

- Should new product development be centrally directed, globally or regionally, or managed by individual subsidiaries?
- If centrally directed, to what extent should resources be channeled to product concepts with broad-based global appeal, as opposed to those with country-specific features?
- To what extent do global product designs or formulations offer an advantage, economic or otherwise, over locally targeted products?
- What are the benefits or risks of leaving branding and packaging decisions in the hands of local management?
- How much would an international standard policy on support services improve the customer-perceived value of the product offering?

Pricing

With the most immediate impact on profitability, pricing remains at the forefront of marketing decisions preoccupying global marketers. Issues in this area involve trade-offs between centrally administered policies and local decisions, risks and impacts of parallel trade, administration of regional or global price coordination including policies on transfer prices, pricing for multinational clients, and use of price as an offensive or defensive tool:

- Given regional or global trends among customers, distributors and competitors, what are the opportunities or drawbacks of centrally coordinating local prices?

- If prices are set to fit local conditions, what are the risks and costs of potential parallel trade – from low-price to high-price countries?
- What should be the pricing policy towards regional or global clients – with or without a central buying function?
- If some degree of international price coordination is deemed desirable, what should be the mechanisms for administering it? When the product is centrally manufactured, what policies on transfer pricing are most appropriate?
- In competition against key rivals, should aggressive local pricing be used selectively to improve share position one market at a time? And how should the company defend itself against the predatory pricing of a local or global competitor in key markets?

Distribution

Issues in distribution have to do with several concerns including speed and cost of market entry, concentration and growth among multinational channels of distribution, the level of channel control and the quality of customer service:

- In entering new markets, what are the trade-offs between establishing one's own distribution network versus utilizing existing local channels of distribution? Which provides a faster coverage? Or a more lasting long-term alternative?
- What are the trends in international wholesaling and retailing? To what extent is the current distribution in line with these trends?
- How is the producer's channel power *vis-à-vis* wholesale or retail establishments changing regionally or globally? What are the implications of such trends for a global marketer?
- What are the benefits or risks in acquiring local agents as a move to upgrade the distribution function or a defense against similar actions by local or global competitors?
- How integral is the customer service function among the activities performed by local distributors? Should a standard global policy towards such services be adopted, or should such decisions be delegated to local management?

Communication

Communication through media advertising or personal selling is often carried out locally. However, relevant questions remain as to the desirability or practicality of having some degree of central direction on *what* is communicated and *how* it is done.

The key issues in *advertising* are:

- Do customers perceive product or service benefits in similar ways everywhere? Do they seek the same values?
- If so, should the advertising message be essentially the same internationally, emphasizing similar themes or value propositions?
- Can a successful campaign in one market be transferred elsewhere?
- What are the opportunities or risks in centrally led brand advertising?

- Are there the trade-offs in using a single advertising agency internationally?

The key issues in *personal selling* are:

- Are buying and selling processes essentially the same in different countries?
- If so, should the national sales forces be expected to undertake identical prescribed selling activities everywhere?
- Are there opportunities for improving sales force performance by adopting similar sales management policies (such as in recruitment and training, sales force organization, compensation, performance evaluation, and so on) in different country subsidiaries?
- What are the advantages or drawbacks in centralizing the personal selling function for multinational (regional or global) accounts?
- What are the opportunities or problems in centralizing certain aspects of sales support functions, such as technical assistance?

Global Strategy: A Framework for Analysis

As the above issues should have demonstrated, global strategy-making is more complicated than treating the world as one homogeneous marketplace. What makes global marketing complex is the fact that not all businesses or marketing decisions lend themselves to central direction. In many markets where significant differences still exist among different countries, as in ethnic food product categories, the room for internationally coordinated marketing is limited. Even where opportunities for coordination or standardization exist, as in many consumer or industrial goods, not all marketing decisions lend themselves equally well to such international streamlining. Many decisions, such as those requiring rapid response to customer demands or involving local tactics, are still best made locally by managers close to those markets. Global marketing thus involves important choices as to who decides what and where.

At the first level of analysis, a global marketer is interested to determine whether common denominators are present among different national markets and, if so, whether such commonalities can be exploited to advantage. Where there are important similarities, and where these can be leveraged for improved operational *efficiency* or strategic *effectiveness*, there is room for centrally driven marketing. Where no such commonalities are present, a locally driven approach is most appropriate.

Even when there are significant commonalities that can be potentially exploited, a global marketer must still discriminate between those decisions which can be made centrally and others best left to local management discretion. This last distinction is critical to the success of the overall strategy as it addresses a typical global marketer's dilemma: how to benefit from central strategy-making without losing local market flexibility or speed of action.

There are no easy answers to the above dilemma. A great deal of judgment is involved in making the right choices. But as an analytical guide to a global marketer's judgment regarding what decisions are best made and managed centrally and, by the same token, what others are best left to those closest to local markets, it is important and useful to distinguish between the **contribution** of a given decision to the overall marketing strategy, and the potential **impact** that might be expected from international integration of that decision. Let us elaborate.

The **contribution** of a marketing decision relates to its anticipated role in the overall success of a given strategy. Not all decisions qualify as high contributors. For the marketing strategy supporting the launch and roll-out of P&G's Wash & Go, cited earlier, only product formulation, positioning and communication, and some elements of packaging were considered key areas for the brand's overall strategy. Other decisions, among them pricing, distribution, merchandising, trade and consumer promotions, were judged as relatively less important. The case of Wash & Go is typical: the list of pivotal decisions judged as high contributors is often shorter than that of low contributors.

The **impact** of international integration is a different variable altogether. It refers to the benefits a global marketer can derive from integration of a given decision across a number of countries, in a region or beyond. Such benefits come about from consolidation or standardization. Decisions that enjoy one or more of the following features qualify as high impact areas:

- *Savings:* Where significant economies of scale exist in consolidating individual country operations, as in upstream manufacturing and logis-

tics, or downstream advertising production costs
- *Spillover:* Where marketing practices in one country market influence the performance in others, as might be the case in pricing of an internationally branded product or advertising with cross-border reach, as in satellite broadcasts
- *International Accounts:* Where decision impacts the same customer in different locations around the world as in the case of global clients of a bank that serves these accounts around the world through its local network of branches.

Not all marketing decisions promise high impact from consolidation or standardization. Many decisions are unlikely to benefit from central direction because one or more of the following features are present:

- *Speed:* Where the speed of response to customers or competitive action is critical to success, as in quick repair service for industrial machinery, or pricing in highly competitive local market conditions
- *Customization:* Where much of the value added is through customization and individualized service, as in tailor-made systems configuration and application development for computers
- *Tactics:* Where short-lived measures are used to address specific local issues, such as in consumer or trade promotions.

Figure 3.3 demonstrates possible categories of marketing decisions along the *Contribution–Impact* dimensions. The matrix shows how different decisions might enjoy different measures of contribution to the overall strategy, as well as their expected pay-off from integration. Each of the four quadrants, labeled for easy reference, is described below.

Leverage

These decisions are not only pivotal in terms of overall marketing strategy, but also promise relatively high benefits from central direction. They are clear candidates for integration across country operations. Center-led standardization or harmonization is in order here.

Fringe

These decisions lie at the other end of the spectrum from those identified above as 'Leverage'. They are neither central to the performance of the strategy, nor likely to benefit in any significant way from international integration. This category represents those decisions best left in the hands of local management. There are no pay-offs from central management or coordination.

Core

This category of decisions represents those that are central to marketing success, yet unlikely candidates for integration. Given their relatively high expected contribution to the performance of a strategy, they need to be managed carefully, but at each and every local country operation. Little benefit can be expected from central direction.

Potential impact from integration

	Low	High
High	CORE	LEVERAGE
Low	FRINGE	SUPPORT

Contribution to Strategy

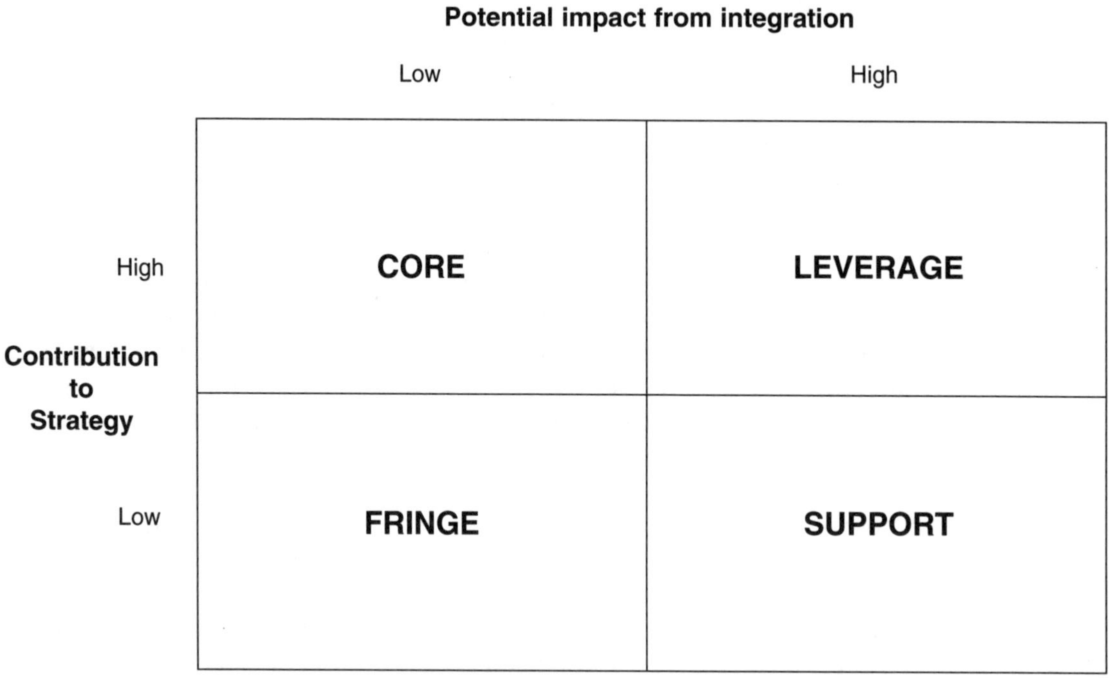

Figure 3.3   Contribution–Impact matrix: an analytical framework for making global priorities

Support

This category represents those decision areas characterized by a relatively low contribution profile in the strategy, yet relatively high potential impact from integration. These decisions would certainly benefit from some form of central direction, but their expected contribution to the overall performance is by definition limited. Whether the global marketer takes on the challenge of consolidation makes only marginal difference to the overall picture.

As a guide for analysis and decision, the Contribution–Impact matrix helps the global marketer to make useful distinctions and priorities for action. For example, while decisions identified as 'Leverage' must carry the high-est priority in terms of cross-market integration, those labeled as 'Fringe' should be left to local management to manage. Similarly left for local management are 'Core' areas, with the difference that such decisions must be given highest priority but only at local operations. Given the low strategic contribution of 'Support' decisions, any benefits from integration cannot carry a significant weight; hence, these constitute low priority areas for the global marketer.

The Case of Integrated Solutions Inc.

Figure 3.4 shows how Integrated Solutions Inc. (ISI), a disguised name

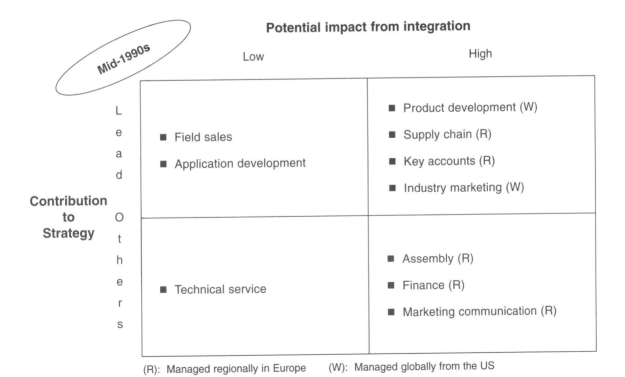

Figure 3.4 Integrated Solutions Inc.: priorities for global or regional management

for a medium-sized US-based computer company, has prioritized its various marketing decisions using the Contribution–Impact model. As with the rest of the industry, ISI has experienced growing trends towards globalization in its customer base as well as among its competitors. Over time, it has responded to these trends by redefining its overall strategy and the marketing component of it. For example, while back in the mid-1980s only hardware product development was considered a 'Leverage' activity deserving worldwide leadership from the center in the US, by the mid-1990s it was joined by one other: industry marketing. The latter activity involved creation of sector-specific solutions (for example for banks or retailing establishments) that involved a great deal of industry know-how and high expenditures in software development. Once created, these platforms could be exploited around the world. Similarly identified as 'Leverage' were two other decision areas delegated to regional management in Europe. These were supply chain decisions, including manufacturing and inventories, and key account management. These decision areas were previously managed by country operations (key accounts) or given a lower status in the strategy as 'Support' (supply chain).

Figure 3.5 shows the changing strategic priorities of ISI over a 10-year time horizon; priorities that clearly tend towards global consolidation. This evolving picture highlights two key features of global marketing integration that deserve to be underscored here. First, the success of integrated global marketing rests in the balance it maintains among different but interrelated elements – the balance between central and local management influence on individual decisions, between centrally controlled pivotal decisions and those that carry less weight, between tight standardization and loose coordination, and between headquarters-led activities and local innovations. Second, the success of global marketing also lies in how well this delicate balance is adapted over time to the changing market and competitive conditions. If trade promotions, for example, are handled in a decentralized manner, the growth in multinational channels may make such locally decided practices less and less appropriate. Similarly, but going in the opposite direction, a regionally coordinated pricing policy may have to be selectively sacrificed to counter the predatory pricing attacks of a competitor in a key subsidiary market. An effective global strategy, as follows, is a moving target: it requires constant vigilance to ensure that it stays responsive to changes in its markets, both local and global.

Cases in Section III

The cases that follow all deal with one or more aspects of marketing in markets that are in different stages of globalization. The first case, Libby's Beverages, highlights the opportunities and challenges of transplanting a successful marketing strategy from one local market to others.

Innovations do travel globally, but there are also barriers, some real and others perceived.

The second case, Hilti series, describes a challenge in the construction

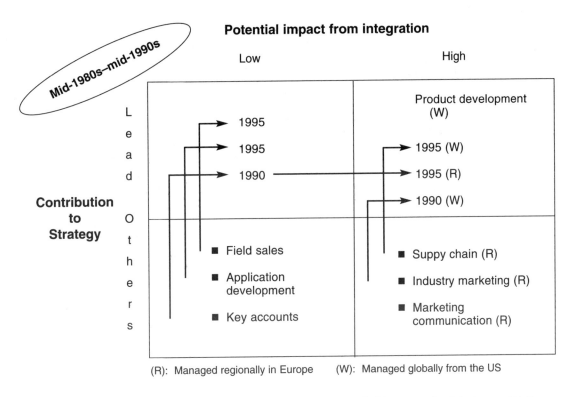

Figure 3.5 Integrated Solutions Inc.: changing priorities towards global consolidation

tools and fasteners industry. The company's successful global distribution strategy of selling its products directly to end-users is being challenged by a country that claims its market conditions demand a different approach altogether. The role of regional management and how much autonomy they should have in interpreting the global strategy are raised. Haaks Europe, the final case, is about creating a strategic marketing plan that promotes consistency between centrally driven European priorities and decentralized local actions.

Learning Points

The students can expect the following learning points from analyzing and discussing the cases in this section:

■ Facility in identifying regional or global market trends that are contexts for integrated regional or global marketing

Learning Points (cont'd)

- Appreciation for opportunities and barriers that respectively promote and inhibit development of integrated international marketing
- Skills in applying the Contribution–Impact model as a tool in making informed distinctions and priorities among different marketing decisions
- Exercise in making important decisions in international marketing, including when to press for regional or global integration, and when to make exceptions to such efforts in the interest of specific market conditions
- Opportunity to set up a planning process that promotes integrated marketing when that is called for, and allows ample room for local initiatives when that is most appropriate

CASE 3.1 Libby's Beverages: Um Bongo Fruit Drink

This case was prepared by Professor Kamran Kashani, with assistance from Research Associate Robert C. Howard. All names have been disguised.

Um Bongo is a success story in the UK, Portugal and Spain and we think the US market should also be ready for it.

> A headquarters beverage executive, Nestlé, Vevey, Switzerland.

Um Bongo has a strange flavor, unfamiliar to the American child's taste buds, and a very unusual commercial with jungle drums and animals and lots of activity all over the place… In tests it lost to Hawaiian Punch, a leading competitor, so the project died right there.

> A Libby's executive, Purchase, New York, USA.

In 1989, managers at Libby's American operation and its parent Nestlé were debating the future of Um Bongo in the US. Um Bongo was a fruit-based drink with 25% juice content specifically developed for children. It was originally introduced by Libby's UK company but later also marketed by the Spanish and Portuguese organizations. Nestlé executives considered the Um Bongo concept of combining 'fun and health' a significant product and marketing innovation with broad international appeal. As proof, they pointed to the success of the brand in three different European markets.

Libby's US managers were less convinced about Um Bongo's general appeal. Initial consumer tests had indicated potential problems with its taste and the TV commercials used in Europe. Besides, they claimed they were busy with another children's brand, Juicy Juice, a 100% fruit juice product. Juicy Juice had been relaunched two years earlier with great success. US management now intended to consolidate Juicy Juice's gains for further growth and improved profitability. The addition of Um Bongo to the product line, these managers argued, would only detract from the tasks ahead.

Background

Libby's was a division of Nestlé, the world's largest food company. With more than $24 billion in sales and 428 factories on five continents, Nestlé and its wholly owned divisions marketed a large variety of products including evaporated milk and infant foods, chocolate, coffee, beverages, culinary products (such as sauces, mixes, soups, and so on), and refrigerated and frozen products. Nestlé's flagship products – such as its 50-year-old Nescafé – were sold in more than 100 countries.

Since the early 1970s, Nestlé had pursued an active acquisition policy in the international food business. In 1970, Nestlé acquired Libby's, one of the largest fruit and vegetable processors in the US. Other major acquisitions that followed were Stouffer (US: 1973), Chambourcy, (France: 1978), Carnation (US: 1985), Buitoni-Perugina (Italy: 1989) and Rowntree (UK: 1989). In most cases, the acquired companies, including Libby's activities around the world, were integrated into Nestlé's local operations.

In 1989, less than 3% of the company's total turnover came from non-food activities including cosmetics and pharmaceuticals. (Refer to **Exhibit 1** for a breakdown of sales by product category and geographic region.)

Each Nestlé country operation was run by a country manager who had full responsibility for profitability and for overseeing all functions including marketing, manufacturing and finance. Many country managers were local nationals who had risen through the marketing function.[1]

Nestlé's corporate structure was organized along five geographic zones and nine product groups. The zones were: Europe; Asia, Australia and New Zealand; South and Central America; US and Canada; Africa and the Middle East. The product groups consisted of beverages (including coffee, mineral water, fruit juices and drinks); cereals, milks and dietetic; culinary; frozen foods and ice cream; chocolate and confectionery; refrigerated products; pet foods; pharmaceuticals and cosmetics; and food services.

Zone managers, who were located in the company's headquarters in Vevey, Switzerland, worked with individual country managers for setting overall sales and profit targets, and monitoring performance. Product directors, and their teams of product managers reporting to them, were also in Vevey. They interfaced with their respective country product managers, who reported to their local executives, to implement global or regional product strategies, to search for new products, and to maximize cross-fertilization of marketing practices internationally. In the beverages group, for example, four product managers looked after Nestlé's worldwide activities in roasted and ground coffee, instant coffee, chocolate and malt drinks, and tea and liquid beverages – including fruit juices and drinks. In Nestlé's matrix of staff product groups and line geographic zones, zone management wielded considerably more influence on local matters. (Refer to **Exhibit 2** for a partial organization chart.)

Nestlé had traditionally been run as a decentralized organization giving much autonomy to country management. Country heads, evaluated on overall results, were thought of as 'pillars of the organization' and allowed freedom to run their 'one-man shows'. Marketing, more than other functions, was considered to be a local activity aimed at capitalizing on the particularities of each market.

---

1. Certain data pertaining to Nestlé's organization are based on the Harvard Business School case study, Nestlé S.A.

Recently, more attention was being paid to global branding and looking for marketing opportunities that cut across traditional market boundaries. Helmut Maucher, Nestlé's CEO, was explicit on this point:

> (Our) aim is to identify market groups and build global brands. These can be sold to the same groups of people all over the world – single households, the health conscious, old people, oriental food lovers, instant coffee drinkers. The idea is to target these segments clearly for maximum sales, and hence become the lowest-cost producer.[2]

Nevertheless, Nestlé believed there were limits to how far a food company could go global and satisfy consumers on five continents. The company aimed to stay close to local markets.

World Fruit and Juice Market

In 1988, the world's total consumption of fruit juices and juice-based drinks[3] amounted to an estimated 27 billion liters, representing a value of $23 billion at manufacturers' prices. These figures included all forms of industrially processed juices and drinks, including nectars, ready-to-drink preparations, concentrates and frozen. Orange juice and orange-based drinks were the best-selling flavors, accounting for nearly one-half of all consumption. Apple was the second most popular flavor with 15%, followed by grapefruit, pineapple and grape. Fruit juice and drinks consumption had grown by about 8% per year since the early 1980s.

Unlike soft drinks, the world market for fruit juices and drinks was fragmented. No competitor appeared dominant internationally, although Coca-Cola held the leading position with an estimated worldwide share of 15%. Coca-Cola's brands were Hi-C, Minute Maid, Five Alive, and Sprite – a carbonated soft drink with 10% of fruit juice content. Other major competitors were Pepsi-Cola (Slice), P&G (Citrus Hill), Seagram's (Tropicana), UK-based Cadbury Schweppes (Sunkist) and Melitta (Granini), headquartered in Germany.

Three countries accounted for more than 60% of the world's volume of juices and drinks: the US, 41%; Japan, 13%; and Germany, 9%. Consumption volumes and patterns differed internationally. For example, one study showed that while per capita consumption in the US surpassed 70 liters annually, in the other Anglo-Saxon countries the volume was in the 20–25 liters range, and in the Latin countries it was below 10 liters. The same study highlighted other differences in how juices and drinks were consumed:

---

2. *Management Europe*, January 16, 1989.
3. 'Drinks' was a term used to refer to fruit-based beverages whose juice content was less than 100%. Most drinks contained 10–50% fruit juices, with the rest consisting of water, sugar, color and flavoring.

Amounts of Consumption (%)

	Anglo-Saxon	Latin
Breakfast	35	10
Lunch/dinner	25	10
During the day	40	80
At home	70	55
Outside the home	30	45

Source: Company Records.

Despite national and cultural differences, Nestlé management identified a number of trends which were influencing the juice and drinks industry worldwide:

- *Health:* Among the industrialized countries, consumers were paying unprecedented attention to their own and their family's health and diet. Fruit juices and drinks were benefiting from this trend as 'healthy' alternatives to modern soft drinks or traditional coffee and tea.
- *Quality:* In major markets internationally, a growing number of consumers were turning to the premium quality fruit juice segment. This factor explained the growth of premium-priced ready-to-drink brands marketed under taste platforms like 'freshly squeezed'.
- *Value:* In large markets, the low-priced 'value for money' segment accounted for an increasing percentage of fruit juices and drinks. The rise in the number and volume of private brands marketed by large food chains in Europe and North America had helped this trend.
- *Advertising:* Media advertising for fruit juices and drinks was on the rise. In some markets it had already surpassed relative expenditure levels of soft drinks, historically a media-intensive category. In 1987, for example, the US media expenditure for fruit juices approached $200 per 10,000 liters versus $100 for soft drinks.

The US Fruit Juice and Drinks Market

Overview

In 1988, the US market for fruit juice and drinks was approximately $9.4 billion at manufacturers' prices. This volume represented only a small portion of a much larger beverage market estimated at more than $112 billion in that year. (Refer to **Exhibit 3**.)

Libby's management divided the juice and drinks products into frozen, shelf-stable and refrigerated segments. The ready-to-drink shelf-stable products were by far the largest segment, accounting for close to one-half of the market. The refrigerated products – typically citrus flavors – accounted for 26% of the market in 1988.

These products had increased their market share by nearly 10 points over the last five years at the expense of the frozen segment.

The juice and drinks market was also segmented by flavor. In the shelf-stable category, blended juices and drinks were leading with about two-thirds share of the dollar volume, followed by apple (17%), grapefruit (5.2%), grape (5.6%) and orange (3.3%). Orange juice was the dominant flavor in both frozen and refrigerated segments, with 61% and 72% respectively.

A variety of packaging was used for fruit juices and drinks. Glass was by far the most dominant form among shelf-stable products, accounting for 47%, followed by cans (31%), aseptic brik packs (16%) and plastic containers (6%). In recent years, both glass and brik packs had grown relatively, while cans had declined. In the refrigerated and frozen segments, paper and plastic cartons were the most common forms of packaging.

The overall fruit juice and drinks market had grown by nearly one-third since 1982 and was projected to reach $11 billion by 1990. The annual growth rates had doubled since the mid-1970s reaching 7% by 1988. Since 1982, the dollar sales in the refrigerated segment had grown 104%, while the frozen product sales had actually declined 6%. With 36% growth during this period, the shelf-stable segment had slightly overtaken the industry average. Among the flavors, orange and blended flavors were the fastest growing varieties in the refrigerated and shelf-stable segments, respectively.

Industry analysts attributed the continued US market growth to the concern with health and fitness by consumers, the growing popularity of new aseptic packaging, and the impact of new products such as blended fruit juices. These combined factors had contributed to a rise in per capita juice and drinks consumption – from 11.5 gallons (52 liters) in the mid-1970s to 15.7 gallons (71 liters) in the mid-1980s.[4]

Competition

Three firms dominated the US fruit juice and drinks market: Coca-Cola Foods, Seagrams, and Ocean Spray. Coca-Cola Foods was the largest juice and drinks marketer with a total 1988 sales of $1.3 billion and a market share of 14%. The company's Minute Maid brand, an orange juice in shelf-stable and frozen forms, accounted for slightly more than $1 billion of sales. Another major brand was Hi-C, a shelf-stable fruit drink with sales of $203 million. Seagrams was the second largest producer in the industry. The firm's 10% market share came almost entirely from its highly successful and fast growing Tropicana brand of refrigerated and shelf-stable orange juice. Ocean Spray, the industry's third largest, had sales of $700 million and a market share of 9%. The company's wide variety of cranberry-based and other fruit drinks made it the largest player in the shelf-stable segment.

Besides the three largest, more than 10 other producers, including divisions of such large firms as P&G, Campbell Soup, RJR/Nabisco, and Nestlé competed in

---

4. US population in 1989 = 247 million.

the industry. Private labels represented a growing segment of the US juice and drinks market, accounting for an estimated 16% in 1988. (**Exhibit 4** provides data on competitors and products in the shelf-stable segment, including Libby's brand, Juicy Juice.)

According to Libby's management, a number of juice and drinks companies had recently entered the 100% blended fruit juice segment, where Juicy Juice was the leading brand. The newcomers had been attracted by the segment's growth which was estimated to be the highest in the industry. Starting with a modest size of $10 million in the mid-1970s, the blended juice market had reached $145 million by 1988. Among the new entrants were Coca-Cola Food's Hi-C100, Seagram's Tropicana Twisters, Motts, and Dole. However, in the opinion of Libby's management, despite 'strong introductions and megabuck expenditures', none of the 'big boys' had seriously damaged Juicy Juice's leadership in the segment. Nevertheless, the management believed that all fruit-based beverages competed with one another directly or indirectly, and Juicy Juice's competition came not only from the 100% blended juice products but also from the single flavor juices and the lower priced fruit drinks. (Refer to **Exhibit 5** for sales and market shares of major brands.)

Juicy Juice by Libby's: '100% Real Fruit Juices'

We turned a 'corporate dog' into a success story, and we did it by following the good old recipe of effective product management.

> A Nestlé fruit juice and drinks executive in Vevey, Switzerland.

We went to market at a time when the juice content of products was becoming important in parents' minds... A lot of people thought Hi-C and Hawaiian Punch were good products; they felt they were giving their kids something that was healthy. Well, we came along and said 'no'; they have only 10% juice, whereas we have 100%. And a lot of people were not aware of that fact...

> A Libby's executive in Purchase, New York.

History

The above comments refer to the turnaround of Juicy Juice, a brand acquired by Libby's in 1984 from Fruitcrest, a regional producer. The brand had been launched by Fruitcrest in 1978 and was distributed in the eastern part of the US. With five different blended flavors[5] targeted at children, from 'Real Red' and 'Yummy Yellow' to 'Golden Good', Juicy Juice enjoyed a sales level of $34 million in 1984.

---

5. A blended flavor was a mixture of concentrates from different fruits. In manufacturing, only water and natural fruit flavor were added to restore the juices to their original strength.

Each product was made up of a blend of 100% fruit juices – including apple, grape and cherry – to give it a distinctive taste and color. Libby's management believed the brand would not be profitable for Fruitcrest.

Libby's own products in 1984 included Libby's Nectars, a range of drinks with 50% juice content, and Hearts Delight, a private label drink with less than 50% juice. Both were targeted at adults and families. In the opinion of many Nestlé executives, prior to the launch of Juicy Juice, Libby's beverage range was 'imbalanced' towards the price-orientated segment of the market. 'Libby's was trying to fight the big brands like Del Monte and Minute Maid in the volume business', explained an executive in Vevey. 'But, with such a small share, the company had no chance.' In the early 1980s, Libby's annual losses amounted to nearly 10% of sales.[6]

In 1985, Libby's launched Juicy Juice nationally with a '100% juice' taste platform, spending $2.5 million on media (70%) and promotions (30%) targeted at children. But, a year later, due to what management diagnosed as 'inferior' taste and a 'weak marketing program', the line was withdrawn from national distribution. Juicy Juice continued to be marketed in its core market, the eastern states (representing 48% of the US). By the end of 1986, the brand's sales were $13 million, or 60% below 1985 level.

In 1986, Juicy Juice was given to Robert Mead, the newly appointed Group Vice President for beverages, and his management team to turn around. (Refer to **Exhibit 6** for Libby's partial organization chart in the US.) The appointment came when, in Mead's words, 'the whole damn Libby's beverage business was going to hell'. In his opinion, the product had failed because of poor taste, its '1950s image' labels, and a positioning which did not differentiate it from competition. Although constrained by limited funds, Mead's team was expected to put new life into Juicy Juice and relaunch it initially in its core markets, then later nationally.

Juicy Juice was relaunched in 1987 following a number of changes. First, with help from Nestlé's research facilities in the US and outside, the formulation and taste of the product was improved dramatically. Consumer research showed that Juicy Juice had a taste superior to the major blended juice brands, Tree Top and Hi-C100. Next, labels were changed to show real fruits on the package and to substitute fruit names (for example, 'Cherry') for what had been color names (for example, 'Real Red'). The new labels clearly identified Libby's as the parent behind Juicy Juice. Also, while the number of flavors was expanded from four to six (cherry, grape, punch, tropical, berry, apple), the pack sizes were reduced from four to two (a 1.4-liter can and a new 0.250-liter brik pack).[7] (Refer to **Exhibit 7** for sample labels.)

According to Libby's management, the most important change from the past was repositioning Juicy Juice from good taste and '100% juice' to 'we are 100% juice and they're not'. (**Exhibit 8** shows a positioning map used by management for locating the repositioned Juicy Juice and its competitors.) As Dennis Scott, the General Manager for Beverages, explained:

---

6. By 1984 Nestlé had sold off Libby's other operations and had kept only the beverages.
7. An option for glass packaging was dropped, initially because of its higher costs.

There is a lot of confusion out there. Some say they are '100% natural', or 'a blend of ten different juices'. Yet they all contain 50% or less of real fruit juice. So when we come along and say 'we are 100% and they are not', that stays in the consumer's mind. Juicy Juice became a point of reference for the consumer against which to compare all others.

The brand carried a significant price premium over drinks leading to relatively higher trade margins. Juicy Juice's $1.59 retail price for its 1.4-liter can, for example, compared with the $.79–.99 price range for similar sizes of Hi-C and Hawaiian Punch. Management believed that the premium prices reinforced the superior quality positioning. 'When you offer something that's unique or with high value added, you ought to be able to get a price for it', argued Mead.

In 1987, the company spent $3 million on advertising in the media to relaunch the product in its core market, but stayed away from excessive price-orientated promotions common in the industry. (**Exhibits 9 and 10** show 15" TV commercial storyboards for Juicy Juice and Hawaiian Punch, a leading drink.)

Juicy Juice's positioning was thought to have contributed to its strength against recent competitive entries such as Coca-Cola's Hi-C100, a 100% blended juice brand extension from Hi-C. 'They came at us with all kinds of ad dollars', recalled Mead. 'But, when they raised their prices for the juice, the consumers refused to pay. They said "you are a drink, a price brand, and I won't buy what you are selling."'

Results to Date

'With this improved product, improved label, improved positioning, and improved everything else', Mead recalled, 'we went to war.'

The results of the relaunch were dramatic. By the end of 1987, a full year later, Juicy Juice sales in its core market had increased by 82% to $23 million. In 1988, when the product was reintroduced to new markets representing an additional 21% of the US, sales increased by another 32% to $31 million. (Between 1986 and 1988, the total shelf-stable blended segment had grown by 20% to $145 million.) Currently, Juicy Juice was being sold in cans (73% of dollar shipment) in addition to brik packs (24%) and the newly introduced glass (3%). It was distributed through more than 28,000 grocery stores in 42 states, representing 80% of national market. Libby's management projected sales of nearly $50 million nationwide in 1989. (Refer to **Exhibit 11** for a consumer profile drawn by management for the relaunched Juicy Juice. **Exhibit 12** shows highlights of the brand's 1989 marketing plan.)

Um Bongo by Libby's: The 'Jungle Juice'

The success of Um Bongo is due to its concept – a product developed specifically for kids. It's not a me-too this or a me-too that which anybody can imitate. It's UM BONGO from nose to tail!

A Nestlé beverage executive in Vevey, Switzerland.

> Um Bongo was one of the few juice drinks targeted at children with a fun overtone; its advertising was very instrumental in getting the product off to a good start.
>
> A Libby's Marketing Manager in Croydon, United Kingdom.

History

Um Bongo was introduced in 1984 by Libby's UK beverages division. It was the company's newest entry in a growing but also highly competitive local market for fruit juices and drinks where price-orientated private brands held more than 50% share. Libby's other products included a line of fruit and vegetable juices and drinks targeted primarily at adults. The company was also producing under private labels. In the early 1980s, the UK company was annually losing approximately 2% on a stagnating turnover of about $15 million. (Refer to **Exhibit 13** for data on the UK market and shares.)

Before Um Bongo's introduction, company-sponsored research had shown that while per capita consumption of traditional beverages such as tea (290 liters), milk (110 liters) and beer (100 liters) had declined over the years, consumption of soft drinks (100 liters), and fruit juices and drinks (14 liters) had risen constantly. Research also showed that 45% of all soft drinks was consumed by children aged 15 years or younger, a segment accounting for only 20% of the population.[8] Furthermore, focus group discussions revealed that fruit juices and drinks, though considered by children as 'good for you', suffered from having an old traditional image compared to the younger and more contemporary soft drinks. Mothers indicated that they wanted a healthier alternative to soft drinks, which they thought to be artificial and 'not good for you'.

'All those facts led to the conclusion that there was a marketing opportunity for a product especially developed for children', recalled Paul Lawrence, the UK Marketing Manager for Libby's beverages. 'Thus was born Um Bongo.'

Um Bongo was a blended drink with 25% juice content. It was launched under Libby's umbrella with one flavor, a mixture of nine juices, and in two brik pack sizes (1-liter and 0.2-liter). Its extraordinary 'jungle name' and its 'jungle juice' positioning were decidedly unique, helping the brand to stand out with its offer of a 'balance of fun and health'. Almost every aspect of the product, including its tropical flavor, color, packaging and cartoon advertising had been designed for and tested with children and their mothers. The 'jungle juice' concept had been developed by Libby's advertising agency to project the 'fun overtone' which management considered important. (Refer to **Exhibits 14 and 15** for samples of packaging and TV commercial storyboard, respectively. **Exhibit 16** shows UK consumer research data on Um Bongo.)

Um Bongo carried a premium price which was 32% over private brand drinks but 10% below equivalent volumes of 100% fruit juices. The launch was supported in

---

8. Population of the UK in 1989 = 57 million.

its first year by $1.5 million in advertising and $1 million in consumer and trade promotions. New flavors (Apple Um Bongo and Orange Um Bongo) were introduced subsequently, thus capitalizing on the largest flavor segments in the juice and drinks category. The company also added a new package incorporating three single-serve briks. In 1988, $230,000 was spent on advertising and $152,000 on promotions.

Results to Date

Um Bongo's factory sales in its first year of introduction were $2.1 million. The brand had grown to $3.9 million by 1988, accounting for 20% of Libby's total sales in beverages. In 1989, sales were expected to grow by about 40%. Um Bongo's performance was a key factor behind the UK division's growth in total sales and the significantly improved profitability since 1984.

Um Bongo's success had led to the entry of what management considered to be imitative drinks – brands such as Kia Ora by Cadbury Schweppes in 1986 and Fruit Troop by Del Monte, a division of RJR/Nabisco, in 1989. Both brands had targeted children and their mothers and, like Um Bongo, had used cartoon characters on packaging and in TV commercials. In mid-1989, Libby's management carefully watched Del Monte's launch of Fruit Troop, which was being supported with heavy advertising.

Um Bongo's performance in the UK had not gone unnoticed by Libby's other European divisions. Since 1987 the Spanish and Portuguese companies had introduced Um Bongo in their markets. The brand concept, including its communication, had been kept intact, and only the product's taste and the language on the label were adapted locally. The drinks were produced from imported concentrates. Both countries had used the UK TV commercials dubbed in the local language.

In Spain, the per capita consumption of processed fruit juices and drinks (less than two liters) had traditionally been limited due to the availability of freshly prepared varieties at relatively low prices.[9] The market was also characterized by low marketing activities and poor quality products. (Refer to **Exhibit 17** for data on the Spanish market.)

Libby's produced a line of fruit juices and drinks targeted at families. Sales had declined by about 25% in volume since the early 1980s to $3.5 million in 1986, or less than 3 million liters. Nestlé executives attributed the decline to poor packaging, unfocused positioning, and the absence of advertising support.

Libby's beverage sales in Spain received a boost with the 1987 test introduction of Um Bongo in the Valencia region, which represented 25% of the national market. Supported by $100,000 in TV advertising, the brand's sales reached $110,000 in the test area, a level several times higher than its target. In 1988, sales in the region had grown to $350,000 and 300,000 liters. The increased marketing activities related to Um Bongo had helped to pull the rest of Libby's business up to a total of

---

9. Population of Spain in 1989 = 39 million.

$4.5 million and 4.2 million liters in 1988. The management projected an additional 90% growth for Um Bongo in 1989 after national introduction.

In Portugal, a smaller market than Spain but with similar features, Um Bongo had been introduced nationally in the spring of 1988.[10] Nestlé's local management had recently concluded that significant growth opportunities existed in the beverages sector where Libby's had not been present. Previously, sales had been limited to only Nestlé's dry grocery products such as coffee and cereals. (**Exhibit 18** provides data on the Portuguese juice and drinks market.)

In the words of Patrick Martin, the Nestlé headquarters product manager for juices and drinks, Um Bongo's introduction in Portugal 'blew up the market'. With an advertising support of $1.2 million, Um Bongo's national sales for the year reached $4.7 million or 4.8 million liters. The first year sales were 240% of budget. By early 1989, with less than one year in the market, Um Bongo had reached what management believed was a significant market position and accounted for close to 5% of total Nestlé sales in the country. The company expected a doubling of Um Bongo sales in 1989.

Reactions in the US to Um Bongo

Convinced that Um Bongo was a global concept with a universal appeal, executives at Vevey had prodded Libby's US management to examine the opportunities for the brand's introduction in the American market. According to one headquarters executive: 'We have a winner and it would be a pity if we couldn't transfer it to the world's largest market – the US.'

Research Results

Recently, Libby's US management had commissioned a study to test the acceptance of Um Bongo by the American consumer. The research consisted of a taste test and interviews with 300 children between the ages of 8 and 18 in four states – Ohio, New York, Arizona and Florida. Um Bongo imported from the UK was tested against the leading drink, Hawaiian Punch. The research also aimed to evaluate the effectiveness of Um Bongo's 'jungle' commercial used in the UK, Spain and Portugal.

The study's overall conclusion stated that 'Um Bongo could be a viable entry in the US fruit juice/drinks market, given certain refinements.' The refinements primarily were making the flavor less 'sour/tangy', and changing the commercial so that the product concept would be more clearly communicated. The product was rated equal to Hawaiian Punch in everything except 'purchase interest' and 'taste', where the latter's ratings were significantly higher. (Refer to **Exhibit 19** for a summary of the study's findings and conclusions.)

---

10. Population of Portugal = 10.5 million.

Management Priorities

'It's hard for Um Bongo to make the jump to the US marketplace because food habits are so culturally dependent', Dennis Scott explained his reactions to the brand's performance in the test. 'To give you a fresh example on how cultural food is, we tested a one-liter (32 oz) brik pack, which is so popular in Europe but doesn't exist here. We thought it made inherent sense for the American consumer. We put Juicy Juice into it, made big supermarket displays with special prices, but the American consumer said, "I don't know what that is, so I am not going to venture out." People are just resistant to change.'

A change in Um Bongo's flavor had been considered by US management. But, according to Scott, 'We just don't have the time or manpower to focus on it right now. We have our hands full.'

Currently, Scott and his colleagues were preoccupied with Juicy Juice's perform-ance on a national level. 'Our aim is to make Juicy Juice a $100 million business in five years', explained Jean Graham, Juicy Juice's Marketing Director. Among short and medium-term actions being planned were completion of the national roll-out, introduction of new concentrated and refrigerated forms, expansion into non-grocery outlets and the addition of glass packaging. Improved household penetra-tion was a prime medium-term objective. With 7.8% penetration, Juicy Juice was trailing Hi-C (16%) and Ocean Spray (34%).

Profitability remained another issue of immediate concern. 'Our biggest challenge is to make this business profitable', explained Graham. 'We have high costs in a low margin industry. Our current gross margin is 35% – which is the number off the production line, before any distribution costs or marketing expenses. That's pitiful compared to other grocery categories such as 65% on tea or 85% on corn chip snacks.'

In 1989, management was looking at ways of reducing the raw material and packaging costs. A target date of 1990 was set for breaking even on Juicy Juice.

Other projects preoccupying Libby's management included a new children's beverage product made from a combination of milk and fruit juices. 'We are looking at "Moo Juice" or some such brand name for a milkshake-like product which means fun to kids and health to moms', explained Graham. The product was in an early phase of development.

Management believed that timing was another factor in favor of innovative new products such as milk–juice mix and against a drink like Um Bongo. 'The Um Bongo idea has severe competition today in the US from companies like Coca-Cola, General Foods, Ocean Spray and RJR/Nabisco', argued Scott. 'If we had introduced such a product a few years ago, it might have had a chance. But, Um Bongo would be entry number five at this point.'

Conclusion

Vevey was aware of the US management's views on Um Bongo. 'There is no secret about our different views concerning Um Bongo's potential in the US', confirmed Patrice Martin, the worldwide juice and drinks product manager. 'While we are totally convinced that it's a good product concept, we also understand their hesitation to take on ideas from outside. It's natural. Even the management in Portugal were initially resistant to the Um Bongo idea, and look what happened there when they tried it. So our attitude is: "Give it a try and prove the idea wrong." Meanwhile, all we could do from here is to build confidence in the product by telling them what is going on elsewhere.'

Martin and his colleagues in Vevey advocated a test marketing of Um Bongo as the next step in the US. 'We would like to see a real market test and not just a consumer taste test', Martin explained. Estimated costs of undertaking such a test in the US ranged from $500,000 to $1 million per city including advertising and promotional expenses. A minimum of two major cities representing at least 2% of the US consumption was considered necessary for representative results.

On the US side, meanwhile, the attention was focused on the future of Juicy Juice. Mead described his views on the next steps:

> My challenge is to identify the three biggest ideas and make sure we execute them. Therefore, I tell my people I don't want to hear about product extensions. You've got big big opportunities still with Juicy Juice that need to be fulfilled. Once you've got the important piece in place, we can always add another. We can always circle back.

EXHIBIT 1

Nestlé's 1988 Sales Breakdown

Sales: 40 billion Swiss Francs

Product Category		Geographic Regions	
Beverages	27%	Europe	46%
Dairy	15%	N. America	26%
Chocolate/ Confectionery	12%	Asia	12%
Culinary	12%	L. America	10%
Frozen Foods/ Ice Cream	10%	Africa	3%
Refrigerated Products	9%	Oceania	3%
Infant Foods	6%		
Pet Foods	5%		
Pharmaceuticals/ Cosmetics	2%		
Others	2%		
	100%		100%

Source: Company Records.

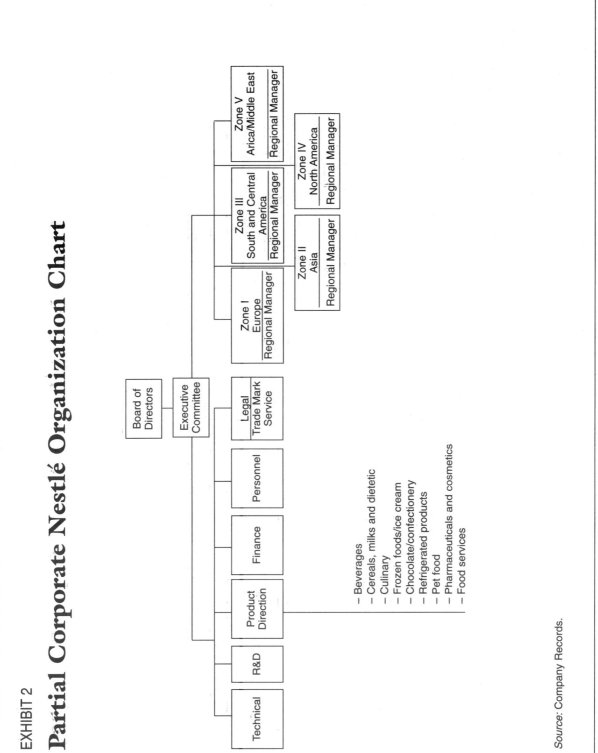

EXHIBIT 2

Partial Corporate Nestlé Organization Chart

Board of Directors

Executive Committee

Technical | R&D | Product Direction | Finance | Personnel | Legal Trade Mark Service

Product Direction:
- Beverages
- Cereals, milks and dietetic
- Culinary
- Frozen foods/ice cream
- Chocolate/confectionery
- Refrigerated products
- Pet food
- Pharmaceuticals and cosmetics
- Food services

Zone I Europe — Regional Manager

Zone II Asia — Regional Manager

Zone III South and Central America — Regional Manager

Zone IV North America — Regional Manager

Zone V Arica/Middle East — Regional Manager

Source: Company Records.

EXHIBIT 3

Segmentation of the US Beverage Market, 1988

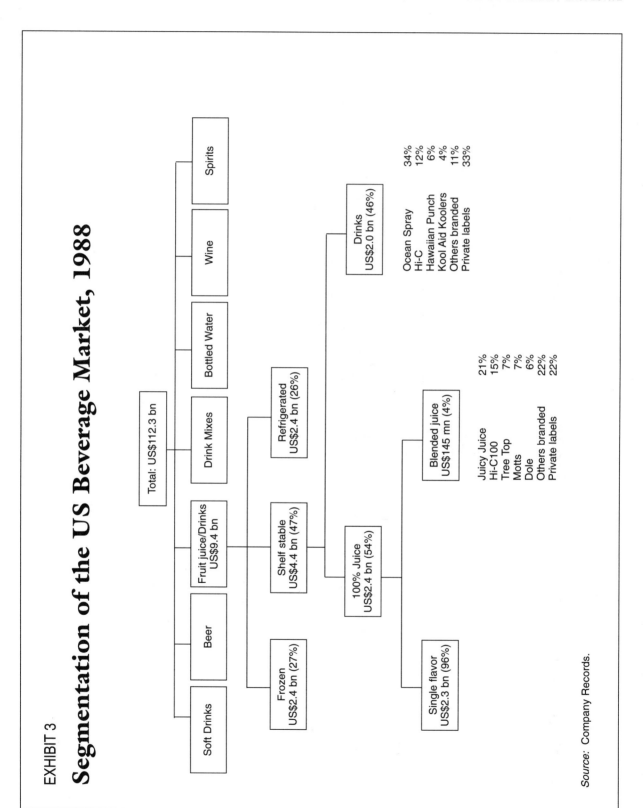

Source: Company Records.

EXHIBIT 4

US Competitive Overview: Who is Who in Shelf-stable Juice

Manufacturer/ Brand	1988 Sales* ($ Million)	Positioning	Product	Retail Price	Packaging	1988 Ad Spending* ($ Million)
Ocean Spray All Brands	**696**	– Refreshment for Adults (Cranberry Juice & Grapefruit)	– Line of Cranberry Juice Cocktails (27% Juice) incl. Concentrates	$1.89–$2.29 (48 Oz)	92% Glass; 8% Brik	21.9
Cranberry Line	562	– Exotic Taste	– Grapefruit Juice cocktail	$0.99–$1.29 (Brik)		
Mauna Lai	41	– Mauna Lai	– Mauna Lai Drinks			
Grapefruit Juice	51		– Crantastic			
Splash	1		– Testing Splash (Carbonated Juice Drink)			
Concentrate	40					
Coke Foods	**239**					
Hi-C	203	– Fun and Good Taste Targeted to Kids	– 10% Fruit Juice	$0.79–$0.99 (46 Oz) $0.79–$0.99 (Brik)	34% Cans; 61% Brik 4% Glass	2.8
Hi-C 100	14	– Family and Kids	– 100% Fruit Juice	$1.19	100% Brik	N/A Part of $25m Umbrella Campaign
Minute Maid	22	– Wholesome Juice	– Brik Pak is only Shelf-stable Item. Offer 100% Juice and Drinks	$0.99–$1.29 (Brik)	Brik	
RJR/Nabisco	**195**					
Hawaiian Punch	114	– Great Taste for Kids	– 10% Juice	$0.79–$0.99 (46 Oz) $0.79–$0.99 (Brik)	60% Cans 23% Brik 14% Glass 3% Plastic	1.8
Del Monte Fruit Blends	81	– Great Tasting Fruit Drink for Adults	– 50% Juice	$1.79–$1.99 (48 Oz)	Glass Brik	0.1
General Foods	**73**					
Kool-Aid Koolers	57	– The Wacky, 'Cool' Juice Drink for Kids – 100% Natural W/ Great Taste	– 20% Juice	$0.79–$0.99 (Brik)	100% Brik	4.6
Tang	16	& Variety Targeted to Kids	– 10% Juice	$0.79–$0.99 (Brik)	100% Brik	2.5

EXHIBIT 4 (CONTINUED)

Manufacturer/ Brand	1988 Sales* ($ Million)	Positioning	Product	Retail Price	Packaging	1988 Ad Spending* ($ Million)
Nestlé	**73**					
Juicy Juice	38	– 100% Juice and They're Not for Kids	– 100% Juice	$1.59 (46 Oz) $1.19 (Brik)	76% Can 21% Brik 3% Glass	2.5
Other Libby's	35					
Tree Top	**177**	– 100% Pure Fruit Juices Targeted to Adults	– 100% Juice Blends Based largely on Apple Juice, Product Inferior due to the Absence of Natural Flavors	$1.79–$1.99 (48 Oz) $1.39–$1.49 (Cans) $0.99–$1.29 (Brik)	Glass, Brik, Can	3.2
Seagrams Tropicana Twisters	13	– Unusual Taste	– Line of 6 Citrus Based Juice Drinks with 30–40% Juice	$1.79–$1.99 (46 Oz)	100% Glass	7.9
Welch's	**268**					
Welch's	200	– Heritage Campaign (100 Yrs)	– 50% Juice	$1.79–$2.09 (40 Oz Glass) $0.99–$1.19 (Brik)	Glass, Brik	2.7 Umbrella Campaign
Welch's Orchard	58					
All Others	10					

*A.C. Nielsen – 1988

Source: Company Records.

EXHIBIT 5

1988 Dollar Volume and Share Trends
Total US Juice/Drinks Category (US$ thousands)

Manufacturer	Brand	1988 Volume ($)	Versus Last Year	Share	% National Distribution
Coke Foods	Total Company	1,254	+6.7%	16.5	
	Minute Maid	1,038	+7.3%	13.7	100
	Hi-C	203	+4.6%	2.7	100
	Hi-C 100	14	−10.8%	0.1	89
Seagrams	Total Company	748	+24.2%	9.8	
	Tropicana	735	+22.5%	9.7	99
	Tropicana Twisters	13	+++	0.1	71
Ocean Spray	Total Ocean Spray	696	+4.8%	9.2	100
Procter & Gamble	Total Citrus Hill	342	+36.1%	4.5	98
Campbell Soup	Total Company	269	+20.4%	3.5	
	Campbells	50	+3.3%	0.7	100
	V-8	218	+25.3%	2.8	100
Welch Foods	Total Company	268	+9.9%	3.5	
	Welch's	200	+12.5%	2.6	100
	Welch's Orchard	58	−2.0%	0.8	84
	All Other	10	+45.3%	0.1	
Quaker Oats	Gatorade	221	+36.0%	2.9	100
RJR/Nabisco	Total Company	195	+7.7%	2.6	
	Hawaiian Punch	114	+0.6%	1.5	100
	Del Monte	81	+19.9%	1.1	99
Tree Top	Total Tree Top	177	+12.5%	2.3	78
Nestlé	Total Company	73	+28.1%	1.0	
	Juicy Juice	38	+51.3%	0.6	45
	Libby Nectars	25	+7.5%	0.3	63
	Hearts Delight	10	+17.5%	0.1	34
General Foods	Total Company	73	+10.2%	0.9	
	Kool-Aid Koolers	57	−12.6%	0.8	99
	Tang	16	+++	0.1	89

Source: A.C. Nielsen – 1988.

EXHIBIT 6

Libby's US Division Reporting Structure

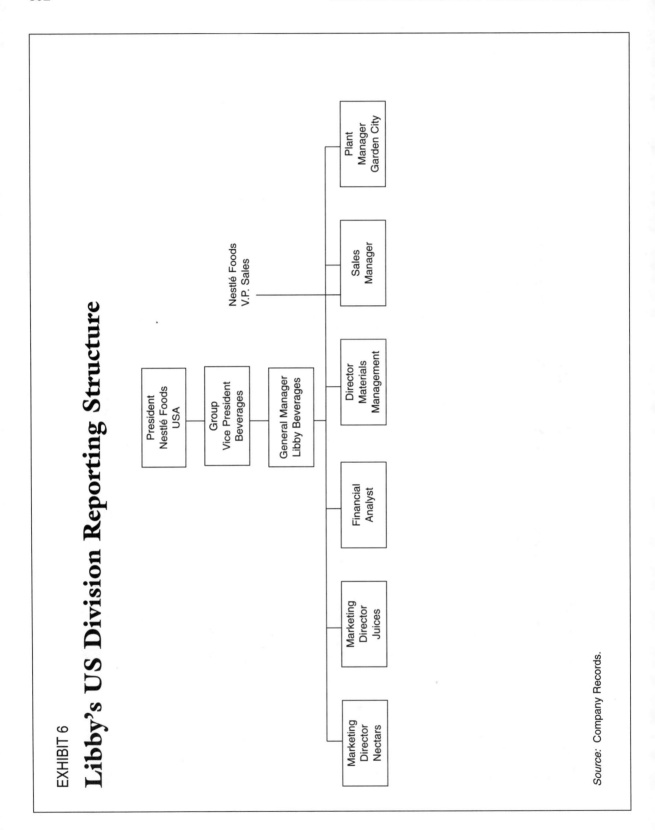

Source: Company Records.

EXHIBIT 7

Juicy Juice: Sample Labels

Source: Company Records.

EXHIBIT 8

Juicy Juice Positioning
(Based on 1987 Creative)

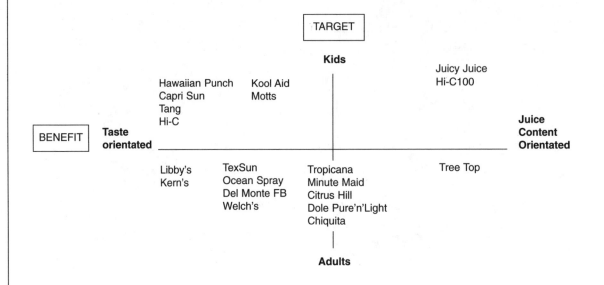

EXHIBIT 9

Juicy Juice Storyboard

Kid 1: You'll never get more than 10% real juice out of those drinks.

No matter how much you pour.

But Juicy Juice from Libby's is 10% real fruit juice.

Kid 2: Wow!

Announcer: Juicy Juice is a juicier juice.

Kid 3: It's 100%.

Source: Company Records.

EXHIBIT 10

Hawaiian Punch Storyboard

1. (MUSIC) CHORUS Hit me with a juice that turns my taste buds loose.

2. How about a nice Hawaiian Punch...

3. a nice Hawaiian....

4. ANNCR: 10% fruit juice, 7 kinds of fruit

5. one of a kind fruit taste.

6. CHORUS: Punch? (MUSIC OUT)

Source: Company Records.

EXHIBIT 11

Juicy Juice Consumer Profile

1. **Demographics**

   Heavy Users:
   - Income: +$25K/yr.
   - Female head under 35 and full-time housewife/mother
   - Household size 3+
   - Users age: 2–11

2. **Purchasing Patterns**

   Juice purchase cycle is short:
   - Purchased every 2 weeks
   - Comparatively, coffee is purchased every 9 weeks

   Juice is a high impulse item:
   - Planned purchase for juice: 39%
   - Planned purchase for coffee: 64%

Source: Company Records.

EXHIBIT 12

Highlights of 1989 Marketing Plan
Juicy Juice

1. Long-term Strategy: Increase sales to $100mn+ via expansion of product into multiple store locations (shelf stable and refrigerated) and through multiple distribution outlets (grocery stores, non-food, convenience stores, vending, food service).

2. Short-term Strategies:
    - Increase household penetration
    - Increase product usage
    - Continue to steal share from juice drinks and 100% juices
    - Continue to improve profitability

3. Target sales: $39 million
    Target spending: $9 million (+13% over 1988)

Ads	$3 million
Consumer Promotion	$1.3 million
Trade Promotion	$4.7 million

4. Pricing: Price at significant premium to kids' 10% drinks, but not at a premium which risks volume. Parity with other 100% juices.

5. Advertising: To create awareness in new markets; maintain awareness in core markets.

6. Positioning: Juicy Juice is the 100% juice blend alternative to kids' 10% juice drinks.

    Target audience: Moms age 25–49 with kids 2–11
    $20,000+ household income

7. Promotions: Consumer   – to maintain current heavy user base
           – to increase household penetration

    Trade   – to increase listings in core market and new expansion markets
           – to focus on gaining displays at reduced price

8. New Products: Continue work on new flavors, packaging and form (concentrate).

Source: Company Records.

EXHIBIT 13

Segmentation of the UK Beverage Market, 1988 (US$ mn)

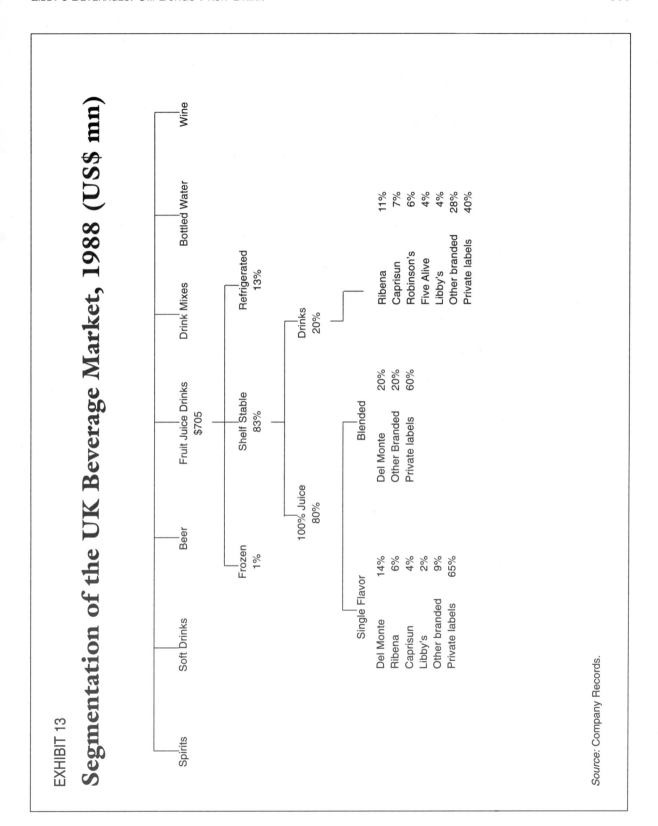

Source: Company Records.

EXHIBIT 14

Um Bongo Brik Paks

Source: Company Records.

EXHIBIT 15

Um Bongo Commercial Storyboard

Sound: Music in
background to end

Chorus singing UM BONGO
UM BONGO

THEY DRINK IT IN THE CONGO

UM BONGO

UM BONGO

THEY DRINK IT IN THE CONGO

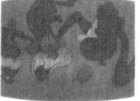

male: LIBBY'S

UM BONGO

BLENDED FRUIT JUICE DRINK
2nd male: YEAH.

Source: Company Records.

EXHIBIT 16

UK Consumer Data on Um Bongo*

Children's Opinion		Children's Agreement with Attributes**		Mothers' Agreement with Attributes**	
Like a lot	53%	Fun	81%	Fun	93%
Quite like it	34%	Something I would buy	79%	Children would ask for it	92%
		Exciting flavor	84%	High quality	80%
Don't like it very much	7%	Good for me	86%	Full of goodness	70%
Don't like it at all	3%	Something mother would buy for me	65%		
No opinion	3%				
	100%				

*   Responses given after product trial and exposure to video of TV commercial
** Percentages do not add up to 100 due to multiple responses

Source: Company Records.

EXHIBIT 17

Spanish Fruit Juice and Drinks Market* 1988

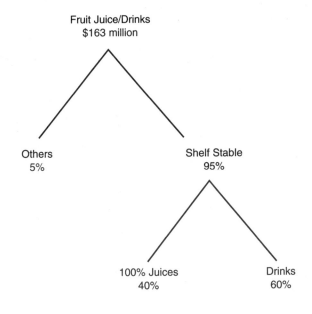

Zumosol	14%	Trinajanjus	16%
Pascual	10%	Zumosol	14%
Juver	11%	Pascual	11%
Libby's	3%	Juver	11%
Large number of		La Verja	10%
other brands	62%	Libby's	3%
		Other brands	35%

* Excludes fresh juices.

Source: Company Records.

EXHIBIT 18

Portuguese Fruit Juice and Drinks Market* 1988

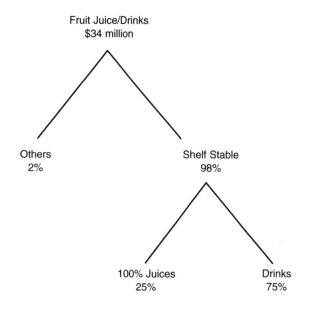

Fruit Juice/Drinks
$34 million

Others
2%

Shelf Stable
98%

100% Juices
25%

Drinks
75%

Compal	11%	Trinajanjus	20%
		Libby's	18%
Large number of		Compalinho	7%
other brands	89%	Other brands	55%

* Excludes fresh juices.

Source: Company Records.

EXHIBIT 19

US Um Bongo Research: Interpretative Summary and Selected Findings

Background and Purpose

The ready-to-drink fruit juice and fruit drink markets continue to be among the fastest segments of the overall US beverage market.

Nestlé has offered Libby USA the opportunity to market Um Bongo – a ready-to-drink fruit juice drink presently being successfully marketed by Libby in the UK.

Management wishes to evaluate the acceptability of the product to the American consumer. Specifically to determine:

1. the acceptance of the Um Bongo product versus Hawaiian Punch (the market leader) on a blind taste basis;
2. the incremental value of the Um Bongo concept (in video form) in heightening the appeal of the product;
3. how well the Um Bongo product lives up to the expectations generated by the concept;
4. the communication ability of the Um Bongo commercial.

Conclusions/Recommendations

Based on the research results, it appears that Um Bongo could be a viable entry in the US fruit juice/drink market given certain refinements.

The strength of the Um Bongo product itself lies in the specific fruit flavors and the strength of those flavors. However, a 'sour/tangy' taste seems to pull down the product's acceptance and would need to be reduced to improve acceptance.

From a conceptual standpoint, the current commercial enhances the product's acceptance and the perception that the product is unique – definitely a plus in the vast sea of fruit juice/drink beverages. However, the commercial needs to communicate the concept in a clearer manner. It is hypothesized that after viewing the commercial consumers are not sure of what to expect and when they taste it they are pleasantly surprised. A more focused and clear explanation of the product in the commercial without diminishing the uniqueness would aid in enhancing the product's acceptance overall.

Key Findings

1. The Um Bongo commercial generated limited interest in trying the product. After trial, however, consumers were more receptive to the product.
2. Positioning the product prior to trial enhanced the product's perception of being unique as well as its acceptance overall.
3. On a blind basis Um Bongo performs similarly to Hawaiian Punch in terms of overall rating and total purchase interest. However, when directly compared, Hawaiian Punch is significantly preferred.
4. Um Bongo's product advantages are seen in its specific fruit flavors and the strength of those flavors. However, its 'sour/tangy' aspect was the major focus for rejection.

EXHIBIT 19 (CONTINUED)

Summary of Findings

Video Impact

1. Within the context of a single viewing, the Um Bongo video produces limited enthusiasm for product trial.
2. The video succeeds in communicating the brand name and places the product squarely in the fruit juice-drink market.
3. Consumers who are reluctant to try Um Bongo have ill-defined concerns apparently based on their difficulty in understanding words in the commercial.
4. Despite these reservations, concept positioning via the video ultimately appears to aid in the actual product's acceptance.

Product Acceptance After Commercial Exposure

1. The product fosters significantly greater buying interest than was considered before trial; it was better than expected.
2. Um Bongo is judged best in terms of its uniqueness; providing a good overall taste through a combination of strong, tangy fruit flavors.
3. Acceptance/rejection, although often expressed in terms of sweetness/tartness levels, ultimately translates into the impact of these physical attributes on beverage benefits; that is, taste satisfying, refreshing.

Blind Acceptance of Um Bongo versus Hawaiian Punch

1. In absolute terms, the Um Bongo product produces ratings approximate to those given the Hawaiian Punch.
2. They are not equal however:
   – purchase interest in Hawaiian Punch is significantly higher;
   – when directly compared, Hawaiian Punch is overwhelmingly preferred to Um Bongo,
3. The sweeter, not too tart flavor of Hawaiian Punch is the dominant reason for its preference.
4. Tanginess is the major point of focus in rejecting Um Bongo.

Selected Tables

Impact of Video

1. The Um Bongo commercial, albeit after a single exposure, produces only limited enthusiasm for product trial.

   Just 5% of children 8 to 10 years of age express a definite commitment to buy. The overwhelming reaction appears to be one of cautious reserve, with 81% indicating a 'probably buy' to 'might or might not buy' purchase interest.

	Post video Purchase Intent
Base: Total Respondents	(150)
	%
Definitely would buy	5
Probably would buy	50
Might or might not buy	31
Probably would not buy	7
Definitely would not buy	7

EXHIBIT 19 (CONTINUED)

2. The video succeeds in communicating the brand name and places the product squarely in the fruit juice-drink market.

- 86% recall Um Bongo as the brand name.
- 84% believe product will be most similar to other fruit juice-drinks – particularly Hawaiian Punch.

One Beverage Most Similar

Base: Total Respondents	(150)
	%
Hawaiian Punch	45
Juicy Juice	22
Hi-C	17
Orange Juice	7
Kool-Aid	4

3. Commercial also positions Um Bongo as most appropriate for pre-teenage children, at other than the formal meal occasions of dinner and breakfast.
- Regardless of age, Um Bongo is perceived as most suitable for young children, particularly those under 8. Few teenagers (19%) see the product directed at them, while 2 of 3 (67%) pre-teens indicate they would be likely to use.
- Non-meal at home occasions are considered best for Um Bongo.

Use/Occasions Appropriateness

		Age	
	Total	8–13	14–30
Base: Total Respondents	(150)	(76)	(74)
	%	%	%
Would be likely to use:			
Children under 8	89	88	89
Children 8–12	73	67	78
Teenagers 13–19	21	24	19
Adults 20 and over	13	17	10
With breakfast	47	51	42
'On the go' occasions	58	54	62
Drink at home	79	87	70
With a snack	79	83	76
With lunch	64	68	60
With dinner	23	29	16
Away from home	60	66	54

☐ = Significant difference at the 90% level of confidence

EXHIBIT 19 (CONTINUED)

4. In spite of these reservations, the video, as the tool for presenting the Um Bongo concept, appears to favorably alter ultimate product acceptance.

    Actual product ratings and interest in buying Um Bongo are uniformly higher when consumers are previously shown the video than when tasting the product occurs without concept positioning.

Video Impact on Product Evaluation

	Um Bongo		
	With Video	Without Video	Difference
Base:	(150)	(75)	
	%	%	+
			−
Purchase Intent			
% Definitely would buy	25	15	−10
Total positive	67	60	−7
Overall Rating			
% Excellent/extremely good	44	33	−11
Mean	3.97	3.80	−0.17
Attribute Ratings (% Excellent/extremely good)			
Is tangy	50	36	−14
Is refreshing	47	39	−8
Has a strong fruit taste	56	49	−7
Is sweet tasting	46	43	−3
Is satisfying	44	40	−4
Is bitter tasting	27	20	−7
Is a good combination of flavors	49	45	−4
Has a good overall flavor	51	41	−10
Leaves a pleasant taste in your mouth	46	43	−3
Has an appealing color	45	43	−2
Is different	59	56	−3
Is a beverage for me	44	41	−3
Is fun to drink	43	33	−10

☐ = Significant difference at the 90% level of confidence.

EXHIBIT 19 (CONTINUED)

Product Acceptance After Commercial Exposure

With product trial, the uncertainties that existed after only concept exposure are clarified, producing a significantly broader base of favourably disposed purchasers.

Tasting the product engenders significantly greater buying interest than was considered before trial.

Purchase Intent

	Post Video Exposure	Post Product Trial	Difference
Base: Total Respondents	(150)	(150)	+
	%	%	−
Definitely would buy	5	25	+20
Probably would buy	50	42	−8
(Total Positive)	(55)	(67)	+12
Might or might not buy	31	15	−16
Probably would not buy	7	7	−
			+
Definitely would not buy	7	11	−4

[   ] = Significant difference at the 90% level of confidence.

Product Acceptance Blind versus Hawaiian Punch

Um Bongo overall and specific product characteristic ratings closely parallel those elicited by Hawaiian Punch. Only in the specific area of fruit taste does Hawaiian Punch garner a higher satisfaction rating.

Nevertheless, in spite of this seemingly similar level of acceptance, purchase interest is significantly greater for Hawaiian Punch.

(Table on next page)

EXHIBIT 19 (CONTINUED)

Blind Test – Um Bongo and Hawaiian Punch

	Um Bongo	Hawaiian Punch
Base: Total Respondents	(75)	(75)
	%	%
Purchase Intent		
% Definitely would buy	15	29
Total positive	60	72
Overall Rating		
% Excellent/extremely good	33	36
Mean	3.80	4.04
Attribute Ratings (% Excellent/Extremely Good)		
Is tangy	36	27
Is refreshing	39	43
Has a strong fruit taste	49	48
Is sweet tasting	43	49
Is satisfying	40	45
Is bitter tasting	20	11
Is a good combination of flavors	45	45
Has a good overall flavur	41	41
Leaves a pleasant taste in your mouth	43	41
Has an appealing color	43	56
Is different	56	43
Is a beverage for me	41	44
Is fun to drink	33	37
Directional Ratings (% Just Right)		
Sweetness	77	80
Color	79	79
Fruit taste	68	84
Too strong	17	11
Too weak	15	5

[box] = Significant difference at the 90% level of confidence.

Source: Company Records.

Hilti Corporation (A)

This case was prepared by Professor Peter Killing.

In the summer of 1993, the new executive board of Hilti Corporation, led by Dr Pius Baschera, was meeting to discuss the less than satisfactory operations of the Hilti company in Hong Kong. Dr Baschera and the other three members of the board would not officially take up their new positions until January 1994, but to ensure a smooth transition, the group began functioning in mid-1993. Whatever decision they came to about Hong Kong would have to be agreed to by Michael Hilti, the current CEO, and other members of the outgoing executive board.

The way forward in Hong Kong was not clear. The country manager was proposing a course of action that was a marked deviation from Hilti's well-proven worldwide strategy of selling construction tools and fasteners directly to end-users. Yet something had to be done. In a market that was growing at least 10% per year, it appeared that Hilti Hong Kong would have 1993 sales and profits 5% to 10% lower than 1992.

Hilti Corporation

The Hilti company was founded in 1941 by Martin and Eugen Hilti in the Principality of Liechtenstein, which is nestled between Austria and the eastern border of Switzerland. The Hilti brothers laid the foundations for the company when they obtained an order to manufacture threaded studs and nails for a pistol-like tool that was intended for fastening work in construction. Although not fully developed, this tool was recognized by the Hiltis as having great potential for the rebuilding of Europe. Patents were obtained, and a product line centered on high-velocity tools was created. (Refer to **Exhibit 1** for a selection of products from Hilti's line of drills, anchoring systems and direct fastening systems.)

By 1960, Hilti had a major production facility in Liechtenstein and was well established in European markets. Martin Hilti's belief that 'market share is more important than factories' had led to a great emphasis on understanding and responding to customer needs. Recognizing that customers would value knowledgeable advice on how to best use Hilti tools, the company had established a direct sales force, rather than using distributors or dealers.

The 1960s and 70s were years of strong growth for Hilti, as construction in the company's major markets of Europe and the United States was booming. Key to Hilti's success were the strong willed entrepreneurs running each country operation who pushed their sales forces for ever better results. As sales and profits grew, production facilities were added throughout Europe, and a plant was built in the USA.

In the early 1980s, however, Hilti was hard hit by a worldwide recession in the construction industry. Sales and profits slumped, and the managers in major markets like Germany, France, and the US informed the head office that little could be done in this adverse economic environment. Market shares were already high, so growth was not an option: they would just have to ride out the storm and wait for better times. One younger manager commented:

> When the markets turned down, we began to realize that these Hilti 'country kings' were not very complete managers. They successfully grew sales volumes in boom times, but they had failed to develop their organizations and their people.
>
> I have to give credit to Schaan (Hilti's head office), as they recognized the problem, and in the next few years replaced most of the country kings. They promoted or brought in from the outside younger managers, better educated, with broader skills.
>
> Of course simply changing the senior managers was not enough, as there were many others in the country organizations also used to doing things their own way. So we brought in McKinsey to perform an overhead value analysis, which resulted in changes in our processes and structures that gave us more flexibility. And we were not happy with central research and development – it seemed to be an empire unto itself – so we also brought in BCG (Boston Consulting Group), and created four divisions at head office that were responsible for developing, manufacturing, and sourcing products that were then sold to the country units for resale to final customers.
>
> These changes went some way to curbing the power of the countries, and improving the innovation process in the company.

Strategy 2000 – The Beginning

In 1984, for the first time, a week-long meeting was held to bring together all senior Hilti managers from around the world. As the thirty or so country managers made presentations on their business, it became clear that, in the words of one of the attendees, 'We had no vision, no strategy, no coherence. We were simply a collection of countries each doing its own thing, and the results were not nearly as good as they could have been.'

A decision was made to begin a major strategy review, again with the help of BCG. The work began in the United States, where Hilti's performance had been suffering. The challenge was both to increase profitability and return to higher rates of growth. A close examination of Hilti customers and their needs made it clear that Hilti's policy of selling direct to end-customers should be maintained. It was also decided that telephone-based customer service should be instituted. Thus, a customer could contact Hilti by phone, or by direct contact with the salesman.

Hilti USA was divided into three business units, each to serve a particular customer segment for the whole country. This was a sharp change from the previous area-based organization in which a salesman sold all Hilti products to all customers in his geographic region. A senior manager commented:

> A change like this is dramatic, because it means that many of our customers are now dealing with a new salesman, and they have to get to know each other. Remember that we are not just selling products; we are also giving advice and training – and it is those things and our product quality that allow us to price our products 20–30% above competitors like Bosch or Makita. So the salesman has to learn his product line in depth, and a market segmented approach encourages that. Once the salesman understands the applications of his product line in the trades he serves very well, he will begin to demand modifications and new products from our product development people.

With the US model in place by the late 1980s, attention turned to Europe. Pius Baschera, head of Hilti's operation in Germany at the time, recalled the situation:

> Germany was (and still is) Hilti's largest operation, and we were performing well. The country was divided into five geographic regions, and within each region the sales force was segmented by trade group – plumbers, electricians, and so on. So we could see the US rationale for dividing the sales force – although we thought they had the trades segmented incorrectly – but we could not see the rationale for creating whole business units for each trade. Our plan was to keep the sales force specialized by trade, but at the management levels above the sales force, we did not see the need for specialization.
>
> There was a lot of pressure on the German management team to make a quick transition to the US model, however. The president of Hilti Western Hemisphere was given the responsibility for the total core business worldwide and, as a member of the executive board, he worked with the new head of Germany (Baschera's successor) to push changes through. There was a lot of resistance: almost no one, for example, thought that the quick move to set up a central customer service function and closing all the regional sales offices was a good idea. Several key managers left the German company.

The Evolution of Strategy 2000

As the roll-out of Strategy 2000 continued in Europe, adjustments were made in a number of areas. Agreement was reached on the best way to segment the sales force, for example, which meant that the US adopted the trade segments used in Europe. The German drive for maintaining regional centers was not supported, however.

In the early 1990s, a diagram was created that captured the heart of the Hilti 2000 strategy on a single page. This chart, shown in **Exhibit 2**, became known in the company as the 'mother of all charts' and was widely displayed in company facilities all over the world. The creation of a common, simply communicated strategy was seen by employees at all levels as extremely valuable, and the items on the chart became a part of everyday communication.

As European countries gradually moved to implement Strategy 2000, the resistance in Germany continued. In the early 1990s, with East Germany opening up,

Germany was growing at 20% per year. Instituting a program of major change did not make sense to many people in the German operation. But by 1991, it was clear that the change would happen; by early 1993, it was largely complete.

A Challenge for New Management

In mid-1993, significant changes were taking place at the most senior levels of Hilti. Michael Hilti, the son of Martin, was to become Chairman of the Board, and Pius Baschera, aged 44, would be the first non family member to take over the CEO role. At the same time, the other two members of the executive board would also change, as Hilti's mandatory age limit of 55 necessitated their retirement.

The Hong Kong situation was the first major issue addressed by the new management team. Pius Baschera commented:

> In 1991, dealer sales accounted for one third of our total sales in Hong Kong. But in 1992, this figure fell to 19%, and is heading for zero in 1993 as Strategy 2000 is fully implemented. To compensate, we have increased our direct sales force, but sales are not increasing yet. Without dealers, we find it difficult to access the small customers – and they are growing in number. We estimate that there were about 6,000 construction companies in Hong Kong in 1983, with an average of about 16 employees. Today, there are closer to 13,000 with an average of fewer than ten employees. So there are more and more small guys in this business, and at the moment, they account for at least 15–20% of the Hong Kong market. In the West, small operators play a less important role.
>
> What the Hong Kong general manager is proposing is that we use a controlled number of 'local sales elements' (the name he gave to dealers) to carry a limited number of our product lines most suitable for small customers. In this way, he argues, we can regain our lost ground, and participate fully in the growth of the market.
>
> Taking a broader perspective, we must remember that while approximately 60% of our two billion Swiss francs of annual revenue comes from Europe, and only about 12% from Asia, our greatest growth prospects are in Asia and Eastern Europe. And we are not currently meeting our targets of double-digit growth in sales and profits – so we need to get our approach to Asian markets just right.

Another member of the new executive board added the following:

> We must bear in mind that there are good reasons for our direct sales approach. First, we are not just selling products. We add value by giving advice and training. Our customers trust us. We can only create such relationships by selling direct. Second, by working with customers, we get valuable ideas for new products and applications. Third, if we have two competing channels, we hurt our sales force. And remember, of the 12,000 people in this company, 4,000 are salesmen! These people live on their commissions, and being an exclusive channel for Hilti products is very much part of their livelihood. We do not want to set up a conflict in the company.

The other risk of using dealers is that we lose control of pricing. We have international customers who can quite effectively take advantage of any global anomalies in our pricing policies. And of course, we lose some of our profit margin by selling to dealers.

And if we do this in Hong Kong, it will only be the beginning. I can name at least three other countries that are just implementing Strategy 2000 who will argue that they too should be allowed to use 'local sales elements'.

A third board member commented:

We will never survive if we just copy what other people are doing. Bosch uses dealers and is very good at it. They have drill bits packaged nicely to be displayed in dealer premises. They have point-of-purchase material, incentive programs for dealers, and so on. We have none of this. It is not our way of doing business. We need to stick with our unique Hilti strengths and approach to doing business wherever we can.

Secondly, I must stress that while the roll-out of Strategy 2000 into Asia is extremely important, we *also* need to extend our Hilti culture to the Asian region. As our small country operations in Asia grow, we need to ensure that we manage our people there the same way as we do elsewhere. We must emphasize worldwide training programs, for example, which will stress the Hilti values of self-responsibility, freedom to take risks, openness, commitment and freedom of choice.

As he sat at the board table with his new team, Pius Baschera reflected on the views of Michael Hilti and his executive team, the people to whom he had to make his new management group's recommendation.

Michael and his executive team have been working very hard to put Strategy 2000 in place. It has not always been easy, as the struggle in Germany shows, but they have been firm and persistent. If we come in as the new management team and as our first act encourage Hong Kong to walk away from Strategy 2000, I do not know how it will be received.

EXHIBIT 1

The Hilti Product Line

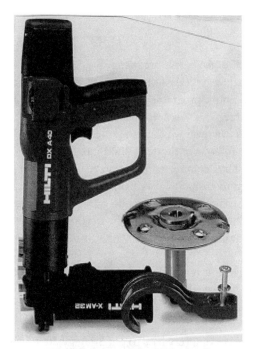

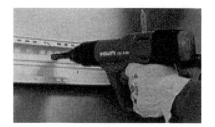

Sources: Top left: 1994 Hilti Corporation Annual Report; Others: 1996 Hilti Corporation Catalogue, *Kompakt-Katalog Producte und Anwendungen.*

EXHIBIT 2

Global Strategy

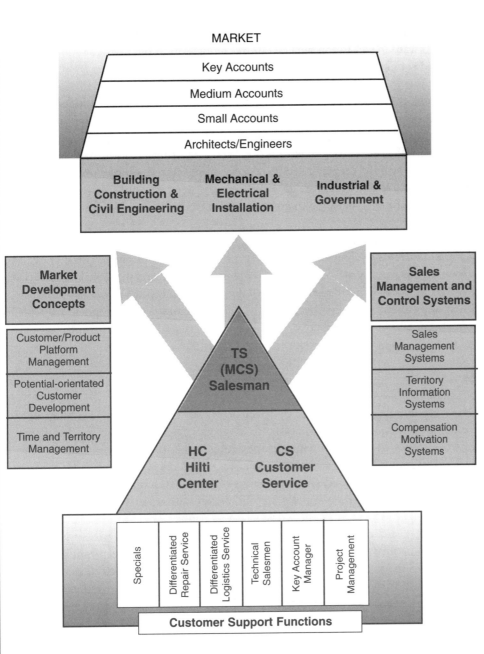

Source: Hilti Corporation Company Document.

CASE 3.3^R **Haaks Europe**

This case was prepared by Professor Kamran Kashani with the assistance of Research Associate Janet Shaner. All names and figures have been disguised.

The days of local marketing for local markets are numbered. We have a responsibility to move forward in pan-Europeanizing our marketing. This is our division's most important goal and your key challenge.

These were the words of Stuart May, the European regional President of Haaks International, a medium-sized food company specializing in fast-moving confectionery and snack products, as he briefed the division's newly appointed European Marketing VP, Hans Viber. The headquarters marketing position had only recently been filled. It still lacked a detailed job description, but the senior European management understood the function's primary role to be establishing better coordination across Haaks' diverse national marketing activities.

Hans, before we begin any regional activity, we need to harmonize our marketing planning across the 15 national organizations. Next month's strategic planning workshop with top local management is our opportunity to present a unified structure for all future country marketing plans. With that structure well understood and accepted, we can then take the first steps towards pan-European initiatives... I'd like to see your proposals for a unified marketing plan in two weeks.

Background

Haaks Europe was the regional division of Haaks International, headquartered in the Netherlands. Haaks International had grown faster than the food industry in general, thanks to a series of important acquisitions in recent years. With sales of US$1.5 billion in Europe and North America, Haaks ranked number 16 worldwide in confectionery and salted snack products. Using a strategy of selective expansion and a focus on key segments, the group management target was to be, within seven years, among 'the top ten' of the world's largest confectionery and snacks companies.

Over the past decade, Haaks Europe's acquisitions had followed a similar pattern. Targets for acquisition were small companies with strong local brands in confectionery or salted snack products, and those which had a well-established local sales and distribution network. Management was particularly interested in 'underperformers', or companies whose potential for high performance had yet to be realized.

Typically, after each acquisition the turnaround came rapidly – through manufacturing rationalization, stronger marketing, and overhead cost control.

By now, Haaks Europe consisted of 15 independent local organizations in as many countries. Eight companies had joined the division over the past five years. Every country had its own manufacturing, sales and marketing structure. Haaks' performance varied considerably from country to country, but its share of confectionery and snacks markets was strongest in central Europe and weakest in northern Europe.

More than 60 confectionery and snacks brands were being locally marketed by Haaks Europe. The brands ranged from the Maxy selection of fruit-flavored candies in Germany, and the Ovation chocolate bar in the UK, to Snax corn-based and spiced crackers in France.

Senior European managers believed that many local brands lacked sufficient marketing support and consumer franchise. The question of whether or not the weaker brands should be dropped from the product line was often the subject of heated debate between the local management and headquarters. On the other hand, a dozen brands were thought to have pan-European potential. These brands enjoyed high local market shares, had differentiated positioning, and were in such growth segments as health-related snacks. It was estimated that by integrating operations and having a more streamlined product line, Haaks Europe's markets could be supplied by half as many plants.

The Market

Over the last decade, the European market for confectionery and snack products had grown at an annual rate of 6%, faster than the growth of the food industry. A number of consumer trends explained this overall higher growth rate:

- Consumers were having smaller meals, but more confectionery and snack products between meals
- More confectionery and snack products were being consumed at work
- Europe's aging population had given rise to a growing 'health segment' in most food categories, including confectionery and snack products.

At the same time, major international food companies were investing significant resources in Europe's growing markets. Nestlé, Unilever, Mars, Philip Morris and Pepsico were among the global food concerns which had increased their activities in confectionery and snack products across Europe. Some of these firms had adopted pan-European strategies for brand development, manufacturing and logistics. Medium-sized food companies were growing more alarmed at the industry consolidation, as it was giving the majors an increasingly large share of the European food markets.

Another trend of significant long-term impact on European food markets was the growth of large food chains and the rising share of private brands. The consolidation in the trade tended to erode the traditional bargaining power of producers of branded products. Similar consequences were expected from the rise of food retailers' own private brands. Pan-European wholesale and retail alliances were a recent development in the food trade.

Marketing at Haaks Europe

At Haaks Europe, where country management was accountable for local performance, marketing was always a local concern. Accordingly, if and when marketing plans were drawn up, they remained in the local organizations. The headquarters received only sales and volume targets and corresponding budgets for marketing expenditures. After discussions between the center and local management, often leading to adjustments in the numbers, these budgets became the basis for each country's annual performance evaluation.

Three years earlier, a study conducted by an international consulting company had proposed the creation of a headquarters coordinating function in marketing. The aim of the new unit was to upgrade the uneven quality of marketing expertise in local organizations, and to promote more consistent local and regional brand strategies.

The consultants' recommendations had been gladly adopted by the then newly appointed European President, Bo Larsson, May's predecessor. However, Larsson had soon found the task of building support for a headquarters-led coordination role hard to implement. Opposition from a handful of powerful country organizations had proved much tougher than expected. He had resigned after only 16 months in the job.

May, on the other hand, had taken a more patient approach. While believing in the need for more coordination, he was careful to build local and group management support for any regional initiative. Viber, hired by May, was told to proceed methodically and build credibility for central marketing. He had no line authority *vis-à-vis* local marketing managers. One of the activities undertaken by Viber was to hold quarterly meetings of local marketing managers. These meetings were purely for information sharing purposes and were considered by the participants as useful for networking across the organization. (Refer to **Exhibit 1** for a partial organization chart.)

Strategic Planning

In line with creating support for center-initiated activities, May had recently sent invitations to senior local managers to attend a two-day strategic planning workshop. The workshop was to prepare the groundwork for Haaks Europe's first exercise in strategic planning. May hoped that through an exchange of information and ideas, agreement could be reached regarding a unified structure for a three-year country plan encompassing all business functions – including marketing, manufacturing, and personnel. Country managers were expected to submit their plans within two months following the workshop.

May considered a marketing plan as the core of each country's strategic planning document. The marketing plan, with comprehensive market analysis and action initiatives for each brand, should provide the basis for other functional plans such as manufacturing capacity, investments, and so on. Additionally, local marketing plans could help highlight opportunities for cross-national brand activities which would then be coordinated from the center. As before, May did not want to impose any structure that could impede local entrepreneurship or creativity and speed of action in Haaks' increasingly competitive markets. At the same time, he believed that a center-led initiative for effective planning would help strengthen the European division's overall performance in the increasingly competitive confectionery and snacks markets.

The Marketing Plan

When Hans joined Haaks Europe a year earlier, he could not find a single marketing plan at Haaks Europe headquarters. Instead, what he found were comprehensive annual country and brand budgets which showed targeted sales, expenses, and profit contributions. He recalled May commenting: 'What we have here is the least important part of any plan – the numbers.'

In preparing for the upcoming workshop, Hans set some objectives for himself. First, he would present the structure of a unified marketing plan to the country managers. The structure would encompass all the essential elements of analysis and action plans for each local operation. Second, besides helping country managers to upgrade local marketing, the plan would highlight opportunities for pan-European coordination. Third, he would not finalize the proposed marketing plan before soliciting and incorporating the ideas and suggestions of workshop participants. Once agreed to by the countries, the plan would become the basis for all future planning exercises in marketing.

Hans saw that a number of details still needed to be worked out. There were many questions to be dealt with. For example: What was the appropriate time horizon for local marketing plans – 1 year or longer? What were the main components of the marketing plan? How detailed should the proposed planning structure be? Should performance targets be set top-down or evolve bottom-up? How should any conflicts between the countries and the center be resolved?

Hans recalled May's final advice:

Propose a plan which is simple and yet disciplined, one that establishes a common vocabulary in the organization and promotes professionalism in our marketing... And let's avoid useless bureaucratic rituals.

EXHIBIT 1

Haaks International
Partial Organization Chart

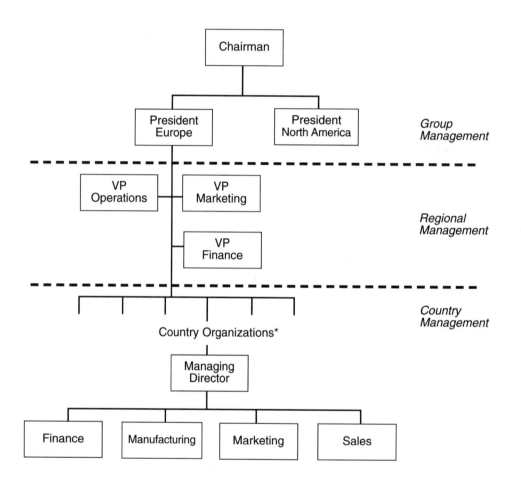

* Haaks Europe consisted of 15 countries: UK, Ireland, Germany, France, Italy, Portugal, Netherlands, Belgium, Switzerland, Austria, Denmark, Norway, Sweden, Finland, Luxembourg.

Source: Company Document.

International Marketing: Strategy Implementation

International Marketing: Strategy Implementation

Implementation is the Achilles' heel of a global strategy. Consider the following illustration.

Parker Pen was a pioneer of global marketing, and one of the first to stumble on poor implementation. Back in the mid-1980s a newly appointed management team embarked on an ambitious path of streamlining Parker's marketing strategy which had previously been left to the company's 154 local country operations to lead. Sitting in Jamesville, Wisconsin, headquarters, the architects of Parker's global scheme wanted to improve the profit margins by pruning the company's vast product line, centralizing manufacturing sites, and internationally standardizing many marketing decisions including packaging, pricing, and brand communication. But in the absence of adequate groundwork, local managers, who had traditionally enjoyed significant autonomy in many such decision areas, did not support the new direction. They questioned the 'global' logic behind the ambitious strategy, and objected to the fact that they were now left out of marketing decision-making. Without the country managers' active support the new strategy fell into a limbo, confusion reigned, and financial results deteriorated.

Only two years into the job, Parker's top global strategists were forced to resign. Reflecting on the demise of their global ideas after some sober-headed soul-searching, the departing managers placed the blame primarily on their own failure to elicit the support of those closest to the markets, the heads of Parker subsidiaries. 'We tried to take massive leaps [but] people weren't brought into it', said one former manager. Another quipped, 'Never globalize the fun... don't take all decisions out of [local managers'] hands.'[1]

Parker's highly publicized early failure to get its global strategy implemented was a warning to all strategists with global ambitions that implementation on an international scale is a complex undertaking indeed. There are several reasons for this. To start, strategies, even the most solid ones, do not implement themselves. Rather, they require concerted management action such as reconciling often conflicting short-term objectives and long-term goals, forging widespread management support for the aims of the strategy, and making sufficient resources available for the activities which need to take place. Without persistent follow-up, strategies have a habit of faltering.

---

1. J.M. Winski and L. Wentz, 'Parker Pen: What Went Wrong', *Advertising Age* (June 2, 1986):1, 71.

Another source of complexity is the fact that global strategy-makers are almost always away from the local markets where the action is supposed to take place. The distances separating the decision-makers and others are not only physical. A center-dominated decision-making process, as global strategy tends to be, has to live with the inherent difficulties of bringing about and coordinating actions of managers who are separated geographically by thousands of kilometers and who, in addition, live in different business and cultural settings. The barriers are many and so are the potential pitfalls.

Also, in trying to implement their global schemes, the marketers often have to labor through highly intricate organizational structures that span across product lines, functions and geographic units, to exert influence on people and resources over which they do not have direct control. Finally, global strategies often call for changes in the way marketing activities are performed, changes that are rarely welcome by those most affected by it. These changes often mean having to move away from traditional local autonomy to an increased level of cross-market coordination. Experienced global strategists are only too aware of the obstacles that such a shift in the decision-making process puts on the path to implementation.

Chapter Coverage

This chapter reviews pertinent issues in implementing global marketing. Some of these issues are related to the organizational *structure* of a firm. Others are *task*- or *process*-related, as they involve the scope and mandate of the marketer's job, and the methods and tools he or she uses for implementation. Still others involve the managerial *behavior* and *skills* of the global marketer. Together these five interrelated sets of issues provide complementary facets of global strategy implementation.

Structure[2]

Organizational structures are tools in strategy implementation. But to appreciate the influence of structure on global implementation, one needs to examine the different types of organization and their features. Although no two organizations are alike, in their 'generic' form most international corporate structures fall into one of four types: **international division**, **geographic**, **product**, or hybrids called **matrix**.

International division structures are common in companies that market a narrow product line and are at the early stages of internationalization, where the home market still accounts for the majority of sales. In such a structure, all international activities are handled by an international division, hence the label, which is responsible for the company's sub-

---

2. Parts of the section on Implementation are adapted from: Kamran Kashani, *Managing Global Marketing*, Boston, Mass: PWS-Kent Publishing Company, 1992, Part Three.

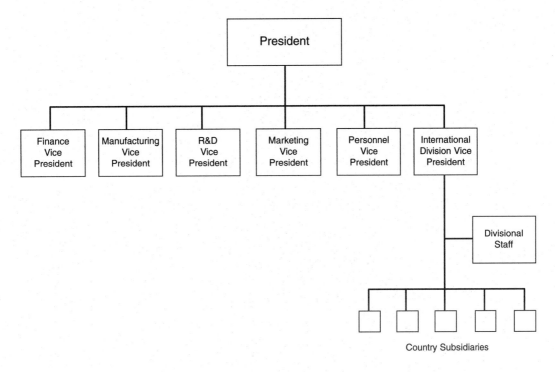

Figure 4.1 International Division Organization

sidiaries in other markets. Typically, the division head has a line responsibility and is accountable for the profitability of international markets. The division and its subsidiaries often enjoy a great deal of autonomy in managing their affairs. Figure 4.1 shows an example of international division organization alongside a functional domestic structure.

Simplicity is this structure's most important virtue. The lines of authority and areas of responsibility are clear. The distinction between home market and international activities is equally clear. Strategy-making and implementation are relatively easy in such a simple structure. But in this pattern's simplicity lies a potential for future problems. As international activities expand, and as the product line grows in its diversity, the international divi-

sion's structure soon exhausts its advantages. The international division managers, for example, may find themselves having to constantly negotiate for adaptations of products which are routinely developed for domestic needs. Also, local independence, often a companion feature of this structure, may prove a major stumbling block when implementing an integrated regional or worldwide strategy.

Geographic structures represent a departure from the simple domestic–international distinction of the previous design. Here the world market is divided into several geographic regions, each responsible for a number of subsidiaries. The home market does not necessarily enjoy a special status as it constitutes or belongs to one of these geographic entities. A key assumption underlying this kind of structure is that

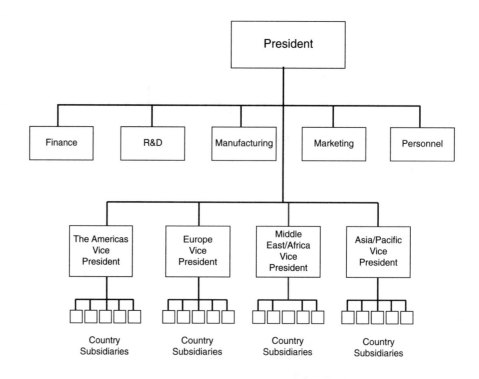

Figure 4.2   Geographic Organization

regional markets are different enough to justify their own dedicated organizations. Regional heads are line managers responsible for results in their assigned geographic markets. They may be assisted by corporate staff or, if the region's size of activities permits, they may provide their own internal services. Figure 4.2 shows an example of a geographic structure assisted by corporate staff functions.

Although geographic structures offer a more balanced orientation to world market opportunities than the international division organization, they still have their limitations. The geographic structure, for example, would be inappropriate for firms with diverse product lines because the focus on national and regional markets tends to override the different strate-gic requirements related to products – their technology, production, marketing, and so on. Similarly, a geographic structure may undermine implementation of a strategy that spans across a number of regions. Regional managers, given their geographic perspective, tend to see more differences than similarities among world markets.

Product structures tend to overcome some of the problems inherent in the previous two models, namely, a fragmented view of world markets and the subordination of product needs to geographic considerations. A product structure is especially useful when the number and diversity of products marketed worldwide are large. The key advantage of this structure is that it gives a group of line managers total control over the fate of a product line

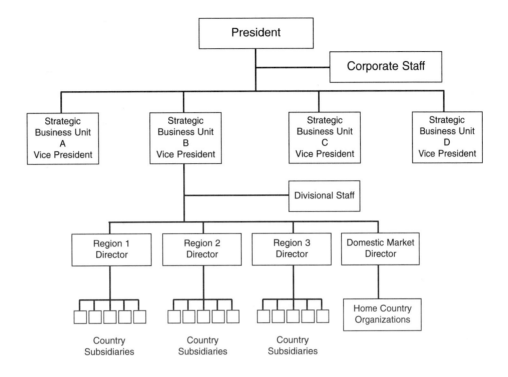

Figure 4.3   Product Organization

or a category of related products. The strategic business unit (SBU) managers, as product managers are sometimes called, typically have worldwide profit responsibility for their assigned lines. If a distinction is made between the home and international markets, it is done within each product organization and not for the entire firm. Country organizations may be grouped by area or region, but report to the head of product division. Product managers may be assisted by corporate staff functions, such as R&D, manufacturing, and so on. Or, if their size and scope of operations permit, product divisions would provide these services internally. Figure 4.3 shows an example of a product organization.

A product organization with worldwide scope tends to be better prepared to deal with global trends than the previous two structures. Division CEOs have the mandate to monitor worldwide developments for their respective product lines and respond accordingly. In their advanced form, product strategies may call for integration of activities and practices across geographic and country organizations. Implementing these strategies is helped by the fact that individual country units are integral to the division's global operation, and that local or regional autonomy, a feature of the previous two structures, is less of an issue in a worldwide product structure.

On the other hand, major drawbacks of product organizations are the absence of synergy among product divisions, duplication of activities,

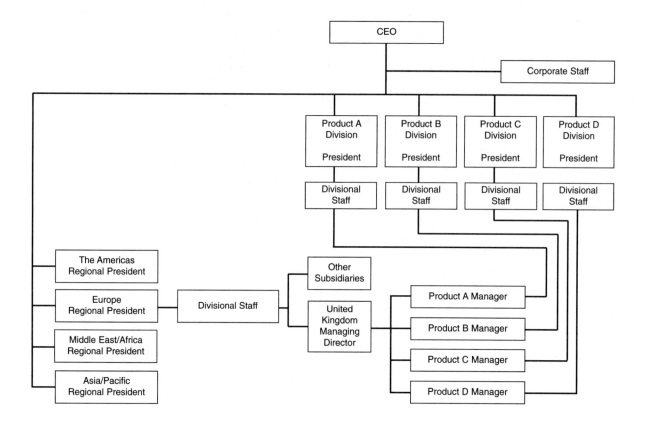

Figure 4.4   Matrix Organization

and a potential tendency to ignore important differences among national markets.

Matrix structures are a hybrid of product, geographic and, to a lesser extent, functional organizations. They are the most common form of organizational design used by major global companies. A prominent feature of matrixes is their dual chain of command: many managers report to two different bosses, one representing, say, the product structure and the other a regional organization. Figure 4.4 shows an example of a matrix structure.

In theory at least, matrix structures facilitate a balanced influence of different perspectives on major decisions.

For example, a global product strategy formulated by a matrix organization would be, by design, the output of the interaction between the worldwide product managers and the regional chiefs of geographic structure. Such a strategy would not only exploit worldwide commonalties among the different regions, but would also recognize the major geographic market differences and incorporate them in its design. Similarly, regional plans would have input from the various product lines in addition to the region's own managers. Such overlapping decision process is of particular value to firms operating in diverse product and geographic markets.

Matrix organizations were once hailed as the answer to a growing need for strategic flexibility. But, in practice, the matrix structures have fallen far short of that promise. Instead, managers have complained about such impediments as role confusion, excessive meetings, and slow decision-making. In the worst cases, implementation of strategic decisions has come to a standstill because of the built-in conflicts in the structure.

Faced with these shortcomings, companies are not abandoning their matrix structures, however. Instead, attempts are being made to refine, simplify and refocus them. In some companies, while the parallel product and geographic market structures are maintained, for a given line of business, one dimension is given priority over the other – thereby recognizing the special needs of that organization. At Nestlé, for example, restructuring has explicitly recognized the different strategic requirements of the company's diverse product lines – from hot and cold beverages, to chocolates, ice creams, prepared dishes and pet foods. The creation of eight strategic business units has signaled a major shift in the balance of power, from traditionally powerful geographic zones to a more balanced sharing of influence. Similarly at Procter & Gamble, the company has recently created global category management units with total responsibility for upstream product creation all the way to downstream brand marketing. As with Nestlé, P&G is re-balancing its matrix structure for more effective implementation of the company's global strategies.

Most recently P&G has reorganized its world structure to give still greater say to global brand management. Dubbed Organization 2005, the new structure proposes to put more weight behind global category management by creating senior level positions which counterbalances the company's traditional regional organization and bias. Each category-led Strategic Business Unit will house global brand managers and will house a multifunctional team, including global brand managers.

Tasks

Not all global marketing tasks are alike. They differ substantially in their scope of responsibility and, as a consequence, in their ability to implement global strategies. Some international marketing positions have a broad scope: their mandates encompass the entire value-adding activities, from upstream product development to downstream marketing and service activities. Others have a far more limited scope, and focus on only one or few downstream activities – such as marketing research, packaging, and advertising communication. For the purposes of our discussion on implementation it is useful to distinguish among at least three types of marketing tasks with global reach: **strategists**, **integrators** and **facilitators**.

Strategists have the broadest mandate. They are often worldwide heads of product divisions or strategic business units focused on product categories or technologies. They tend to control the entire value-adding chain in their organization including R&D, manufacturing, logistics, sales and marketing. As general managers, they typically have a line function in their organization and are accountable for profitability of their assigned lines of business worldwide. Although marketing is one element of their responsibility, their global strategies are often centered on key marketing choices such as segments, products, brands, and so on. Strategists can be found in product and matrix structures.

At ABB, the job of formulating regional or worldwide strategy is the responsibility of some 30-odd Business Area Managers – strategists who lead diverse businesses such as gas turbines, cables, transformers, and automation products and systems. They are also responsible for implementation. In the latter capacity, they see to it that local actions are brought in line with the global priorities. They also monitor local operations against overall performance targets. Implementation is very much driven from the center.

Integrators do not enjoy the full job scope of strategists. They have a far more limited task, although still important to global strategy and its implementation. As integrators these managers aim to rationalize local marketing practices towards more uniform practices across diverse local markets. Their aim might be to reduce costs, upgrade marketing practices, or transfer local innovations to other markets. In this context, integrators work within the framework of locally decided strategies; their mission falls short of unifying those strategies, but only elements of it. Integrators are found in most international structures, often in staff positions working closely with those we have identified as strategists.

At Nestlé, where routine business strategies are still decided by country organizations, the eight headquarters-based strategic business units exert their growing influence through worldwide harmonization of branding practices for many of the company's more than 800 brands. As integrators of brand strategies in a decentralized Nestlé structure, the SBU's contribution to the health of these global strategic brands – like Nescafé, Maggi, and Perrier – is considerable. The expected payoffs are stronger brands and greater associated equity – no small returns for a company built on the strength of its brands.

Facilitators have the narrowest task, and the least ambitious marketing mandate. Located in the headquarters, their contribution is often limited to providing specialist know-how, or a clearinghouse of information for a company's many local operations. Centralized expertise in product development, marketing research, packaging or advertising are examples of specialist know-how offered by facilitators. They also help reduce duplication of effort, such as through centralizing collection and dissemination of market and competitive information. Unlike the strategists or integrators, whose mandates call for taking proactive initiatives *vis-à-vis* the local operations, facilitators tend to offer their services only upon request from subsidiary management. Facilitators are present in all international organizations, and their influence on global strategies or implementation is limited.

What the preceding discussion makes evident is the fact that certain global marketing tasks are more effective instruments of implementation than others. Strategists have the broadest organizational scope to devise long-term strategies and see them implemented in structures which they often head or have great influence on. At the other end of the scale are facilitators whose narrow mandates prevent them from actively pursuing a global agenda. In between the two extremes are the integrators whose effectiveness in devising and implementing global marketing strategies is tightly dependent on the support they receive from the rest of the organization, notably the general management. With genuine support, integrators can pursue an active global agenda, and be effective instruments for implementation. In the absence of such support, the job of integrators is a frustrating one. The following words of an International Product Manager, responsible for harmonizing local marketing practices at a major global pharmaceutical company, capture the frustrations of an integrator whose broad job mandate is not matched with adequate organizational support for implementation:

'At times I felt like standing in the middle of chaos waving my arms and shouting, while everybody did their own thing.'

Process

Organizational structures are inert elements of strategy implementation. By themselves they are no more than the hardware around which the living action takes place. What influences the live action are management processes managers actually employ to reach decisions and implement them. Processes encompass a wide array of formal management tools and methods, including planning and target setting, performance measurement, management appraisal and rewards. They also include informal processes such as the level and quality of interaction among decision-makers and implementers, ways internal conflicts are recognized and resolved, and how broad-based support is built for certain actions. Together, the formal and informal processes help to determine the outcome of strategic decisions.

Research on process-related issues in marketing has shown that the particular methods used are indeed instrumental to the success or failure of global implementation. The same study has highlighted a number of process tools that global marketers might use to overcome barriers to implementation, often in the form of resistance from local country operation.[3] Among these tools are: **championing**, **consultation**, and **discerning exceptions**.

Championing. The study shows that managers who visibly and energetically champion global marketing strategies contribute a great deal to the adoption of those strategies by the larger international organization, and their implementation. They do so by overcoming the implementation bottlenecks in the organization, both at the headquarters and in the local subsidiaries, and by gradually building up

---

3. See: Kamran Kashani, 'Beware of Pitfalls of Global Marketing', *Harvard Business Review* (September–October 1989): 91–8.

support for the global concept where it would be lacking otherwise.

A champion's role is often twofold: they minimize initial management resistance to the changes necessitated by the harmonization of marketing practices, and ensure continued management support for the strategy and access to needed resources over time. Both tasks are important, especially in firms where the management has traditionally had a decentralized concept of its business, thereby allowing local management a great deal of autonomy, or where the structure of the firm is not conducive to central initiatives. Thus the choice of a candidate to carry out the implementation of a strategy becomes a critical decision. Some of the requisite managerial skills of qualified champions are described later in this chapter.

Consultation. Although global marketing requires elements of central coordination, research shows that without local management input into global decisions the risk of failing to implement those decisions is high. At issue here is the openness of decision-making to local management influence.

As Parker Pen learned the hard way, genuine consultation with local management helps in the implementation of global decisions at a later stage. But what is even less appreciated is the fact that consultation also improves the quality of those decisions as they are refined and enriched with front-line insights. As time-consuming as international consultation process tends to be, nothing can substitute for it as a process tool.

A coordinating mechanism can help in institutionalizing the process of consultation in an organization. Such mechanisms are often extra-organizational, *ad hoc* task forces whose membership consists of representatives from key local operations. Given such titles as Councils or Boards, coordinating mechanisms aim to channel a healthy dose of local inputs for global decision-making, and provide a forum where thorny implementation issues are discussed and resolved.

Discerning Exceptions. Global marketing has a bias towards inflexibility when it comes to implementation. Local organizations are often left with little choice but to go along with a scheme concocted for everyone – without exception. The argument usually put forward by the head-office marketers in favor of an unbending and uniform implementation of their global design is a persuasive one: to be true to their objectives, decisions must be enforced without exception or else nothing will remain of the global programs. There is an element of truth in this argument, but only an element.

For most global marketing strategies, as we have seen in Section III, only a few unified decisions are critical to their success. These strategic variables, which we have labeled 'Leverage' decisions, qualify for integration and enforcement across local organizations. Other decisions do not. But even here, certain local conditions may argue against blanket enforcement. For example, a well-conceived communication strategy for a global brand may have to be abandoned in a given market where the advocated positioning is already used by a local competitor. Allowance thus must be made for exceptions, as implementing a long list of standardized practices just for the sake of international uniformity is likely to be counterproductive.

Room for local judgment and discerning exceptions to global decisions should be built into strategy implementation. A manifestation of this principle is the guiding rule of thumb used by the top regional management of US-based Johnson Wax in harmonizing their European national marketing practices: 'As unified as possible, as diversified as necessary.' In their case, the burden of proof was placed on local managers who had to make a compelling case for a discerning exception to the global rule.

Behavior

The global marketer's job is a complex one. The complexity, as we have already noted, has to do with the diversity of local markets, cultural barriers, absence of direct line authority over local operations and, at times, lack of adequate top management support. For example, the territory assigned to the Vice President of Marketing at SmithKline Beecham consists of 147 countries, a vast geography spanning four continents and multitudes of local cultures. Through dotted lines to local marketing organizations this global manager and his small staff in London aim to influence in an informed fashion brand and product strategies in every country. Their actual influence on what really happens in the field is almost always tempered by local general managers and other line functions in the organization.

Recent research confirms that a global manager's **behavior** in reducing the inherent complexity of the job, and overcoming the endemic problems of distances – organizational, geography and cultural – has a lot to do with his or her success in implementation.[4] The research highlights three such behaviors: **selective focus**, **teaming up**, and **proactive learning**.

Selective Focus. Deciding what the overriding strategic priorities of a given business are is the first step towards managing the cross-national complexity. The fact is, managers can be overwhelmed by the diversity that exists in the markets they are responsible for, and by the local management's natural desire to do things their own way – almost regardless of global priorities. In such a typical atmosphere any strategy that aims to do too much, to align local action too tightly, is bound to fail – for lack of local support and also possibly for disregarding real and important local differences. Instead, the global manager, with a mandate of strategist or integrator, should focus his or her attention on those few strategic priorities that matter. We have already identified these as 'Leverage' and, to a lesser extent, 'Core' decisions. That means the global marketer must rise above local fire fighting by identifying a select number of strategic variables to focus his or her attention on – those strategic priorities that make the most difference in the long-run.

---

4. Joseph Franch and Kamran Kashani, 'The Rise of the Cross-National Manager,' *Financial Times Mastering Management Review* (May 1998): 36–9.

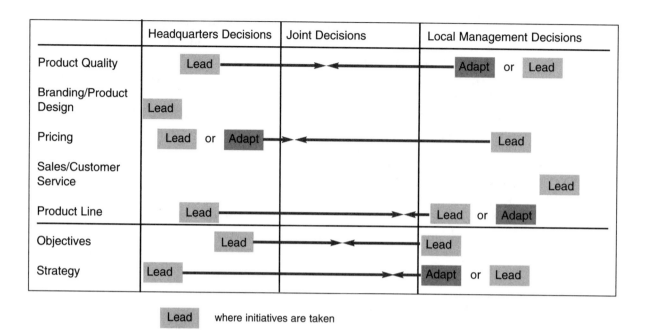

Figure 4.5   Henkel's Global Decision-making Map: Lead, Adapt and Joint Decisions

The selective focus that comes with such prioritizing helps to reduce unnecessary complexity, and allows for local discretion and contribution outside of the short global priority list. Furthermore, the approach has one other important advantage: it focuses everyone's attention on what is important and strategically of consequence. To help shape a common perspective, some global marketers have devised formal 'decision-making maps' that lay out, in clear terms, the division of responsibilities between the center and local operations, and provide a road map for resolving potential conflicts.

Figure 4.5 is one such instrument devised by a division of Henkel, the German makers of industrial and household sealants and adhesives. The chart, used by the entire division as a guide to action, shows clearly which decisions are to be made solely at the headquarters (for example branding and product design), or local subsidiaries (for example sales and customer service), and where joint decision-making is in order. In addition, the chart assigns 'lead' and 'adapt' roles to signal where initiatives might come from, or whose responsibility it is to adapt to someone else's lead. By signaling that, in a good number of areas, leadership might well come from both local operations as well as headquarters, Henkel's chart is promoting continuous dialogue between the center and periphery leading to frequent joint decision-making. In this respect the chart becomes an effective tool in implementation.

Teaming Up. A global marketer as strategist or integrator needs local management support to turn overall global priorities into appropriate local actions. But experience shows that local support, however critical, is rarely automatic. Distances, conflicting priorities, and diverse market conditions all contribute to center–periphery divergence on priorities. The more effective global managers overcome the local support hurdle by creating a 'virtual team' of geographically scattered national managers who help to define the strategic priorities at the outset, and then push for their local implementation at a later phase. These multinational teams are almost always off the formal organization chart. They are the creations of global managers as unofficial tools for cutting through the formal hierarchies and winning support for cross-national initiatives deep inside the local organizations. Networking skills, put into practice through frequent contacts with local markets, are a prerequisite for creating these virtual teams as instruments for implementation.

Proactive Learning. A good part of creating a supportive team of local managers with a common set of goals is the global manager's willingness and ability to educate himself or herself about the realities of their markets. That means, at the outset, appreciating the fact that there is no such thing as an 'average' market, and that each local scene is unique in its own way. That also means overcoming the natural barrier that sheer dis-

tances create through frequent visits to local organizations to listen and learn firsthand about their markets. Experienced global marketers see no substitute for such time-consuming personal visits where local managers are met personally and data are gathered firsthand.

Proactive learning about local markets should be a permanent part of the global marketer's on-the-job behavior. In the words of two global managers: 'You need to be humble [and realize that] you need to learn what they know [in the local markets] because you can't know it all', and 'If you stop learning… you start to become a liability to the organization'. It is such openness towards listening to the markets and proactive learning that paves the way for respect and trust from the local managers.

Skills

As the preceding discussion demonstrates, 'right' management behavior is the essence of effective implementation, and individual skills in producing that behavior can make a big difference on the fate of a strategy. The list of implementation skills can be very long, but for the purposes of this discussion the essential skills are grouped into two interrelated categories: **cross-cultural communication** and **interpersonal skills**.

Cross-cultural communication skills have to do with distortion-free interaction between people of different cultural backgrounds. Ineffective cross-cultural communication has been blamed for routine misunderstandings in international business contacts. The phrase 'We will study your proposal' may mean just that in the US or Germany. But in other countries, say Japan or France, it may mean something quite different – such as 'We are not ready to talk any further about your proposal', or simply and politely, 'No thanks, we are not interested'. Experts on cross-cultural communication have categorized most world cultures as either high or low context. In high context cultures what is not said can be as important as what is said. In France, Spain, Saudi Arabia, China and Japan – examples of high context countries – communication tends to be both direct and indirect. What is verbally communicated is often of general orientation, approximations lacking fine details. Such cultures put more emphasis on non-verbal communication, including body language or physical distance between sender and receiver.

Low context cultures, in contrast, put more emphasis on what is said than what is not. In the US, Germany, Sweden, Switzerland and the UK – examples of low context countries – straightforward communication is considered good business behavior. Generalities are avoided, factual information is prized, and candid communication is respected. In dealing with counterparts from high context setting, unprepared low context people often find themselves searching in vain for concrete meaning in what they hear. They also ignore or are distracted by non-verbal communication. To avoid misunderstandings, one expert says, 'low context communicators must learn to listen not only with their ears, but with their eyes as well'.

Interpersonal skills, the other set of managerial competencies for effec-tive implementation, encompass a wide assortment of attributes. Those directly related to implementing global strategies include:

- Ability to influence others in an organization without the benefit of direct line authority. This attribute includes being skilled at moving with relative ease up and down the company's far-flung organizational structure as well as laterally across geographic boundaries. It also includes, as we have seen earlier, skills at building 'networks' of like-minded individuals and cooperative relationships, and at using the networks to accomplish specific tasks. Such skills are vital, especially when implementation involves a well-coordinated participation of managers from several parts of the global organization.

- Ability to resolve conflicts. This skill belongs to the 'survival kit' of any global marketer since implementation, as we have observed, is a minefield of organizational friction. The conflicts are at times built into the structure. For example, 'turf wars' between product and geographic divisions are typical of the inherent tensions in a worldwide matrix organization. At other times, the conflicts are generated by the changes in marketing practices called for by a global scheme. Whatever their source, a marketer's ability to move around these obstacles has a direct bearing on the success of implementation.

- Negotiating skills. Global marketers are often required to negotiate creative solutions to unavoidable problems of conflicting interests in the organization. Creative negotiated solutions – also called win-win strategies – can make a difference between success and failure in implementation.

- Ability to endure strenuous work while performing at high physical and emotional energy levels. The complexity of the global implementation task puts a heavy burden on those responsible for its outcome. This burden is often manifested by high pressure and deadline-driven assignments, crowded agendas, and seemingly never-ending travel for meetings and discussions in different parts of the world. Despite the widespread availability of electronic communication, experienced global managers still underscore the importance of face-to-face interaction which only extensive international travel can offer.

Cases in Strategy Implementation

The two comprehensive case series that follow this discussion, Alto Chemicals and Sony Europa, deal both with the interrelated issues of strategy formulation and implementation. To separate strategy from its implementation would be artificial, and neither of these two learning vehicles tries to draw this artificial line. While both case series take place in Europe, they fit the definition of global marketing as the scope of strategies and their implementation crosses many divides of individual country markets, cultures, and organizational units each with its own agenda. The global managers at the center of each

case face personal and managerial battles that they must win in order to implement their chosen strategies. Their battles are external to their organization as well as internal. Externally, they face market and competitive challenges to their business which they must effectively respond to; internally, they have to deal with people and organizational tensions which, if left unattended, could derail their work.

Together, the Alto Chemicals and Sony Europa cases offer the student ample opportunity to put into analysis and decision-making many of the topics covered in this chapter. They include:

- Operating in complex organizational structures, and having to work through many layers and interest groups to build support for a chosen strategy
- Examining the true nature of the global marketing task, as strategist or integrator, and defining its critical elements
- Defining appropriate processes for implementation, and diagnosing the process-related issues in the actual conduct of global managers
- Focusing on the managerial behavior of key executives and how it contributes or hinders implementation
- Assessing the actual implementation skills brought to bear on management actions or, alternatively, their absence
- Proposing comprehensive implementation plans based on the above analysis.

Learning Points

The student can expect the following learning points from analyzing and discussing the cases in implementation:

- Develop an integrative view of global marketing which combines strategic decisions with their prerequisites for implementation
- Appreciation for structure- or process-related issues of marketing through the labyrinth of a complex worldwide organization
- Seeing how different global marketing tasks contribute to developing action plans around a short list of global priorities
- Skills in identifying behavioral obstacles to implementation
- Practice in devising creative solutions to eliminate or minimize conflicts inherent in strategy implementation
- Exposure to cross-cultural factors that can hamper global marketing

CASE 4.1^R **Alto Chemicals Europe (A)**

This case was prepared by Professor Kamran Kashani.

Eberhard Graaff had held the position of headquarters marketing manager for stabilizers at Alto Chemicals Europe (ACE) for only two months when problems with subsidiary sales managers began to surface. It was December 1990 and the end of an 8-week period in which Graaff had spent time studying the industry and the company's several European subsidiary sales organizations to familiarize himself with the challenges of his new job. In the preceding week, a number of important decisions had been made by Graaff which would have long-term strategic implications for ACE's stabilizer business. He had informed the subsidiary sales organizations that stabilizers, a chemical used in making plastic products, were no longer to be sold based on low or even competitive prices, and that share gaining at the expense of profitability of sales was no longer an acceptable policy. They were also informed that headquarters marketing was to take on a more active role in setting prices and determining target sales volumes for the various subsidiaries.

Reactions from the field to Graaff's decisions were immediate. Subsidiary sales managers were unanimous in their opposition. Expressions used by the managers to describe the new headquarters policies ranged from 'unworkable' and 'contradictory' to 'theoretical' and 'dictatorial'. What the sales managers appeared to resent most was the notion that their own local judgment on sales matters had to be subordinate to that of headquarters. In the past, they had enjoyed relative autonomy in these areas.

Graaff was not overly perturbed by the negative reaction of the sales organization. He was, however, concerned about the steps needed to assure sound implementation of the revised strategy for stabilizers.

Company Background

ACE was the regional headquarters for Alto Chemicals Corporation's operations in Europe. Alto was a major North American-based multinational whose principal activities included production and marketing of commodity and specialty chemicals. With its headquarters and production facilities located in Switzerland and France, ACE accounted for more than a third of Alto's global production and sales volume.

Nine wholly owned subsidiaries, each serving one or more countries in Western Europe, reported to ACE.[1] The products produced and sold by the subsidiaries in the region ranged from finished compounds such as agricultural chemicals to 'building blocks' used in the production of other products such as solvents, elastomers and stabilizers.

ACE's headquarters organization was by product group. Five directors, each responsible for one or more products, reported to the company's president. Functions such as marketing, manufacturing and planning were included under each product organization. Every director, in addition to having a region-wide product management responsibility, also supervised one or more of Alto's subsidiaries in Europe. The subsidiary managing directors, who reported to their assigned 'associate' director, were in turn responsible for ACE's operations in their respective national markets. These included sales of all products produced in the region as well as any local production. The subsidiaries were typically organized by function.

The headquarters–subsidiary interaction was best described as a matrix relationship. The 'dual boss system' was a common expression used to portray the dual sources of influence on product and subsidiary management.

Stabilizers

Stabilizers were a category of chemicals used to make plastic products. When mixed with PVC (polyvinylchloride) resins and dyes, the stabilizers helped prevent the breakdown of polymers in the finished product caused by environmental factors such as temperature, light and general aging. A plastic product not adequately treated with stabilizers was likely to become brittle and discolored over time. For example, the plastic covering of an electrical cable would lose its flexibility and disintegrate eventually if not protected by stabilizers. Management estimated that close to 40% of all PVC uses in Europe were in applications requiring the addition of a stabilizer.

Product management had identified eight end-use and process segments for the stabilizer market. These segments produced a wide range of goods from plastic bags and upholstery to wall covering, cables, hoses and shoes. Although the share of each segment in total market varied from one country to another, the three largest segments accounted for more than 50% of the market Europe-wide (refer to **Exhibit 1**).

In 1990, an estimated 600,000 tons of stabilizers of all types, valued at approximately $600 million, were sold by the industry to approximately 1,100 plastic fabricators in Europe. This was considered as one of the most fragmented markets served by ACE. Stabilizers had experienced an annual growth rate averaging less than 3% in tonnage during the 1980s. The market was expected to remain stagnant, however, for most of the 1990s. As one member of product management explained,

---

1. Alto's subsidiaries operated in the UK, France, Belgium, W. Germany, the Netherlands, Italy, Spain, Portugal and Sweden.

'Stabilizers have matured as an industry. All potential applications have been discovered and we do not see any prospect for rapid growth among the existing uses.'

The recessionary conditions prevailing in many European user industries during the past year were blamed for the 15% decline in total consumption from the 1989 level. The industry's unutilized plant capacity was estimated at about one-third.

More than 20 companies competed in the European stabilizer market. The four largest producers were: Ciba-Geigy (Switzerland); ACE; Berlocher (W. Germany); and Lankro (United Kingdom). Together they accounted for approximately one-half of the market in 1990. ACE management pointed out that most competitors had a home base where they were particularly strong. All companies, however, tried to sell their stabilizers regionwide.

The chemical properties of the stabilizers produced by ACE differed from those made by others in Europe. The company's variety was referred to in the trade as 'Tin' (Sn) – the generic name representing its chemical structure. The stabilizers most frequently produced by competitors had a different structure and were generically referred to as 'Barium' (Ba). Both varieties were general purpose products with large end-use applications. Differences in properties – such as heat and light resistance, and weathering and oil absorption – were considered by many in management to be minor between the two varieties. Although, in theory, general purpose stabilizers could substitute for one another in most applications; in practice, plastic fabricators could not switch easily from one type to another, as the process technologies required were considerably different. Barium was by far the most commonly used stabilizer in Europe.

Entry Strategy

ACE's decision to enter the European stabilizer market was made in 1980. The original strategy called for a step-by-step penetration of the market towards a long-term market share objective of 20%, projected at 160,000 tons by 1989. The main elements of the entry strategy are described below:

1. *Market Exploration:* As ACE did not have any working knowledge of the European stabilizer industry, the first few years after entry were to be spent exploring 'the possibility of becoming a major fully-integrated stabilizer supplier by 1990'.

   The long-term choice of stabilizers for ACE was Tin, for which the company's European subsidiaries had ample feedstock or the needed raw material. However, beginning in 1980, ACE entered the market with Barium purchased from European producers.

2. *Third Party Production:* Due to the high level of start-up investment in production facilities, ACE's supply of Barium initially, and of Tin later on, was to be secured through production agreements with established European producers. A member of the management closely involved with supply negotiations referred to the process as 'difficult – something you can do when you have a strong heart

and lots of guts'. The company foresaw eventual European production once sufficient sales volume was attained.

3. *Conversion:* Barium was to be an entry product in Europe; ACE management intended to gradually convert its customers to Tin. Conversion was to be encouraged through lower initial prices, but also through assuring better product performance. Initial discounts of 2–3% below Barium prices were deemed necessary, as conversion required changes in process and machinery which had to be justified economically.

4. *Segmentation:* Product management was keenly aware of the differences among various segments in the stabilizer market. For some, performance was more important than price; for others, the reverse held true. In wire and cables, for example, stabilizer costs were less than 2% of the total cost. As a result, these producers were less sensitive to price than those in flooring for whom the cost ratio was around 10%.

    Size also played an important role: large firms purchasing in excess of 500 tons per month paid lower prices than small and medium-sized firms purchasing one truckload or more at a time. The difference in price could be as large as 5%.

    The entry strategy placed its sales emphasis on those segments for which price played a relatively more significant role. As one subsidiary sales manager explained, 'We had to get the attention of people when we first started up. We used the tools we had, and price was an important tool.'

Selling Stabilizers

ACE's Tin stabilizers, branded as Polystab, were sold through a specialized sales force in all the subsidiaries. They were assisted in technical matters by the staff from technical service located in Geneva. The service was thought to be of particular importance for small and medium-sized clients who did not have one in-house. Management believed that the specialized sales people and the highly competent technical service, both unique in the industry, had allowed the company to gain and build in-depth knowledge of the various industries and processes using stabilizers.

For selling purposes, the subsidiaries grouped their accounts according to the following classifications:

- *Base:* Regular Polystab customers mostly converted from Barium
- *Strategic:* Important prospects; usually trendsetters in their industry, currently using Barium
- *Swing:* 'In and out' customers; price orientated.

In 1990, the *Base* accounts provided the bulk of Polystab sales. The *Strategic* accounts, on the other hand, were key targets for conversion and, hence, long-term sources of sales. They required intensive attention from management and often a highly technical type of selling. The *Swing* accounts were usually converted, but could not be counted on as regular customers because of their low-price orientation.

The task of converting from Barium to Tin fell on the sales force. The sales management pointed out that selling revolved around establishing tangible advantages for the client to justify the changes in equipment and process that were usually needed. They also mentioned that in certain applications conversion held only small benefits that were hard to demonstrate. In all cases, conversion was a time-consuming process. Product management estimated that it took, on average, 18 months to convert an account. The actual time spent could vary from six months to several years. In every case, a minimum of eight to ten visits from the Technical Service staff in Geneva were required.

For all the subsidiaries, the proportion of selling time spent on conversion had declined since the mid-1980s. In a typical case, in 1990 the sales force spent only a quarter of its time on conversion prospects, whereas in 1985 the ratio was close to 60%.

Since ACE was not the sole supplier of Tin in the market,[2] most converted customers compared prices before placing an order – usually done on a monthly basis. The sales force, therefore, was intimately aware of the importance of price in making sales.

One subsidiary sales manager explained the buying behavior of stabilizer customers, 'The larger companies have a professional buying practice. They check with two or three regular suppliers and then place their order. The smaller firms, on the other hand, tend to contact a multitude of producers, trying to negotiate a low price. They often wait till the middle or end of the month hoping for a general deterioration in prices.' He added that Barium producers were the price setters in the market and, therefore, a knowledge of their prices, as well as those for Tin, was essential in selling. 'Prices do fluctuate during the month, depending on the level of demand and the producers' eagerness to sell their inventory. So timing is critical. When you set your prices high at the beginning of the month and you don't get an order by the tenth, you get pretty nervous. You can easily overreact and then destroy your average price level for the rest of the month.' Typically, about two-thirds of each month's sales were made in the first two weeks of the month.

A stabilizer salesman in the subsidiaries had between 10 and 25 accounts to look after. His days were spent partly in the office, preparing reports and reaching customers by phone, and partly on the road, visiting companies. Some sales managers insisted on visiting each account a minimum of once a month.

Stabilizer Marketing Organization

(The marketing organization for stabilizers is shown in **Exhibit 2**. Partial job descriptions for key executives in the organization are given in **Exhibit 3**.)

Graaff, who was new to the stabilizer organization, described the matrix structure as one built on 'interaction and positive confrontation'. Another executive, Peter

---

2. For all other producers, Tin accounted for a minor share of their stabilizer sales, as they did not have their own feedstock required for its production.

Hansen, director for stabilizers, referred to the 'dual boss system' as working well. 'In the old days before the system arrived, the subsidiaries wouldn't even let us into their offices!' A sales manager with many years in the company also commented on the system, 'The dual boss relationship can be useful or painful. It depends on the chiefs.'

Headquarters marketing had profit responsibility for stabilizers. Graaff described the product line's profitability as a function of production costs, average prices received by the subsidiaries and the total volume of sales. Management at the subsidiary, on the other hand, was held accountable primarily for the volume of sales generated in its market, in addition to the cost of selling and the level of receivables. Subsidiaries paid a transfer price for stabilizers sold in their market.

The performance of sales managers was evaluated jointly by the subsidiary managing director and headquarters marketing manager. Whenever a manager was responsible for the sales of a number of products, a joint performance appraisal would be undertaken for each line. Company executives pointed out that a superior overall performance could mean an increase in annual salary of up to 10% for the sales managers. This merit raise was said to be a 'big carrot' and an important incentive.

Before Graaff joined stabilizer marketing, quarterly and annual sales quotas were used as bases for performance evaluation. Quarterly meetings in Geneva between the marketing and sales managers compared the progress in stabilizer sales against quotas.

By company policy, all ACE executives and members of the sales organization were compensated by a fixed salary. This policy also applied to the 10-man specialized stabilizer sales force in Europe, whose salaries and performance evaluation procedures were determined at the subsidiary level.

Eberhard Graaff

Eberhard Graaff had been with Alto for 15 years before being assigned to stabilizer marketing. A chemical engineer by training, he had filled various positions in Europe and the Far East as a business analyst, design engineer, plant supervisor, and subsidiary sales manager. This was his first appointment in Geneva; his predecessor had recently retired from the company. In 1990, Graaff was 40 years old and the second youngest member of the stabilizer marketing organization.

'We felt we needed a man with positive leadership', explained Peter Hansen, Graaff's immediate boss. Graaff's outstanding performance as sales manager in France was considered as one factor in his promotion to the marketing position. Graaff himself believed that his 'tough name' in the company was also instrumental in his selection.

ACE executives were aware of the difficulties inherent in Graaff's new assignment. Hansen explained, 'The job of headquarters marketing is complicated not only by the different market and competitive conditions of each subsidiary, but also by the diversity in personalities and cultures of their management.' He felt that the job required, in addition to marketing expertise, skills in establishing a dialogue with the subsidiaries and in building a sales team.

Strategy Revised

The stabilizer strategy set in motion in 1980 had achieved most of its objectives by 1990. ACE's stabilizer share in Western Europe was nearly 18%. Predictably, the proportion of Barium in total company sales had declined over the years. As of mid-1989, Tin stabilizers were being produced by the company's own facilities in France. In that year, the stabilizer sales force was calling on a total of 170 accounts in the region.

Graaff's first couple of months in the new job was taken up with visits to each of the nine subsidiaries and a review of marketing and sales practices region-wide. By December, Graaff had reached a number of conclusions regarding the current Polystab strategy as implemented in the field:

1. *Over-reliance on Price:* Selling was too price orientated; Barium prices were matched or undercut by 2–3 percentage points even for the converted Tin accounts.
2. *Narrow Market Base:* Price-orientated selling had led to emphasis on those segments where it played an important role, that is, the larger companies and Swing accounts.
3. *Low Profitability:* Low prices in the region meant low profitability for the stabilizer business. The current regional average contribution margin of $40 per ton was deemed as an unsatisfactory return for the recently completed facilities in France.
4. *Price Discrepancies:* In the absence of central coordination, differences in subsidiary prices were encouraging the larger geographically diversified clients to buy their entire requirements from cheaper subsidiaries and transfer them for use to other subsidiary markets. Price differentials among subsidiaries were partly due to different average market prices in each country. Traditionally, for example, German stabilizer prices were a few percentage points above those of other European countries.

Graaff commented on the conclusions of his 8-week study:

The picture became rather clear to me. We are a volume-orientated organization, from here all the way down. This is a legacy of the original strategy which gave us a chance to compete in this market. So, as long as the quarterly sales quotas were met, nobody complained. And to meet the quotas, subsidiaries had a fairly open hand in setting prices. Headquarters' price guidelines were only good for the first few days of each month. Afterwards, the sales pressure from the field forced the people in Geneva to give in, leading to low average prices for the whole month. This cycle would repeat itself 12 times a year.

Graaff was convinced that a revision of the successful stabilizer strategy was in order. 'Product management and top ACE executives have been increasingly concerned with the return on our heavy investment in stabilizer facilities', he explained. 'My understanding of this market leads me to believe that improved profitability is possible, provided we have the right segments and selling approach.'

In December 1990, Graaff communicated in writing the following elements of the revised stabilizers strategy to the subsidiary sales managers and asked them to incorporate these points into their future sales plans. A summary of the revised strategy follows:

1. *Non-Price Selling:* Price to play a subsidiary role in selling; instead, emphasis to be placed on areas where ACE held a competitive edge such as expert sales force, superior technical service, and general corporate reputation for supplier reliability.
2. *New Accounts:* Selling aimed at conversion of new accounts to receive added impetus; new accounts to come primarily from small and medium-sized firms, and segments that were less price sensitive such as wire and cable.
3. *Price Leadership:* Discounting or merely 'meeting Barium prices' will no longer be an acceptable pricing policy for converted accounts; sales management to watch for opportunities to initiate price leadership *vis-à-vis* other suppliers.
4. *Central Coordination:* Geneva was to take a more active part in setting price and volume targets for subsidiaries; the highly competitive low price markets were to receive less sales emphasis than those enjoying higher average prices; headquarters coordination to aim at regional optimization.

The average price improvement was expected to yield immediate results. For the 1991–92 planning period, Graaff was projecting a doubling of contribution margins to $80 per ton.

In his communication to the sales organization, Graaff also mentioned that, although he was willing to accept a slight short-term drop in sales due to price improvement, the longer-term objective remained a growth in volume. This, he maintained, was essential if the new stabilizer plant were to operate at an economical utilization rate.

Sales Management Response

Reactions from the field were not long in coming. Communicating their sentiments to Graaff mostly by phone, sales managers were unanimously against the announced changes in the business strategy. 'To speak of price improvement at a time when the whole market is declining is just absurd', was a typical comment from the field. Another manager responded, 'Your strategy of improving both price *and* volume is unrealistic and contradictory.' Still another commented, 'The smaller accounts take the same amount of selling time as the larger ones. If we added them to our customer list, we would be running after more accounts for the same volume of sales. That wouldn't make sense.' Another manager labeled the revised strategy as 'not market orientated, but rather inward looking'.

Sales management also expressed concern about their future relationship with clients. One manager explained:

> We have gained our customer base through conversion and the promise of savings to the client. They did not scream when we gradually raised our prices to the Barium level during the past few years. At least they know that they won't be paying more than their Barium-using competitors. Now, if you were a user of Barium for 25 years and I succeeded in converting you, how would you react if I came around a few months later and told you that from now on you will be paying a premium over their prices? You'd probably ask me – whatever happened to the savings you promised? The money is in your pocket not mine!

This executive added that problems of this kind would have a detrimental effect on sales force motivation.

Underlying most managers' complaints was another concern – that the initiative in key decision areas was shifting away from subsidiaries towards Geneva. One subsidiary sales manager explained what was felt by many:

> So far, we have succeeded in stabilizers because of local initiative; we knew our markets well enough to have confidence in headquarters marketing. They trusted our best judgment. We are professionals in this field and should be allowed to harmonize our own performance. Headquarters can help by synthesizing and giving broad guidelines. That's all. Rigid rules go against management harmony.

Implementation

Graaff was not surprised by the sales organization's reactions to his proposals. He explained, 'I myself was in the subsidiaries for a number of years, so I know how they feel.'

Graaff intended to take steps towards implementing the strategy which he believed was sound and consistent with market realities. 'I am convinced the strategy will work', he added in defense of his decisions. 'It aims at changing our customer mix, which in turn allows us some pricing leverage in the long run. It also aims at enlarging the base, which reduces our risk with a few large customers and, finally, it takes a regional view of the stabilizer business, where all competitors and a number of customers are operating in more than one national market. A regional strategy gives us the flexibility of shifting our volumes towards those markets where we earn better margins.'

Graaff did not minimize the implementation task ahead of him: 'The job won't be easy, but I have always been sent into jobs with difficult problems.' He added that, although he believed Hansen was in favor of improved profitability, he had not cleared the specifics of his strategy with the director and was certainly not going to ask for his help in implementing it in the field. 'I am not the type who would seek advice from the boss on everything', he emphasized. 'I have always followed the things I believe in.'

EXHIBIT 1

Stabilizer Market Segments (1989)

	Sample Products	Consumption (% of total)	No. of Fabricators (estimate)
End-use Segments			
Coated Fabrics	Upholstery	17	180
Flooring	Cushion Flooring Sheets / Tiles	20	160
Wire & Cables	Cable Jackets and Insulation	17	235
Compounds	Shoes	11	55
Process Segments			
Plastisole	Wall Covering Gloves, Balls	5	90
Calendering	Very Broad: Dresses, Housing, etc.	13	180
Extrusion	Hoses	11	130
Injection Molding	Shoes	6	70
		100%	1,100

Source: Company Records.

EXHIBIT 2

Stabilizer Marketing Organization

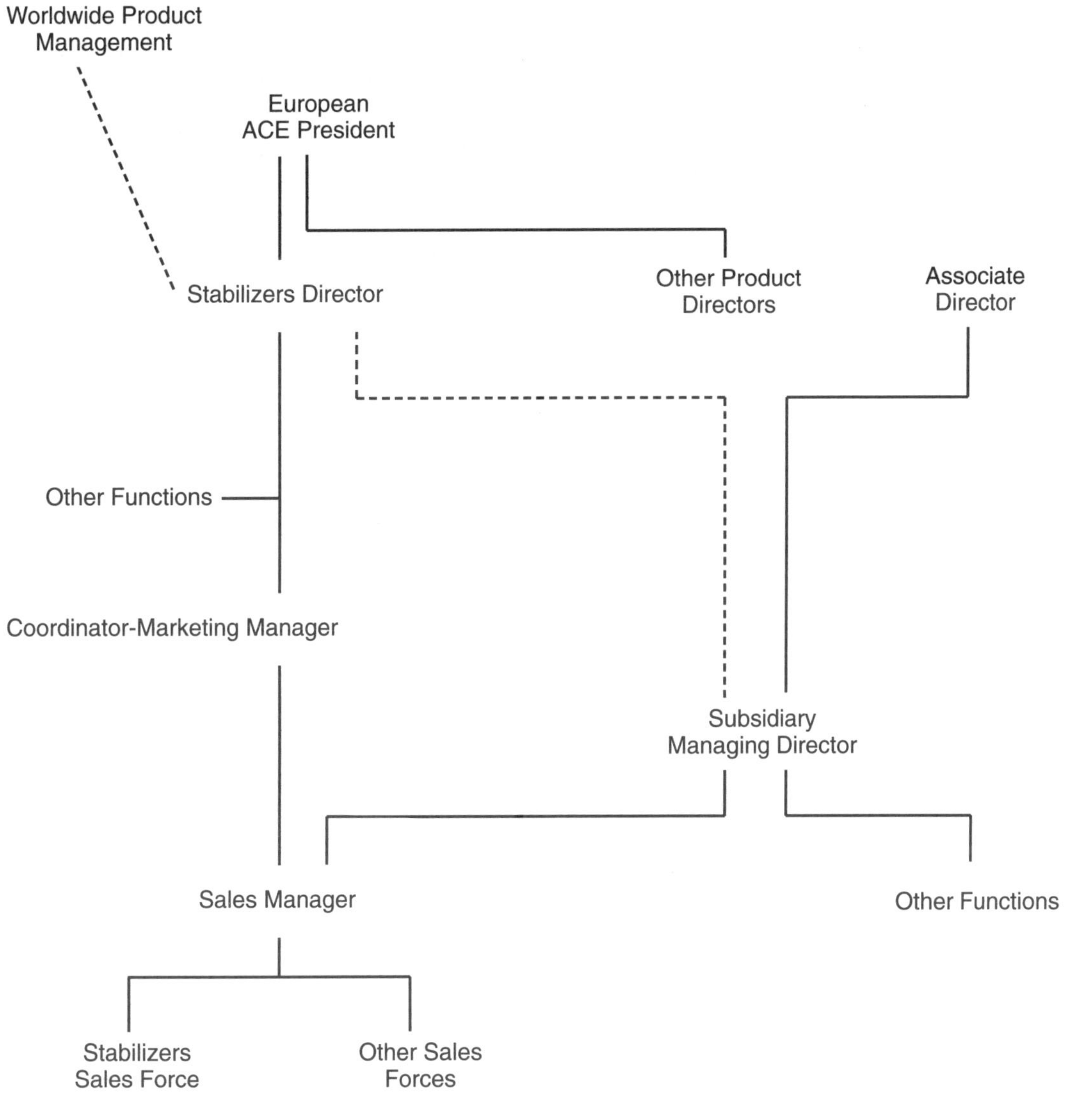

Worldwide Product Management

European ACE President

Stabilizers Director

Other Product Directors

Associate Director

Other Functions

Coordinator-Marketing Manager

Subsidiary Managing Director

Sales Manager

Other Functions

Stabilizers Sales Force

Other Sales Forces

Source: Company Records.

EXHIBIT 3

Partial Job Definitions

Director, Stabilizers	Serves as Regional Product Manager, responsible for all phases of the region's stabilizer business, including technology, manufacturing, marketing and supply and transportation; establishes regional goals, objectives, plans and action steps and works with Worldwide Product Manager to assure that these are consistent with the worldwide plan and resources; responsible for proper execution of approved plans; must coordinate his conduct of business with and seek guidance from Worldwide Product Line Manager and the regional President.
Stabilizers, Marketing Manager	Responsible for all marketing activities within stabilizers; consults subsidiary marketing and sales personnel to develop the marketing inputs for the stabilizer business plan; responsible for proper execution of approved marketing plan and region-wide results; shares responsibility with subsidiary sales manager for development of sales staff.
Subsidiary Managing Director	Is accountable for all of the chemical businesses in the subsidiary; shares responsibility with each of the regional product line directors for planning and conduct of each of the businesses within the subsidiary.
Subsidiary Sales Manager	Shares responsibility with each of the regional product line marketing managers for planning and conduct of the businesses within the subsidiary; must play an important role in high level contacts with key customers; will advise on overall strategy within the country including the economic outlook as well as opportunities for new businesses; will encourage a close working relationship between salesmen and the regional product line marketing managers.

Source: Company Records.

CASE 4.1ᴿ Alto Chemicals Europe (B)

This case was prepared by Professor Kamran Kashani.

In the first six months of 1991, Graaff had undertaken a number of steps which he believed were necessary to implement the revised stabilizers strategy. He was reviewing the results to date with the purpose of deciding what to do next.

Graaff's Actions

Between January and June of 1991, Graaff had taken the following measures.

HQ Presentation

Early in January, Graaff invited the subsidiary sales managers to a planning meeting where he made a presentation on the main elements of the revised strategy. Central 'monitoring' on price and volume, in addition to new emphasis on smaller accounts for the less price-sensitive segments, were highlighted in the presentation. He also underlined that selling should become more technical in nature, with emphasis on quality and performance arguments. The need for closer collaboration between the sales force and technical service staff was similarly underscored.

Monthly Meetings

Subsidiary sales managers were asked to meet monthly with Graaff at headquarters to set price *and* volume targets and review progress to date. Graaff explained later, 'The meetings were necessary to have better control of the business but also to give the subsidiaries a chance to talk to each other and see the whole picture.'

Account Targets

Along with price and volume targets, the monthly meetings resulted in a 'rolling list' of named accounts for each subsidiary's sales force to pursue. The accounts were segmented by size, end-use, and whether they deserved a special effort for conversion. Accounts known for 'price cutting' were left off the list, even the larger ones.

Some rules were established for division of the selling effort between old accounts and new ones.

Volume Redistribution

To improve average prices received in the region, lower sales targets were set for historically competitive markets such as Holland. With higher target volumes for less price-orientated markets such as Germany, Graaff intended to shift the total volume towards the more profitable subsidiaries.

Results to Date

Although Graaff considered the first six months were too short a time to determine the effectiveness of the new strategy, a few results had begun to surface. The company had gained a number of new accounts among the medium-sized and smaller companies. This had been achieved despite the absence of discounts. On the other hand, several medium-sized and large accounts had been lost, some going to competitors and others reverting to Barium.

The overall impact on total volume of changes in the customer base was difficult to assess, as the industry sales had declined by about 8% during this period. Also, in some markets the contribution margins had increased slightly, in others not.

Meanwhile, the relationship between Graaff and the subsidiary sales managers had deteriorated significantly. The monthly meetings had often turned into shouting matches between Graaff and the more outspoken sales managers. The complaints voiced by the latter centered around the inherent wisdom of the new strategy and its impact on short-term results. Typical among these complaints were:

- You show us numbers and ratios to argue why a higher price is better than a lower price. But, the market doesn't have to follow your logic. Our customers don't understand our ratios; they don't even care. What they want is a lower price.
- For every key account I lose, I have to run after several smaller ones.
- You are destroying what took me years to build.

Conclusion

Graaff did not enjoy his monthly encounters with the sales managers, but he was not overly concerned. He felt it was 'part of the job'. What was beginning to concern him, however, were signs that his boss was losing patience. On some recent occasions, Hansen had mentioned that sales force motivation should not be sacrificed for the sake of a strategy and that a more consensus-orientated approach might be more effective in winning subsidiary support. Evidently, some subsidiary managing directors had been in touch with him regarding complaints from the field.

Although agreeing with the merits of a consensus approach, Graaff was not totally convinced that it would work in this situation: 'Consensus is fine. But, at the end of the day someone has to make a difficult decision and, in this case, that someone is me.' Graaff was, however, more profoundly concerned about whether or not Hansen really believed in what he was trying to accomplish. 'There are times I think even Hansen doesn't believe the strategy is going to work. It's difficult to change things when people have been around a long time and used to a different thinking', he complained.

Despite certain signs of unease, Hansen had not tried to stop Graaff. On the contrary, he had given him a free hand to proceed.

CASE 4.2 **Sony Europa (A)**

This case was prepared by Professors Kamran Kashani and J.B.M. Kassarjian.

In October 1994, the top management of Sony's European operation, Sony Europa, was pondering over the recent reorganization of the group and the ensuing developments. Seven months earlier, Sony Europa had restructured its organization to achieve several objectives including operating efficiencies, more effective pan-European marketing, and a unified posture *vis-à-vis* Sony Europa's parent in Japan. Dubbed the 'Big Bang', the new structure was an important change in the history of Sony's operations in Europe.

Jack Schmuckli, Sony Europa's Chairman and Chief Executive Officer, saw the reorganization as a necessary step in the growth of his company: 'In the old days when we were younger and less experienced, we were entrepreneurial; we took big risks and we succeeded. But as we have grown we have become less entrepreneurial and more bureaucratic; we have learned to find reasons why big things can't be done any more... To grow further we have to rediscover the old spirit.'

The market for consumer electronics in Europe was evolving rapidly. The industry was consolidating, and the increasing power of large retail chains and cross-border buying groups was changing the structure of trade. As a result, prices and margins were coming under unprecedented pressure. Sony's country sales companies, which had traditionally enjoyed considerable autonomy in launching a stream of innovative products developed in Japan, were facing new challenges from increasingly mature markets and lower-price competitors. Some senior managers felt that it was time for Sony to change from being a collection of country operations to become a truly pan-European organization.

Underscoring the need for change, Ron Sommer, Sony Europa's President and Chief Operating Officer, commented on the challenges facing his management: 'Consumer electronics is changing in big ways and if we don't learn to change with it, we'll become "an also ran" of the 21st Century!'

Since the reorganization, a number of issues had surfaced that called for management attention. But the most immediate concern was the departure of a senior manager from a key HQ marketing post in the new organization and the consequent need to appoint a replacement. Among the list of candidates for the job was a highly qualified country manager who had previously objected to many of the new organization's central functions, including pan-European marketing. The questions were whether he should be offered the position and, if so, whether he would change the course of the reorganization.

History

The history of Sony is a story of innovation; from its inception Sony was forced to innovate to survive intense competition from older, larger Japanese, US and European competitors.[1]

Tokyo Tsushin Kogyo KK,[2] later renamed Sony, was founded by Masaru Ibuka and Akio Morita in 1946. With very little capital, and working out of a modest room in a burned-out department store in Tokyo, the founders adopted 'Research Makes the Difference' as the company slogan. In the foundation prospectus of 1946, they declared: 'We shall create our own unique products.'

With a determined approach often characterized by the phrase 'We Do What Others Don't', he and his team of engineers established a tradition of consumer electronic products based on new technologies.

In addition to using new technologies for innovative products, from its inception the founders envisioned the company as an international enterprise based in Japan, that would aggressively pursue markets all over the world.

Sony was the pioneer[3] in a large number of product categories, and gradually many of its competitors would wait to gauge market acceptance of these products before launching their own imitations. Throughout its history, market research was not viewed as an effective way to lead in this industry; instead, the product development effort at Sony was driven by a guiding principle: *new products create new markets*. (Refer to **Exhibit 1** for a list of product introductions.)

Sony in Europe

The 1960s were characterized by product development and manufacturing in Japan, and aggressive sales throughout the world. In Europe, Sony Overseas S.A. was established, in 1960, to provide certain financial services and general support to the increasing number of independent distributors that were signed up to carry Sony products.

The independent distributors in Europe enjoyed considerable autonomy in sales and marketing. As one European independent Sony distributor (whose company was later acquired by Sony) described this period:

We were picked because of our entrepreneurial drive, and the name of the game was to grow the business selling the products they gave us. I would typically go to Tokyo twice a

---

1. This quote and some of the data for this section are taken from two company publications titled, *SONY Innovation* and *SONY – 30 Years In Europe*.
2. Means 'Tokyo Telecommunications Engineering Company' in Japanese.
3. In addition to being a pioneer in technology and product innovation, Sony was the first major Japanese corporation to appoint, in 1989, two foreign nationals to its Board of Directors – one of whom was Jack Schmuckli, a Swiss national who was Chairman of Sony Europa.

year to negotiate prices and shipping dates, but I could run my sales operation pretty much as I wanted – so long as I produced the results I had promised.

By 1970, Sony's European sales had gown to over DM150 million, with a total of 200 employees.

Entrepreneurial Growth Phase

For Sony, the 1970s were characterized by aggressive expansion of sales and marketing companies, closely followed by the establishment of Sony manufacturing operations in various European countries. In some countries, an existing independent distributor was acquired by Sony. In others, Sony set up a new operation and hired European staff to run it.

The country manager was often the former head of Sony's distribution company. Typically, he came to view his Sony operation as a private kingdom, with a direct supply line from the plants in Japan. He would travel to Japan to negotiate product selection and volumes, general price levels, and new product offerings to promote. He would also have to make some firm commitments about results to be achieved in his country. Having settled the supply of products, he was mostly free to determine marketing plans, promotion activities, and sales policies. He was essentially an entrepreneur, constrained only by product choice and availability, who could run his business in the way he thought best to gain market share and to produce profits.

Starting in the mid-1970s, manufacturing operations for selected products were gradually transferred from Japan to Europe. These new European plants were kept on a tight leash by the product groups in Japan. Product development and product modifications were typically initiated in Japan, as was the control of manufacturing processes.

The global economic recession of 1981–82, combined with the proliferation of Sony sales companies and plant facilities all over Europe, highlighted the growing need for more effective coordination of these widely dispersed operations. Under the leadership of Norio Ohga, the new CEO of Sony Corporation, Product Business Groups were organized in Japan to take global responsibility for product positioning in all markets.

As the head of a small but very profitable country stated, 'The name of the game was still fast growth. A lot depended on our sales companies – if I could realize 20–30% annual growth, they would let me run my show to reach the goals we had negotiated, using common sense.'

Another manager remembered a comment by Jack Schmuckli on why Europe was more profitable than the US or Japan: 'In Europe we have 15 country managers who worry about profitability. In the US and Japan, there are only a few people who do that.' At the same time, there was little interaction among the European country managers. As one senior manager recalled later: 'There was no curiosity to find out how the other countries were doing. They were just interested in their own market.'

The Committee Phase

By 1986, with 12 sales companies and 6 manufacturing facilities operating across Europe, there was a growing need for regional coordination. Jack Schmuckli, a Swiss national who had been the country manager in Germany (Sony's largest European market), was appointed Chairman of Sony Europa GmbH, and a new European headquarters was set up in Cologne, Germany. The initial mandate for the new headquarters organization was to coordinate the activities of the country operations, but especially to build an efficient infrastructure for all units, particularly the rapidly growing manufacturing presence.

The more significant changes started with the creation of pan-European committees, typically headed by a senior country manager, who would tackle particular problems on a Europe-wide basis. An important one was the Consumer Sales and Marketing Committee, where all the Consumer Products[4]-related people were brought together to develop a common distribution strategy.

As a country manager, who had headed one of the committees, commented with some conviction:

> The key to this process was that everyone was involved; the committees brought people together, we discussed proposals and made decisions that produced results. And the actions were no surprise to anyone. You know, it takes about a year after people start talking together for them to believe each other!

Another facet of the European committees was a growing rivalry among the country managers. One senior HQ manager recalled: 'There was a competitive spirit emerging among the countries. Each wanted to outperform the others. It was healthy.'

Global Localization in Europe

By the mid-1980s, as the pace of new plant openings increased, and country sales companies secured more of their supplies from European plants that were still tightly controlled from Japan, the debate between *localization* and *globalization* became more vehement.

At the annual European Management Conference held in Rome in March 1988, having listened to this heated debate for some time, A. Morita stepped in with an inspired resolution:

> The answer is to have a policy of 'global localization'. Having the philosophy 'think globally and act locally' will allow us to explore and develop the unique features of each country while at the same time benefiting from the strengths of a global enterprise.

---

4. Although Sony had introduced Professional Products, Computer Peripherals, and Recording Media into Europe, Consumer Products produced by far the highest proportion of sales.

The practical implications of this apparent resolution still remained to be discovered in actions on critical decisions. By the early 1990s, Sony's European TV operation was completely self-sufficient in both engineering and manufacturing. The operation was producing some two-and-a-half million TV sets annually, with more than 90% local value added. (Refer to **Exhibit 2** for a chronological listing of Sony's operations in Europe.)

Sony's growing manufacturing operations in Europe provided visible evidence that Sony was becoming a truly *European company*. But at the same time, country managers of all European countries – large and small – still had to travel to Japan for the all-important Line-up Meetings (for products with Business Groups still in Japan), where product mix, pricing, market positioning, and decisions about new features had to be negotiated. (Refer to **Exhibit 3** for the evolution of the relationship between European country management and Sony Tokyo in the 1970s and 80s.)

By 1994, Sony was making considerable progress towards 'global localization'. Europe accounted for some 28% of Sony electronics sales worldwide. However, while already 40% of the products sold in Europe was produced locally, only 15% of product development and 10% of R&D activities were conducted in Europe.

The European Market for Consumer Electronics

In 1994, Europe was beginning to come out of a recession that had seen sales and profits in the consumer electronics sector plummet for three years. While between 1988 and 1990 the total market had grown 29% in value to DM72 billion, by 1994 it had declined 21% to DM57 billion and remained stagnant. (Refer to **Exhibit 4** for total market size and shares of major producers in Europe.)

With the economic boom of the mid-to-late 1980s, and the introduction of a number of innovative new products such as camcorders and CD players, consumer electronics had grown by double-digits for most of the last decade. However, the recession in the early 1990s had dampened consumer demand and retail sales; the industry was facing over-capacity in manufacturing, both in Europe and in Japan. (Refer to **Exhibits 5 and 6** for European sales trends by product category and by country. **Exhibit 7** shows per capita expenditures on consumer electronics in Europe.)

The consumer electronics market was characterized by rapid new product introductions and obsolescence. An estimated 60–70% of all new products was expected to become obsolete within a 10-year cycle. Color TV sets, the largest of the consumer electronic products, were already a mature market. With European household penetration reaching 100%, growth in color TV came primarily from replacements and upgrades. Camcorders had grown dramatically prior to the recession, but had stalled at household penetration rates below 15%. Similarly, video recorders, or VCRs, had achieved respectable penetration rates of more than 40%, but were not expected to repeat the double-digit growth rates of the 1980s.

Some observers believed that the pace of innovation in consumer electronics had slowed down in recent years. Since the introduction of CD technology and home video products, including VCRs and camcorders, no new breakthrough products had reached mass market proportions. Recent product innovations were mostly in design and features. For example, Sharp Electronics was the first to launch a camcorder with a built-in LCD screen, soon to be followed by others including Sony. Newly introduced technologies were wide-screen TV, digital compact cassette players and mini-disk players. All faced uncertain mass market acceptance.

Competition

More than 20 players in the global consumer electronics industry competed in Europe. With 17% share of the European market, Sony was the leading consumer electronics firm, followed by Philips with 11%, Panasonic with 8% and Grundig with 6%. All had manufacturing units in both Europe and elsewhere.

In recent years, market stagnation and manufacturing over-capacity had led to increased price competition among numerous brands in the market. Average unit prices had declined for TV sets, VCRs and camcorders. This trend was especially noticeable in large markets such as Germany, France, and the UK.

Faced with declining prices and profit margins, the industry was rationalizing its manufacturing operations. The Dutch-based Philips, which suffered its first major loss in the early 1990s, had announced a number of plant closures in Europe. Similarly Matsushita, the parent of major brands such as Panasonic and JVC, planned a major restructuring of its Japanese and European operations following a sharp drop in its reported profits. All major Japanese companies were actively shifting their production out of Japan to the low-cost countries in the Far East. They were also establishing new production sites in Europe.

A process of consolidation was changing the structure of the European industry. Unable to compete, smaller firms were being absorbed by the larger ones. Throughout the 1980s and early 1990s, Philips had acquired a large number of European companies including, most recently, the German-based Grundig. The ongoing process of consolidation promised the creation of a few efficient and resource-rich multi-brand European firms competing for market dominance against each other and against the major Japanese companies.

In the crowded and increasingly competitive European market, Sony enjoyed a brand image unmatched by its rivals. A recent general survey conducted by *TIME Magazine* in 14 European countries showed that Sony had the highest public confidence for a long list of dimensions – including overall corporate image, good management, high quality of products and services, and good value for money. Philips, the only other electronics company on the list, ranked well below Sony on all dimensions.

Distribution

The structure of trade channels in consumer electronics varied considerably by country. For example, while small and medium-sized independent retailers dominated the market in Italy and Spain, in the UK more than half of all retail trade was channeled through specialist electronics chains. The differences in trade structures were in turn reflected in retail prices and trade margins. In countries where smaller independent retailers dominated, store prices and margins were higher than in those markets with a significant presence of large chains. Likewise, manufacturer margins were better where trade channels were fragmented. (Refer to **Exhibit 8** for market shares by channel.)

The country differences notwithstanding, a number of trends in distribution channels were evident across Europe.

Consolidation

The share of total European sales represented by independent retail outlets was in decline. In their place, specialist and non-specialist chain stores were accounting for an ever-larger volume of total business.

Private Labels

With the advance of large chains, a growing volume of consumer electronics was sold under the retailers' own brand. Such private labels, typically produced under contract in the Far East, were priced lower than the established manufacturer brands. In 1994, retailers' own labels accounted for 15% of all consumer electronics sales in Europe.

Buying Groups

Voluntary buying groups were increasingly active in Europe. Representing the interests of their affiliated independent retailers and smaller chains, the buying groups aimed to reduce the cost of sales through central purchasing and streamlined logistics. Like the chains, the buying groups were considered by many producers to be increasingly well informed and well managed.

While in 1994 Sony Europa served 10,000 authorized dealers representing 32,000 outlets, 37% of the company's total sales was channeled through its top 10 chain (19%) and buying group (18%) customers. The top 20 accounts represented 43% of Sony Europa's sales.

Cross-border Channels

While the emergence of large chains and buying groups was mostly a national phenomenon, a small but growing number of such organizations were expanding across borders. Among Sony's top 20 European accounts, all but two were present in more than one country. Multinational retailers and buying groups were known to shop around Europe for 'best deals', sometimes playing a producer's country sales organizations against one another.

Reorganization of Sony Europa

The belief that a major change was needed at Sony Europa, one that aimed for greater European consolidation, had been fermenting for some time. The recession in Europe had put Sony's sales and margins under pressure. In 1993, net sales declined by about 10% over the previous year (this included the strengthening of the DM itself). During the same period, the net profit before taxes fell by 25%. Senior managers, including some in Tokyo, believed that the potential for savings from a more streamlined operation in Europe was untapped.

The gradual cross-national initiatives that started in the mid-1980s were believed to have run their course. The 'committee phase' had paid off well in terms of creating a greater awareness at Sony of pan-European opportunities. Some tangible results had followed. But further incremental steps were considered by senior European management as inadequate to confront the new market realities.

Sony's European management saw one other important reason for pan-regional consolidation: speaking to Tokyo with one voice. Sony Europa's Director of Corporate Planning, Noby Maeda, explained: 'Although Sony Europa contributes considerably more than its sales share to Sony's global profits, given our country-by-country contacts with Tokyo, our influence on Tokyo's priorities is modest. The US and Japan have far more influence than we do.' Another manager echoed the same sentiment: 'Compared with the US and Japan – which speak to Sony headquarters with a single voice, fragmented Europe is more like a second-class citizen.'

The 'Big Bang'

In April 1993, Jack Schmuckli, the Chairman of Sony Europe, took the first step towards launching the most important change in the history of Sony's European operation. He invited Ron Sommer, then the President of Sony USA, back to Europe to head the newly created position of Chief Operating Officer (COO). Sommer's mandate was to spearhead a realignment of Sony Europa's organization for, in Schmuckli's words, a 'completely new way to manage the key decision-making processes in Europe'. Sommer was given a free hand to reshape the European organization.

Sommer, who had been Sony's country manager in Germany before going to the US in 1991, had joined the company in 1980 from a position at Nixdorf. Many at Sony believed Sommer's choice to head the reorganization was an obvious one: he knew the European operation, and had seen in the US how an integrated operation could achieve efficiencies. One other factor was also considered in Sommer's favor: his international background. He had been born in Israel, his parents were Hungarian and Russian, he had grown up in Austria, worked in several countries in Europe as well as in the US, and he spoke a number of languages.

Following fact-finding visits to country operations by Sommer, a new structure was formally announced in October 1993. Signed by both Schmuckli and Sommer, the announcement heralded the start of a new phase in Sony Europa's development aimed 'to reverse the negative [sales and profits] trend and… to generate a new dynamism within our organization'. The announcement concluded by seeking everyone's 'positive understanding and strong support in carrying out this reorganization'. (Refer to **Exhibit 9** for the new organization chart. A partial text of the announcement appears in the **Appendix**.)

Sony Europa's reorganization was quickly dubbed the 'Big Bang' by many because of the major changes it represented. Highlights of these changes were:

Consumer Marketing Europe

A new HQ function, Consumer Marketing Europe (CME), was created to consolidate the European marketing activities, and the head of CME would report to the COO. CME consisted of five product group heads (designated marketing directors), who were given P&L responsibility in their respective lines in addition to being made accountable for line-up decisions, pricing, advertising and promotions, purchasing and inventory management – the areas previously under country management control.

Consumer Sales

Another new HQ function was Consumer Sales. It was organized along four geographic sales regions to which country sales managers were expected to report. The four regional sales directors would also report directly to the COO, and they were responsible for all sales and dealer relationships in their respective geographic territories.

Support Operations

The three functions of information systems, logistics and customer service were organized into a new HQ Support Operations unit. European support managers were expected to aim for 'pan-European optimization through greater economies of scale, utilization of capable resources, and elimination of duplications'. This unit was headed by a director of support services, also reporting to the COO.

Country Operations

Sony's local country operations were to continue to represent the firm's legal interests in each of the 22 West and East European countries. According to the October 1993 announcement, the country managers – officially reporting to the COO (with a dotted-line to the regional sales managers) – were 'to become even more important under the new organization structure… and, as the extended arm of the COO, [they] will be responsible for effecting a smooth implementation of the structure change and… optimizing operations in the country'.

Jack Schmuckli, as Chairman and CEO, was to hold overall responsibility for Sony Europa and directly supervise all Corporate HQ Functions, Engineering and Manufacturing Operations, and Eastern Europe & Eurasia Development.

The Logic

Ron Sommer had extensive discussions with Jack Schmuckli, senior management in Tokyo, and key country managers in the European organization, before announcing the reorganization. Tokyo was concerned that the new structure would distance the product groups in Japan from those closest to the markets – the European country management. That relationship had proven particularly important to product groups in Japan. Also, Sony Japan preferred a simpler structure. Tokyo was concerned that the new set-up would dilute the strong sense of commitment that country managers made to carry out certain plans at the conclusion of individual line-up meetings in Japan.

For Jack Schmuckli, the logic of the new organization and the modified decision processes were driven by a need to put greater emphasis on European profitability:

> In the past, European product management was attached to the product groups, a fact that led to an emphasis on volume targets and setting prices to meet those targets. Profitability was a country management problem. For this reason Ron insisted on a separation of European marketing from engineering and manufacturing.

Two areas targeted by the reorganization were line-up decisions and logistics, including inventory management. Both tasks were previously controlled by country management. Under the new structure, '22 single country deals' – as one Sony Europa manager called it – would be replaced by one European line-up decision reflecting consolidated individual country requirements. Similarly, by centralizing logistics, Sony Europa was aiming to reduce the total inventory levels of more than 3,000 items in Europe.

Other reasons for the new structure were dealing with the growing complexity of doing business in Europe and re-energizing the organization. Sommer elaborated:

> The choices we had were simple: either leave it the way it is, or consider ways to stir up people, take away the safety net from beneath and see who can swing under the new conditions. I think we needed the big change for many reasons, but also to stir the people up and increase the adrenaline!
>
> My objectives were to keep the entrepreneurial spirit of each small country team and be able to move as an army, with a clear decision pyramid. That way when something goes wrong, we will not wait to see who would come to the rescue! There is also an increasing number of *European* decisions to be made. We have a growing number of European customers, and trans-shipment of goods from one country to another is a real problem. We at the center can deal with big international dealers better than any one country management. This is *not* a matter of centralizing power, or creating a more complex matrix, but just the reality of doing business in Europe today.
>
> You can't run Europe with consensus among 22 country managers. If we do some things centrally, it frees up the local people to focus on truly local issues. For a line-up meeting, do we really need 100 people to go to Tokyo?
>
> Maybe we can get SGA (sales and general administration expenses) down to 10% of sales from today's 16%. Some say 'that's stupid, you'll never get there'. I say we have a chance if we do things on a European scale.

Sony Europa's consolidation of its Nordic country markets in 1992 was considered by some as a small-scale model of the potential benefits from the reorganization. Previously, the four countries of Denmark, Sweden, Norway and Finland were managed independently, each representing a full-scale country operation. Jorn Aspelie, then head of Norway and later the Managing Director of Sony Nordic, remembered:

> Before 1992, we had four country managers, four marketing managers, four computer systems and four of everything else. When we created the Nordic region, we needed only one of each. The result was that we cut headcount by 20%, reduced SGA to 16% from 22%, passed the savings along in reduced prices, and increased sales and profits.

Aspelie underlined that Nordic consolidation was not liked by everyone. 'You have to convince people, or they have to find another place to work', he remarked.

Mid-range plans for Europe had already targeted operational efficiencies by 1996. The SGA-to-sales ratio was to drop by a full two percentage points and headcount by 10%. The reorganization was also meant to change Sony Europa's traditional operating philosophy. Sommer explained:

> In the past we followed a 'watering can principle', spreading equal but small amounts on each country. The result: we didn't grow fast enough. Now if Tokyo asks me 'What's wrong with Germany?' I say, 'Don't ask about Germany, ask about *Europe!*'

Implementation: From Big Bang to Reality

Dismantling the old structure, in Jack Schmuckli's words, of 'country kings' was more difficult than initially anticipated: 'People had their doubts about whether the new organization was really necessary. Some were saying "it was nice before, why change jobs, or reporting relationships?" Under the surface I could sense a certain silent resistance.'

Some country managers resented the process of introducing the changes, more than the intended objectives. One experienced and successful country manager voiced his concerns:

> The October '93 announcement (as to when the new organization would actually become effective) came in the mail! Maybe a 'Big Bang' was necessary, but such a big change requires extensive communication. People have to find out how they are going to fit into the same boat!

Appointments

The initial hesitations notwithstanding, by March 1, 1994, most appointments to new positions had been made. A number of country managers were given visible positions in the new structure. The important position of VP CME was assigned to a highly successful country manager from northern Europe. Two of the new European product managers had formerly represented Tokyo's product groups in Europe. Two country managers, for Germany and Portugal, were given the additional assignments of European product management for Mobile Electronics and Hi-Fi Products.

The position of VP Consumer Sales was left vacant pending the appointment of a qualified individual. Meanwhile, regional sales directors were selected from among country sales managers or managing directors. Helmut Rupsch, responsible for the Central Region, was the only regional sales director without a country responsibility. Before the appointment, Rupsch had held the sales and support function responsibilities in Germany. All regional sales directors reported to Ron Sommer.

Appointments to HQ functions, including VPs, directors and their staff support, involved nearly 50 different positions. By mid-1994 some ten positions were still vacant.

Reflecting on the appointments, Sommer believed that the new structure, while constrained by a shortage of qualified people, had opened up new opportunities for the young managers in the organization. 'We've tried to give big jobs to young people', he said. 'We will see how they succeed.'

Shaping the Mandate

In early March 1994, Sony Europa's senior management (country managers and European HQ staff – both old and new) gathered in Lausanne, Switzerland, to translate the intentions of the new organization into concrete action. Opening the workshop, Jack Schmuckli offered his colleagues an unambiguous mandate:

> The fate of our attempt to rejuvenate Sony's operations in Europe will ultimately depend on the people in this room. Ron and I have given you the framework, now it is up to you to clarify elements of the reorganization, to pinpoint specific tasks and responsibilities, in a word – to make it work!

At the end of the workshop, the 21 participants made a presentation to Schmuckli and Sommer under the overall theme of 'We Will Make It Happen!' Under the sub-theme of 'Getting Closer to the Customer', one group of managers expressed their new realization that: 'We have to manage the paradox of conflicting objectives: be more *centralized*, yet more effectively *decentralized*.' A second group offered what they called 'The Butterfly Concept': how ideas and information would start with dealers and consumers and go through the country sales companies and converge at CME, to be conveyed to the Tokyo Business Groups in 'one voice'. Still another group proposed '**SymphONY Europa**' as a metaphor for harmonious operations in Europe. They also presented a detailed Decision Map, adopted later by the participants, specifying primary and secondary responsibilities for key decisions. (Refer to **Exhibits 10 and 11** for copies of the Butterfly Concept and the **SymphONY Europa** decision map.)

Emerging Issues

Almost a year after the announcement of the new structure, a number of issues were coming up for management attention. These issues concerned many elements of the new organization and certain decision processes.

Country Managers

While the October 1993 announcement had left the specific role of country managers open, it was beginning to take shape in practice. In most cases, the country heads were assigned the additional function of national sales director for consumer products. In their redefined roles, the country managers were no longer directly involved with marketing decisions, including line-up decisions, which were assigned to national marketing managers. The latter group reported to both their country manager and their respective product group managers at headquarters. As national sales managers, country managers were responsible for profit and loss.

Commenting upon his new role, one country manager said: 'By taking away brand building from local management, we are promoting a narrow distribution mentality.' Another country manager reflected: 'I used to represent my country at line-up meetings in Tokyo because I knew my market better than anybody else. Now I am no longer in the driver's seat.' Both managers were absent from the two line-up meetings which had taken place in 1994. One suggested that under the new structure there was a risk that a country manager's job might be reduced to 'organizing Christmas parties'.

One other concern about the redefined role of country management was expressed by Shin Takagi, the head of Sony UK. Criticizing what he believed was over-centralization, Takagi was worried that the new order would demoralize the people in the markets, the people who, in his words, 'put their heads and hearts into their jobs. What worries me is that the more we centralize here, the more the picture from each country gets blurred particularly to the Tokyo Business Groups.' He remembered the critical role played by line-up meetings in Tokyo, where individual country managers negotiated with business groups: 'These were tough meetings. You arrive with jet lag, the meeting room is not nice, and then you go through a tough grilling. If you had done well, your track record went up; if not, you had to defend yourself and make new commitments.'

CME

Related to the changing role of country managers was the debate about what CME could contribute under the new organization. Headquarters product managers were expected to assist country operations in marketing, and to represent Europe as a single entity in discussions with engineering and manufacturing in Tokyo. Some country managers thought that in its current capacity CME was becoming, in the words of one, 'a huge layer of bureaucracy' that had neither local market know-how nor credibility *vis-à-vis* Japan, which still preferred to deal directly with the big markets. Many wondered if CME could ever fulfill its ambitious mandate.

A very different view was expressed by a recently appointed country manager: 'What I am expecting from CME is to optimize the total operation beyond TV, Audio and so on, and to look at Sony in Europe. CME has to guard and enhance the Sony image, stay abreast of consumption patterns, and keep in contact with Japan. And finally we need a referee – but only if we can't agree!'

Product Management

Under the former structure, European-based product managers were part of Sony's product development and manufacturing functions. In that capacity, they helped with aligning production in Japan with country-level sales. At Sony, this process was called 'Seihan' and was considered an important influence on the profitability of the consumer business. Product managers did not control local prices or inventory levels and were not responsible for the profitability of their lines in Europe.

Sony Europa's reorganization had significantly changed the product managers' job: they had been made part of CME, which would represent the markets and be separate from the upstream activities. The only exception was TV product management, which already had a fully integrated European operation. Furthermore, for the first time product management was given responsibility for decisions involving procurement from Japan, positioning, pricing, and logistics including inventory which, according to the original plan, was supposed to be managed centrally.

The new product management structure had put additional demands on the organization. A country manager with a small but profitable market was frustrated by the additional paperwork: 'One of my people was working late on consecutive nights, and it turned out that he was re-doing all the budget numbers because a product manager at HQ had revised his numbers up by 6% and was trying to squeeze a bit from every country! There is more paperwork but no benefits are seen, no clear progress.'

An exception to the concerns expressed about product management was the contribution of Sony Europa's TV group. Having had a fully integrated operation in Europe for a number of years, which included product development and manufacturing, the TV product group was considered by many as a workable model for European integration. Ichiro Mihara, the HQ marketing director for TV, explained how his unit worked: 'I've got engineering and manufacturing in Europe; it is relatively easy to integrate those operations with central marketing. This is not the case for the other product groups which have to rely on Tokyo for products.' He insisted that his central marketing managers were instructed 'not to bother the local managers' for information. Rather it was their job to do the necessary 'footwork' to keep track of local developments. For Mihara, 'footwork' meant trade visits, getting different views on each market, and having an 'eye' for reliable information.

Another source of concern was the profit-and-loss responsibility assigned to product management. One senior HQ manager wondered if 'countries were not relaxing now that they have a shared profit responsibility with the HQ product management It's fuzzy.' Others thought that without responsibility for results, product management lacked substance. Still others felt that shared responsibility was a big step forward. Jean-Michel Perbet, managing director of Sony France, commented on his new relationship with the TV group:

> We have shared responsibility now, where *I* have to worry about Mihara's P&L, and *he* has to worry about my P&L. This is a big change… The real enemy is outside, we can't afford to fight each other, while Philips is out selling its products every day!

Regional Sales

The European consumer sales, divided into four regions, was not a function that was well understood in the new organization.

A key role of sales regions was to manage a growing number of cross-border trade and channel issues. In that capacity, regional sales directors, working with country managers, were to promote harmonized pricing and commercial conditions. Still other activities falling under regional sales were joint promotional campaigns utilizing central concepts and vehicles, regional market logistics, and customer service. Regional sales directors were to have profit responsibility for their region.

The contribution of regional sales was not well understood by everyone. For one thing, there appeared to be some overlap with the activities assigned to CME and its local marketing arm. They included the so-called 'net-net' pricing (or final dealer prices), local promotions, and inventory management. For another, some doubted if the existing scale of cross-border trade justified such a visible central function. One country sales manager commented:

> Pan-European dealership is an illusion. What we have are pan-European buying groups with more than a 1,000 members across Europe. But even here the final decision belongs to the independent local dealers. If locals don't place an order, the buying center doesn't buy.

Counterbalancing these doubts was the argument that since CME was by definition orientated towards product marketing, Sony Europa needed another function which focused on dealers and field sales. This point was especially clear for Helmut Rupsch, who represented the central sales region:

> I am convinced we need a counterpart to CME. Without it we will have a power imbalance in the organization – an unfortunate development at a time when we see distributors growing larger and becoming more active in cross-border trade,

Management Talent

During the process of management appointments, it became clear to Jack Schmuckli and Ron Sommer that Sony Europa lacked sufficient depth in management, the type of people who could operate in the complex organization that the new structure represented. Schmuckli observed: 'We need a new type of manager to get us there. What we have are mostly home-grown, those who have learned their trade hands-on. They lack the higher degree of sophistication needed for strategic thinking.' Others agreed. Shin Yamamoto, director of logistics, pointed out that the new matrix organization called for skills in cross-national communication that some lacked: 'Coming from Japan, we are not used to debates in meetings, and that's very useful in a global company. So, we have to learn quickly how to do it.'

On the positive side, the reorganization had opened up promotion opportunities for the younger managers. Noby Maeda, director of corporate strategy, commented: 'Thanks to the pan-European vision, younger managers are now given higher responsibilities faster than would have been possible in their own markets.'

Pace of Change

While the pace of change at Sony Europa was too fast for some managers, it was not fast enough for others. Jack Schmuckli belonged to the latter category: 'Some big countries have stepped back and are waiting to see what happens next. Meanwhile they are doing as before; others are letting the business run into the wall.' Aspelie, managing director of Sony Nordic, agreed: 'A lot of people would like to see things go back to the old days, especially the key managers in the larger countries.'

A number of managers attributed the uneven pace of change to insufficient groundwork before the October 1993 announcement. Pearson, the UK sales director also responsible for the North Region, explained: 'Not enough *nemawashi* was done prior to the announcement.[5] The Big Bang approach and an inadequate preparation of people have exacerbated the problem.' Yamamoto, the newly appointed logistics director, concurred:

> The reasons for the reorganization were never made clear to everyone. People didn't know if it was the market or the expected economies in SGA that was driving the reorganization. The process got ahead of the goal; the reorganization became an objective in itself.

Jack Schmuckli thought that potential problems associated with the Big Bang had been underestimated:

> More than the logic of putting the new organization together, there was a need to explain that logic to those most affected. The announcement was not enough. So a lot of people have come to me distressed... I've spent a lot of my energies showing people why a change was needed. They came to me because I was the only constant in the organization. Everything else had changed.

Some country managers were concerned that unless more rapid progress were made, the entire reorganization could lose its momentum. Aspelie remarked: 'If we don't move faster at the local levels, especially in big markets, we risk having quick and dirty decisions made at the top imposed on the organization. That would not be a healthy development.'

Taking Stock

Reviewing the first few months under the new organization, Ron Sommer understood many of the issues that had been raised:

---

5. *Nemawashi* refers to the Japanese word for consensus building prior to an official announcement. The often informal process taking place outside of normal channels is meant to reduce the element of surprise and possible opposition once a new idea is formally announced.

The good thing about all the complaints is that they help you identify the problem and fix it. After all, how do you prepare people for a big change? One way is to let them learn by doing. The previous organization didn't allow people to grow. It will take another two years till we reach a level where I feel we have self-momentum. It's like an old railroad station with a lot of different cars; at first you move each one by yourself, then when they are more or less lined up, you start getting the momentum.

Maeda commented on Sommer's approach:

Ron is a super manager. He aims higher than the goal he wants to hit so that he can get somewhere close to it. And he tells everyone 'I want you to be aggressive and make noise. If you don't complain you won't get promoted!'

Recent Developments

In October 1994, the VP of Consumer Marketing Europe (CME) resigned from his position, less than a year after his appointment. Ron Sommer believed that mistakes were inevitable in such a major reorganization:

We could've spent a long time thinking about all aspects before taking a first step. We could've waited another five years to find or develop the right people for the job. In Europe we often think too long before acting; the US is better at it. My bias is action, not thinking. The point is that you must have the guts to make changes even when you know you don't have all the right people. There is the risk that you might fail to develop the people you need on the job, but I am not afraid to take that risk.

The sudden departure of the first VP-CME had opened up a key post for a new appointment. In the search for suitable candidates, Ron Sommer had consulted a number of senior country and corporate managers. One name that had been cited often was Shin Takagi, the current country manager for the UK, who was also favored by Jack Schmuckli. Takagi was among the most senior managers at Sony Europa, where he had served since 1976 as a deputy or country manager in Germany, Italy, and Spain. In 1987 he had moved to Sony-US, and in 1990 was appointed president and CEO of the Sony Recording Media Group in the US. Upon his return to Europe in 1993, he had led the UK country operation. (Refer to **Exhibit 12** for Shin Takagi's career history.)

Takagi's qualifications for the CME job were undisputed. As one country manager commented: 'Shin is the only one who can really do the job. His seniority and his world experience make him the ideal candidate.'

The main concern expressed by some senior HQ managers was Takagi's explicitly different vision of the role of CME in the new organization. In a number of meetings attended by both HQ and country managers, Takagi had openly criticized the central role that the first incumbent advocated for CME, and he had questioned the feasibility of pan-European marketing in the near future. As one country manager put it: 'Takagi is a heavyweight; if he gets the job, he will probably pursue a very different agenda from his predecessor.'

Conclusion

Aware of Takagi's reserved opinions on European integration, and convinced about the relevant experience that Takagi could bring to the job, Sommer was wondering if the UK country manager should be approached for the CME position. He was also not sure whether Takagi would accept it. Sommer was weighing Takagi's solid qualifications with his less than enthusiastic view of centralization under the new structure.

EXHIBIT 1

Sony Product Innovations

1950	Japan's first tape recorder
1955	Japan's first transistor radio
1960	The world's first all-transistor TV set
1962	The world's first transitored video tape recorder
1965	The world's first home-use video tape recorder
1968	The world's first Trinitron TV set
1971	The world's first color video cassette format
1975	The world's first VCR (Betamax)
1979	The world's first personal stereo, Walkman
1981	The world's first portable video tape format
1981	The world's first high-definition video product
1982	The world's first CD player
1983	Introduced the new world standard 3.5" floppy disc
1985	The world's first universal video camcorder format
1986	The world's first component digital VTR
1988	The world's first composite digital VTR
1992	The world's first blue laser
1992	The world's first digital disc home recording format

Source: Company Records.

EXHIBIT 2

History of Sony's Operations in Europe

Headquarters and Support Functions

1960: Sony Overseas S.A., Baar, Switzerland – Financial Services

1971: Sony Logistics Europe B.V., Vianen, Netherlands

1973: Sony Service Center (Europe) N.V., Londerzeel (Brussels), Belgium

1986: Sony Europa GmbH, Cologne, Germany – Management Headquarters
Basingstoke Technology Center, Basingstoke, UK

1987: Stuttgart Technology Center, Fellbach, Germany

Since 1990:

Sony Brussels, European Affairs, Belgium
Sony Financial Services (Europe), London, UK
Sony Europa B.V., Badhoevedorp (Amsterdam), Netherlands – Operations Center
Sony European Computer Services, Düsseldorf, Germany
Sony Telecom N.V., Brussels, Belgium

Business Group and Manufacturing Organizations

Consumer Products:

1974: ● Sony Manufacturing Company UK, Pencoed (TV) and Bridgend (CRT), UK

1975: ● Sony-Wega Produktions-GmbH, Fellbach, Germany

1982: ● Barcelona Plant, Viladecavalls, Spain

1986: ● Audio/Video Manufacturing Europe, Alsace Plant, Ribeauvillé, France

1987: ◆ TV, Europe, Staines, UK

1990: ◆ Consumer Video Europe, Badhoevedorp, Netherlands

Since 1990:

◆ Audio Sector Europe, Badhoevedorp, Netherlands

◆ Business Group Organizations
● Manufacturing Facilities

Source: Company Records.

Sales and Service Companies

1968: Sony United Kingdom Limited, Staines (London), UK

1970: Sony Deutschland GmbH, Cologne, Germany

1973: Sony France S.A., Paris, France
Sony Espana S.A., Barcelona, Spain
Sony Italia S.p.A., Cinisello (Milan), Italy

1974: Sony Danmark, Taastrup (Copenhagen), Denmark

1977: Sony Belgium N.V., Brussels, Belgium

1979: Sony Austria Ges.m.b.H., Vienna, Austria
Sony Nederland B.V., Badhoevedorp (Amsterdam), Netherlands

1986: Sony Portugal Lda., Lisbon, Portugal
Sony Schweiz AG, Schlieren (Zürich), Switzerland

Since 1990:

Sony Praha, Prague, CR
Sony Finland, Espoo (Helsinki), Finland
Sony Hellas S.A., Psychiko (Athens), Greece
Sony Ireland, Tallaght (Dublin), Ireland
Sony Nordic a/s, Taastrup (Copenhagen), Denmark
Sony Norge, Oslo, Norway
Sony Poland sPzoo, Warsaw, Poland
Sony Moscow, Moscow, Russia
Sony Sverige, Spanga (Stockholm), Sweden
Sony Turkey, Caglayan (Istanbul), Turkey

EXHIBIT 3

Relations Between European Country Management and Sony Tokyo

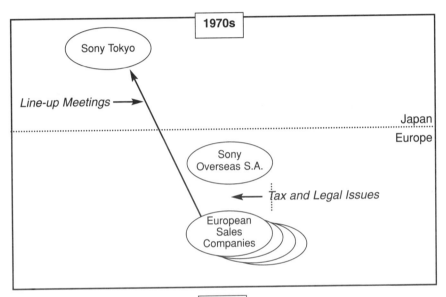

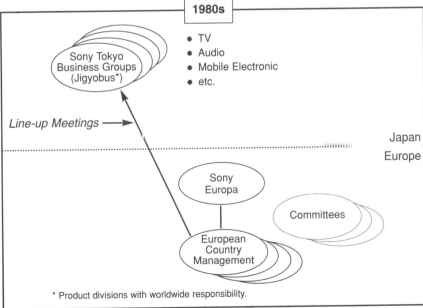

* Product divisions with worldwide responsibility.

Source: Casewriters' interpretations.

EXHIBIT 4

European Consumer Electronics Market Size and Shares of Major Producers

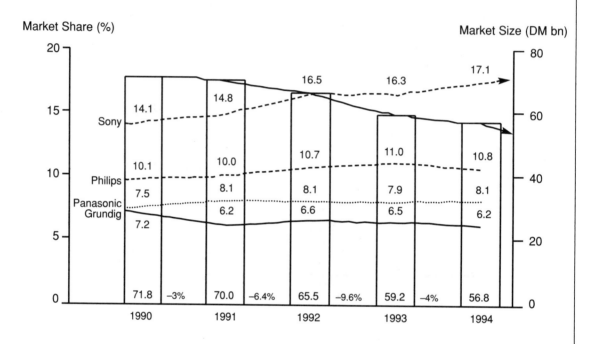

Source: Company Records.

EXHIBIT 5

European Consumer Electronics Sales Trends by Product Category

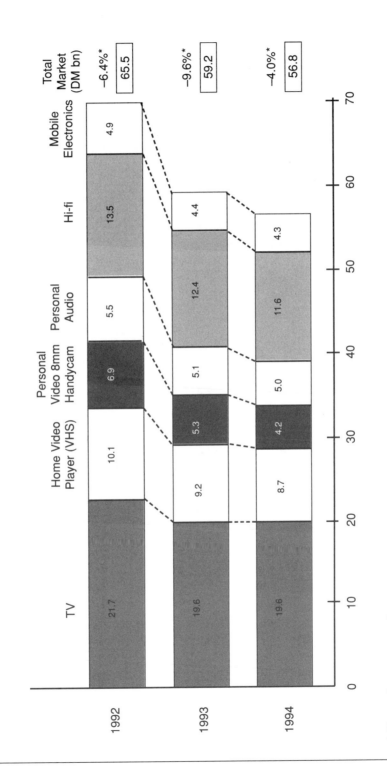

Year	TV	Home Video Player (VHS)	Personal Video 8mm Handycam	Personal Audio	Hi-fi	Mobile Electronics	Total Market (DM bn)	
1992	21.7	10.1	6.9	5.5	13.5	4.9	65.5	−6.4%*
1993	19.6	9.2	5.3	5.1	12.4	4.4	59.2	−9.6%*
1994	19.6	8.7	4.2	5.0	11.6	4.3	56.8	−4.0%*

* Change from a year earlier.

Source: Company Records.

EXHIBIT 6

European Consumer Electronics Sales Trends by Country and Region

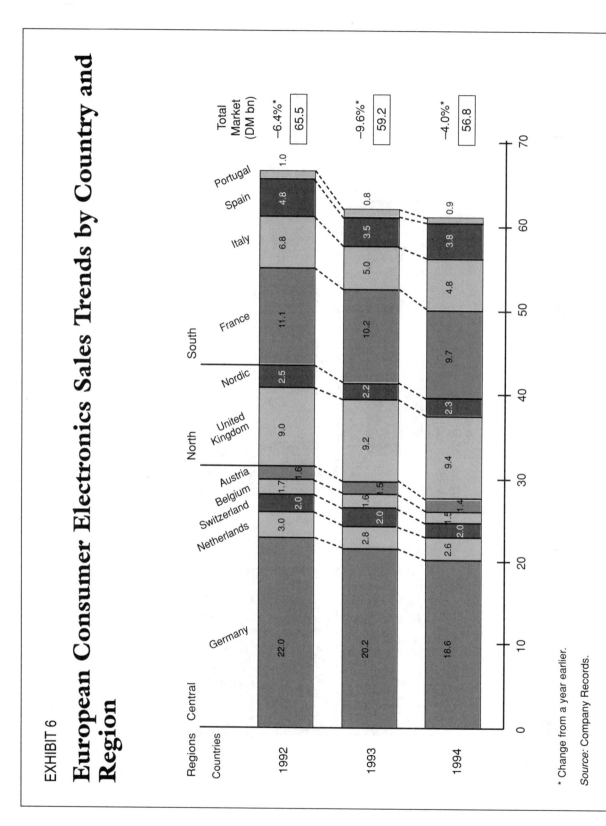

* Change from a year earlier.

Source: Company Records.

EXHIBIT 7

Per Capita Expenditure on Consumer Electronics (1992)

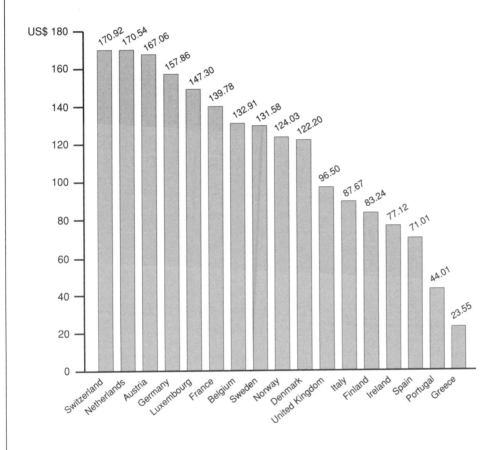

Country	US$
Switzerland	170.92
Netherlands	170.54
Austria	167.06
Germany	157.86
Luxembourg	147.30
France	139.78
Belgium	132.91
Sweden	131.58
Norway	124.03
Denmark	122.20
United Kingdom	96.50
Italy	87.67
Finland	83.24
Ireland	77.12
Spain	71.01
Portugal	44.01
Greece	23.55

Source: Euromonitor.

EXHIBIT 8

Shares of Consumer Electronics by Channel

| | Specialists | | | | Non-specialists* | |
| | Independents/Buying Groups % | | Chains % | | % | |
Country	1990	1993	1990	1993	1990	1993
Germany	56	50	9	13	35	37
France	30	25	39	43	31	32
UK	34	32	51	58	15	10
Italy		>85		<5	11	10
Spain	45	35	10	15	45	50
Netherlands	62	61	29	33	9	6
Sweden	67	55	25	40	8	5
Norway	90	85	6	10	4	5
Finland	71	69	19	23	10	8
Denmark	49	45	35	42	15	13
Switzerland	50	50	25	25	25	25
Belgium	62	55	20	25	18	20
Austria	53	45	37	45	10	10
Total Europe	54	49	22	27	25	24

* Non-specialists consist of all general merchandise outlets including department stores, hypermarkets, etc.

Source: Company Records.

EXHIBIT 9

Partial Organization Chart: European Sales and Marketing Operations

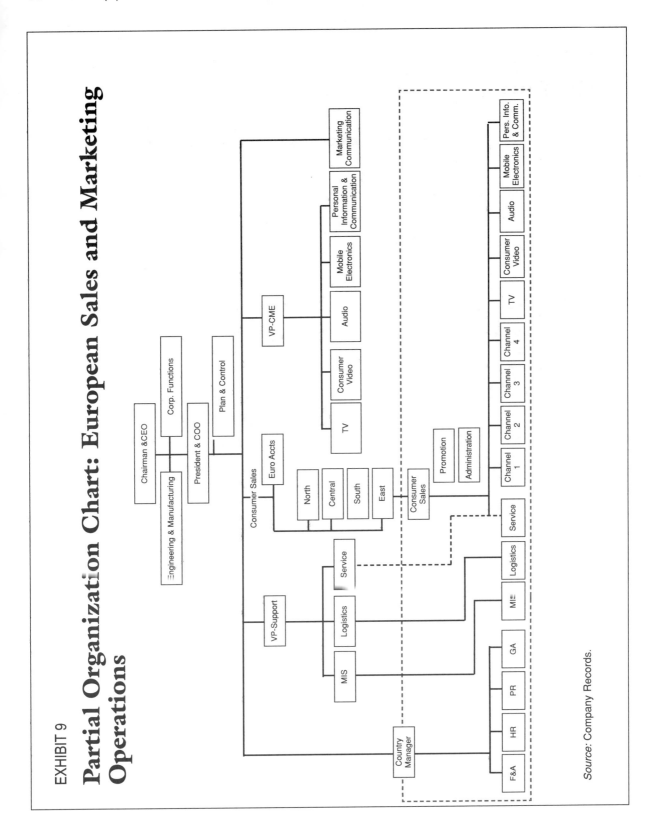

Source: Company Records.

EXHIBIT 10

The Butterfly Concept

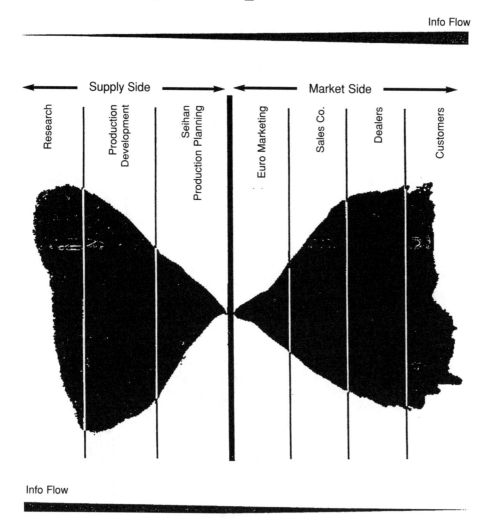

Info Flow

Supply Side

Market Side

Research

Production Development

Seihan Production Planning

Euro Marketing

Sales Co.

Dealers

Customers

Info Flow

Source: Company Records.

EXHIBIT 11

SymphONY Europa

	CEO/ COO	European HQ	CME	Sales Regions	Country
Pricing					
Transfer Price			●		
Dealer Net/Net			●		
Guideline Retail Price			●		
Final Retail Price					●
Procurement			●		✳
Inventory			●		✳
P&L					
Horizontal				●	●
Vertical – Europe-wide			●		
Overall	●				
Ad & Pro					
Pan-European			●		
Local					●
Budget Approval					
Horizontal				●	
Vertical – Europe-wide			●		
Overall	●				
Negotiation with Tokyo			●		
Euro Accounts				●	✳
Support Functions		●			✳
Finance		●			

● Primary

✳ Secondary

Source: Company Records.

EXHIBIT 12

Shin Takagi's Career History at Sony

1973:	Joined Sony Corporation in Japan
1976:	Sony Deutschland: Jack Schmuckli's special assistant, involved in Marketing, Purchasing, Sales Manager, etc.
1979:	Sony in Italy: for three years with the distribution company in Italy
1980:	Vice President of newly established Sony Italia
1982:	Managing Director of Sony Espana S.A., instrumental in buying out Spanish shareholders
1986:	Managing Director of Sony Portugal Lda.
1987:	With the Sony US Consumer Video Company
1989:	Sony-US Telecom and diversified group: nine new business ventures in industrial products
1989–90:	Attended Harvard Business School 'Advanced Management Program'
1990:	President and COO of Sony Recording Media Group in the US: he established this unit, including two plants, Production, Distribution and Marketing, reporting to M. Morita
1993:	President of Sony UK

Source: Company Records.

APPENDIX

Partial Text of Organization Announcement

New European Operations Structure

During the past few years European Operations enjoyed impressive sales growth, accompanied by high profitability, thereby attaining and subsequently consolidating our No. 1 position in Europe.

Recently, however, a number of factors have been adversely affecting our business, resulting in negative sales growth and tightly squeezed profits.

We now urgently need a new impetus to reverse the negative trend and return to double-digit sales growth – not only by increasing our market share, but also by expanding the market as a whole – and to achieve healthy profitability to allow us to invest for future expansion.

We are therefore pleased to announce today a new European Operations structure which is intended to generate a new dynamism within our organization to realize these crucial goals.

The size of Sony's operations today and the increasing integration of the European market require strong European sales and marketing functions to aggressively drive our business forward and support local companies in strengthening their sales / distribution channel management and service operations. At the time, in order to achieve improved efficiency and productivity, it is imperative that we also take full advantage of the benefits our changing environment is offering by integrating operational support functions on a European level.

While we appreciate that change is never easy, we are convinced that our ability continuously to readjust our organization in line with our ever-changing operating environment is undoubtedly a key competitive asset.

We believe that the organizational changes described in detail in the following pages will enable us to drive our business forward. Your full support in pursuing these objectives will be highly appreciated.

Best regards,

Mr J. Schmuckli
Chairman & CEO

Dr R. Sommer
President & COO

Cologne, 7 October 1993

Source: Company Records.